India Studies in Business and Economics

The Indian economy is considered to be one of the fastest growing economies of the world with India amongst the most important G-20 economies. Ever since the Indian economy made its presence felt on the global platform, the research community is now even more interested in studying and analyzing what India has to offer. This series aims to bring forth the latest studies and research about India from the areas of economics, business, and management science. The titles featured in this series will present rigorous empirical research, often accompanied by policy recommendations, evoke and evaluate various aspects of the economy and the business and management landscape in India, with a special focus on India's relationship with the world in terms of business and trade.

More information about this series at http://www.springer.com/series/11234

Kumar V. Pratap · Rajesh Chakrabarti

Public-Private Partnerships in Infrastructure

Managing the Challenges

Springer

Kumar V. Pratap
Ministry of Finance,
Government of India
New Delhi
India

Rajesh Chakrabarti
Jindal Global Business School
O P Jindal Global University
Sonipat, Haryana
India

and

Sunay Policy Advisory Pvt. Ltd.
Gurugram, Haryana
India

ISSN 2198-0012 ISSN 2198-0020 (electronic)
India Studies in Business and Economics
ISBN 978-981-10-3354-4 ISBN 978-981-10-3355-1 (eBook)
DOI 10.1007/978-981-10-3355-1

Library of Congress Control Number: 2017948623

Printed on acid-free paper

This Springer imprint is published by Springer Nature
The registered company is Springer Nature Singapore Pte Ltd.
The registered company address is: 152 Beach Road, #21-01/04 Gateway East, Singapore 189721, Singapore

Foreword

India is the second most popular market for Public–Private Partnerships (PPP) in the developing world as per the Private Participation in Infrastructure database of the World Bank. However, given the infrastructure deficit in the country, PPPs need to be scaled up across sectors and geographies. In this environment, this book that starts with infrastructure challenges, talks about options for infrastructure financing, and discusses the transaction structure, is timely and should prove useful to the uninitiated as well as professionals to enter into such partnerships. This book should be especially useful to students who need to understand the nitty-gritties of the PPP transaction process. The many case studies in the book emphasize its real-life flavor, which should enhance understanding of the complex subject.

However, not everything is sanguine about PPPs. Owing to the resource crunch faced by countries, they have invited the private sector for provisioning of infrastructure. Increasingly infrastructure projects are being renegotiated squandering the gains from private participation in infrastructure. This trend is catching up across the world, including India.

My own research for Latin America and Caribbean region shows that infrastructure contracts are becoming more fragile with time: incidence of renegotiations for the region has increased from 30% to 68% between 1985–2000 and 1988–2010; time to renegotiate has decreased from 2.2 years to 1 year from start of commercial operations; and the sectors most vulnerable to renegotiations are transport and water and sewerage where the incidence has increased to 78% and 87% respectively, making renegotiations the rule rather than the exception.

Renegotiation of infrastructure projects for reasons other than incompleteness of contracts or poorly designed contracts are bad in principle and practice. The Government of India and the infrastructure regulatory agencies would be well advised to make renegotiations not a matter of routine but exceptionally difficult. There exist many mechanisms to accomplish this, like asking the private party to pay a fee linked to the total project cost for applying to the public authority for renegotiations, which would be forfeited in case the renegotiation request is rejected; requiring a hefty performance bond in the form of bank guarantee; declaring and acting upon the pledge that the public authority would not entertain a renegotiation request within the first 5 years of commercial operations of the project, etc. All these measures would deter opportunistic bids and preserve their sanctity.

While India is doing well in terms of the stock of PPP projects, there are sectors such as water and sewerage where there is immense scope of private participation, but with a realistic dose of caution. Water is under-priced in India, like in the rest of the world, and any effort to bring in private players would have to be accompanied by an increase in water retail tariffs, which makes the effort politically sensitive. However, there exist examples across the world (Manila Water Company, to name one) where tariff increase has come with much better service delivery, making the initiative politically palatable. India would be well advised to follow such examples to augment infrastructure services at a rapid pace and maintain its position as the fastest growing large economy in the world.

I commend the authors for a balanced and comprehensive exposition of the various facets of infrastructure PPPs and hope the book finds a wide readership.

Washington DC

Prof. J. Luis Guasch
Professor of Economics at University of California
San Diego
Formerly Head of the Global Expert Team on Privatization
The World Bank

Preface

This book is an attempt to better understand the broad realities and challenges of managing infrastructure Public–Private Partnerships (PPP) in developing countries with a special focus on India. It is meant to be a text for the students of infrastructure and PPP design, as well as an operating manual for the practicing manager or government official in charge of making such large and expensive projects work out right. Consequently, our attempt here has primarily been to focus on the key decisions and design aspects of these projects as identified in the literature and the recent global PPP experience. However, we also discuss the context and the broad historical and economic principles of PPPs here, since a failure to understand these principles would limit the readers' understanding of the challenges.

The central questions that the volume seeks to shed light on include: what is a PPP and why is it gaining popularity? What broad needs does it fulfill for its many stakeholders? What are the different ways of structuring and financing PPPs and with what implications? What are the observed flashpoints of conflicts that arise in PPPs? How can better design of PPP contracts avoid such problems and help resolve them? What roles do regulatory structures play in helping PPPs? What are the implications of renegotiating PPPs?

Our broad approach in writing this book has been to move away from abstract theoretical discussion of these issues to elucidate the always complicated issues involved with case studies and in-depth examples. We have, therefore, included several case studies from India as well as many other developing countries to bring out the nuances of contract design and enforcement, the clash of private and public objectives, and the time inconsistencies and incomplete contracting issues that frequently crop up in large scale infrastructure PPP projects.

Apart from helping PPP students and practitioners in their jobs, we also hope to stimulate research interest in contemporary PPP reality in India and other emerging markets. We recognize that the field of infrastructure PPPs is an evolving one. There is no last word here and new knowledge is being created every day around the world as innovations are tried out in contracting, financing, structuring and (re)negotiating contracts, and the experiences recorded. Also the multidimensional nature of the issues involved—the shifting politico-economic environment, the technical issues, the sometimes unanticipated environmental challenges—leave room for reinterpretation of events in the recent past as well. Our attempt here, therefore, is to capture, organize, and present the reality of PPPs as we understand them now to help practitioners to learn from experience and avoid the errors of the past in engineering future partnerships. But this is only a step in the never-ending journey of seeking knowledge.

The extent to which this volume encourages further research in infrastructure PPPs and informs the PPP practitioner—in governments, private sector, transnational organizations, or any other stakeholder—in making better decisions would, therefore, be the litmus test of the value of our efforts.

New Delhi, India

Kumar V. Pratap
Rajesh Chakrabarti

Acknowledgements

Several people contributed in myriad ways to the long project that finally culminated in the present volume. We apologize in advance to those whom we would doubtless fail to mention despite our best efforts.

We, particularly Dr. Pratap, owe a massive debt of gratitude to Prof. N.R. Prabhala of the University of Maryland, Clive Harris of the World Bank, Carol Graham of the Brookings Institution, Mark Hugo Lopez of the Pew Research Center, Gajendra Haldea and Ravi Mital of the Planning Commission, and Madhusudan Prasad of the Ministry of Urban Development, who helped form and organize our thoughts on the subject. Our association with the Indian School of Business (ISB), Mohali and Hyderabad has also helped coalesce the material into its present shape. We would like to thank ISB and the Bharti Institute of Public Policy for the opportunity. We would also like to thank the five batches of students at ISB for the questions and discussion that have helped us make our arguments more robust. We also learnt a huge amount from our discussions with Prof. Richard Neufville of MIT.

We would like to particularly thank Prof. V. Raghunathan of Varalakshmi Foundation as well as the GMR top management for the support and access that they provided to us in writing the case study on the Indira Gandhi International Airport at Delhi. Mandar Kagade and Aadhaar Verma at the Bharti Institute provided great help in creating the initial draft of the case study.

Sagarika Ghosh and Nupoor Singh of Springer shepherded the project in the most encouraging manner. Praveen Kumar and other Springer team members provided great support without which this project would never have been completed.

The OP Jindal Global University has been the academic home of Prof. Chakrabarti for much of this project. Special thanks to the Vice Chancellor, Prof. Raj Kumar and the Dean, Jindal Global Business School, Prof. Tapan Panda for their support.

We alone remain responsible for the errors and shortcomings that we are sure have crept into and remained in the book despite our best efforts. We can only appeal to the readers' indulgence and kind feedback here.

Kumar V. Pratap
Rajesh Chakrabarti

Contents

About the Authors[1]

Dr. Kumar V. Pratap is currently Joint Secretary (Infrastructure Policy and Finance) at the Department of Economic Affairs, Ministry of Finance, Government of India. Earlier, he has worked with the Prime Minister's Office, Ministries of Finance and Urban Development, and Planning Commission (New Delhi, India), and the World Bank and Embassy of India (Washington DC, USA). He has lectured at various reputed institutions, both in India and abroad, and is also a visiting faculty at the Indian School of Business, Hyderabad and Mohali. He has been part of many Government of India committees in the infrastructure sectors including the Task Force for setting up a Road Regulator and the chair of the Committee writing the Model Concession Agreement for Public–Private Partnerships (PPPs) in the Urban Water Supply sector. He is on the Board of Directors of Indore Smart City Development Limited. He has published with Oxford University Press, the World Bank, *Economic and Political Weekly*, and the popular press. He is a recipient of a letter of appreciation from the Indian Prime Minister, and fellowships from the University of Melbourne's Emerging Leaders program, and University of Maryland's John J Sexton and doctoral programs. He has a MBA from Indian Institute of Management, Lucknow, India (1987) and a PhD from the University of Maryland, College Park, USA (2011).

Dr. Rajesh Chakrabarti is Professor and Executive Vice Dean at the Jindal Global Business School, Jindal Global University, Sonipat, India, and co-founder of Sunay Policy Advisory based in Gurugram, India. He has taught finance for over a decade and a half—at the University of Alberta, Canada, Georgia Tech, USA, and the Indian School of Business (ISB). As the founding Executive Director of the Bharti Institute of Public Policy at ISB's Mohali campus, he helped design and launch one of India's leading public policy programs. He has also been Executive Vice President, Research and Policy at the Wadhwani Foundation. Rajesh has held visiting positions at various institutions including Indian Institute of Management (IIM) Calcutta, Indian Statistical Institute (ISI) Delhi, India Development

[1]Views are personal and may not correspond with the views of the organizations with which the authors are affiliated.

Foundation (IDF) Gurgaon, ICN Business School, Nancy, France, and the Federal Reserve Bank of Atlanta. He has authored or edited eight books, in addition to authoring several book chapters and articles on finance, economics, and management in leading international scholarly journals. He has been a columnist with the *Financial Express* and is frequently quoted in the media. His current research interests are in the areas of management and public policy. Rajesh is an alumnus of Presidency College, Kolkata, and IIM Ahmedabad, and earned his PhD from the University of California, Los Angeles, USA.

Abbreviations

AAI	Airports Authority of India
AC	Average Cost
ACS	Average Cost of Supply
AERA	Airports Economic Regulatory Authority
ALM	Asset-Liability Mismatch
AMI	Advanced Metering Infrastructure
AMSS	Amarchand & Mangaldas & Suresh Shroff & Co
AP	Andhra Pradesh
APTEL	Appellate Tribunal for Electricity
ARR	Aggregate Revenue Requirement
AT	Average Tariff
AT&C	Aggregate Technical and Commercial Losses
BGT	Biwater Gauff (Tanzania) Limited
BHEL	Bharat Heavy Electricals Limited
BOO	Build–Own–Operate
BOOT	Build–Own–Operate–Transfer
BOT	Build–Operate–Transfer
BRICS	Brazil, Russia, India, China, South Africa
BRPL	BSES Rajdhani Power Limited
BSNL	Bharat Sanchar Nigam Limited
BTC	Baku–Tbilisi–Ceyhan
BYPL	BSES Yamuna Power Limited
CA	Concession Agreement
CAG	Comptroller and Auditor General of India
CCGT	Combined Cycle Gas Turbine
CCI	Cabinet Committee on Infrastructure
CDPQ	Caisse de depot et placement du Quebec
CERC	Central Electricity Regulatory Commission
CESCO	Central Electricity Supply Company of Orissa
CGPL	Coastal Gujarat Power Limited

CIL	Coal India Limited
COD	Commercial Operation Date
CoS	Committee of Secretaries
CPI (UNME)	Consumer Price Index for Urban Non-Manual Employees
CPPIB	Canada Pension Plan Investment Board
CRR	Cash Reserve Ratio
CSA	Coal Supply Agreement
CSO	Civil Society Organization
CWS	City Water Services Ltd
DAME	Delhi Airport Metro Express
DAMEPL	Delhi Airport Metro Express Private Limited
DAWASA	Dar-es-Salaam Water and Sewerage Authority
DAWASCO	Dar-es-Salaam Water and Sewerage Corporation
DBFOT	Design–Build–Finance–Operate–Transfer
DERC	Delhi Electricity Regulatory Commission
DESU	Delhi Electricity Supply Undertaking
DF	Development Fee
DIAL	Delhi International Airport Limited
DMRC	Delhi Metro Rail Corporation
DPC	Dabhol Power Company
DPR	Detailed Project Report
DVB	Delhi Vidyut Board
EAP	East Asia and Pacific
EBIT	Earnings before Interest and Taxes
EC	Evaluation Committee
ECB	External Commercial Borrowings
EGoM	Empowered Group of Ministers
EMIO	Emerging Market Investors and Operators
EMP	Enhanced Monitoring Period
EP	Equator Principles
EPC	Engineering, Procurement and Construction
EWURA	Energy and Water Utilities Regulatory Authority
FARAC	Fideicomiso de Apoyo al Rescate de Autopistas Concesionadas
FC	Financial Consultant
FDI	Foreign Direct Investment
FII	Foreign Institutional Investment
FRBM	Fiscal Responsibility and Budget Management
GCF	Gross Capital Formation
GCR	Global Competitiveness Report
GDP	Gross Domestic Product
GDR	Global Depository Receipt
GETE	Group of Eminent Technical Experts
GNPA	Gross Non-Performing Assets
GoI	Government of India
GoM	Group of Ministers

GoT	Government of Tanzania
GRC	Government Review Committee
GTA	Global Technical Adviser
HAM	Hybrid Annuity Model
HOT	High Occupancy Toll
HPEC	High-Powered Expert Committee
HSR	High-Speed Rail
ICR	Interest Coverage Ratio
ICSID	International Centre for Settlement of Investment Disputes
IDF	Infrastructure Debt Funds
IDP	Initial Development Plan
IE	Independent Engineer
IFC	International Finance Corporation
IGIA	Indira Gandhi International Airport
IIFCL	India Infrastructure Finance Company Limited
IMG	Inter-Ministerial Group
INFRA	Infrastructure Recovery and Assets
IOC	Indian Oil Corporation
IPO	Initial Public Offer
IRDA	Insurance Regulatory and Development Authority
IRFC	Indian Railway Finance Corporation
IRSDC	Indian Railway Station Development Corporation
JICA	Japan International Cooperation Agency
JNNURM	Jawaharlal Nehru National Urban Renewal Mission
JV	Joint Venture
JVC	Joint Venture Company
kWh	Kilowatt hour
L&T IDPL	L&T Infrastructure Development Projects Limited
LAA	Land Acquisition Act, 1894
LAC	Latin America and Caribbean
LC	Legal Consultant
LD	Lease Deed
LNG	Liquefied Natural Gas
MA HSR	Mumbai–Ahmedabad High-Speed Rail
MC	Marginal Cost
MCA	Model Concession Agreement
MCP	Mandatory Capital Project
MERC	Maharashtra Electricity Regulatory Commission
MES	Military Engineering Services
MMTPA	Million Metric Tonnes Per Annum
MoCA	Ministry of Civil Aviation
MoEF	Ministry of Environment and Forests
MoF	Ministry of Finance
MoU	Memorandum of Understanding
MR	Marginal Revenue

MSEB	Maharashtra State Electricity Board
MSEDCL	Maharashtra State Electricity Distribution Company Limited
MSS	Mahan Sangharsh Samiti
MSW	Municipal Solid Waste
MTNL	Mahanagar Telephone Nigam Limited
MYT(O)	Multi-Year Tariff (Order)
NAFTA	North American Free Trade Agreement
NBFC	Non-Banking Finance Company
NDA	National Democratic Alliance
NDMC	New Delhi Municipal Council
NDPL	North Delhi Power Limited
NDTL	Net Demand and Time Liabilities
NGO	Non-Governmental Organization
NHAI	National Highways Authority of India
NHDP	National Highways Development Project
NOIDA	New Okhla Industrial Development Authority
NPA	Non-Performing Assets
NPC	Net Present Cost
NRHM	National Rural Health Mission
NRW	Non-Revenue Water
NTBCL	Noida Toll Bridge Company Limited
NTDPC	National Transport Development Policy Committee
NUWA	National Urban Water Authority
O&M	Operation and Maintenance
ODA	Official Development Assistance
OECD	Organization for Economic Cooperation and Development
OMDA	Operation, Management and Development Agreement
OPIC	Overseas Private Investment Corporation
P	Price
PAP	Project Affected Persons
PC	Planning Commission
PCEL	Pink City Expressway Private Limited
PE	Private Equity
PFC	Power Finance Corporation
PFI	Private Finance Initiative
PGCIL	Power Grid Corporation of India Limited
PLF	Plant Load Factor
POG	Procurement of Goods (Contract)
PPA	Power Purchase Agreement
PPI	Private Participation in Infrastructure
PPP	Public–Private Partnership
PSC	Public Sector Comparator
PSL	Priority Sector Lending
PSP	Private Sector Participation
PSU	Public Sector Undertaking

PV	Present Value
PwC	Price Waterhouse Coopers
QCBS	Quality-cum-Cost Based System
R&R	Rehabilitation and Resettlement
RAM	Rational Actor Model
RBI	Reserve Bank of India
REC	Rural Electrification Corporation
RFCTLARR	Right to Fair Compensation and Transparency in Land Acquisition, Rehabilitation and Resettlement (Act, 2013)
RfP	Request for Proposal
RfQ	Request for Qualification
RGPPL	Ratnagiri Gas and Power Private Limited
RIL	Reliance Industries Limited
RLNG	Regasified Liquefied Natural Gas
RoFR	Right of First Refusal
ROT	Rehabilitate–Operate–Transfer
SAR	South Asia Region
SBD	Standard Bidding Documents
SBI	State Bank of India
SCM	Smart City Mission
SEB	State Electricity Board
SERC	State Electricity Regulatory Commission
SHA	Shareholders Agreement
SIPE	Supply and Installation of Plant and Equipment (Contract)
SLR	Statutory Liquidity Ratio
SoE	State-owned Enterprise
SPV	Special Purpose Vehicle
SSA	State Support Agreement
SSA	Sub-Saharan Africa
STM	Super Doll Trailer Manufacture Co. (T) Limited
SWM	Solid Waste Management
T&D	Transmission and Distribution
TAMP	Tariff Authority for Major Ports
TAPI	Turkmenistan–Afghanistan–Pakistan–India
THSRC	Taiwan High-Speed Rail Corporation
TINA	There Is No Alternative
ToD	Time-of-Day (tariff)
TPC	Total Project Cost
TPDDL	Tata Power Delhi Distribution Limited
TRAI	Telecom Regulatory Authority of India
UDAY	Ujwal Discom Assurance Yojana
ULB	Urban Local Body
UMPP	Ultra Mega Power Project
UNCITRAL	United Nations Commission on International Trade Law
UPA	United Progressive Alliance

USD	United States Dollar
VDOT	Virginia Department of Transportation
VfM	Value for Money
VGF	Viability Gap Funding

Prologue: The Delhi Noida Toll Bridge

Since its opening to traffic in February 2001, the Delhi Noida Toll Bridge across the River Yamuna has vastly improved the quality of commute and hence life itself for millions in India's capital. It was one of the first major Public–Private Partnership (PPP) projects in the country, and with its majestic eight-lane span, cloverleaf interchange, and modern approach road system on the Noida side as well as its connect to the Ashram flyover on the Delhi side, the 6-km-long bridge pretty much introduced modern planned road system structure in the country.

Many would argue that the bridge contributed much more to India than just the resulting ease of transport. As one of the very first PPP projects in the country, it literally provided concrete proof of the concept in the nation that would soon catapult to hosting the second highest number of PPP projects in the developing world. It provided functioning evidence that private capital could be effectively harnessed to provide public services. And with a series of firsts to its credit, it had opened multiple doors across sectors.

The construction of the mammoth structure was completed in 25 months, 4 months ahead of schedule. This was almost an unheard of accomplishment in the Indian setting, where time overruns in creating public infrastructure is a generally assumed feature. It was also completed within its budget of approximately Rs. 4.08 billion. More than anything else, it underlined the efficiencies of private project management, the mainstay of the PPP argument.

The project broke new ground in India's still fledgling capital markets by making an Initial Public Offer (IPO) of Deep Discount Bonds, first by any green-field infrastructure company. Its ability to raise funds from the market again proved the viability of the model on the financing side. It succeeded in raising money abroad as well through a Global Depository Receipt (GDR) issue. It was the first private infrastructure project to be listed on a stock exchange.

But this is only part of the story. In 2007, India's erstwhile Planning Commission, the key backer of infrastructure PPPs in the country, released a review with a scathing criticism of the manner in which the Toll Bridge was contracted and what that has implied for the exchequer.

The saga of the Delhi Noida Toll Bridge is both long and instructive. In April 1992, the government of Delhi, UP's New Okhla Industrial Development Authority (NOIDA), and the private sector infrastructure financing entity, IL&FS had signed a Memorandum of Understanding (MoU) to create the Toll Bridge. IL&FS created a subsidiary, Noida Toll Bridge Company Limited (NTBCL) exactly 4 years later in April 1996. The Concession Agreement (CA), or the contract defining the project, got signed another year and a half later, in November 1997. It granted the NTBCL the right to Build, Own, Operate, and Transfer (BOOT) the Toll Bridge for 30 years, extendable if certain conditions were not met. NTBCL was entitled to charge tolls to passing vehicles, the quantum of which would be revised periodically in step with inflation by a committee with representatives of all major stakeholders. Importantly, NTBCL will receive an assured post-tax return of 20% on the entire capital employed—project cost, repair costs, and the shortfall from the assured return in the previous year. NOIDA could give IL&FS Land Development Rights to make up for the shortfall in assured returns. Two months later, the governments of Delhi and UP signed "support agreements" to facilitate construction of the bridge and approach roads, respectively. By December 1998, Intertoll Services Management BV of Netherlands, subsidiary of an eponymous South African company, was brought in as the maintenance partner. Construction started within a few months.

Upon inauguration in 2001, however, the commercial reality did not live up to the projections. The expected traffic growth, particularly of the commercial traffic, did not take place, and the project continued to make losses for the next 5 years adding up to over Rs. 1.20 billion. Within a year of start of the operations, the company approached the institutional lenders and obtained a debt restructuring and succeeded in obtaining judicial approval in 2005 to alter the terms of its Deep Discount Bonds. The debt restructuring also triggered use of the land development rights granted under the CA. The cumulative shortfall of the assured 20% return meant an extension of the life of the concession well beyond the 30 years.

The disappointing financial performance and the fiscal burden it imposed on the public partners prompted a relook at the Concession Agreement itself. The 2007 Planning Commission review strongly criticized it for being biased to the private partners. Among other things, it argued that the central clause of 20% assured return to the project on capital employed was at the core of many of the problems since (i) without any cap on project cost it incentivized overinvestment; (ii) the interest rates being in the 12–16% range and the project being heavily leveraged, as is typical of project-financed infrastructure, it provided an unjustifiably high rate of virtually risk-free return on equity in excess of 30%; (iii) the inclusion of the shortfall of assured return in the capital employed, the base of the assured return, transferred the entire risk to the public partner with no incentive for the private partner to improve financial performance. It also pointed out several provisions that gave the project sponsor undue influence in setting terms in its own favor. One of its strongest objection was that the project award mechanism used a single-party negotiated contract rather than a public tender to private partners which would have allowed competitive forces to reduce the burden on the public sector.

A 2012 review of the project by one of the authors found that the total project cost would increase to over Rs. 830 billion (over 200 times the original project cost) by the end of the original contract period in 2031 on current traffic trends. In addition, since the project would never make as much money as guaranteed by the CA, it would last till perpetuity.

In October 2016, the Allahabad High Court, citing several reasons, including compromising public interest,[2] directed that, henceforth, the Concessionaire, Noida Toll Bridge Company, shall not impose or recover any user fee/toll from the commuters for using the Delhi Noida Toll Bridge.

With the Delhi Noida Toll Bridge, India had entered the era of infrastructure PPPs. It epitomized the PPP experience, both in its success in terms of swiftly delivering a swanky, well-maintained twenty-first century public asset, and its challenges and controversies, including over-optimistic (in hindsight) growth projections and acrimony over a flawed concession agreement. The sector and the country would have to learn to resolve these challenges and craft projects more efficiently over the years to come. For, despite all its challenges and roadblocks, infrastructure PPPs are here to stay.

[2]The Allahabad High Court judgment dated 26.10.2016 says "The action of NOIDA in awarding the Concession Agreement dated 10.11.1997 in favour of NOIDA Toll Bridge Company i.e. the Concessionaire fails to satisfy the test of reasonableness and public interest".

Chapter 1
Infrastructure and Public–Private Partnerships: Overview and Key Issues

1 Infrastructure and PPPs—An Overview

It is well accepted that investment in infrastructure is essential for growth. Infrastructure investment expands the productive capacity of a nation, on the one hand by increasing resources, and on the other, by raising the productivity of existing resources.[1] Infrastructure investment also crowds in private investment leading to more growth, jobs, and economic well-being. Surveys of prospective foreign investors show that availability and quality of infrastructure is a critical factor in selecting potential investment sites. At the macro-level, it is seen that countries with good roads, railways, airport and port connections, telecommunication networks, and power supply have lower costs, higher competitiveness, attract significant investments, create more jobs, all this leading to higher growth and incomes through a virtuous circle.

As a corollary, inadequate infrastructure is a major hindrance to growth. Power shortages lead to dependence on expensive captive power, which in turn implies higher costs and lack of competitiveness for the economy. Inadequate transport infrastructure leads to bottlenecks both in the supply of raw materials as well as movement of finished goods to the marketplace. Poor connectivity could also hinder "just-in-time" delivery of products increasing the inventory costs. The price that farmers get for their produce is depressed if there is no connectivity through good quality rural roads, which in turn keeps rural incomes suppressed negating the fruits of high overall growth performance. For all these reasons, provision of adequate infrastructure is essential for growth and for making this growth inclusive.

[1]Munnell (1992)

K.V. Pratap and R. Chakrabarti, *Public-Private Partnerships in Infrastructure*, India Studies in Business and Economics, DOI 10.1007/978-981-10-3355-1_1

1.1 Infrastructure Deficit in Developing Countries

Several countries, particularly those in the emerging markets, today witness yawning infrastructure gaps when compared to the industrialized nations. Apart from affecting the lives of their citizens, the infrastructure deficit significantly reduces their ability to attract private investment holding back growth. The high positive correlation in the *Global Competitiveness Report*'s ranking of nations and availability of infrastructure points to the close connection between the two. Both directly, in terms of its effect on productivity and indirectly, through reducing attractiveness to foreign investors, infrastructure deficits are a significant drag on growth.

1.2 Who Should Provide Infrastructure

The history of shouldering the responsibility of infrastructure provisioning between the public and private sectors has gone through a cycle. Till the middle of the twentieth century, private participation in infrastructure was more the norm rather than exception. Private turnpikes and toll roads were common in the US, for instance.

The three decades from 1950 to 1980 saw the public sector capture the "commanding heights" of the economy, including infrastructure, around the world—through nationalization and, particularly in the newly independent third world, in the public works that began to create the sorely missed infrastructure.

The tide began to turn in the 1980s in consonance with the Reagan–Thatcher pushback to public sector and, almost everywhere, because of the paucity of state coffers to fund infrastructure projects, Public–Private Partnerships (PPPs) made their emergence and became increasingly common around the world, particularly in the developing countries and emerging markets.

1.3 How Public–Private Partnerships (PPPs) Can Help

Broadly speaking, PPPs are commercial transactions between public and private parties where the latter performs a traditionally "public" function for a substantial period of time, assumes related risks—construction, commercial, and operational—and receives a payment for its services, paid either by the public party or the users, or both.

PPPs can play a useful role in augmenting infrastructure and addressing many concerns. However, PPPs have to be carefully structured and implemented for them to be able to provide infrastructure in a sustainable fashion.

Addressing Resource Crunch of Governments

The starting point of Public–Private Partnerships in most countries is the resource crunch of governments. PPPs can help increase infrastructure funding through, for example, charging users for services and improving asset utilization, thereby creating additional revenue streams.

However, the benefit of PPP in terms of additional revenue streams is less clear if it is completely funded by deferred government expenditure, for example, as in a PPP annuity project. The net present value of a PPP project financed through government annuity payments may not be too different from that of similar publicly funded project. Nevertheless, even in such cases, PPPs can help governments overcome annual budget constraints as the capital cost of the PPP project is spread over its lifetime through annuity payments, rather than incurred at the beginning. This would make it possible for governments to fund more new infrastructure projects within annual budgetary restrictions.

There are other ways in which the competitive and business-oriented nature of PPPs help.

Project Selection: Since project selection under conventional procurement is essentially a political process, many inappropriate projects could be chosen for political economy reasons. Since a PPP project has to be financially justified for it to be able to raise private finance, it is harder to select inefficient projects in the PPP mode.

Infrastructure Management: Publicly provided infrastructure is plagued with inefficiency because of lack of accountability, poor incentives, and agency issues. As a result, publicly provided infrastructure often suffers from time and cost overruns in construction, and high-cost and poor-quality services in operations. PPPs are generally more efficiently managed. Studies have shown that more PPPs have been delivered within time and budget than traditionally procured projects and in cases where time and cost over runs are there, the extent is lower. There are stronger incentives for private companies to bring projects in operation on time and on budget as their returns are dependent on it—such incentives are usually absent under traditional procurement.

Maintenance: Traditionally, public sector prefers new investment to maintenance expenditure for political economy reasons. Maintenance projects may have a much higher rate of return than new investments, but are often less politically appealing. PPPs generally combine construction and maintenance into a single contract, thus incentivizing high-quality construction by the private company upfront as well as regular maintenance of the asset. This is because revenues through user charges depend on providing superior services to users.

Customer Service Orientation: Many private sector infrastructure providers depend on user fees for servicing their investments and as such need to provide superior customer service. This is often not the case with public sector providers.

In addition, PPPs enable governments to focus on their core business. Thus, the core business of schools is to teach children. PPPs in schools can be developed in a way that the private sector takes care of the school building, cleaning, security, grounds maintenance, and information technology within these schools, allowing school teachers to spend most of their time on the core business. This focus on core business is expected to improve efficiency in provisioning of infrastructure.

PPPs also release governmental resources from commercial sectors by transferring these responsibilities to the private sector, enabling governments to focus on noncommercial sectors like rural roads.

1.4 Not Always a Perfect Solution

However, benefits from PPPs are not automatic and the project and the contracts have to be carefully structured and monitored for benefits to flow from them. There are many cases where PPP projects have either stalled or backfired and/or ended up costing the public exchequer exorbitantly while protecting private interests. There are instances of private companies getting bankrupt as well, with the asset in question either never coming up or functioning unsatisfactorily owing to failure from the public side to live up to its promises.

1.4.1 Renegotiation of Long-Term Infrastructure Contracts

Owing to its lumpy, politically visible nature as well as its often natural monopoly feature, public authorities are often forced to renegotiate when PPP projects are stressed, particularly if the stress is caused by a factor not completely under the private party's control. Renegotiations, however, vitiate the sanctity of the contract and their outcomes generally end up against the public sector.

The very idea of inducting the private sector into infrastructure from the public sector perspective is to see that the government gains through risk transfer, especially construction and commercial risks, to the private sector. If that does not happen, through renegotiations, for example, then the public sector may find the contract too onerous, perhaps building up the case for its premature termination in public interest. Unviable PPP projects should be allowed to fail rather than make efforts to prolong their life with unviable renegotiations at great cost to the public sector.

2 What Lies Ahead—The Plan for the Rest of the Book

This introduction only touches upon a few of the themes covered in this volume to provide the proverbial 30,000 feet view of the flight path. The rest of the book is structured as follows.

The book is divided into two parts. The first part comprising Chaps. 2 through 8 cover the concepts associated with PPP projects as well as the broad evidence pertaining to PPPs from around the world, with a tilt towards the emerging markets.

It includes detailed case studies from various parts of the world to support and elucidate its message. The second part, comprising Chaps. 9 through 11 focus on infrastructure PPP issues in a single specific emerging market—India—to get a more in-depth understanding of the nature of issues that dog the world of infrastructure PPPs.

Chapter 2 discusses the special economic features of infrastructure investment particularly the large externalities associated with them and their "public good" nature that make them a special class in themselves. It also presents the broad history and evolution of infrastructure provisioning between private and public sectors to create the background and context for the subject of this volume.

Chapter 3 covers issues with infrastructure finance. Many private infrastructure projects are implemented on a project finance basis, which implies a highly leveraged balance sheet. However, bank finance is the main source of debt which causes an asset-liability mismatch for the banking sector given that infrastructure assets are long-term while the liabilities like time deposits are relatively short term.

Chapter 4 deals with PPP concepts and brings out that optimal risk allocation between the public and private sectors is at the heart of PPPs. While PPPs can help mitigate resource constraints of the public sectors, and bring about other benefits like construction of infrastructure assets without time and cost overruns and efficient delivery of infrastructure services, the benefits of PPPs are not automatic. These expected benefits of PPP provided infrastructure services would fructify depending on how well the contracts are written and enforced. The chapter includes an analysis of the Delhi Airport Metro Express as an example of a contract gone wrong.

An appendix to Chap. 4 deals with the important concept of Value for Money (VfM) that ought to be paid attention to, for ensuring that appropriate projects are selected for implementation in the PPP mode and they are structured properly to provide value to the government.

Chapter 5 deals with alternative PPP models and issues associated with each of the models. There could be a number of private participation arrangements, beginning with management contracts where minimal risks are shared by the private sector, and continuing up to Design–Build–Finance–Operate–Transfer models, which involve substantial risk sharing by the private sector. It has been shown that higher degrees of risk transfer to the private sector produces better results for the public sector, but there could be a number of reasons why the public authority prefers management contracts, say in the water and sanitation sector. A case study on Dar es Salaam Water and Sewerage Services as an example of a lease contract is also a part of this chapter.

Chapter 6 deals with the sectoral spread of PPPs and we find that while PPPs are quite widespread in the telecom and energy generation sectors, there are few PPP projects in water and power distribution sectors. This is mainly because the tariffs in the latter sectors are way below costs, and while the private sector can bring in efficiencies, the initial cost under-recovery may be too wide to bridge with politically feasible tariff increases. A case study on the Mexican Toll Roads attempts to help exemplify the issues involved.

Chapter 7 focuses on designing and managing PPP transactions. Here, the best practice is to have competitive bidding as opposed to negotiations to select the winning bidder. For such high-value transactions as infrastructure projects, the best practice is to have a two-stage bidding process: Request for Qualification (RfQ) stage where the technical and financial capacity of prospective bidders is evaluated so as to qualify for the Request for Proposal (RfP) stage. In the RfP stage, competition should generally be based on a single bidding parameter among prequalified bidders. The draft Concession Agreement should form part of the bidding documents to be given to the prequalified bidders at the RfP stage.

Chapter 8 covers regulation of infrastructure. Many infrastructure sectors like power and water distribution are natural monopolies. There is a need for price and quality regulation in these sectors because competition cannot regulate these parameters. Four regulatory institutions have come up in the infrastructure sectors of India: electricity (CERC and SERCs), telecom (TRAI), ports (TAMP), and airports (AERA). But, there is no uniformity in the powers, recruitment rules, conditions of service, etc., of these regulators. So, the government is thinking of regulatory reforms, which would also enhance the accountability of these regulators.

Chapter 9, the first chapter of the second part of the book focusing on India, deals with the policy framework of PPPs in India and its role in determining their relative prevalence across sectors. India is second in the developing world in terms of both the number of PPP projects as well as associated investments. But most PPP projects have come in the road and power generation sectors. Like the rest of the world, there are very few PPPs in power and water distribution, mainly because of political economy issues that prohibit financial feasibility as we discussed in Chap. 6. This chapter would also discuss the land acquisition issue and the issue of environmental clearances, which are responsible for a number of stalled infrastructure projects.

Chapter 10 is on Renegotiation and Cancellation of Infrastructure PPPs, once again with a strong focus on the Indian experience. All PPP contracts are incomplete contracts as it is difficult to foresee developments over a 20–30 year contract period. Therefore, renegotiation of PPP contracts may, at times, be inevitable. However, renegotiations also give rise to a number of issues, including corruption, which queer the pitch for all PPPs. The chapter looks at some examples of renegotiations in the Indian context. Lately, the incidence of PPP project cancelation has gone up in India to catch-up with the rest of the world. However, this is not necessarily a bad development as canceling projects rather than renegotiating them would give rise to more realistic bids and lesser renegotiations.

Chapter 11 presents an assortment of in-depth analyses and detailed case studies in an attempt to flesh out the real life nature of infrastructure PPP projects in India. It begins with an analysis of all PPP projects under India's National Highways Development Program (Phase I) and finds that the value for money to the government from these projects is mildly positive after allowance is made for the transfer of construction risk to the private sector. Then it presents three in-depth and distinct case studies: the Dabhol Power Project in Maharashtra; the Delhi Power Distribution Project; and the Delhi International Airport Limited project.

Part I
Infrastructure PPPs—Concepts and Evidence

Chapter 2
Infrastructure Challenges

In this chapter, we describe infrastructure and its characteristics, and how these characteristics have been instrumental in their provisioning, which even now is primarily provided by the government. However, for various reasons, numerous challenges have emerged that need to be addressed so that infrastructure does not become a binding constraint to economic development. The chapter is divided into two parts—the first focuses on understanding the key characteristics of infrastructure, while the second delves into understanding the implications of these characteristics on infrastructure investment.

Part I: Understanding Infrastructure

This part is divided into three sections: attempting a definition of infrastructure; examining the key characteristic features of infrastructure; and focusing on the macroeconomic implications of infrastructure—the link between infrastructure and development.

1 Defining Infrastructure

Infrastructure—literally the "underlying structure"—is surprisingly hard to define. Apparently, the word has its roots in French and was first used in English in 1927 and, hard to believe today, did not gain currency in economic discussions till well into the last quarter of the twentieth century. Harvard University's law department conducted a survey in 2011 of pension fund investors on what they understand by the term (See "Infrastructure—Defining Matters"). The definitions that seemed to

K.V. Pratap and R. Chakrabarti, *Public-Private Partnerships in Infrastructure*,
India Studies in Business and Economics, DOI 10.1007/978-981-10-3355-1_2

receive a reasonable degree of unanimity were "that which provide[s] services and support that are basic to the functioning of a community, organization, or society and crucial to its economic productivity" with "what are the basic physical and organizational capacities and resources needed for the operation of a society or enterprise or are necessary for an economy to function" coming second.

It is important to note that the key elements of these definitions stress: (1) physical (hard) or organizational/social (soft); (2) criticality to functioning of economy. Broadly speaking, therefore, the following industries would generally be included by the term:

A. Economic Infrastructure: Energy projects (power generation, transmission, and distribution projects, natural gas projects, renewable energy projects); Telecom (telecom services, network, broadband network and internet services); Transport (roads, bridges, railways, ports, inland waterways, airports); Urban infrastructure (metro system, water supply—both water treatment plants and water distribution network, solid waste management, and sewerage);
B. Social infrastructure: Construction and management of educational institutions and hospitals. Social infrastructure is a more recent broadening definition of infrastructure. Education and health have characteristics similar to economic infrastructure like significant externalities, large investments, long gestation period, and most importantly, criticality for economic development.

Apart from these, pockets of entrepreneurial support like industrial parks, and special economic zones, as well as chunky critical inputs to agriculture like irrigation and storage, are also included in the definition of infrastructure in many contexts.

A few almost essential features of infrastructure—particularly physical infrastructure—that may help define it are listed below[1]:

- Capital goods, providing essential services, not products consumed directly;
- Lumpy, not incremental or divisible: If you need to build a 300-ft bridge, a 30-ft structure will not provide 10% of the benefits;
- Long-lived (some European cities still use Roman structures, Indian metros, British-era sewerage system); this is related to it being capital goods, but even among capital goods they tend to be very long-lived;
- Generally stationary, linked to location, immobile;
- Capital intensive and often requiring relatively long to create.

We examine the nature and implications of these characteristics in greater detail in the next section.

[1]Prud'homme (2004).

2 Infrastructure Characteristics

Infrastructure has certain characteristics, which largely determines how it is provided. Let us look at some of these infrastructure characteristics, which are broadly applicable to all infrastructure sectors.

2.1 Lumpy with Large Upfront Investments

Infrastructure investment tends to be huge and "lumpy" (i.e., spaced apart). Thus, at an average of $1 million per Mega Watt (MW) of capacity, a 4,000 MW coal-based power project [the Ultra Mega Power Projects (UMPPs) in India are each of 4,000 MW] may cost up to $4 billion, which is a huge investment for a single project. This investment has to be brought in the construction period, which is typically 3–4 years. So, there is a huge investment requirement, which needs to be brought upfront without any expectation of return in the first 3–4 years construction period. This level of investments requires providers with deep pockets, which in many emerging markets, may only be from the public sector or foreign investors.

2.2 High Sunk Costs

Infrastructure investments are generally sunk. Thus, investments in networks of piped gas supply, piped water supply, and transmission lines cannot generally be converted to other uses or moved elsewhere, and are therefore mostly irrecoverable, unlike, for example, the investment in a vehicle. Once incurred, these costs are "sunk." Such costs arise when, for instance, means of production (e.g., buildings, machines, infrastructure) are so use-specific that they cannot—completely or effectively—be used in other markets segments (Gent et al. 2004).

Large sunk costs are an important source of natural monopoly. Where the unit costs of producing an extra unit of good or service or servicing an additional user fall over a wide output range, economies of scale are created, which is an important source of "natural monopoly."

2.3 Long Gestation Period

Construction of infrastructure projects entails a long gestation period. For example, in general, construction of a coal-based power generation project may take up to 5 years, while construction of a greenfield four-lane road project may take up to 3 years. This implies that the construction agencies, whether public or the private sector, should have the technical and financial capacity to sustain the project for the long gestation period in which no returns may be forthcoming.

2.4 Long Payback Period

Infrastructure entails large capital investments. The need for keeping user charges reasonable implies that the payback period should also be long. This is facilitated by the fact that life of infrastructure assets often is 30 years or more, e.g., for example, road, airport, or power projects. Such long payback periods make infrastructure difficult to finance. However, it is also true that steady long-term returns of infrastructure assets may be attractive to pension and insurance funds.

2.5 Public Planning, an Important Aspect

Infrastructure has strong linkages to growth and development. Therefore, governments plan for augmenting infrastructure so that it does not become a binding constraint to growth. However, this also entails additional risks as many infrastructure services are essential services and their provisioning and pricing is politically sensitive. There is also a bias towards high-visibility new construction projects over more sustainable, longer term solutions for political economy reasons, hiking costs and reducing the cost competitiveness of economies.

2.6 Natural Monopoly Characteristics

A monopoly describes a market structure where a single firm caters to the major part of the market. A natural monopoly is characterized by large economies of scale, which implies that the larger the scale of output, the lower the costs. This arises when the marginal (or extra) cost of producing another unit keeps declining as output rises, giving an advantage to larger producers ultimately leading to a natural monopoly. This acts as a barrier to entry for industries with natural monopoly characteristics, which in turn perpetuates the monopoly. This tends to be the case in industries where capital costs predominate, creating economies of scale that are large in relation to the size of the market: examples include public utilities such as water services and electricity or transportation services (Perloff 2012). This also underlines the need for independent regulation to mimic the outcomes of a perfectly competitive market (reasonable user charges, etc).

2.7 *Non-tradability of Output*

For many infrastructure sectors, services have to be provided in situ, e.g., road services. While electricity can be imported from abroad (India imported 5.1 billion units of electricity from Bhutan in 2014–15), the same does not hold for roads as they have to be provided in situ. Since users cannot generally substitute infrastructure services with imported services, there would be a need to develop domestic capacity in the public and private sectors and provide a conducive business environment to foreign investors to invest in the host country.

2.8 *Large Externalities*

Infrastructure assets are generally associated with significant positive and negative externalities. Good transport and communication facilities may crowd-in private industries as they would benefit from lower costs. Similarly, rural roads, education, and health may have large positive externalities. One of the common examples of negative externality is higher pollution that may follow road expansion. Allowing unfettered market forces to provide infrastructure services with significant externalities would result in under- or over-provision of services. Managing externalities requires market intervention through thoughtful regulation and, in the case of economically beneficial but financially nonviable projects, government support. In India, the Viability Gap Funding scheme is designed to provide support to projects that produce positive externalities and are economically viable but do not cross the standard thresholds of financial viability.

2.9 *Interconnected System*

Infrastructure assets form interconnected networks and have strong cross-cutting effects, e.g., unstable power supply can severely affect transport modes dependent on electricity like the Delhi Metro Rail Network. Infrastructure, therefore, needs to be managed, as large, partially integrated systems—there is a need for close coordination among infrastructure institutions. But, today, responsibility for infrastructure provision tends to be scattered across local (water supply services in Indian cities), provincial (power distribution), and national (railways) jurisdictions and various infrastructure authorities (like a public sector undertaking, NTPC supplying about a quarter of India's electricity through mainly thermal power projects) that administer different asset classes. Thus, while electricity distribution is managed by three private and one public sector distribution company in Delhi,

Delhi Metro is managed by the public sector, Delhi Metro Rail Corporation (DMRC).

2.10 Some Public Good Characteristics

Table 1 below shows a broad typology of goods and services based on their two major characteristics: rivalness and excludability. In contrast to private goods where consumption by one user reduces the supply available to other users (think in terms of ice cream available to me after a friend bites into it), being non-rival in consumption means that consumption by one user does not reduce the supply available to other users, e.g., availability of road for car users up to congestion limits. Being non-excludable means that a user cannot be prevented from consuming a service once it has been provided, e.g., good law and order.

Market mechanism works best in providing pure private goods or services, which are both rival in consumption and excludable. Examples of private goods would be food, clothing, cars, personal electronics, etc. Toll goods, which are excludable but non-rival up to congestion limits are cinemas, private parks, and toll roads—tolls are used to restrict access to these services by non-paying users, while also serving as a method to cover costs. Similarly, examples of common pool resources, which are non-excludable but rival, are fish stocks, timber, and coal.

Pure public goods are both non-rival in consumption and non-excludable. The all-time favorite example of a pure public good is a lighthouse. Since its services are both non-excludable (one cannot prevent non-payers from enjoying the benefits of the service) and non-rival, nobody would want to pay for it, giving rise to the free rider problem. As such, pure public goods may only be expected to be provided by the state. Other examples of such goods could be rural roads, and national defense.

In many cases, infrastructure services have public good characteristics, e.g., road services up to congestion limits. However, use of technology has enabled provision of these goods by the private sector. For example, television broadcasting was considered a public good in that it was both non-excludable and non-rival. However, improvements in technology have enabled to make it excludable: satellite broadcasters collect a subscription, and in return provide a card that unscrambles the signal to enable viewing. So, there is a possibility of price exclusion in infrastructure facilitated by technology. In this way, market mechanism could be used to supply "quasi" public goods but this will require careful regulation.

Table 1 Typology of goods and services in terms of rivalness and excludability

		Rivalrous?	
		Yes	No
Excludable?	Yes	Private goods	Toll goods
	No	Common pool resources	Public goods

Because of the above characteristics, infrastructure poses multiple market failures and would be typically inefficiently provided if there is complete dependence on market mechanism. For example, to the extent that specific infrastructure activities entail natural monopoly elements, they will not be provided efficiently by an unfettered market. However, differences related to both technology and economics of production create the possibility of "unbundling" the segment that involves natural monopoly from those that can be provided more competitively, e.g., power sector with generation, transmission, and distribution as distinct economic segments. The network segment of the sector (power transmission) can, therefore, be separated (unbundled) from the more competitive segment (power generation), with regulation to ensure fair and nondiscriminatory access to the network. Infrastructure activities that create externalities may also warrant some regulation.

3 Infrastructure and Development

It has been found that infrastructure is positively and significantly correlated to economic growth and poverty alleviation. A 1% increase in telephone lines per worker, for instance, is estimated to be associated with a GDP growth of 0.19 percentage points (see Table 2 below). Good telecommunication facilities provide wider access to data, enabling quicker decisions, and reducing transport and transaction costs by allowing people to conduct business remotely, all this leading to improved efficiency.

Ports and airports are critical for facilitating producer connectivity with markets, especially export markets, as also providing "just-in-time" delivery of products saving on inventory costs. Surveys of prospective foreign investors show that the quality of infrastructure is an important factor in ranking potential sites for location of direct investment, which contributes to economic growth. Paving roads has helped double school attendance by girls in Morocco. Road networks also provide links to global and local markets. With better roads, raw materials can reach factories faster and finished products can reach markets quicker (especially perishable produce). This has implications for rural poverty and off-farm employment, and ultimately inclusiveness of growth and economic development.

Table 2 Effect on GDP Growth of a 1% Increase in Infrastructure Assets (%)

Type of asset	Direct effect	Indirect effect (via K)	Total effect
Power generation capacity per worker	0.07	0.02	0.09
Paved roads per worker	0.05	0.02	0.07
Telephone lines per worker	0.14	0.05	0.19

Note The K effect refers to the impact via capital accumulation
Source Calderon and Serven (2003)

Infrastructure is also a key ingredient for achieving all the Millennium Development Goals, and thus is an important input to human development. Safe drinking water and improved sanitation arrest the spread of a range of serious diseases like diarrhoea, the prime cause of child mortality and malnutrition. Electricity provides critical support to health and education services and strengthens the productivity of small businesses. There is evidence that infrastructure quantity and quality is linked to the reduction in income inequality.[2]

A World Bank study notes "…across Africa, infrastructure contributed 99 basis points to per capita economic growth from 1990 to 2005, compared with 68 basis points for other structural policies. That contribution is almost entirely attributable to advances in the penetration of telecommunication services. The deterioration in the quantity and quality of power infrastructure over the same period retarded growth, shaving 11 basis points from per capita growth for Africa as a whole and as much as 20 basis points for southern Africa."[3]

The relationship between growth and infrastructure, however, is a two-way process. While availability of infrastructure facilitates growth, growth, in turn, raises demand for infrastructure. The elasticity of demand for total infrastructure stock to GDP has been calculated as 1.0,[4] implying that if India aims to grow at 9–10% of GDP per annum, the stock of infrastructure has to increase by 9–10% of GDP per annum.[5] If India does not spend as much for augmenting infrastructure, there would be excess demand for infrastructure manifested in congestion on roads, railways, ports and airport runways, pollution, lack of access to basic services, power outages, and ultimately the slowing of economic growth—pretty much what we are seeing today. When economies consume resources, rather than invest, say during an economic boom, the problems that result from inadequate infrastructure

[2]Chong and Calderon (2001).

[3]Foster and Briceno-Garmendia (2010).

[4]However, each constituent of infrastructure has different elasticity of demand to GDP as compared to elasticity of demand of total infrastructure stock to GDP. For example, the elasticity of demand for water and paved roads have been estimated at less than 1 (more specifically, water: 0.3 and paved roads: 0.8), while that for power and telecom as greater than 1 (power: 1.5 and telecom: 1.7) (Source: World Bank (1994). *World Development Report 1994: Infrastructure for Development*).

[5]See for example, Mohan and Kapur (2015). Pressing the Indian Growth Accelerator: Policy Imperatives. Washington DC: IMF. It says National Transport Development Policy Committee (NTDPC 2014) projects that overall infrastructure investment will need to increase substantially from around 5.4% of GDP in 2011–12 to around 8% during the 2020s and beyond—levels consistent with the economic growth and transformation experiences of South East and East Asian countries. It had indeed reached 6.2–6.3% in 2008–10. So, aiming for 7% in the medium term and ascending to 8% later is realistic. These infrastructure numbers are based on estimates for gross domestic capital formation (GDCF) according to National Accounts Statistics (NAS) and are typically lower than those usually made for infrastructure by the Indian Planning Commission. For example, expenditures made for buying land in the process of making infrastructure investments are not included in GDCF as these are regarded as transfer payments in the GDP context. This and other factors could lead to an underestimation of infrastructure estimates in NAS classification by 1–1.5% of GDP (NTDPC 2014).

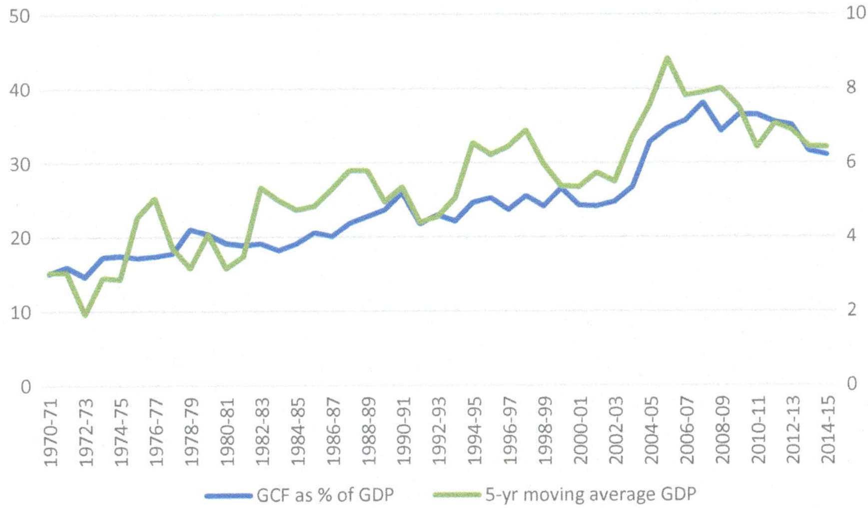

Fig. 1 Growth and Investment in India (1970–2015). *Note* Data sourced from Ministry of Finance, Government of India (2016). *Economic Survey 2015–16*

become inevitable and pull down the growth rate over the longer term as inadequate infrastructure becomes a binding constraint to growth.

However, establishing causality is difficult—the connection between infrastructure investment and growth is usually bidirectional. Moreover, there are usually other factors driving both variables that are not fully taken into account. However, it is widely accepted that infrastructure and growth are significantly correlated.

Let us look at the relationship between GDP growth and infrastructure in India. Figure 1 plots India's investment rate (gross capital formation as percent of GDP) and the 5-year moving average annual GDP growth and clearly shows the link between investment and growth for India. It is evident that the two lines track each other very closely, quite in keeping with the expected relationship between investment and growth discussed above.

3.1 *The Infrastructure-Competitiveness Connection*

As per the World Economic Forum's Global Competitiveness Report (GCR) 2014–15, India is ranked 71st out of 144 countries—ranked lowest among the BRICS countries. What is more worrying is that India is steadily losing its competitiveness —down from 48th rank in the GCR 2007–08 and the rank differential with China is 43, up from 14 in 2007. One of the most problematic factors for doing business in India has been identified as the inadequate supply of infrastructure. Quality of overall infrastructure is one of the 12 parameters considered in the rankings and has been ranked at 87th out of 144, which implies that quality of infrastructure is pulling down the overall Indian competitiveness. The quality of electricity supply is ranked at a lowly 103. So, Indian infrastructure is a cause of concern.

Though things have improved in 2015–16, there is a long way to go. Thus, as per GCR 2015–16, India ranks 55th out of 140 countries, but it continues to be ranked lowest among the BRICS countries except for Brazil.[6] Though the rank differential with China has narrowed to 27, it is still nearly double the rank differential in 2007. Though the quality of overall infrastructure rank has improved to 81 out of 140, it is still pulling down the overall Indian competitiveness, particularly quality of electricity supply which has still been ranked quite low at 98.

Infrastructure is also linked to competitiveness in numerous other ways. For example, infrastructure levels and quality are strong determinants of inventory levels. In the US, businesses hold inventory of about 15% of GDP, while in many developing countries, inventories are twice as large, and raw materials are often more than three times as large. Carrying extra inventories has associated financial costs, and other costs, such as insurance, obsolescence, and storage, which raises firm unit costs and therefore has a significant adverse impact on country competitiveness and productivity. Rough calculations indicate that if the interest rate for financing inventory holdings is 15–20%, a conservative estimate in many developing countries, then the cost to the economy of the additional inventory holdings is greater than 2% of GDP. A key determinant of this excess inventory is poor economic infrastructure exemplified by roads and ports.[7]

4 Supply and Demand of Infrastructure Around the World

4.1 Investment in Infrastructure

McKinsey reckons that in 2007–12, investment in infrastructure in rich countries was about 2.5% of GDP per annum when it should have been 3.5%. In 2013, government spending on infrastructure in USA, at 1.7% of GDP, was at a 20-year low.[8]

In Africa, it has been estimated that about $93 billion is required to be invested on infrastructure per annum. This is 10% of their GDP. Another 5% of GDP is

---

[6]World Economic Forum's Global Competitiveness Report 2015–16 ranks China at 28, Russia at 45, South Africa at 49, and Brazil at 75. The ranking is based on the assessment of 140 countries on 12 parameters such as infrastructure, macroeconomic environment, institutions, health and education, among others. The Report states that after 5 years of decline, India jumps 16 ranks to 55th place. As per the Report, this dramatic reversal is largely attributable to the momentum initiated by the election of Narendra Modi, whose pro-business, pro-growth, and anti-corruption stance has improved the business community's sentiment towards the government.

[7]Guasch and Kogan (2001).

[8]The Economist (2015).

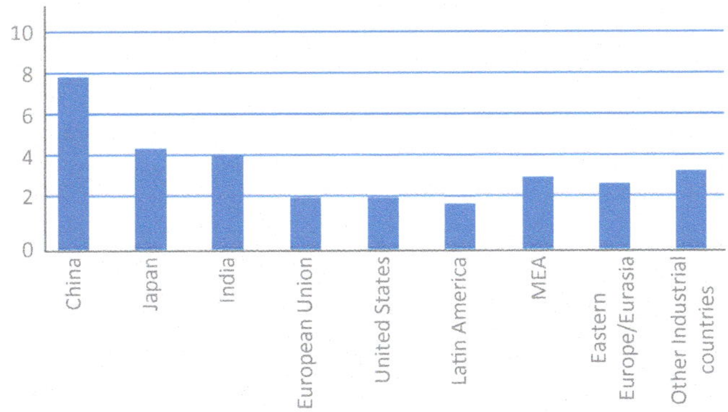

Fig. 2 Infrastructure Investment as Share of GDP (%) (Average annual Infra spend during 1992–2011 as % of 2010 GDP). *Source* McKinsey Global Institute (2013). *Infrastructure productivity: How to save $1 trillion a year*

required in operation and maintenance. Another estimate suggests that Democratic Republic of Congo needs to invest about 70% of its GDP on infrastructure.

In China, Thailand, and Vietnam, total infrastructure investment exceeds 7% of GDP. In other Asian countries with high growth, public investment in infrastructure is in the range of 5–7% of GDP. Added to this is private investment in infrastructure. Historical evidence appears to suggest this to be broadly the optimal range for high and sustained growth.[9]

As shown in the figure above (Fig. 2), China is the leading investor in infrastructure in the world having overtaken the US and the European Union. In the 20-year period from 1992 to 2011, India spent 4.7% of GDP on infrastructure. However, as already stated, for India to grow at 9–10% per annum, India would need to spend about 9–10% of its GDP on infrastructure. In infrastructure distressed countries, the requirement of investment in infrastructure could be much more.

4.2 Distribution Between Public and Private Infrastructure Investment Worldwide

Infrastructure investment can come from public and private sources. Figure 3 below shows that the global infrastructure investment averages about $2.7 trillion per year. It also shows the distribution of public and private investment worldwide. It would be apparent from the figure that the major part of infrastructure investment in the world still comes from the public sector—roughly two-thirds coming from the public sector and the balance third coming from the private sector.

[9]World Bank (2008).

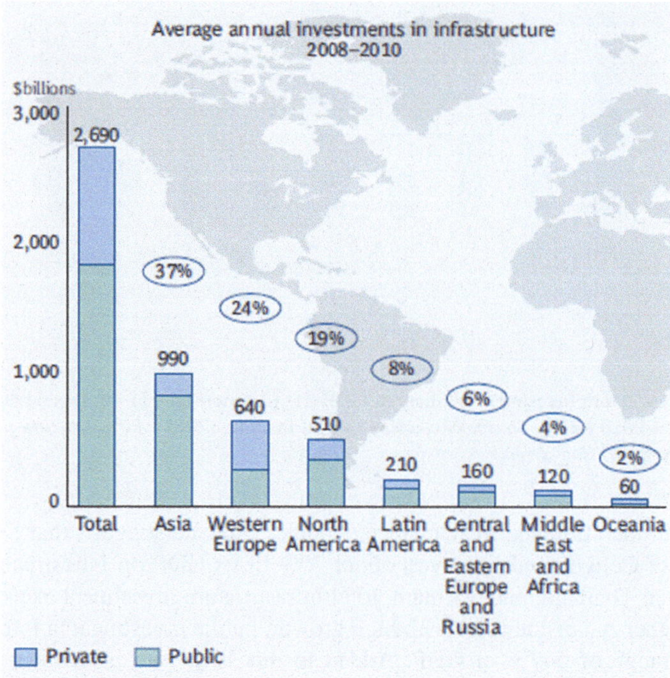

Fig. 3 Distribution between public and private infrastructure investment worldwide. *Source* Boston Consulting Group (2013). *Bridging the Gap—Meeting the Infrastructure Challenge with Public–Private Partnerships*

4.3 Infrastructure Deficit

Notwithstanding the impressive investment in infrastructure, large parts of the world today suffer from serious infrastructure deficit. It is estimated that 1.2 billion people in the world do not have electricity; 780 million are without clean water; 2.5 billion do not have basic sanitation; 1.5 billion do not have reliable phone service; and 1 billion live more than 2 km away from an all season road.

The South Asia Region (SAR) lags behind all but Sub-Saharan Africa (SSA) in access to infrastructure services as shown in the table below. It is apparent from the table that SAR's access to infrastructure services closely resembles SSA, even though its economic growth is second only to East Asia and Pacific (EAP) region. Therefore, infrastructure deficit is possibly emerging as the binding constraint to economic growth in SAR.

Tables 3 and 4 indicate that the infrastructure deficit in India is quite pronounced as a constituent of the South Asia Region as also in relation to other South Asian countries. There is a big range among SAR countries in access to infrastructure services. Sri Lanka and Maldives have the best access rates in the SAR region (much above India).

Table 3 Infrastructure access across regions

	Avg GDP Growth (2000–2012)	Urbanization Rate (2012)	Telecom Access (per 100 people) (2011)	Electricity Access (% of pop.) (2010)	Access to Improved Sanitation (% of pop.) (2011)	Access to Improved Water (% of pop.) 2011
East Asia and Pacific (EAP)	8.9%	50	98	92	67	91
Europe and Central Asia (ECA)	4.4%	60	157	100	94	95
Latin America and the Caribbean (LAC)	3.1%	79	125	94	81	94
Middle East and North Africa (MNA)	4.2%	60	105	94	89	89
South Asia Region (SAR)	6.7%	31	72	71	39	90
Sub-Saharan Africa (SSA)	4.7%	37	54	35	30	63
World	2.5%	53	103	78	64	89

Source Biller et al. (2014). *Infrastructure Gap in South Asia.* Washington DC: The World Bank

While the developing countries suffer an infrastructure deficit, the disease afflicts the developed world as well. For example, one in three railway bridges in Germany is over 100 years old as are half of London's water mains. In USA, the average bridge is 42 years old and the average dam 52. ASCE (American Society of Civil Engineers) rates about 14,000 dams as "high hazard" and about 150,000 bridges as "deficient." In USA, traffic jams on urban highways have been estimated to cost over $100 billion in wasted time and fuel per annum, airport congestion $22 billion and power outages, $150 billion.[10]

On an annual basis, while the demand for infrastructure is about $4 trillion worldwide, the supply is only about $2.7 trillion leading to a deficit of $1.3–$1.5 trillion (in 2010 constant dollars).

The implications of infrastructure deficit are indeed severe, including slower growth. One of the ways in which the problem can be resolved is through increased investment in infrastructure. McKinsey estimates that $57 trillion would be needed

[10]The Economist (2015).

Table 4 Infrastructure access across countries in South Asia Region

	Telecom Access (per 100 people) (2011)	Electricity Access (% of pop.) (2010)	Access to Improved Sanitation (% of pop.) (2011)	Access to Improved Water (% of pop.) (2011)	Total Road Network (km per 1000 people)	% Paved Roads
Afghanistan (AFG)	54	30	29	61	1.6	29
Bangladesh (BGD)	58	47	55	83	0.1	10
Bhutan (BTN)	69	65	45	97	9.7	40
India (IND)	75	75	35	92	3.5	50
Maldives (MDL)	173	95	98	99	0.3	100
Nepal (NPL)	47	76	35	88	0.8	54
Pakistan (PAK)	65	67	47	91	1.5	72
Sri Lanka (LKA)	104	77	91	93	5.5	81

Source Biller et al. (2014). *Infrastructure Gap in South Asia.* Washington DC: The World Bank

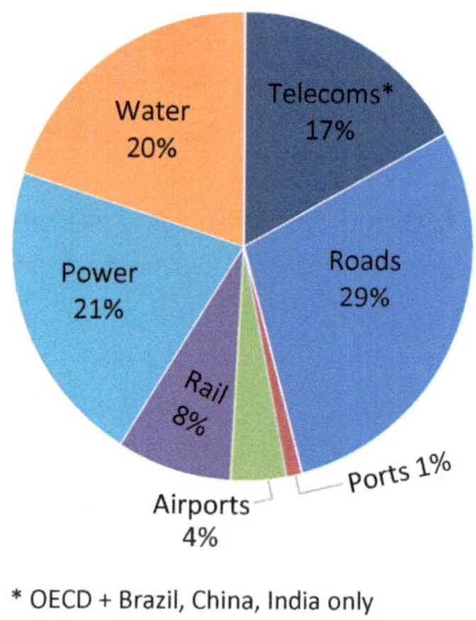

Fig. 4 Required Global Infra Investment: $57 trn (2013–30, 2010 prices). *Source* Based on McKinsey Global Institute estimates

in the 18-year period (2013–2030) for investment in infrastructure worldwide (see Fig. 4). As is apparent from the figure, road and power sectors account for half of the required infrastructure investment. However, as per McKinsey, this estimated requirement would be sufficient to support projected economic growth between 2013 and 2030 and maintain current levels of infrastructure capacity and service relative to GDP. However, it would be insufficient to address backlogs and deficiencies. This estimate would imply that there is a need to step-up infrastructure investment by about 60%.[11]

4.4 *High-Cost Infrastructure*

Partly emanating from the massive infrastructure deficit, infrastructure is too expensive in many developing countries. In the power sector, for example, infrastructure deficit is reflected in frequent unscheduled black-outs, leading to higher costs, and dependence on alternative and expensive sources of power. Thus, while the energy generation costs of coal-based power were Rs. 1–2 per unit, the costs were over Rs. 10 per unit for diesel-based alternative power in India in 2009. If current trends continue, McKinsey estimates that India could suffer a GDP loss of $200 billion (about 10% of its GDP) in fiscal year 2017 (end of the 12th Plan period) because of infrastructure deficit. In terms of GDP growth rate, this would imply a loss of 1.1 percentage points (Table 5).

Table 5 Power Generation Costs in India by Energy Source (2009)

Energy Source	Energy Generation Costs in Rs/kWh ($/kWh)	Source
Coal	1–2 (0.02–0.04)	McKinsey (2009). Powering India: The Road to 2017 (unpublished)
Nuclear	2–3 (0.04–0.06)	Same as above
Large Hydro	3–4 (0.06–0.08)	Same as above
Gas	4–6 (0.08–0.12)	Same as above
Diesel	10+ (0.20+)	Same as above
Wind (onshore)	3–4.5 (0.06–0.09)	Industry experts
Small Hydro	3–4 (0.06–0.08)	Industry experts
Biomass	4–5 (0.08–0.1)	Industry experts
Solar (CSP)	10–15 (0.2–0.3)	Industry experts
Solar (PV)	12–20 (0.24–0.4)	Industry experts

Source National Renewable Energy Laboratory (2010) *Indian Renewable Energy Status Report—Background Report for DIREC 2010*; McKinsey (2009). *Powering India: The Road to 2017* (unpublished)

[11]McKinsey Global Institute (2013).

Table 6 Africa's High-Cost Infrastructure

Infrastructure sector	Sub-Saharan Africa	Other developing regions
Power tariffs ($ per kilowatt-hour)	0.02–0.46	0.05–0.10
Water tariffs ($ per cubic mater)	0.86–6.56	0.03–0.60
Road freight tariffs ($ per ton-kilometer)	0.04–0.14	0.01–0.04
Mobile telephony ($ per basket per month)	2.60–21.00	9.90
International telephony ($ per 3-min call to the United States)	0.44–12.50	2.00
Internet dial-up service ($ per month)	6.70–148.00	11.00

Note Ranges reflect prices in different countries and various consumption levels
Source Foster and Briceño-Garmendia (2009). *Africa's Infrastructure—A Time for Transformation*. Washington DC: The World Bank

Africa, which suffers from a massive infrastructure deficit, is characterized by high-cost infrastructure compared to global standards (see Table 6). Both high costs and high profits contribute to Africa's higher prices.[12]

Part II: Investment in Infrastructure

5 Who Funds Infrastructure—A Quick Survey of Recent History

Broadly speaking, there have been three phases as shown in the figure below (Fig. 5), when public or private investment has played a major role in provisioning of infrastructure. We discuss these phases below.

5.1 Private Participation was Important in Nineteenth Century and the First Half of the Twentieth Century

Between 1790 and 1850, perhaps as many as 20,000 miles of private toll roads were built in the US, although these roads all but disappeared with the arrival of railroad competition in the last half of the nineteenth century. In the US, some states issued land grants to private turnpike companies to help them capture a portion of gain in property values and thus cover capital costs during the early years when traffic volumes and revenues from tolls were likely to be small. In the 1930s and 1940s,

[12]Foster and Briceño-Garmendia (2009).

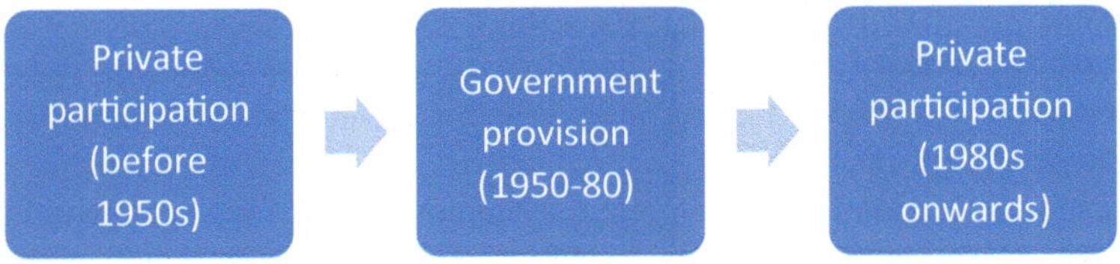

Fig. 5 Who funds infrastructure?

toll charges reemerged to underwrite the building of major limited access roads outside of urban areas—the turnpikes in Pennsylvania, Ohio, New Jersey, and Massachusetts. Private firms have also been involved primarily as operators of food and fuel concessions at turnpike rest areas and as engineering and construction contractors.[13]

Private companies initially developed England's rail network with a focus on freight rather than passengers, while the competing, canal network, was state-owned, although private operators ran steamboats. Foreign companies initiated rail networks of China and India in the late nineteenth century.[14]

5.2 *Widespread Nationalization of Infrastructure After World War II Till Early 1980s*[15]

World War II marks a break from the past and there was widespread nationalization of infrastructure since then. The public sector dominance in infrastructure since the 1950s has arisen for several reasons: recognition of the economic and political importance of infrastructure; a belief that governments needed to be actively involved in supplying technology; and a faith that government could succeed where markets appeared to fail.[16] There were also other factors like customer fears that firms will use their market power to overcharge matched by apprehension of firms that governments will use their regulatory power to prevent them from covering their costs. Public sector ownership was also viewed as a way to ensure broader access. Besides, infrastructure characteristics like higher upfront costs, long payback periods, and presence of externalities meant that infrastructure provisioning suffered from market failure and was more amenable to being provided by the public sector.

[13]Jacobson and Tarr (1995).

[14]National Transport Development Policy Committee (2013).

[15]This section is built on and borrows considerably from the material in Pratap (2011). Sustaining Privatization (http://drum.lib.umd.edu/bitstream/handle/1903/11549/Pratap_umd_0117E_12145.pdf?sequence=1&isAllowed=y).

[16]World Bank (1994).

There are various theories that explain this trend of increasing nationalization in the 1950–80 period. Vernon (1971) put forth the concept of "obsolescing bargain" and argued that foreign investment is welcomed initially for bringing in new technologies, good management, and capital. Over time, as the recipient country becomes wealthier, and develops better technological and management skills, its perception of the bargain changes in nature. Outright expropriation may occur, though creeping expropriation, for example, through emphasis on local inputs, might be more likely.

Gomez-Ibanez (1999) reviewed the nationalization of electric utilities in Latin America over the period 1943–1979, covering the experience of Argentina, Brazil, Colombia, Mexico, and Venezuela. Foreign private investment in their power sectors was often associated with the development of complex engineering projects (hydroelectric plants) or the large scale of infrastructure finance required. As cities were initially electrified, the investment was welcomed. However, as access to electricity became more widespread, concerns about natural monopolies, and perceptions that investors, in particular, foreign investors, were making excess profits grew and began to impact the regulatory framework. He notes that the few electric utilities not nationalized by the 1980s were domestically owned; all foreign-owned utilities had been nationalized. He also notes that where the sector was regulated at the national level—in Brazil, Colombia, and Mexico—the regulatory frameworks were more robust but still not strong enough to provide continued incentives for investment. In Argentina, utilities were regulated by municipalities and were the first to be nationalized. Finally, he notes the impact of macroeconomic factors on the financial viability of utilities, given the reluctance of regulators to allow prices to rise to reflect inflation and currency devaluation.

Klein and Roger (1994) emphasize the role of other factors in nationalization of private infrastructure, including reactions against colonialism, and public investment associated with this in newly independent countries (in India, it was felt that "commanding heights" of the economy should be in the public sector as per the Industrial Policy Resolution of 1956), and the belief prevalent in the middle of the last century that the public sector could provide these services more efficiently. They highlighted the fact that many infrastructure services would continue to be provided in monopoly settings. The regulatory systems designed to oversee these (see Fig. 6 below) would be vulnerable to political pressure and this could lead to a vicious cycle of a decline in profitability, underinvestment, and deterioration in services and ultimately nationalization. They highlighted the role that competition *for* the market could play in reducing demands for this type of regulation, as well as the possible role of repeated competitive bidding of natural monopoly concessions.

Much of infrastructure was a "natural monopoly" and a sustainable regulatory approach that allowed investors satisfactory returns while being perceived to charge fair prices to consumers would be challenging. This might over time lead to the exit of the private sector, as a cycle of political pressure on prices leads to less investment, lower quality of services, further downward pressure on prices and so on until the government steps in taking over the assets and service responsibility. Some of these apprehensions proved credible as private investment in infrastructure

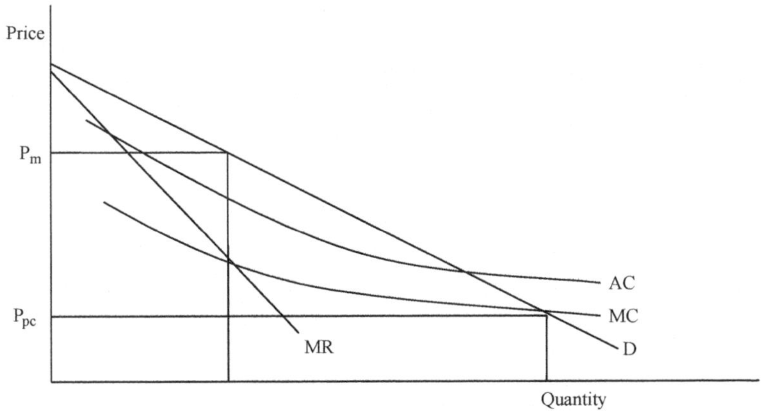

Fig. 6 Sustainable regulatory regime in infrastructure is problematic. *Source* Author's conceptualization

showed a downward trend from 1997 to 2003. Subsequently, it stabilized and began to increase, but has not done so in water sector, where the political economy problems associated with pricing are often the greatest.

The above argument is illustrated in the figure above. Natural monopolies are characterized by downward sloping average cost curves. The socially optimal price is at P_{pc}, where P = MC.[17] While the monopolist would want to set the price at the level of P_m, where MC = MR, the regulator would want to set the price near P_{pc} or at the most where P = AC, thus allowing only normal profits to the monopolist provider of infrastructure services. These regulatory concerns may lead to a vicious cycle of a decline in profitability, under-investment, deterioration in services and ultimately nationalization.

Macroeconomic crises have also been instrumental in nationalization of infrastructure assets. Private infrastructure projects in Mexico were adversely affected by the 1994 Mexican peso crisis, in Indonesia by the 1997 Asian Financial Crisis, and in Argentina by the large devaluation of the peso in 2002. The macroeconomic crises reduced the demand for services from these projects and increased the cost of financing, as foreign currency loans were extensively used. Macroeconomic shocks were not the only issue with some of these projects. In the case of the Mexican toll roads, Ruster (1997) noted that indirect guarantees by the government to the investors and lenders funding the projects might have reduced the extent of due diligence on these projects.[18]

[17]One of the most important objectives of regulatory systems is to mimic the outcomes of a perfectly competitive market in the absence of such markets. In perfectly competitive markets, firm equilibrium occurs at the point where Price = Marginal Costs.

[18]Pratap (2011).

Some examples of public provision of infrastructure are:

- In India, the entire electricity sector (including generation, transmission, and distribution) was in the public sector (State Electricity Boards). Even after the functional separation of the power sector into individual generation, transmission and distribution companies in most Indian states now, the power distribution companies are predominantly in the public sector.
- In the telecom sector, government-owned monopolies were dominant, including BSNL and MTNL in India. However, now public providers have been reduced to bit players in a market dominated by private providers.
- Water and sewerage, almost wholly, is in public sector in India even now.

5.3 *Full Circle—Back to Private Provision of Infrastructure*

While the predominant trend in the period 1950–80 was public sector ownership and operation of infrastructure, in more recent years, it is back to private provision of infrastructure. Some reasons are: growing demand gap, fiscal pressures and mounting dissatisfaction with public services, change in the prevailing views about markets and private sector to the effect that ownership matters and incentives are better in private sector, which leads to higher efficiency of service delivery[19]; deregulation, competition, and liberalization would produce improved outputs and outcomes. This implied that network utilities should be vertically unbundled, with potentially competitive segments separated from natural monopoly components. In the power sector, this meant that the restructuring has focused on delinking the vertically integrated utilities, separating the structurally competitive segments of generation and supply from the monopolistic segments of transmission and distribution. Large-scale privatization began in the UK in 1984, when 51% of British Telecom was sold to the private sector.

Between 1991 and 2003, the number of countries with state-owned telecommunications declined from about 150 to 79. At the same time, the number of telecommunication regulators, usually an indicator of the entry of private participants, rose from 12 to 123.[20] Private participation in infrastructure is more popular today (see Table 7) with the maximum number of projects seen in the energy sector (further break-up of the energy sector would reveal that the maximum number of projects are in electricity generation, where the political economy issues are lower than in electricity distribution). The maximum amount of investment is in the telecom sector where there is adequate cost recovery. The least amount of

[19]Performance contracts with incentives and independent external audits have become dominant features of the reform process for governance of state-owned enterprises, for both electricity and water but with little success in terms of reducing losses and fiscal drain.

[20]World Bank (2004). Global development finance – Harnessing cyclical gains for development.

Table 7 Private participation in infrastructure (developing countries, by sector) 1990–2015

	Number of Projects	Investment commitment ($ billion)
Energy	3,185	832
Telecom	847	1,034
Transport	1,609	473
Water and sewerage	906	80
Total	**6,547**	**2,419**

Source Private Participation in Infrastructure database of the World Bank (ppi.worldbank.org)

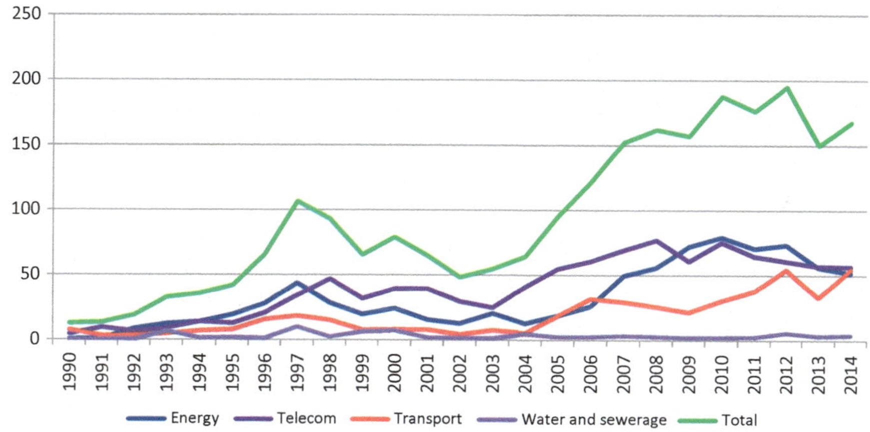

Fig. 7 Trends in Private Participation in Infrastructure in developing countries. *Source* Based on data from the Private Participation in Infrastructure database of the World Bank (ppi.worldbank.org)

investment is in the water and sewerage sector, where the political economy problems associated with pricing are often the greatest.

Figure 7 shows the remarkable growth in private participation in infrastructure in developing countries where it added up to over $2 trillion since 1990. As the figure shows, the trend in privatization is not uniform across years. While annual private investment in infrastructure projects was close to $20 billion in 1990–92, it quickly increased during the first part of that decade to peak at $107 billion in 1997. This rapid rise was driven by investment in power projects in East Asia and privatization of telecommunications and electricity utilities in Latin America. The decline in investment began with the East Asian Financial Crisis, which impacted many of the independent power projects that had commenced. Further crises in Russia and Latin America led to a decline almost as swift as the earlier increase.[21] After a period with no real discernible trends, investment levels have increased

[21]Pratap (2011).

again over the 2003–2012 period to come down again in 2013 due to the Eurozone crisis. If we look at the composition of the increase, we find that the energy, telecom, and transport sector investments converging at about $50 billion each in 2014. However, the water sector has seen no discernible increase with the sector accounting for just about 4% of the total private infrastructure investment in developing countries owing mainly to low-cost recovery and any effort to improve cost recovery being subject to immense political sensitivity.

6 The Rationale and Challenges of Public Funding of Infrastructure

(A) *Rationale: Why do Governments fund infrastructure?*

Traditional economic theory argues for public or government provisioning of what are known as "public goods." Non-excludability[22] and non-rivalrous consumption[23] characterize public goods. Classic examples are clean air, national defense, good law and order, and lighthouse. Markets work best in providing pure private goods or services, which are both rival in consumption and excludable.

If nobody can be excluded from the benefits of a good or service and its supply is not adversely affected by another user joining in, such goods and services would be marked with severe free rider problem (nobody would be willing to pay for them). Since no one can be excluded, it is impossible to extract a price from anyone since non-payment would not deprive the person of the good.

Because of these features, particularly the challenge of pricing stemming from non-excludability and the widespread benefit to entire society, it is generally held that the market system would fail to produce such goods in socially desired quantities, since suppliers of such goods will not be rewarded to an extent commensurate with the social value of such goods.

Market failure can also occur in situations when the good or service in question, even if not a pure public good, has one or more of these other features—externalities, decreasing costs, and merit goods. Externalities imply a situation when one person consuming it affects the welfare of another. Decreasing cost implies that average cost keeps falling with increasing scale leading to a natural monopoly rather than multiple producers being the socially optimum outcome. Merit goods refer to a class of goods, consumption of which creates more value for the society as a whole than to the individual consuming it (who would therefore not pay to

[22]Non-excludability means that a user cannot be prevented from consuming a service once it has been provided.

[23]Non-rivalrous consumption means that consumption by one user does not reduce the supply available to other users, e.g., availability of road for car users up to congestion limits.

Table 8 Infrastructure related services and market failure

Infrastructure related service	Cause of market failure
Power, gas	Natural monopoly
Water supply and treatment	Natural monopoly, externality
Rail transport	Natural monopoly, merit good
District heating	Natural monopoly
Garbage collection and disposal	Public good, externality
Cable	Natural monopoly, merit good
Roads	Quasi-public good, externality

Source Adapted from Prud'homme (2004). *Infrastructure and Development*, available online at: http://siteresources.worldbank.org/DEC/Resources/84797-1251813753820/6415739-1251814066992/remy1-12.pdf

consume "enough" from a social point of view) unless its price is subsidized to a point where his chosen consumption level is indeed the social optimum.

Strictly speaking, infrastructure is not, usually, a "pure public good." It is possible to exclude non-toll-payers from using roads and bridges, and when traffic volumes reach the capacity of a road or bridge, one user's benefit can certainly come at the cost of another. However, in most cases, infrastructure is related to market failures stemming from externalities, decreasing costs, and merit goods. The above table summarizes the key market failures often associated with infrastructure services (Table 8).

These "alleged" market failures ("alleged" because establishing the nature of these failures is often not beyond dispute) are central to justifying the conventional practice of public sector funding of infrastructure projects. Since the point is quite central to the present volume, it is pertinent to note that the likelihood of market failure does not necessarily imply the optimality of public funding. Some commentators have likened this to judges in a beauty pageant looking at one contestant (the "market") and crowning another (the "public sector").

Notwithstanding this distinction, infrastructure has generally been publicly funded across countries. By far the most important reason for governments to spend on infrastructure is that such investment is associated with economic growth and development, an aspect of infrastructure we have discussed at some length in Part I of this chapter. A few other reasons for pervasive government investment in infrastructure are listed below.

6.1 *Residents' Quality of Life*

Infrastructure is essential to improving residents' quality of life. We all require electricity to run our offices, businesses, and households and we also know that power cuts are a big nuisance. Public transport like metro systems facilitates movement without much pollution and congestion. Telecom facilitates information exchange without having to go everywhere physically. Safe drinking water is essential to life.

6.2 Macroeconomic Stimulus

Many countries, including India, US and China have used infrastructure-based fiscal stimulus in times of economic and financial crisis, for example in 2008, when the world was confronted with the Global Financial Crisis. Every G-20 nation implemented substantial stimulus in 2008–09 with an unweighted average of 2% of GDP—US spent 2% of GDP as fiscal stimulus while China spent 3.1% of GDP. India launched stimulus packages in December 2008 and January 2009, together amounting to about 3% of GDP, which included substantial funds for infrastructure spending. The focus on infrastructure reflects the generally held view that these efforts will ultimately have the strongest impact on growth and are largely cost effective, unlike the usual Keynesian remedy of digging a pit and filling it up in times of an economic depression.

6.3 Concerns About Natural Monopoly

If the industry is such that there is place only for a monopoly supplier (say in power transmission or airport), concerns about possible exploitation of consumers have pushed the government to become the only monopoly supplier. However, technology has enabled the introduction of competition even in the erstwhile monopoly markets. Thus, the power market has been segmented into power generation, transmission, and distribution and it has been possible to introduce competition in generation, while ensuring that power generators have nondiscriminatory access to the monopoly transmission provider.

6.4 Assembling the Right of Way for Linear Projects Under Its Powers of Eminent Domain

Land acquisition for infrastructure projects, where the land requirements are typically large, has always been contentious, more so now. If the government acquires land under its own name for infrastructure projects, it is generally easier than otherwise. Therefore, linear projects like railroads, power transmission, and telephone lines may be easier to implement and therefore owned by the public sector.

The sovereign's power to acquire land (though with compensation) under the concept of "eminent domain" is well recognized in law worldwide. There is also strong justification for it in the theory of political economy as a resolution to certain types of market failure. First, there is the "hold up" problem where an individual can stall development projects requiring a block of land, by refusing to sell or demanding a disproportionate price, even if the majority of land owners are willing to sell. Second, as in Indian conditions, imperfect land titles discourage market transactions. Government acquisition of land statutorily cures title defects and the allottee gets clean title. Thus, provisions for compulsory acquisition of land by the government are essential to economic development in many cases.[24]

6.5 Economic Development and Equity Considerations

In social infrastructure projects like health and education, where there is direct consumer interface, investment per service unit is typically low and returns are risky. These characteristics of social infrastructure generally make them unattractive to the private sector with the result that such projects are generally implemented by the Government. Thus, in India, almost the whole of primary health and education infrastructure is provided by the public sector. Similarly, rural roads, which have many characteristics of public goods in terms of non-rivalness and non-excludability, are generally operated and implemented by the public sector. These types of infrastructure (rural roads, basic education, and health) need to be provided on equity considerations also and therefore are provided by the government.

(B) *Challenges associated with Public Provision of Infrastructure*

6.6 Poor Maintenance

Roads deteriorate, renewal energy projects languish, water pumps break down, sanitation systems overflow, and installed phone lines fail, in many cases, because of poor maintenance. On average, estimated returns on projects involving primarily maintenance are twice as high as those on projects involving mainly new construction.[25] However, maintenance is not fashionable, new construction is, because of political economy issues.

---

[24]Government of India, Ministry of Finance (2014)

[25]World Bank (1994).

Political economy issues relate to politicians' and bureaucrats' desire for ribbon cutting and bribes which favor new construction over adequate maintenance. More corrupt countries seem to spend more on public investment in roads and other infrastructure, but less on maintenance, resulting in poorer quality roads.[26] Another reason for relatively poor maintenance is that the effect of reducing spending on maintenance manifests with a lag, making it easier for politicians to escape the resulting fallout.[27]

It has been estimated that the cost of addressing Africa's infrastructure needs is around $93 billion a year, about one-third of which is for maintenance. It has also been estimated that $1 spent on road maintenance saves $4 on rehabilitation. This calls for some reallocation of resources from new investment to maintenance, particularly in low-income countries with negligible maintenance spending.[28]

6.7 Fiscal Drain—High Subsidies Due to Low User Charges and Inefficiency

Many publicly provided infrastructure services have huge financial losses due partly to low user charges and also because of inefficiency of provision. The figure below highlights low-cost recovery, especially in the water and power sectors (Fig. 8).

Estimates point out that in the early 1990s, mispricing and technical inefficiency in water, railroads, roads, and electricity contributed to annual losses of about $180 billion in developing countries—nearly as much as annual investments in these sectors.[29] On the eve of the handover of Delhi power distribution companies to the private sector as Public–Private Partnerships (2001–02), the annual subsidy to Delhi Vidyut Board, the precursor public sector entity, was about Rs. 1,200 crore because of its persistent losses. Every unit (kWh) of power supplied in India results in a loss of Rs. 0.81 adding up to Rs. 60,000 crore as distribution losses per annum in the country.

Prices are often held well below costs in the name of the poor, i.e., cost recovering tariffs would be unaffordable to the poor. But, the really poor are very often not connected to piped water supply or grid based electricity and end up paying a much higher price for infrastructure services (see Fig. 9).

As shown in Fig. 9, the really poor have limited access to organized infrastructure services. Low prices are presented as necessary to help the poor, but the poorest members of the community often miss out on the access to the service provided. For instance, a study of the "lifeline" electricity tariffs in Honduras, found

[26]World Bank (2004).

[27]Deloitte. *Closing the Infrastructure Gap: The Role of Public–Private Partnerships.*

[28]Foster and Briceño-Garmendia (2010).

[29]Kessides (2005).

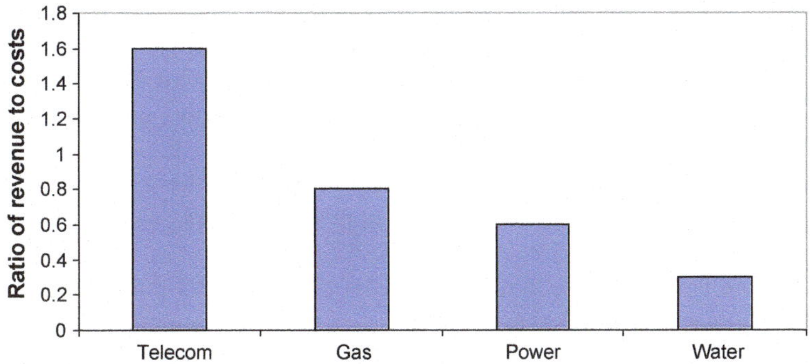

Fig. 8 Cost recovery in Infrastructure Sectors. *Source* World Bank (1994). *World Development Report 1994: Infrastructure for Development*

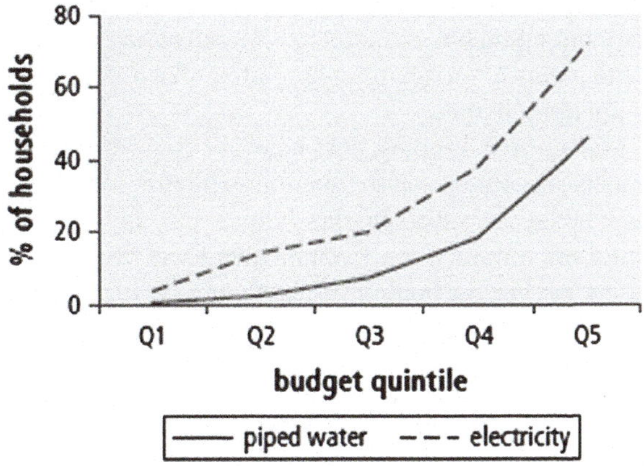

Fig. 9 Infrastructure access by quintiles. *Note* Q1 = first (or poorest) budget quintile; Q2 = second budget quintile; Q3 = third (or middle) budget quintile; Q4 = fourth budget quintile; Q5 = top (or richest) budget quintile. *Source* As quoted in Foster and Briceño-Garmendia (2010). *Africa's Infrastructure—A Time for Transformation*. Washington DC: The World Bank

that about 80% of the subsidies went to non-poor households.[30] Thus, relatively better-off households frequently capture any subsidy to residential services. In fact, targeting works so poorly that a completely random process for allocating subsidies across the population is likely to perform three times better at reaching the poor. Subsidies are therefore highly regressive and usually bypass the intended poor.[31] Another implication is that the main beneficiaries of subsidies are the affluent sections, e.g., users of diesel guzzling Sports Utility Vehicles.[32]

[30]World Bank (2004).

[31]Foster and Briceño-Garmendia (2010).

[32]Till sometime ago, diesel was heavily subsidized in India in the name of providing help to agriculture as subsidized diesel would help in drawing groundwater for irrigation. However, among the major beneficiaries of this subsidy were the diesel guzzling sports utility vehicles driven by the ultra-rich.

Direct subsidies using various targeting mechanisms have been proposed as an alternative (Direct Benefit Transfer to the bank accounts of the poor). These alternative mechanisms have the advantages of being transparent, explicit, with minimum resulting distortions in the behavior of the utility and its customers. Targeting based on broad characteristics like location or housing features can substantially reduce subsidy leakage and help in reaching the intended recipients. Moreover, targeted consumption subsidies appear to perform worse than targeted connection subsidies.[33]

Inadequate tariffs are often compounded by poor financial management. It also results in a low reliance on internal revenues to finance investment and therefore an inability to expand or improve service.[34] And very often the poorest segment of the market is rationed out—thus producing a dramatically opposite result of a public policy measure than originally envisaged (keeping low tariffs to benefit the poor).

This has implications about subsidy design whereby operating cost recovery should be a feasible objective, with subsidies limited to capital costs and giving connection subsidies as opposed to consumption subsidies. Subsidizing connections is more equitable and effective in expanding coverage. The affordability problems with connection charges are often much more serious[35] than those with consumption charges.

Given that keeping cost recovery low for the poor is a false premise, governments should emphasize that infrastructure services have to be paid for, either from the budget or user charges. Since the government cannot keep on paying for infrastructure services given its own fiscal resource crunch, there is no alternative to users paying for quality infrastructure services.[36]

6.8 Unresponsiveness to User Demand—Poor Quality of Publicly Provided Infrastructure

Inefficiency and poor maintenance of infrastructure leads to *low-quality* and unreliable services that alienate users. Examples are Delhi airport before it was given out to the private sector and the customer service provided by Indian public sector telecom providers, MTNL and BSNL. Unreliable quantity or quality of power leads to enormous investments in alternative sources that are especially costly to those who can least afford it.

---

[33]Kessides (2004).

[34]World Bank (1994).

[35]Foster and Briceño-Garmendia (2010).

[36]In the Government of India's Smart City Mission, citizen consultation designed to elicit their willingness to pay for quality infrastructure services is a major evaluation criteria for selection as smart cities with the provision of all basic infrastructure services.

6.9 Time and Cost Overruns

Time and cost overruns is a major problem associated with traditional public procurement. There are political economy reasons for starting a large number of projects, which get allocated a limited amount of funds in the annual budget cycle leading to massive time (and cost) overruns. This outcome is also because of poor incentives and accountability in public procurement.

The time and cost overruns are not restricted just to public procurement in developing countries. Bain, in a survey of over 14 studies for UK, Australia, France, and Norway, found that the average construction cost overrun in conventionally procured projects is 25%, and the range of outturn costs is significantly high from −9% to as high as 98%.[37]

6.10 Limited Resources Are Often Spent on Wrong Projects

The reasons why limited resources are often spent on wrong projects or projects built for reasons other than economic rationality could be related to the following factors, all pointing towards political economy: tied aid—the Bullet Train being built between Ahmedabad and Mumbai has massive tied aid; political projects—power stations taken up despite not being justified financially; railway lines on many uneconomic routes, etc.

Very often, many projects are over-engineered, which lead to inefficiency in the deployment of limited resources.[38] Thus, the T3 terminal of Delhi International Airport Limited (DIAL) has large excess capacity with the result that DIAL is among the most expensive airports in the world both in terms of aircraft landing charges as well as user development fees. If the built excess capacity had been lower catering for demand in the medium term (say 5 years), it is likely that the capital costs would have been lower leading to lower user fees. Similarly, the Gurgaon–Jaipur Highway, which has suffered from large time and cost overruns has over 90 structures like flyovers in its 250 km length and it is likely that had traffic norms for construction of flyovers been followed, unnecessary structures would not have been built leading to lower time and cost overruns. Thus, the antidote is adopting lower cost technologies that provide reasonable levels of service at an affordable price—to both consumers and the government.[39]

[37]Bain (2010).

[38]Though spent by the PPP concessionaire in the below mentioned cases, the incidence ultimately falls on the users and the government as these investments are serviced by them.

[39]Foster and Briceño-Garmendia (2010).

6.11 Inefficiency in Operations

Broadest indicator of inefficient performance by an infrastructure system is the extent of output lost in delivery.[40] In the power sector, this inefficiency is reflected in high Aggregate Technical & Commercial Losses (AT&C losses[41]). In the Water sector, this inefficiency is reflected in high Non-Revenue Water (NRW). Another manifestation of inefficiency in infrastructure provisioning is related to overmanning and redundant manpower.

Investment gap in countries can partially be met through addressing these inefficiencies. However, there are political economy issues while tackling these problems. And investment may also be required for addressing the inefficiencies (for example, reducing distribution losses in power or water sectors). Such investment should be prioritized to reap relatively higher returns.

7 The Case of India

(A) *Infrastructure Shortfall*

- Power: There is a peaking power deficit of 3.2%, energy shortage of 2.3%, and Aggregate Technical & Commercial (AT&C) losses of 25%. AT&C losses are constituted by Transmission and Distribution (T&D) losses and Collection Efficiency. With T&D losses of 21%, India is 15th worst in the world and in the company of Nepal (34%) and Haiti (55%). The comparative T&D numbers for the developed world are Germany (4%), US (6%), and UK (8%) while for other constituents of BRICS, they are—Brazil (16%), Russia (10%), China (6%), and South Africa (8%).
- Roads: There are 100,000 km of National Highways (NHs) constituting 2% of the road network, but accounting for 40% of the traffic as these roads are extensively used. However, though these roads are best in the country, only 24% of the NHs are four lane or more, 52% are two lane, and 24% are single lane, which means that if two cars have to cross, one has to get down to the shoulder to allow the other to pass implying worrying road congestion and wastage of time and fuel.
- Airports: There is inadequate capacity in terms of runways, aircraft handling capacity, and terminal buildings given the high growth of traffic experienced in recent years. The Delhi International Airport Limited (DIAL) has more than one

[40]World Bank (1994).

[41]AT&C loss is the difference between the energy input into the system and the revenue realized. As an illustration, if 100 units of electricity are input into the system and the power distribution company is able to realize payment for only 73 of these units, the AT&C losses are 27%. AT&C losses can be measured as 1 − (Billing Efficiency * Collection Efficiency).

airport movement per minute during peak hours and more than 950 aircraft movements per day.

- Ports: This sector is afflicted with inadequate berths, railroad connectivity, and shallow draft. The average turnaround time for ships in Indian ports is slightly less than 3 days while it is about 10 hours for Singapore.
- Railways are characterized by saturated routes and slow average speeds. In many sections of the Delhi–Kolkata route and the Delhi–Mumbai route of Indian railways, the capacity utilization is over 150% pointing towards immense congestion and resulting slow average speeds.

(B) *Infrastructure Investment*

The best 5-year period for private participation in infrastructure in India is the Eleventh Plan period (2007–12) when average investment per annum reached about 7% of GDP (see Fig. 10 below). The figure also shows that public sector remains the dominant source of infrastructure investment even in India, in consonance with rest of the world.

Figure 10b shows that while public investment as a percent of GDP is flat in India (because of the fiscal resource crunch), private investment is increasing. So, all the variation in total infrastructure investment is largely because of increasing private investment during the Eleventh Plan period. Given the fiscal realities in India, where the Government is bound by the fiscal limits provided in the Indian Fiscal Responsibility and Budget Management (FRBM) Act, the public sector resources are constrained and so it is inevitable that the private sector contribution to any stepped up infrastructure investment increases.

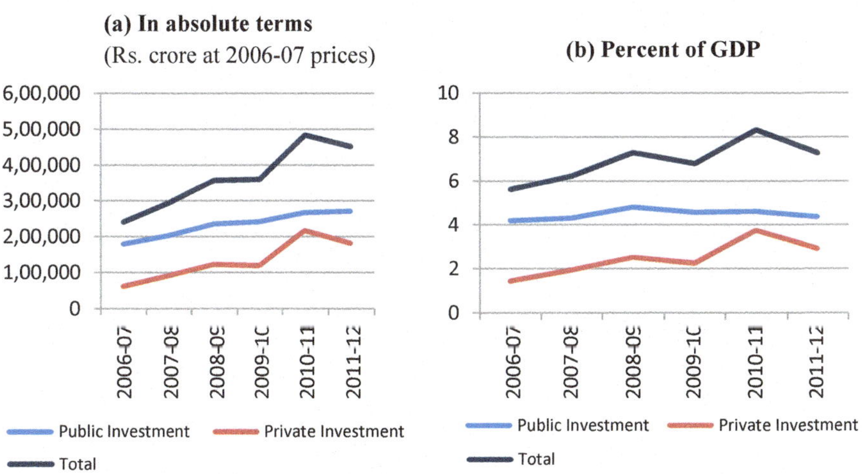

Fig. 10 Infrastructure Investment in India. *Source* Government of India, Planning Commission (2012). *Interim Report of the High Level Committee on Financing Infrastructure*

8 Public–Private Partnership—Match Made in Heaven or Marriage of Convenience?

As we have discussed, historically and especially in the period 1950–80, infrastructure has been provided almost exclusively by the government around the world as well as in India. Public spending on infrastructure expands investment opportunities and raises the returns to private investment. Thus, power projects, roads, and ports enhance the availability of quality power and connectivity, crowding-in private investment. By facilitating setting up of new industries, public investment is also a crucial aid to structural transformation and export diversification.

Given its importance, governments should recognize the indispensability of their own infrastructure investments as a complement to private endeavors. The public investment function is unlikely to be fully replaced by private providers, resulting in often ineffecient and poorer delivery of basic services to the public.[42]

However, governments also have funding constraints. Excessive public investment can crowd out private investment through say, higher interest rates. In India, the government has historically used the Statutory Liquidity Ratio (SLR) requirement of banks to have access to funds at lower-than-market rates, but such solutions have distortionary effects at the financial system level, and the fiscal limits of infrastructure investment are significantly lower than the needs of the growing economy. Private investment also has a better record of on-time and within-cost delivery, especially when there is full transfer of construction risk to the private sector through fixed price contracts with liquidated damages. Private investment is also expected to be more closely aligned with customer needs. In addition, private investment can provide competitive benchmark to public sector for performance improvement. Because of these reasons, governments are increasingly turning towards the private sector to provide infrastructure in recent times.

PPP holds the promise of combining the best of both worlds—the "public purpose" angle that government can bring in as well as the efficiency in execution and delivery expected of the private sector and access to the private funding possibility. But this happy combination of advantages can easily get derailed in reality unless the two parties—public and private—interact and cooperate seamlessly and in a trusting manner to deliver the goods and services. Carefully crafted contracts ensure this, but only partially. In the world of "incomplete contracts" (i.e., where the possible "states of the world" are too numerous and unpredictable to be anticipated and contracted), the two parties need to continue to work together and discretionary issues are likely to come up regardless of how detailed the contracting is.

This chapter discussed the background and rationale of the nature of infrastructure and the issues involved in public and private funding of it. The chapters to follow will delve deeper into these issues and analyze key benefits and challenges involved in structuring and implementing infrastructure PPPs.

---

[42] World Bank (2008).

Chapter 3
Financing Infrastructure

Globally, infrastructure is a growth sector with massive unmet demand. The annual world demand for infrastructure at around USD 4 trillion,[1] far outstrips the supply, around USD 2.7 trillion. A major part of this gap, about USD 1 trillion annually is expected to occur in developing countries. India, for instance, spent over USD 500 billion in the 11th Plan (2007–12) period and plans to spend twice the figure in the 12th Plan (2012–17) period.

How is this massive investment financed? That is the subject matter of this chapter. Broadly, there are four major sources of funding infrastructure investments around the world:

- Direct Budgetary Support/dedicated funds from the national/state government (Public)
- Internal and extra-budgetary resources of public sector undertakings (quasi-public)
- Private investment (Private)
- International funding from donors, multilaterals and commercial finance (quasi-public or private)

While the above classification is based purely on the nature of the funder, one may also classify modes of financing based on the nature of the funding contract/mechanism—equity, debt or project finance. Each kind of financing (mechanism as well as source) brings its own set of advantages and challenges. In this chapter, we would like to point out some of these issues.

The chapter is structured in the following manner. The next section provides a broad discussion of the issues connected with the various funding *sources*—public, quasi-public, and private. The section following that discusses the nature and implications of the three major *mechanisms* of financing—debt, equity, and project finance, with particular emphasis on the last mode, which is a mode of financing

[1]World Economic Forum. *Shaping the Future of Long-Term Investing, Infrastructure and Development*

K.V. Pratap and R. Chakrabarti, *Public-Private Partnerships in Infrastructure*,
India Studies in Business and Economics, DOI 10.1007/978-981-10-3355-1_3

commonly associated with infrastructure projects. The next section provides a broad overview of the financing patterns of infrastructure projects in India in recent years. The final section discusses the challenges associated with financing of infrastructure in the Indian context.

1 Sources of Infrastructure Finance

1.1 Government Budgetary Support

Despite the rapid growth of private investment in recent times, Government budgetary support continues to be a key source of infrastructure finance. This comes in the form of direct budgetary support or dedicated funds. Governments generally provide direct budgetary support to implement priority infrastructure augmentation programs. Consider, for instance, the Smart City Mission of the Government of India that has a large infrastructure component with a direct budgetary support of Rs. 48,000 crore ($\sim$\$8 billion) over a five-year period (2015–20).

Fiscal prudence ties the hands of governments in providing direct budgetary support. For instance in India, the government's ability to fund infrastructure directly is limited by the bounds defined by the Indian Fiscal Responsibility and Budget Management[2] (FRBM) Act (2003) in terms of the fiscal deficit target and the determination of the government to adhere to these limits. Thus, despite competing demands, the Government of India's fiscal deficit in 2015–16 was limited to 3.9% of GDP, the revised estimate of the fiscal deficit for 2016–17 is 3.5% of GDP, and the budget estimate of the fiscal deficit for 2017–18 is 3.2% of GDP.

Nevertheless, government budgetary support is likely to play a major role in infrastructure financing in future for reasons discussed at length in Chap. 2: market failure in certain infrastructure industries due to externalities, public good characteristics, natural monopoly characteristics, huge sunk costs, and merit goods (for example, water distribution and education). Given the visibility of large infrastructure projects, public sector funding for infrastructure investment is also politically salient—efficiently constructed and managed projects stand as monuments of governance, while leaving long-standing needs unmet gives fodder to the opposition.

Government budgetary support to infrastructure may also be in the form of dedicated funds. For instance, there is a dedicated fund for implementation of the ambitious road development program of the Government of India christened the National Highways Development Project (NHDP) built through levy of cess at the rate of Rs. 6 per liter on diesel and petrol, which adds up to about Rs. 43,000 crore per annum.[3] The government further leverages this cess revenue through market

[2]FRBM Act (2003).

[3]India's annual consumption of diesel is 68.4 million tons while petrol consumption stands at 17.1 million tons.

borrowings using capital-gains-tax-exempt bonds and other tax-free bonds. The key argument for the central road dedicated fund is *better targeting* in the sense that only current road users pay for road development. It also lowers the need for direct budgetary support and is environment-friendly in that it promotes energy conservation. A disadvantage is the reduction in budgetary flexibility as the cess proceeds can only be used for defined purposes including road development. Besides, one can argue that it also leads to inter-generational inequity as the current road users pay for an asset that is going to last for 30 years or more thus also benefitting future generations.

1.2 Internal and Extra-Budgetary Resources of Public Sector Undertakings

Another important source of infrastructure finance is internal and extra-budgetary resources of public sector undertakings (PSUs). In India, internal resource generation (retained earnings) in the public sector is low because of low profitability of PSUs. There were 235 Central PSUs (CPSUs) as on March 2015 making cumulative profits of Rs. 103,003 crore for 2014–15[4]: 157 units earning a cumulative profit of Rs. 130,363 crore[5] and 77 suffering losses totaling Rs. 27,360 crore in the same year (one was in a no-profit no-loss state).

A key source of infrastructure finance that augments internal funds is ***tolls*** (user fees) on road projects. Tolls are an example of user fees for economic infrastructure (a counterpart for social infrastructure would be tuitions). Tolls add to investment in that a new revenue stream is created where none existed earlier. Indian toll roads collected as much as Rs 13,236 crore in 2013–14[6] and Rs. 14,700 crore in 2014–15. The design of tolls in the road sector in India provide for uniform toll rates for publicly funded as well as PPP projects, partial indexation of toll rates to inflation, and partial exemption for local users.

Tolls and user fees can be an elegant solution if rates are set on the basis of objective principles like wear and tear caused to the road surface, saving in vehicle operating costs, acceptability and willingness of users to pay, and differentiating among user classes like trucks being charged more than cars. User charges can also have environmentally benign effects. User fees on toll roads are not just about raising revenue—they also reduce congestion by affecting both the supply and demand of road space. The conventional solution to excess demand is to keep expanding an infrastructure asset as it reaches capacity constraints. However, some demand management can be done without erosion of user benefits (at least to the same extent) using pricing through tolls. Variable tolling, for instance, can incentivize driving at

[4]Government of India, Department of Public Enterprises (2016).

[5]Crore is a unit of Indian currency (Rupees abbreviated Rs.) and is equal to 10 million.

[6]Lok Sabha Unstarred Question No 802, answered on 27 November 2014, 16th Lok Sabha, Government of India.

off-peak times. Similarly chaining trips (combining multiple tasks on a single trip), shifting onto public transport, telecommuting, or carpooling are other outcomes that can be promoted through tolls.

However, it is difficult to introduce tolls on an existing facility that commuters feel has already been paid for through taxes, when it is in a poor state or is not managed very well. People used to free infrastructure services (like water, power and roads) may take up direct action (preventing providers from charging tolls, as in the Delhi-Noida Toll Bridge), adding to political risks faced by private infrastructure projects.[7] The recent dismantling of toll booths in India (on the Delhi–Gurgaon NH8, for instance) has increased political risks in PPPs. Such political risk includes expropriation, non-convertibility and non-transferability. Not allowing concessionaires (the private party building and operating the road) to charge agreed-upon user fees effectively amounts to expropriation of assets. Regulators may also be setting user fees below costs, as in the Indian power distribution sector, for political, social fairness, and affordability concerns. These political and regulatory risks would be reflected in higher risk premium charged by the investors, thereby increasing costs and returns required from investment projects.[8] Three critical enablers for widespread use of user fees are public education and consultation, effective enforcement, and the need to address concerns about access and equity.

1.3 Private Investment

Private investment has emerged as a major source of financing infrastructure in India in recent times. It is estimated that 22% of the $225 billion infrastructure investment in the 10th Plan period (2002–07) came from the private sector, which went up to 38% in the 11th Plan period (2007–12) when Indian infrastructure investment is estimated at $500 billion. The total 12th Plan period (2012–17) infrastructure investment was estimated at $1 trillion out of which roughly half (47%) was expected to come from the private sector. So, not only is the share of the private sector increasing with successive plan periods (from 22% to 38% to 47% in 10th, 11th, and 12th plan periods, respectively), but the size of the overall pie is expanding as well ($225 billion to $500 billion to $1 trillion in 10th, 11th, and 12th plan periods, respectively).

The major sources of private infrastructure finance are internal accruals ploughed back (retained earnings), equity—both domestic and foreign, tolls, and borrowings

[7]Pratap (2015).

[8]Infrastructure services should be paid for, from user charges or the budget. The former is, of course, key to compensating investors in toll-based infrastructure projects. If the user charges must be kept below cost of provision of these services, the government should provide explicit subsidies. Otherwise, there may be problems as in the water and sewerage sector, where 6% of the projects, accounting for 21.6% of investment in the sector, have failed.

from multilaterals[9] and domestic market. Borrowings by private players would play a major role in financing their rising share of a growing pie.

1.4 *International Finance—Donors, Multilaterals, and Commercial*

International sources have played a critical role in funding developing country infrastructure in the past and continue to do so now. Official development assistance (ODA) from organizations like the World Bank Group amounts to about $125 billion a year. In countries like Mongolia and Mali, funds for infrastructure from donors and multilaterals are very significant (in Mali, for example, such funds could account for 80% of infrastructure investment). In India in contrast donors/multilateral finance as a proportion of total infrastructure investments is relatively low.[10] Nevertheless, World Bank has provided a loan of $1 billion to India Infrastructure Finance Company Limited (IIFCL) for infrastructure projects while PGCIL, the biggest power transmission company in India, has been provided over $1 billion by the same institution.

Besides direct financing, multilaterals also improve creditworthiness of projects through endorsement—provide comfort for other providers of long-term finance, investors, and contractors, particularly with regard to perceived political risks, especially projects involving multiple countries. Involvement of multilaterals helps make the deals credible, especially for countries that have poor creditworthiness. Consider for instance the 1800 km-long TAPI (Turkmenistan–Afghanistan–Pakistan–India) pipeline with a capacity to carry 90 million standard cubic meters of gas a day (mscmd) for a 30-year period. India and Pakistan will get 38 mscmd each and Afghanistan 14 mscmd. The pipeline would pass through a politically fragile region and security would be a key concern. The project would cost about $10 billion. The involvement of the World Bank in the project is key to attract financing for the project from other investors.

Most multilaterals are also able to provide specific political risk insurance and partial risk guarantees. Risk mitigation instruments usually depend on full or partial coverage of potential loss for the lender or investor—covering credit risk issues to support *debt funding*, or covering investment risk issues to back *equity funding*. Risk cover would also depend on the nature of the risk—political (or other non-project-related) or *project risks.*[11]

---

[9]Private sector can be funded by specialized multilateral agencies like the International Finance Corporation (IFC) that provide equity and debt support to private infrastructure companies—something we discuss in the next subsection.

[10]In contrast to donor and multilateral finance, India is receiving a sizeable amount of international commercial finance in the form of Foreign Direct Investment and Foreign Institutional Investment (FDI and FII) in infrastructure, especially in the telecom sector.

[11]Farquharson et al. (2011).

Box 1: Risk Mitigation Instruments in Infrastructure Projects

The various types of risk mitigation instruments used in infrastructure financing are as follows:

- ***Partial-Credit Guarantees***: These increase the borrower's access to long-term credit markets by sharing the credit risk between lenders and the guarantee provider. Multilaterals usually issue these guarantees, particularly to cover the "tail-end" repayments of a long-term project-finance loan. This helps private sector banks do project lending, even if they desire a shorter maturity.
- ***Full-Credit or "Wrap" Guarantees***: The entire project debt can be guaranteed by another entity. Then, the lender cares primarily about the credit risk of the guarantor and no longer that of the project itself. Before the global financial crisis of 2008–09, large private insurance companies called monoline insurers provided such guarantees. Such covers enable non-conventional funders like pension funds support projects. Here the lending instrument is usually a bond that investors can hold or sell to one another, rather than a direct bank loan.
- ***Export Credit Agencies***: Export credit agencies provide a more common credit risk cover. Expanding from originally covering political risk only, they now cover commercial risks as well. These are usually export-promoting government entities, covering long-term loans used to finance the purchase of their exports. Consequently, such cover is often, "tied" to the value and nationality of the exports for the project or the lender involved. It can be up to 100% of the political and commercial risk associated with the underlying cost being financed. Apart from the risk cover, these entities may also help with competitive long-term interest rates.
- ***Debt Underpinning***: The public authority itself may guarantee repayment of a portion of the project debt even if the cause of the potential default lies with the private sector partner. Clearly this approach only works if the long-term creditworthiness of the public authority is good enough for the lenders. Here it is important that the *unguaranteed* portion of the debt is enough to ensure that the lenders will have enough funds at risk to be concerned with the performance of the project.
- ***Political Risk Guarantees***: As the name implies, political risk guarantees or insurance protect lenders and investors against losses due to defined political events, such as currency non-convertibility or transfer risks, expropriation, or war, as distinct from the commercial risks of the project itself. Multilateral or bilateral institutions or private insurance companies provide such cover.

Source Adapted from Farquharson et al. (2011).

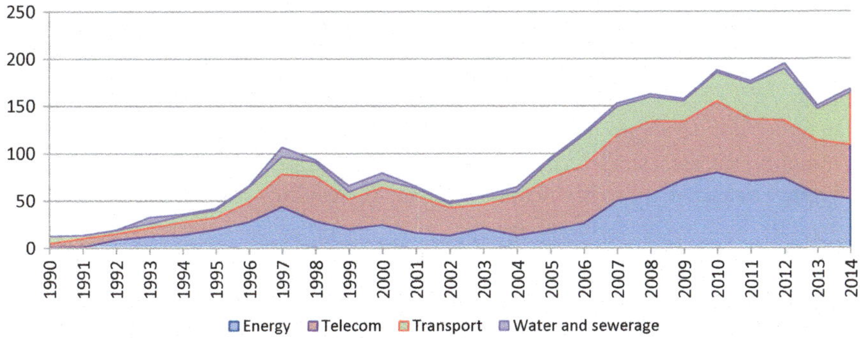

Fig. 1 Trends in private participation in infrastructure in developing countries ($billion). *Note* Data sourced from Private Participation in Infrastructure database of the World Bank (http://ppi.worldbank.org)

Apart from donor and multilateral finance, international commercial finance is becoming an increasingly important source of infrastructure financing for several countries. Figure 1 presents the trend of private participation in various infrastructure sectors in developing countries over the years.

While private investment in infrastructure projects was close to $20 billion in 1990–92, it rapidly increased during the first part of that decade to peak at $107 billion in 1997. Investment in East Asian power projects and privatization of Latin American telecommunications and electricity utilities drove this rise. The East Asian Financial Crisis (1997) started the decline in investment, affecting many of the independent power projects already underway. Continued crises in Russia and Latin America culminated in a fall as sharp as the earlier rise.[12] The effect of macroeconomic crises on international infrastructure finance is discussed in Box 2. After a period with no real discernible trends, investment levels have increased sharply again quadrupling in the decade since 2002, with a few hiccups. If we look at the composition of the increase, we find that the investment in energy, telecom and transport sectors have converged at around $50 billion in 2014. However, investment in the water sector has seen no discernible increase with the sector accounting for only about 4% of the total private infrastructure investment in developing countries.

Box 2: Impact of Macroeconomic Crises on Infrastructure Finance
In the real economy, macroeconomic crises are associated with infrastructure project failures. Where foreign financing is used, required revenues for servicing foreign debt increase as the domestic currency loses value, but experience indicates it is very difficult to increase user charges for

[12]Pratap (2011).

infrastructure services at the time of a macroeconomic shock. The real effect of a macro-shock also reduces demand for infrastructure services causing further financial stress to the affected project.[13] For all these reasons, international infrastructure finance is severely affected by macroeconomic crises. Macroeconomic crises lead to increase in host-country risks (country and project risks); increase in interest rate spreads, resulting in increase in cost of capital; flight of funds to safety, etc.

The significant drop in private participation in infrastructure investments between 1997 and 2003 corresponded with the increase in sensitivity to country risks in the wake of financial crises. In 1997–98, investments in East Asia and in Europe and Central Asia plummeted, as the sovereign credit ratings crashed in those regions. Investments and credit ratings in Latin America followed a year later.[14] As Fig. 2 shows, equity requirements and the cost of capital had increased for many infrastructure projects in the wake of the Global Financial Crisis of 2008. The combined effects of a lower leverage ratio and the higher cost of debt as shown in the figure would increase the cost of capital for infrastructure in the years ahead.

Very often, multilaterals take counter measures in the wake of macroeconomic crises. For example, the World Bank designed the Infrastructure Recovery and Assets (INFRA) Platform in September 2009 as its infrastructure response to the Global Financial Crisis. The INFRA Platform was designed to support counter-cyclical spending on infrastructure and to protect existing assets and priority projects of the client countries to help rapid recovery, job creation, and long-term growth.[15] This vulnerability of infrastructure finance to perception of heightened host-country risks underlines the need of macroeconomic stability measures in developing countries.[16]

2 Modes of Infrastructure Financing—Debt, Equity, and Project Finance

2.1 Debt Financing

With government budgetary support and major components of internal and extra-budgetary resources of public sector undertakings virtually capped, there is

[13]Pratap (2011).
[14]World Bank (2004).
[15]World Bank (2009).
[16]World Bank (2004).

Fig. 2 Effect of a macroeconomic crisis: Debt-Equity Ratio and Cost of Debt in two US infra projects. *Source* McKinsey Global Institute (2013).

increasing need for borrowings for the government to meet the public sector infrastructure obligations at the central level. The sources of borrowings could be international—bilateral and multilateral (World Bank, Asian Development Bank, etc.)—as well as domestic. For example, the Government of India has secured loans from the World Bank and the Asian Development Bank ($0.5 billion each) for its Smart City Mission. A sweetener for facilitating domestic borrowings by specialized infrastructure agencies in India (like National Highway Authority of India, NHAI; Power Finance Corporation, etc.) is allowing them to issue tax-free bonds, that lets them borrow at lower than market rates, though this is an indirect way of getting fiscal support (by foregoing tax revenue). However, given the size of the infrastructure deficit, debt availability for government is quite small.

Debt Funding Gap: Government of India estimates a debt funding gap of 6% of the total infrastructure funding requirements in the 12th Plan period (2012–17). Of the total projected infrastructure investment, 55% is expected to come from debt while 45% is expected from non-debt sources. This 45% is from equity, government budgetary support, and retained earnings (Table 1).

Sources of debt finance include domestic bank credit, Non-Bank Financial Companies (NBFCs), Pension and Insurance companies, and External Commercial Borrowings (ECBs). It may be significant to note that domestic bank credit is the most important source of debt finance and over half of the total debt finance to infrastructure is contributed by this source. However, as apparent from Fig. 3, the rate of growth of bank credit to infrastructure is sagging especially in more recent years.

Table 1 Debt funding gap in the total infrastructure investment requirement in the 12th plan period in India

Estimated requirement of debt	55%
Total estimated debt resources	49%
Debt funding gap	6%

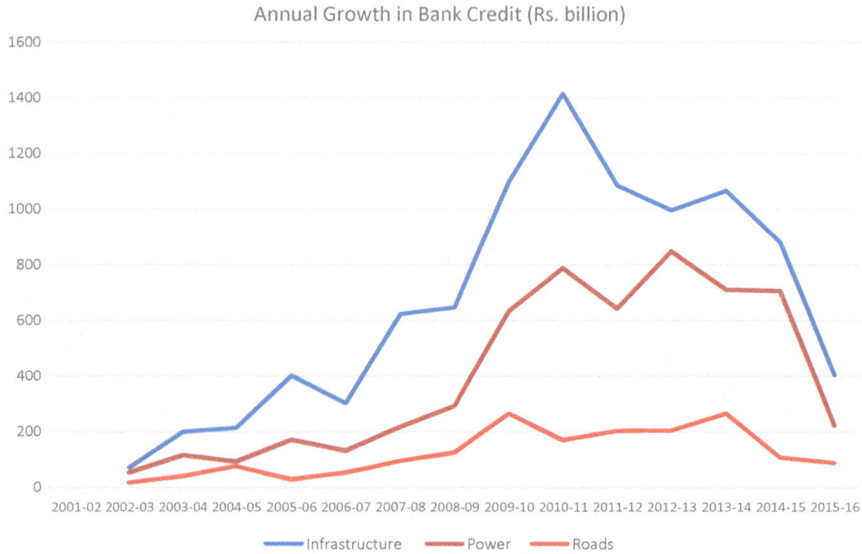

Fig. 3 Growth in bank credit to infrastructure in India

Indian Banks have financed a total of Rs. 9.6 trillion (~$160 billion at current exchange rate) of infrastructure till March 2016. Out of this, 60% is accounted for by power sector, 18% by roads, 9% by telecom, and 12% by other infrastructure. The annual growth of bank credit to infrastructure has slowed in recent years (while it was about 43% in the period 2000–11, it has come down to less than 20% in the last couple of years).

Bank loans are not particularly suitable for infrastructure projects though, owing to the "asset-liability mismatch". Bank deposits (liability) are usually less than ten years in maturity on average, whereas infrastructure projects (assets) are typically more than twice this in duration. This mismatch exposes bank balance sheets to risk, making bank finance an inferior source of infrastructure financing.

2.2 *Equity Financing*

Infrastructure financing requires both debt and equity. Equity funding is necessary as the lenders need some cushion between the cash flow from the project less operating and maintenance costs and the debt service requirements. Equity therefore plays a vital role in absorbing project risk and facilitating debt funding.[17] However, fresh equity investment in infrastructure has decelerated of late leading to

[17]Farquharson et al. (2011).

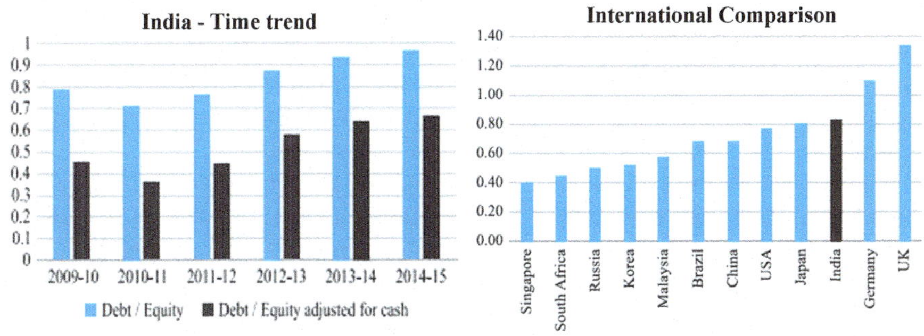

Fig. 4 Debt–equity ratio of non-financial Indian firms. *Source* Ministry of Finance (Government of India) (2015)

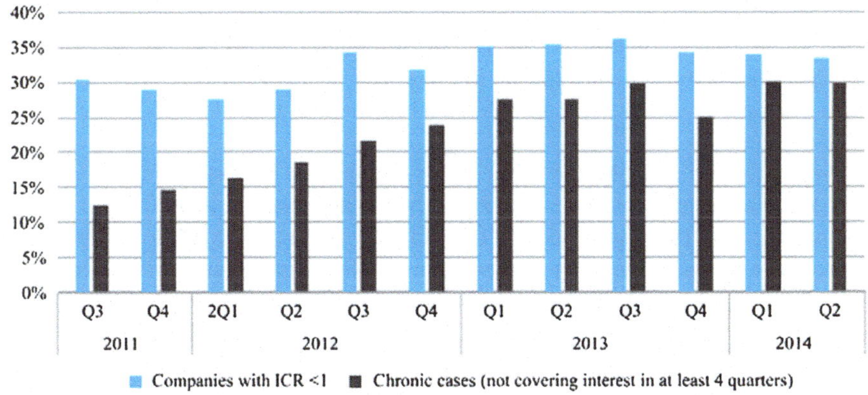

Fig. 5 Companies with interest coverage ratio of less than 1 (percentage of total sample). *Source* Ministry of Finance (Government of India) (2015)

over-leveraged balance sheets (see Figs. 4 and 5) preventing many domestic players from investing further. In contrast, international markets, are flush with liquidity and have a strong preference for infrastructure assets, with stable long-term risk adjusted returns. Therefore, developing countries need to not only allow but proactively seek infrastructure FDI by assuring investors a level playing field and following international best practices.[18]

Debt to equity is a measure of financial leverage that indicates the proportion of debt and equity used by the company to finance its assets. Figure 4 shows that the debt–equity ratio for Indian non-financial corporates has been rising at a fairly rapid rate over time and is significantly higher when viewed against other comparator countries (with the caveat that some of the Indian infrastructure firms are included in this database and others may not be included).

[18]Government of India, Planning Commission (2014).

The implication of the high leverage of non-financial firms in India is the low interest coverage ratio of Indian firms. Interest coverage ratio (ICR) is defined as the ratio of Earnings before Interest and Taxes (EBIT) to Interest expenses. An ICR of less than one demonstrates high risk for the lenders and emphasizes serious weakness in the company's ability to meet its debt obligations.

Figure 5 shows the percentage of companies in a large sample of 3700 listed companies in India that have ICR < 1. Credit Suisse reports that of the total debt of US$450 billion in the sample, US$ 140 billion (about 33%) is currently with companies with ICR < 1. Four years ago, only 17% of the debt was with such companies.

2.3 *Project Finance*

Most private sector infrastructure is project-financed. This is also a mode of financing that is by and large special to this sector. Hence it is imperative we spend some time and effort early on to understand the nature, benefits, and limitations of project financing.

Project finance involves the financing of one specific project by an entity that is created with the sole purpose to design, build, and manage that specific infrastructure (Special Purpose Vehicle, SPV). On the contrary, in traditional corporate finance, one company typically carries out multiple simultaneous initiatives that get financed as a portfolio of projects. In project finance, project company's obligations are ring-fenced from those of the equity investors and thus facilitate off-balance sheet financing. In project finance, therefore, lenders and investors rely either exclusively ("non-recourse" financing) or mainly ("limited recourse" financing) on the cash flows generated by the project to repay their loans and earn a return on their investments.[19] "Recourse" refers to access to other, i.e., non-project, assets of the company promoting the project as collateral for the loan in question. In non-recourse financing, debt repayment comes exclusively from the project company (a SPV set up only for the lifetime of the project with the mandate to exclusively undertake the project), rather than from any other source.

In limited recourse debt, debt servicing carries a repayment guarantee by the promoter up to a time, a fraction of the principal or till a milestone is reached. The distinguishing feature is that at least some portion of the debt eventually becomes non-recourse. This is unlike corporate lending where the strength of the borrower's balance sheet protects lenders. Since senior lenders (debt A is "senior" to debt B if A needs to get repaid before B) do not have access to sponsors' financial resources in project-financed transactions, cash flow, and adequate debt service coverage are critical and they need to secure this through watertight contracts.

[19]European Investment Bank (2015).

Fig. 6 Project finance contractual structure. *Source* DeJongh (2009)

Unlike in normal bank lending collaterals, sponsor guarantees and covenants do not work in capital-intensive infrastructure projects where such security/guarantees would not be able to cover the large quantum of project debt. The principal security for debt here, therefore, is the revenue streams of such projects, and the banks lend primarily on the strength of such security. This is true for India as well.[20]

What makes infrastructure suitable for project finance? Infrastructure is characterized by stable, predictable operating cash flows making it amenable to project finance. Stable and predictable operating cash flows occur because infrastructure is characterized by long-term assets with long economic life; low technological risk; provision of key public services like power and water supply, which have strong non-elastic demand; high entry barriers—natural monopoly or quasi monopoly markets; frequently user charges are hedged against inflation; and low correlation with traditional asset classes and overall macroeconomic performance.

Project Finance contractual structure: A typical project finance contractual structure is shown in Fig. 6

PPPs are associated with a complex set of contracts because of the presence of different actors with different goals, objective functions and interests, the need to reconcile or harmonize these varying objectives to meet a particular infrastructure goal, the presence of many risks[21] affecting Public–Private Partnership (PPP) projects and the need for agreement on risk allocation and management. To protect the interests of all stakeholders, there have to be watertight contracts with all of them. In fact, large deals involve highly complicated contractual bundles with hundreds of documents. For example, when the $3.6 billion Baku-Tbilisi-Ceyhan

[20]Government of India, Planning Commission (2014)

[21]Llanto (2008).

(BTC) pipeline project closed in 2002, it involved more than 200 documents with 17,000 signatures from 78 different parties.[22]

Typically, a Special Purpose Vehicle (SPV) company is created for the sole purpose of implementing the project (see Fig. 6). This company would have a Shareholders' Agreement with the project sponsors. Thus, Coastal Gujarat Power Limited, a subsidiary of Tata Power, is the SPV that has been created for implementing the 4000 MW Ultra Mega Power Project in Mundra in Gujarat, India. The sponsors (Tata Power) would have the Shareholders' Agreement with the SPV. The SPV would typically enter into an Engineering, Procurement and Construction (EPC) contract with specialized construction companies and transfer the construction risk to the specialized EPC companies. The SPV would enter into an Operation and Maintenance (O&M) contract with a specialized O&M company, thus transferring the O&M risk to the specialized O&M company. In the case of a power generation project, there would be a Fuel Supply Agreement with the fuel (coal) supplier like Coal India Limited (CIL), thus transferring the fuel supply risk to CIL.

The government or public sector agency gives a *concession* (or contract) to the SPV for operating the project for the duration of the concession period. Thus, Delhi International Airport Limited (DIAL), the SPV for the Delhi Airport, has been given the concession for 30 years to operate the Delhi Airport by the Airports Authority of India. Given that infrastructure often has a single purchaser or few buyers, there is often a significant demand risk associated with the project. To address the demand risk for a power project for instance, there may be a Power Purchase Agreement (PPA) with the off-taker (or buyer, typically a power distribution company). Thus, power generation projects (Coastal Gujarat Power Limited) generally have PPAs with off-takers (power distribution companies of Punjab, Haryana, Rajasthan, Gujarat, and Maharashtra). Since lenders have to depend on revenue streams of just the project (non-recourse financing, typical in a PPP project), rather than the credibility of the project sponsors, they may insist on all revenues of the project to be put in an escrow account on which the lenders would have first charge. In addition, lenders may want the following defined in a watertight contract (concession agreement, CA):

- source of revenue like user fees or budgetary payments,
- indexation of user fees to inflation,
- discounts and penalties related to performance,
- termination payments, etc.

The various contracts associated with a project finance contractual structure seek to transfer risk from the SPV to entities who have more control over the risk factor.

Features of Project Finance: There is a wide variety of project finance structures. But, there are certain common features underlying the project finance approach:

[22]Esty (2011).

- A 'ring-fenced' project implemented through a SPV whose only business is the project;
- Usually raised for a new project rather than an established project;
- High debt–equity ratio (leverage or gearing)—debt may cover 70–90% of project cost. Project losses are borne first by the equity investors, with lenders suffering only after the loss of the equity investment. Equity investors therefore accept a higher risk and need a higher return on their investment. Minimizing the cost of project finance is the primary aim of financial structuring for the project. Given the higher cost of equity, leverage becomes the typical answer[23];
- No guarantees from sponsors in the SPV (non-recourse financing) or limited guarantee (limited recourse financing[24]) for project finance debt—lenders rely on future cash flows to be generated by the project for debt service;
- Main security for lenders is the project company's contracts, licenses, or ownership rights to natural resources—much more valuable than the physical assets;
- Project has a finite life, based on such factors as length of the contract or license; therefore, project finance debt must be fully repaid by end of this life.
- Project Finance differs from Corporate Finance, where loans are against balance sheet of an existing diversified business and projections from past cash flows and profit record can be made; corporate finance also assumes that the company will remain in business indefinitely as compared to limited life of project-financed projects.
- Whether or not ownership of the project is transferred to the public sector (as in Build–Operate–Transfer (BOT), Build–Own–Operate–Transfer (BOOT) project), or remains indefinitely with the private sector (as in Build–Own–Operate, BOO), makes little difference from the project finance point of view. This is because the lenders rely on cash flows generated from the project and the discounted value of such cash flows becomes quite small after the concession period of 30 years or more. However, any long-term residual value in the project (as there may be in a BOO) may be of relevance to the investors in assessing their likely return.

Why use Project Finance?—Investors: There are several reasons why investors would prefer Project Finance.

[23]Heshmati et al. (2013).

[24]In some cases, a project company may be unable to raise finance on a non-recourse basis. One option is for a major project sponsor to provide a partial or full guarantee on the project debt. For example, in 1997, a concession for the eastern section of metro Manila was awarded to the Manila Water Company, a consortium led by the Ayala Corporation of the Philippines, with interests from United Utilities, Bechtel, and the Mitsubishi Corporation. In the wake of the Asian Financial Crisis, the Manila Water Company was unable to raise debt to finance investments on a non-recourse project finance-basis; so, Ayala provided a corporate guarantee to back up the project company. (Source: World Bank, Asian Development Bank, and Inter American Development Bank 2014).

Table 2 Benefit of project financing to investors

	Low leverage	High leverage
Project cost	100	100
(a) Debt	20	75
(b) Equity	80	25
(c) Revenue from project	10	10
(d) Interest rate on debt (per annum) (%)	4	6
(e) Interest payable [(a) * (d)]	0.8	4.5
(f) Profit [(c) − (e)]	9.2	5.5
(g) Return on equity [(f)/(b)] (%)	11.5	22

- Project finance is associated with higher leverage. High leverage improves investor returns as debt is cheaper than equity. Since interest is also tax deductible, the advantage of lower cost of debt persists at the profit after-tax stage as well.
- Table 2 shows an example of the benefits of leverage on investor returns. Both low-leverage (20% debt) and high-leverage (75% debt, typical level of debt for project finance) columns relate to the same investment of Rs. 100 which produces revenue of Rs. 10 per annum. The low-leverage column shows the return on equity at 11.5% while the high-leverage column shows the return on equity at 22%, despite an increase in the cost of debt from 4 to 6% reflecting the higher risk for lenders.
- Interest is also tax deductible. If the tax rate is 30%, the after-tax profit in low-leverage case is 6.44 (9.2 * 70%), which translates into an after-tax return on equity of 8.05%, whereas in high-leverage case, it is 3.85 (5.5 * 70%), or an after-tax return on equity of 15.4%.
- Off-balance sheet financing: A major characteristic of project finance is non-recourse financing, which increases an investor's borrowing capacity, enabling the investor to undertake several major projects simultaneously. Project finance structure may allow the investor to keep debt off the investor's balance sheet as the debt would belong to the SPV. This would be beneficial to a company's position in the financial markets. However, a company's shareholders and lenders should consider the risks of off-balance sheet activity, which appear in notes to the published accounts. So, project finance should not usually be undertaken purely to eliminate debt from the investor's balance sheet.[25]
- Risk limitation and spreading across stakeholders: In project finance, sponsor's risk is limited to the amount of equity investment in the SPV. This preserves the credit rating of the sponsor. In addition, projects using project finance may be too large for one investor (e.g., the Coastal Gujarat Power Limited project is a $4 billion dollar project). SPV may have O&M operator, EPC contractor, and

[25]Yescombe (2014).

off-taker to share risk, thereby making it possible to implement the large infrastructure project with limited risk to the sponsor.

- Long-term finance: Project finance loans typically are longer maturity than corporate finance. It is a result of high capital cost assets, as in infrastructure, that cannot be recovered over a short term without pushing up the user charges for the project's end product or service to infeasible levels. Mexico was on a massive road building spree in the 1990s. However, the bidding parameter that was used was the length of the concession period, with the result that some of the winning bids had a concession period of 3.5 years for an asset (roads) that was going to last for 30 years or more which resulted in unsustainable user charges. The rule of thumb is that the term of the loan should be equal to the concession period in PPP projects. Many of these Mexican projects failed, partly because of the short length of the concession period and consequent short-term financing.
- Enhanced credit: If off-taker has a better credit standing than the project sponsor, debt may be raised on better terms. In the Indian road sector, for example, there are annuity-based road projects for which payments are made by the public authority (NHAI) based on availability. Since the credit rating of NHAI is AAA, companies like GMR Infrastructure that have much lower credit rating, can raise debt on much better terms for its annuity-based project-financed road projects.

Why use Project Finance?—Third Parties: Third parties also benefit by using project finance. For example, project finance facilitates lower cost of product or service by using a high level of debt (see Table 3).

- Lower cost of services: Suppose the required return is 15%, then as Table 3 shows, a revenue of 12.8 is needed using low-leverage corporate finance, but only 8.25 using high-leverage project finance, reducing the cost to the off-taker or end user. Hence the preference for the latter with the off-taker or end user. Many of the infrastructure sectors are under-priced (exemplified by low cost recovery in power and water sectors in developing countries, including India). The lower cost of services associated with project finance financial structure may be the crucial difference between providing these services and not providing them at all in these countries.

Table 3 Benefit of project financing to third parties

	Low leverage	High leverage
Project cost	100	100
(a) Debt	20	75
(b) Equity	80	25
(c) Required return on equity [(b) * 15%]	12	3.75
(d) Interest rate on debt (pa) (%)	4	6
(e) Interest payable [(a) * (d)]	0.8	4.5
(f) Revenue required [(c) + (e)]	12.8	8.25

- Additional investment in public infrastructure and crowding-in of private investment: Project finance facilitates additional investment in public infrastructure as typical debt–equity ratio in such projects is 70:30. So, the total investment would be higher with the same level of equity. Investment in power, telecom, road, and ports also crowds-in private investment thus raising the investment rate and consequently the growth rate.
- Risk transfer especially cost overrun: Public sector project implementation is notorious for cost overruns. When the public sector has a fixed price contract with the private sector with liquidated damages, the risk of cost overrun is effectively transferred to the private sector. It has also been found that even if there is cost overrun in private implementation of public projects, private sector companies with strong balance sheets and reputations would absorb this, thus effectively shielding the public sector from the risk of cost overruns.
- Transparency and third-party due diligence: Many large infrastructure projects may be implemented for political rather than financial/economic reasons. However, if the private sector is implementing the project, the analysis would be more transparent in that it is a ring-fenced project being implemented by a SPV and there is likely to be third-party due diligence (by lenders, for example, who would be providing most of the project costs and would be depending on the cash flows generated by the project and not on the balance sheet and profit and loss statements of a diversified company). Therefore, project selection in a project financed project may be more objective.

Project Finance: Global Market Trends: One estimate of global market trends in project finance is shown in Fig. 7. The size of the market is $400 billion in a normal year—this was the approximate level in 2007 and 2008 as well as in 2010–13. Project finance is also disproportionately affected by financial crises—the total project finance market slumped to about $250 billion in 2009 in the wake of the Global Financial Crisis. Overall, project-financed deals have a mean size of $541

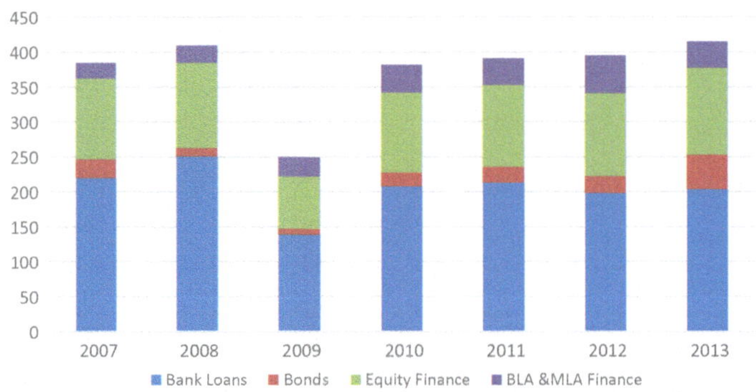

Fig. 7 Global market trends of project finance ($billion) *Note* Equity finance is estimated assuming debt-to-total capitalization ratio of 70%; *BLA* bilateral lending Agencies; *MLA* multilateral lending agencies. *Source* Esty et al. (2014)

million and a median size of $160 million, once again illustrating the importance of very large projects (Fig. 7).

As we have seen, project finance is extensively used by infrastructure firms, which implies that these firms would have high debt–equity ratios. Generally debt–equity ratio in project financed infrastructure projects is 70: 30. Given the scale of planned infrastructure investment projections in countries like India ($1 trillion in 2012–17), finding required equity could be a major issue. However, Government of India's main concern is for ensuring debt financing.

Project sponsors usually provide equity, but contractors building and operating the project as well as financial investors [like Private Equity (PE) funds] can contribute as well. In India, in early phase, there is predominance of sponsor equity. Most investments by PE/Infrastructure Funds into infrastructure are being structured as convertible instruments with option to investors to seek a 'take-out' from developers in case of failure to list at the end of a prespecified period.

3 Infrastructure Investment in India in Recent Years

3.1 Infrastructure Investment in the 11th Plan (2007–12)

India invested about $500 billion on infrastructure in the 11th Plan period. This was roughly 2.2 times the investment on infrastructure in the 10th Plan period (2002–07). The share of private investment in the 11th Plan period was 38% of the total infrastructure investment compared to 22% during the 10th Plan. Starting from a higher base of 5.6% of GDP in 2006–07, the 11th Plan infrastructure investment reached 8.3% of GDP in 2010–11. This dipped slightly to 7.3% of GDP in the final year of the 11th Plan period, chiefly owing to the slowdown in the telecommunication sector. The total infrastructure investment during the 11th Plan period was 7.2% of GDP compared to 5% during the 10th Plan period (all numbers at 2006–07 prices and exchange rate).

The share of private sector in total infrastructure investment rose to 2.7% of GDP in the 11th Plan period from 1.1% of GDP in the 10th Plan period. However, the public sector even now remains the dominant source of infrastructure finance in India and most countries of the world. Public sector infrastructure investment was about 4.5% throughout the 11th Plan (see Fig. 8b). In fact, public investment as a percent of GDP has stagnated in India, while private investment is increasing. The sharp increase in total infrastructure investment during 11th Plan can be attributed largely to the rapid rise in investment by the private sector, which in turn was an outcome of the enabling environment fostered by the policy and regulatory framework.

Share of Private Investment in Infrastructure Sectors—11th Plan: It would be seen that private participation varies widely across sectors. The sectors that are not amenable to private participation (like rural roads) would have to be funded through

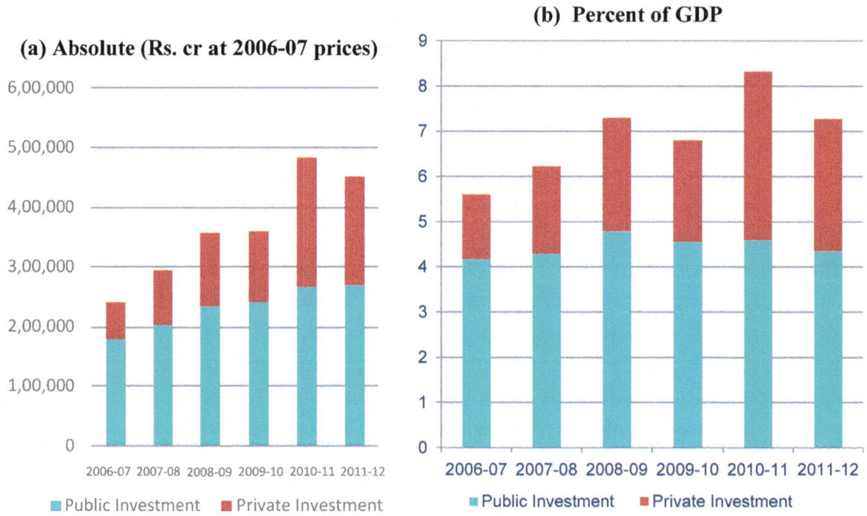

Fig. 8 Infrastructure investment in the 11th plan period (2007–12) in India **a** Absolute (Rs. crore at 2006–07 prices) **b** Percent of GDP *Source* Government of India, Planning Commission (2012)

government budgetary support. Private participation in more commercial sectors enables the government to divert more resources to such non-commercial sectors.

Private investment is now well established in commercially viable sectors such as ports, telecom, airports, national highways, generation of electricity, oil and gas pipelines, etc. (see Fig. 9). As a result, the government can now effectively direct its resources to less commercially viable sectors like irrigation, water supply and sanitation, inland waterways, and rural roads in the short-term, while in the long-term, make efforts to attract private investment in these sectors.

3.2 Infrastructure Investment in the 12th Plan (2012–17)

The original plan in the 12th Plan was to invest \$1 trillion on infrastructure in the 2012–17 period. Private sector share of total infrastructure investment was expected to rise to nearly half (47%) from slightly over a third (38%) in the 11th Plan. Public sector share of infrastructure investment was expected to experience a corresponding fall. The share of the Centre as part of the public sector share in the overall infrastructure investment was likely to decline slightly to 31% in the 12th Plan from 35% in the 11th Plan. The share of States was likely to decline to 22% compared to 28% in the 11th Plan. Average infrastructure investment in the 12th Plan period was projected at about 8.2% of GDP compared to 7.2% during the 11th Plan period.

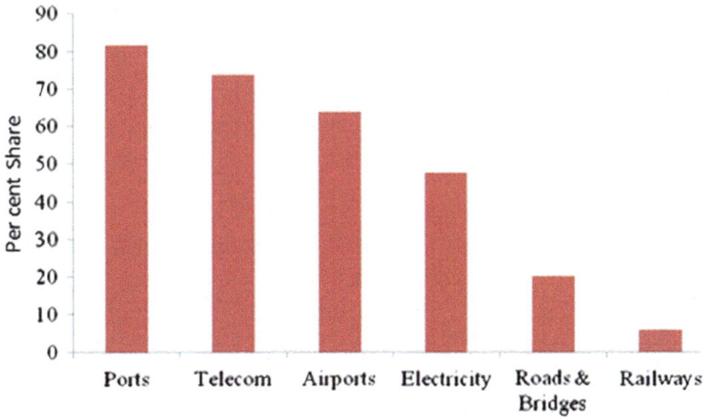

Fig. 9 Share of private investment in infrastructure sectors in the 11th Plan period in India *Source* Government of India, Planning Commission (2011)

It was felt that with the success of private participation in infrastructure during the 11th Five-Year Plan, continued emphasis on private investment would be necessary for bridging the investment gap. The private sector share in total infrastructure investment of around 47% overall, is far higher in some sectors, for instance, in non-conventional sources of energy, telecommunications, ports, airports and storage where over 70% of the investments would be private. For that to happen, large infrastructure projects needed to be structured on sound commercial principles within an enabling policy and regulatory environment. If these initiatives succeeded, India would deliver an unprecedented program of PPPs, even by international standards.[26]

Actual Infrastructure Investment in the 12th Plan: Actual investments have fallen far short of these projections. In 2012–13, infrastructure investment was way below target and lower than even in 2011–12. While the target was Rs. 7.5 lakh crore (or Rs. 7.5 trillion), the estimated infrastructure investment was only Rs. 4.9 lakh crore (or Rs. 4.9 trillion), which works out to 66% of the targeted investment. In comparison, actual infrastructure investment in 2011–12 was Rs. 5.61 lakh crore. In terms of shortfalls in individual sectors, there were substantial shortfalls in electricity, roads, and telecom sectors.

Even in 2013–14, infrastructure investment was way below targets, thus leading to a loss of investment momentum during the initial two years of the 12th Plan. With these developments, it looks doubtful that 12th Plan (2012–17) targets would be achieved. However, the infrastructure momentum seems to have been regained in the last two years of the 12th Plan. The government has implemented a major public infrastructure investment program to remedy the deficiency in private investment.

[26]Government of India, Planning Commission. *Eleventh Five Year Plan.*

4 Challenges in Infrastructure Financing

Given the distinctive characteristics of infrastructure financing and the Indian financial sector, infrastructure financing in India is associated with several challenges. The key ones are discussed below.

- High fiscal deficit
- Challenges emanating from infrastructure characteristics—huge investment requirement, long payback period, etc
- Issues in bank financing of infrastructure. This is important as banks are the most important source of infrastructure finance
- Issues with the use of pension and insurance funds for infrastructure
- Underdeveloped bond markets
- Impact of externalities—economic viability versus financial viability
- Issues with Project Finance
- Low user fees in many infrastructure sectors like power and water

4.1 High Fiscal Deficit

The figure shows Indian federal government fiscal deficit as a percent of GDP over the last several years. The fiscal deficit in India has generally stayed around the 4% mark over the years. This is a whole one-third higher than the world average of 3% in 2015. Adding the fiscal deficit of the state governments, the total fiscal deficit (federal and states) is close to 8% of GDP, which is a very high number. However, since 2015–16, the fiscal deficit is sub-4% of the GDP partly because of the limits placed by the Indian Fiscal Responsibility and Budget Management Act, 2003 (Fig. 10).

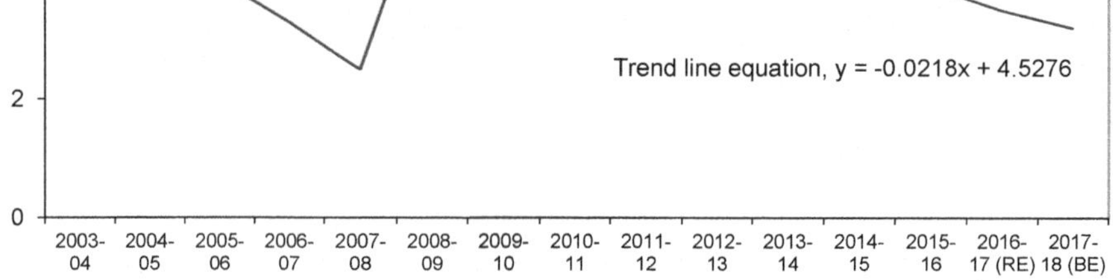

Fig. 10 Indian federal government fiscal deficit as a % of GDP *Source* Data sourced from Government of India (Ministry of Finance). Budget 2017–18 and previous year budget documents

A high fiscal deficit has a direct impact on the availability of resources for infrastructure investment through budgetary support. The high fiscal deficit shows that there is very little fiscal space for infrastructure investment through budgetary support. Therefore, there is growing importance of borrowings and private participation in infrastructure in financing of infrastructure in India.

4.2 *Challenges Emanating from Infrastructure Characteristics—Huge Investment Requirement, Long Payback Period, etc.*

A power generation project costs about $1 million per MW of generating capacity. Thus, a 4000 MW Ultra Mega Power Project (UMPP) is likely to cost $4 billion. There are very few companies in India that can raise this magnitude of funds for implementing such projects. In fact, the Indian Model Request for Qualification for Public–Private Partnership projects has a rule of thumb that the net worth of a company eligible for bidding should be 25% of the total estimated project cost, which translates into a net worth of $1 billion as an eligibility condition for bidding for a UMPP.

Infrastructure projects are also characterized by long payback periods—for example, the payback period of a typical road project could be 30 years because the user charges also have to be reasonable. These infrastructure characteristics may lead to market failure and in an underdeveloped market, these projects may be amenable to only public sector provisioning as was the case in the early years of Indian independence when large projects were implemented by the public sector.

4.3 *Issues in Financing by Banks*

Given the non-recourse characteristic of infrastructure financing, the major concerns of project lenders including banks are: certainty of debt service coverage of project cash flows; reliability of public sector obligations; reliability of PPP legal frameworks; enforceability of the PPP-related contracts; faith in the regulatory regime; step-in rights in case of project failure and availability of alternative contractors; management quality of contractors; reliability of contractors and quality of contractor guarantees; risk allocation among stakeholders; reputational fallout of the project (environmental, social), and availability and effectiveness of insurance cover.

The main issue in bank lending to infrastructure is the asset-liability mismatch (ALM), as mentioned earlier. Tenure of infrastructure loans is inadequate as bank deposits (liabilities of banks) are short term and infrastructure assets are long term.[27]

[27]Banks normally lend for a maximum tenure of 12–15 years even if the concession period of a PPP project is 30 years.

The short tenure of loans increases risk, raises costs, and user charges. If a road project, which has a typical life of 30 years is financed with a loan of 15 years, there is an additional risk that it may not be able to raise finances for the rest of the period (refinancing risk) and any effort to repay the loan in this short period may cause the user charges to rise above politically feasible levels.

In addition, banks are also exhausting their prudential limits in terms of sector, borrower and project exposure. As we have seen, the total project cost of each UMPP is about $4 billion. Reliance Power has been awarded 3 of the 4 UMPPs that have been bid out till now. This is leading to high sector, borrower and project exposure for banks. As per the Reserve Bank of India (RBI, the country's central bank) norms, the single borrower limit is 15% of a bank's capital, but can be raised to 20% if the additional exposure is on account of credit to infrastructure projects. Bank Boards have the discretion to raise this further to 25%. Corresponding numbers for group exposure norms are 40, 50 and 55%. In the case of SBI, three companies—IOC, BHEL and Reliance Industries Limited—have already breached the single borrower exposure limit of 25%.

Single and group exposure limits come in the way of the huge funds requirement in infrastructure projects. There is not much scope to increase these given the internationally accepted norms. Indian banks have low capital base and exposure limits of banks are fixed in relation to their capital funds. Even though RBI has allowed relaxation of 5% in case of single borrower limit and 10% in case of group borrower limits, banks have already reached the maximum group exposure limit to large industrial houses and cannot fund their projects. Besides borrowers also seek out a few large banks worsening the exposure limit constraints.[28]

The counterargument is that the group exposure norm for banks, binding for normal corporate lending to business group companies, should not be applied in the case of project lending since the group assets are not available as security for such loans. Further, such limits would quickly disable Indian companies and groups to participate in infrastructure projects, bringing down the level of competition in the sector. Therefore, the High Level Committee on Infrastructure Financing (2014) recommended non-application of group exposure limits by the Reserve Bank of India for projects financed on limited- or non-recourse basis. This would, of course, require stricter project appraisal and approval processes as a substitute, as is the global best practice.[29]

Banks in India are also suffering from the growing problem of Non-Performing Assets (NPAs), partly on account of their infrastructure portfolio. Gross Non-Performing Assets (GNPAs) of public sector banks have soared to Rs. 6.2 lakh crore at the end of Q3 FY17—an increase of over 56% over the previous year. GNPAs of public sector banks are now at a staggering 11.2% of their advances. For some banks, the situation is worse—GNPAs of five banks namely Indian Overseas Bank (22.4%), UCO Bank (17.2%), United Bank (16%), IDBI Bank (15.2%), and

[28]Chakrabarty (2010).

[29]Government of India, Planning Commission (2014).

Bank of Maharashtra (15.1%) are now over 15%. While at the aggregate level, GNPAs of private sector banks are only 3.5% of advances, some banks have much higher levels of bad loans, e.g., ICICI Bank (7.9%), and Dhanlaxmi Bank (7.6%).

Use of refinancing facility has also has been suggested to mitigate asset-liability mismatches. Under this arrangement, other long-term funds will be borrowed (through take-out financing and Infrastructure Debt Funds) and used to refinance infrastructure loans of banks and specialized Non-Banking Finance Companies (NBFCs).

The Indian Budget 2014–15 has taken some steps to facilitate long-term bank finance to infrastructure. Banks have been encouraged to issue longer maturity debt to infrastructure with greater flexibility in structuring to deal with potential problems—sometimes referred to as the "5/25" structure. A 5/25 structure allows banks to lend to a project for 25 years, with an option of revising the terms of the loan ("reset" in banking parlance) or transferring it to another bank or financial institution after 5 years. It is therefore structured to allow its tenure to match the life cycle of the underlying asset. It aims to improve debt servicing capacity and viability of projects. On their liability side, banks have been permitted to raise long-term funds earmarked for infrastructure sector with minimum regulatory pre-emptions like Cash Reserve Ratio (CRR), Statutory Liquidity Ratio (SLR[30]), and Priority Sector Lending (PSL) obligations.[31]

Committed long-term funding over the life of a project, that may be as long as 30 years, may not be available in many markets like India. As the events of the global financial crisis (2008) have shown, it may be a challenge even in mature PPP markets. Therefore, refinancing may be necessary. It is possible to share the benefits from refinancing the existing debt on improved terms between the equity investors (who take substantial project risks) and the public authority (who, arguably, has facilitated the improved environment).[32]

4.4 *Issues with use of Pension and Insurance Funds for Infrastructure*

The long life of infrastructure assets is a perfect match for the long-term liabilities of insurance and pension funds. The implication is that such funds can finance infrastructure without asset-liability mismatch. Returns of infrastructure projects offer reliable cash flows, act as a hedge against inflation, have low volatility,

---

[30]The 2014–15 budget, allows for long-term bonds issued by commercial banks for financing infrastructure and housing to be exempted from computation of net demand and time liabilities (NDTL) and they would therefore not be subject to CRR and SLR requirements. Minimum regulatory pre-emption on such bonds will reduce their cost by up to 120 basis points according to some estimates.

[31]Government of India, Ministry of Finance (2014).

[32]Farquharson et al. (2011).

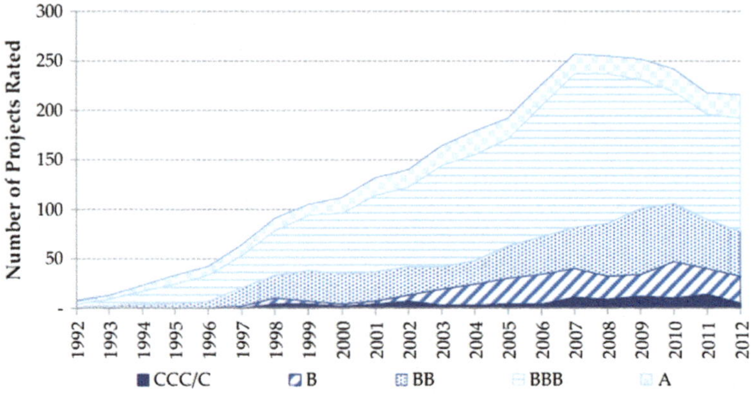

Fig. 11 Rating of project finance debt, 1992–2012 *Source* Esty et al. (2014)

and are generally not correlated with other assets, which can help with portfolio diversification.

As we have seen, banks, which are currently the most important lenders to infrastructure, lack long-term liabilities to match such long-duration loans. Globally, the best practice is to let the banks fund the projects for an initial period and then switch to refinancing from alternative source. This combines the advantage of the bank appraisal particularly in the construction and early operation phase with the lower risk aversion of long-term funders like insurance and pension funds.[33]

In the aging developed world, unprecedented levels of savings in the form of pension, insurance and other institutional funds are seeking stable, predictable, long-term returns that Indian infrastructure could ideally offer. Worldwide, pension funds, sovereign-wealth funds, insurance companies, and other institutional investors manage over $106 trillion of capital. Only 1.6% of this is currently allocated to infrastructure and there is a massive opportunity to increase this proportion.

However, in practice, these funds have shied away from infrastructure investment, scared by the scale, complexity, and political risks involved in such projects.[34] Likelihood of corruption and currency crises have also played a part in preventing such funds from making infrastructure investments. Regulatory guidelines also constrain the participation of insurance companies and pension funds in infrastructure. For example, the Indian Insurance Regulatory and Development Authority (IRDA) requires insurance companies to invest in debt paper with a minimum credit rating of ‘AA’. This automatically excludes investment by insurance companies in debt paper of most private infrastructure companies, which have been set up on project financing basis. A typical non-recourse infrastructure project is rated BBB (see Fig. 11).

[33]Government of India, Planning Commission (2014).

[34]Public insurance firms in India are inherently risk averse and invest more than required in government securities—LIC invested 50% against the minimum prescribed requirement of 25%.

Some Pension Fund Investments in India: In 2014 Canada Pension Plan Investment Board (CPPIB) and Caisse de depot et placement du Quebec (CDPQ) teamed up with Oman's State General Reserve Fund (SGRF) to invest Rs. 2000 crore in L&T Infrastructure Development Projects Ltd (L&T IDPL). L&T IDPL operates a portfolio of infrastructure assets that includes road projects, ports and the Hyderabad Metro Rail Project. The CPPIB investment is in preference shares of L&T IDPL, compulsorily convertible into equity shares by 2018. Post conversion, CPPIB would hold a minority stake in L&T IDPL. This was the first foreign pension fund directly investing in Indian companies. PSP Investments, a pension fund again from Canada, partnered with IDFC PE and Abu Dhabi's National Energy Company to buy out two hydel projects operated by Jaiprakash Power Ventures in 2014. PSP Investments put in Rs. 1560 crore for a 39% stake in the two hydel projects.[35]

4.5 Debt Financing of Longer Tenure—India Infrastructure Finance Company Limited (IIFCL)

IIFCL was incorporated by the Government of India in 2006 for providing long-term loans for financing infrastructure projects. IIFCL provides financial assistance up to 20% of the project cost. The channels include direct lending to project companies and refinancing of banks and financial institutions. IIFCL has sanctioned Rs. 67,823 crore for 389 projects and has disbursed Rs. 30,251 crore to date.

Take-out Financing by IIFCL: IIFCL has been recognized as a special agency to extend takeout financing scheme in 2010. A takeout financing scheme involves the project company, the lender and the "taking over institution" (bank/consortium of banks/ Financial Institution). Under the scheme, the taking over institution enters into an agreement by which the lender transfers a part/whole of the outstanding debt to it on predetermined terms. The scheme would enable banks to reduce exposure to existing borrowers, free up their capital and avoid reaching the exposure limits. The idea of takeout financing has gained global acceptance as a best practice to release long-term funds for financing infrastructure projects.[36] Banks can seek takeout financing immediately after the commencement of commercial operations of the project. Build–Operate–Transfer projects of National Highway Authority of India (NHAI) are eligible for the scheme.

Reinventing the role of IIFCL: IIFCL was originally set up by the Government of India in 2006 to provide long-term debt for infrastructure projects as the commercial banks were plagued with asset-liability mismatch. Since then, IIFCL has given loans to several projects on roughly the same terms as banks, but with a marginal increase in the loan tenure. It has raised long-term resources on the strength of sovereign guarantees. Use of scarce sovereign guarantees for sustaining lending operations similar to normal banking operations requires some rethinking.

[35]Business Standard (2014).

[36]FICCI and Ernst & Young (2012).

Since sovereign guarantees are scarce and also subject to a cap under the FRBM Act (Fiscal Responsibility and Budget Management Act, 2003), efforts should be aimed at leveraging the available guarantee space to the maximum, especially for raising long-term debt. IIFCL has largely duplicated the role of commercial banks, which was not its mandate. IIFCL can provide guarantees for specified infrastructure bonds to enable them to be rated as 'investment grade', which would attract insurance and pension funds, household savings and FIIs. Where IIFCL undertakes direct lending, it should lend for tenures of 20 years or longer.[37]

4.6 Underdeveloped Bond Markets

Bond markets fare better than bank finance in terms of longer maturities, tradability, and back-weighted repayment structures that help boost equity returns. Infrastructure project bonds appeal to institutional investors, like insurance companies and pension funds in particular, whose long-term liabilities find a match in these long-term loan assets.[38]

The primary bond market in India comprises issuances by both Central and State governments, Public Sector undertakings, other government bodies, Financial Institutions, banks and corporates. ASEAN + region's local currency bond market was at $6.2 trillion of which China was $2.4 trillion in 2012. Indian local currency bonds outstanding were $0.6 trillion (10% of regional total and 0.9% of the world total). Another BRICS country, Brazil had $1.6 trillion of local currency bonds outstanding, which is much higher than India. Limited investor base, few issuers and inclination for bank finance over bonds are among the main obstacles to the development of a deep and liquid corporate bond market in India.

The main characteristics of the Indian bond market are:

- Constituted mainly by Government bonds[39] including issuance of tax-free infrastructure bonds[40] by public sector organizations like NHAI, REC, IRFC, and IIFCL;
- Few corporate bond issuers (e.g., Reliance Holdings, SBI, ICICI Bank);
- Corporate debt market constrained by detailed primary issue guidelines, lengthy processes, and absence of long-term investors;

[37]Government of India, Planning Commission (2014).

[38]World Bank (2004).

[39]Government of India (GoI) bonds are medium- to long-term debt securities issued by the Reserve Bank of India (RBI) on behalf of the federal government to finance its budgetary expenditures and infrastructure projects. The Indian bond market is dominated by government bonds, which constitute about 70% of the total bond issuance in India. The balance is constituted by mainly corporate bonds. Market participants have mentioned that GoI securities and treasury bills are relatively liquid and bid—ask spread at 0.6 basis points for Government of India bonds is low.

[40]Issuance of tax-free bonds for Rs. 30,000 crore during 2011–12 established the feasibility and credibility of raising infrastructure finance through bonds.

- Low issue size[41]—average for corporate bonds (US$48 million) compared to $147 million for the region;
- Bond market primarily functions as a private placement market as the public issues of bonds have been found to be difficult, slow, expensive as well as risky.

Government has recently taken some initiatives for development of bond markets including enhancing the limit for Foreign Institutional Investors (FIIs) to invest in corporate bonds issued by infrastructure companies, and notifying guidelines for Infrastructure Debt Funds (IDFs).

Infrastructure debt funds (IDFs): IDFs are designed to raise low-cost long-term funds to refinance infrastructure projects past the construction stage. Through a package of credit enhancements, IDFs would channelize funds to infrastructure projects with a government 'buy-out' guarantee. The advantages of IDFs include the following: (a) project sponsors would refinance their debt while sharing gains with the government/users; (b) IDFs would help release scarce lending space of the banks, enabling them to lend to new projects; (c) IDFs would help create a secondary market for debt bonds.

Structuring of IDF: IDF will be set up by one or more sponsors like IIFCL, SBI, ICICI, LIC, IDFC, UTI, an infrastructure NBFC (Non-Banking Financial Company) or an investment bank. Sponsors may also include multilaterals such as IFC or ADB in order to enhance the credibility of the IDF to foreign investors.

The first Indian IDF was launched in February 2013. ICICI Bank, Bank of Baroda, Citibank and LIC sponsored the India Infra Debt Limited (Infradebt). The shareholding was as follows: ICICI Bank (together with a wholly owned subsidiary) 31%; Bank of Baroda 30%; Citibank 29%; and LIC 10%. The mandate of Infradebt is to raise debt from domestic as well as foreign markets and invest in infrastructure PPP projects with at least one year of operations. It is hoped that Infradebt will help expand and diversify the domestic and international sources of debt funding for the infrastructure sector in India.

IDFs, through innovative means of credit enhancement, are expected to bypass the asset-liability mismatch challenge of banks and provide long-term low-cost debt for infrastructure projects, bringing down the cost and tariff of infrastructure services. Further, buy-out guarantee from Project Authority will protect the IDF-NBFC from NPAs. The taking over of existing bank debts by IDFs, in turn, would release fresh lending by banks to other infrastructure projects.[42]

Who will be the borrowers?: Any PPP project that has: (a) provision for compulsory buy-out by paying predetermined termination payment; (b) been operational for at least 1 year, without any material default in debt service or other

---

[41]Transaction size is a useful measure of market depth, given that it is an ex-post measure of the quantity of bonds that are traded at the bid or ask price. ADB has estimated that average on-the-run transaction sizes (US$ equivalent) for government bonds ranged from lows of US$1.7 million and US$1.8 million in India and Indonesia, respectively, to a high of US$23.2 million in the China.

[42]Press Release on the occasion of the launch of the first Infrastructure Debt Fund (19 February 2013) (http://pib.nic.in/newsite/erelcontent.aspx?relid=92319).

obligations; (c) been awarded through competitive bidding (carrying the assurance of a sustainable price discovery). Non-PPP projects will not be eligible for borrowing as they are likely to miss these risk-reducing features.

Credit enhancement: Given that PPP concessions typically provide a takeover by the public entity against a termination payment even in the event of termination on account of default by the concessionaire, and this payment amount normally covers much of the project debt, this provides for an implicit guarantee on the debt. For example, in the case of national and state highways, the concessionaire would be entitled to receive 90% of the project debt which forms part of the agreed project costs. This may enable the Fund to take over a significant proportion of the existing debt with minimal risks.

The Fund's subscription to the project bonds will be backed by a tripartite agreement among (a) the Fund; (b) the project company; and (c) the project authority (such as NHAI or a state government in the case of highways) making the bonds virtually risk-free and attractive to insurance and pension funds.[43]

Some New Developments: Because of government initiatives[44] and inherent advantages of bonds, companies are increasingly turning to bond markets to source debt at lower interest rates. In April–June 2015, corporate bond placements increased by 215% over previous year to Rs. 1.69 lakh crore. The increased activity in corporate bonds helps explain some of the dichotomy between high GDP growth projections and low bank credit.[45] Most of this was raised at interest rates between 7.75 and 9%, which is below the base rate of banks. Masala bonds[46] and Green bonds[47] are also being issued.

To sum up, the tenure of debt is a critical issue in financing infrastructure owing to the longer payback period. Typically, the tenure of debt should be as much as the expected life of the project to keep user charges reasonable. But, actually the tenure is much less. Insurance and pension funds have stayed away owing to regulations and their risk perception. Bond markets in India continue to be shallow. IIFCL was

---

[43]Haldea (2010a).

[44]Bond issues have also become easier in regulatory terms.

[45]The growth of the real economy in the financial year 2016–17 is expected to be about 7.1%. However, the annual rate of growth of bank credit is low (4.9% as on February 2017) and nowhere near the rates of growth that have been seen in the Eleventh Plan (2007–12) period.

[46]Masala bonds allow Indian entities to raise money from foreign markets in rupees (rupee-denominated bonds), and not in foreign currency. By doing so, masala bonds help internationalize the rupee and deepen the Indian bond market. By issuing bonds in rupees, an Indian entity is shielded against foreign currency risk, typically associated with borrowing in foreign currency. As masala bonds raise money in rupees, foreign investors will be taking the currency risk. Housing Development Finance Corporation (HDFC) has raised Rs. 3000 crore in July 2016 from masala bonds at 8.38% coupon rate—first such issuance by an Indian company.

[47]Green bonds are like ordinary corporate bonds, except that they are used to fund environment-friendly projects. The Indian capital market regulator, SEBI is finalizing its guidelines for listing of green bonds, which would facilitate raising of funds for investment in renewable energy. For India, Green bonds would be the key to meeting the ambitious target of building 175 GW of renewable energy capacity by 2022.

set up for providing long-term debt and is a partial success. NBFCs provide over a quarter of infrastructure debt but not for long tenures. External Commercial Borrowings (ECBs) also provides limited tenures. Government has taken some measures in this regard and there is a pick up in corporate bond activity lately, as we have seen.

4.7 Impact of Externalities—Economic Viability Versus Financial Viability

The major difference between economic and financial viability is externalities. Viability Gap Funding (VGF) Scheme was launched in 2006 to enhance financial viability of competitively bid infrastructure projects with attractive economic returns but insufficient financial returns. Under this scheme, grant assistance of up to 20% of capital costs is provided by the Central Government to PPP projects thus leveraging budgetary resources to access a larger pool of private capital. 324 central and state projects with an investment of Rs. 2,51,298 crore have been approved with a VGF commitment of about Rs. 50,000 crore so far.

4.8 Issues with Project Finance

The non-recourse or limited recourse financing nature of infrastructure projects adds to their financing challenge. Investment protection is through concession agreements providing for user fees, indexation, termination payments, dispute resolution, and autonomous regulatory institutions. In this context, Model Concession Agreements (MCAs) have also been developed across infrastructure sectors in India.

Risk allocation is at the heart of structuring a PPP project. Foreign exchange risk mitigation may be achieved by increasing local currency financing as project revenues are generated in local currency in most infrastructure projects. But, risk mitigation in other areas may not be as straightforward. For example, fuel price and availability risk is borne by the private sector in the old Standard Bidding Documents (SBDs) of the Ministry of Power for power generation projects. But, the private sector had represented that it cannot manage this risk—higher imported coal prices had made the Tata Mundra UMPP unviable. However, the new SBDs of Ministry of Power in which fuel price is a pass through is also problematic. This is because when retail tariffs are politically capped[48] any increase in (pass-through)

[48]Low user charges across infrastructure sectors are immensely politically appealing and governments do not want retail tariffs to be increased.

input costs would only be reflected in increased losses of distribution companies, which are predominantly in the public sector.

4.9 Low User Fees in many Infrastructure Sectors Like Power and Water

In the power sector, there is a loss of about Rs. 1 per unit of electricity sold in India resulting in an annual loss of nearly Rs. 60,000 crore in the power distribution sector (see Fig. 12 for state-wise data on average tariff (AT) and average cost of supply (ACS)). As is apparent, in several states like Rajasthan (RJ), Tamil Nadu (TN), Jharkhand (JH), Madhya Pradesh (MP), and Uttar Pradesh (UP) (the top ranking states in losses) AT is lower than the ACS. We adjust the ACS for high Transmission and Distribution (T&D) losses in these states in order to exclude these costs. Yet, AT continues to stay below this adjusted level of ACS in most states. Mainly because of low cost recovery in the power sector, total accumulated debt of Indian distribution companies is Rs. 3.17 lakh crore. Water is so under-priced and politically sensitive that there is little private investment forthcoming despite immense need. In the transport sector, it is becoming politically difficult to raise toll rates though the contract provides for this (e.g., Delhi-Noida Toll Bridge before the adverse court ruling of October 2016). There is resistance to paying cost-recovery charges in social infrastructure with the malady of low tuitions universally afflicting public sector institutions of higher learning.

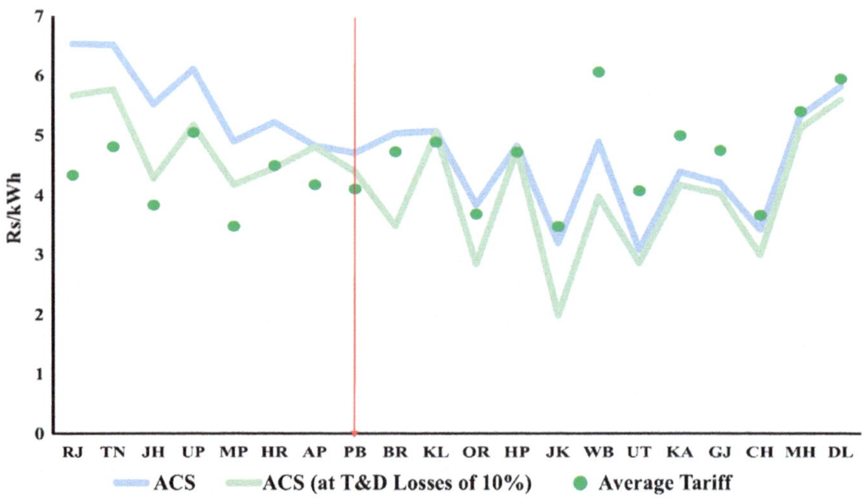

Fig. 12 Average tariff and average cost of supply in Indian states (Rs./kWh). *Source* Government of India, Ministry of Finance (2016)

Infrastructure services have to be paid for—either by the government or the users. With a PPP project, the arrangement has to be clarified and cannot be shrugged under the carpet, as happens when government is providing these services. But, users are willing to pay more if they are provided better services. For example, residential and commercial consumers of electricity frequently use diesel gen-sets as alternative source of electricity at a cost of Rs. 12–14 per kilo Watt hour (kWh). They would be willing to pay more for more reliable grid-based power where the comparative rate is about Rs. 5 per kWh. In fact, the Smart City Mission of the Government of India plans to implement smart cities only in those areas where people are willing to pay for good-quality urban infrastructure services.

In this chapter, and in the previous one we have looked at the various characteristics of infrastructure projects and their implications for financing with special reference to the Indian situation. In the next chapter we take a look at the concept of Public–Private Partnership (PPP) projects, their characteristic features and how they help in infrastructure provision.

Chapter 4
Public-Private Partnership (PPP) Concepts

1 Introduction

In Chap. 3 we have referred to PPPs as a method of financing infrastructure projects. PPPs have become increasingly popular in the last two decades and are now used in more than 134 developing countries, contributing about 15–20% to total infrastructure investment.[1] In this chapter we will take a close look at the concept and nature of PPPs and try to understand some of the key issues associated with them.

First, Public-Private Partnerships are more general than just physical infrastructure projects. They are widely used in managing the provision of several goods and services of a quasi-public nature that are seen as the responsibility of government, like waste management. The first section of this chapter looks at the general concept of PPPs around the world, distinguishing it from outsourcing and privatization and outlining some of the key conditions related to its successful operation.

The second section focuses on the role of PPPs in infrastructure provision pointing out how it facilitates it and how it can combine the strengths of both public and private sectors enabling better implementation. It also underscores the conditions necessary for it to work.

The last section provides an in-depth look at a specific case study—the problem-ridden and controversial Delhi Airport Metro Express project—as an example of the various issues and challenges PPPs face. The intent here is to get a better sense of what often goes into structuring and implementing an infrastructure PPP. The chapters that follow will deal with various aspects of such infrastructure PPPs.

---

[1]The World Bank (Independent Evaluation Group). *World Bank Group Support to Public-Private Partnerships—Lessons from Experience in Client Countries, FY02–12.*

K.V. Pratap and R. Chakrabarti, *Public-Private Partnerships in Infrastructure*,
India Studies in Business and Economics, DOI 10.1007/978-981-10-3355-1_4

1.1 Public-Private Partnerships—What They are and What is Needed to Make Them Tick

A. **What are PPPs?**

(i) ***Defining PPPs***

There is no single universally accepted definition of a PPP. And the impact of this lacuna can be more than academic. For instance, Brazilian and French laws make a distinction between "user-pays" and "government-pays" projects. The former (if 100% user-funded) are governed by the 'Concessions Law', while the rest are governed by the 'PPP Law'. Consequently, only the latter are commonly referred to as 'PPP'.[2]

We attempt a broad definition capturing the essential elements of a PPP here. PPPs are commercial transactions between a public and a private party wherein the private party:

- provides a service for a substantial period of time (that is *usually delivered by the public sector*);
- takes on *risks*—construction, operational and commercial; and
- gets *paid*, either directly by the public authority, or through user fees, or a combination of both.

Let us discuss each of these essential elements of a PPP. Traditionally, infrastructure services like roads, electricity, telecom, and water supply have been provided by the government. Because of quality issues associated with publicly provided services, the large demand gap, and the fiscal crunch underlying the inability of the public sector to provide these services, provision of such services is sought to be transferred to the private sector as Public-Private Partnerships. This transfer of service provision is for a comparatively long period—typically 30 years for a road project and more for projects in other sectors like the Delhi airport project that has been transferred as a PPP for 30 years with an option of extending the concession for a further period of 30 years.

Risk transfer is at the heart of structuring a PPP project. Optimally, risks should be transferred to that party which has more control over the risk factor. On the basis of this principle, risks that are within the control of the private sector should be transferred to it. Thus, post-transfer of infrastructure service provisioning responsibilities, construction, commercial and operational risks should be transferred to the private sector. Cost and time overruns in construction are a major bane of public procurement and the public sector would optimally want to transfer these risks to the private sector through fixed price construction contracts with liquidated damages. Risks associated with operating infrastructure is often costly for the

[2]The World Bank (2014).

government. Offloading some of these risks to a private party capable of managing it better can reduce the project's overall cost to government.[3]

Infrastructure services have to be paid for either by the government or the users or both. This question is not very important when infrastructure is provided by the public sector where there is thin dividing line between the Government and the public sector service provider. However, when it is the private sector providing infrastructure services, this question needs to be addressed clearly and if the Government wants to keep user fees low, the private sector would need to be compensated through direct budgetary payments. Thus, if the Government of Delhi wants to extend lifeline tariffs to those households who consume less than 400 units of electricity per month, direct budgetary subsidies would have to be provided to the private sector electricity providers for them to be able to sustain their operations.

Clearly PPPs are complex and vulnerable to various risks that can delay or derail them. Below we provide a broad and general discussion of a few of the characteristics that need to be managed well to ensure success of the PPPs. But, first, how do PPPs differ from Privatization and Outsourcing?

(ii) ***How are PPPs Different from Privatization and Outsourcing***

PPPs are mid-way house between fully public and fully private ownership (privatization) and provision of services. Privatization normally involves withdrawal of the government in favor of market-based operations while government continues to be engaged with the PPP operator.

- ***PPP versus Privatization***

The crucial differences between PPP and Privatization are:

- PPPs generally involve only the right to use the assets and *not the sale or transfer of ownership of physical assets*,
- Under a PPP, accountability for provision of the service rests with the public sector, with a contract setting the terms of the relationship between the government and the private sector provider. A good PPP contract helps the government retain *oversight and control* over all crucial parameters of performance and outcomes, making payments against services delivered. In contrast privatization usually implies, transfer of immediate accountability for providing the service to the private provider.[4] In this context, PPPs may he seen to be a midway house between fully public and fully private provision of services.
- In a PPP, Government retains a substantial role as the: purchaser of infrastructure services; ultimate service provider if private sector exits the project; or to which the assets revert after the concession period.[5]

---

[3]As quoted in The World Bank (2014).

[4]Farquharson et al. (2011).

[5]Pratap (2011).

So, it would seem that there is continuous engagement of the Government with the PPP operator as opposed to privatization, when this engagement ceases after privatization of the assets.

- PPP contracts are for a limited period—usually 15–30 years or more, which is not the case with privatization. Privatization normally involves withdrawal of the government in favor of market-based operations for an indefinite period.
- Public planning is an important aspect in a PPP. For example, it has been estimated that required infrastructure investment in India in the 12th Plan period (2012–17) would be about $1 trillion, of which nearly half would have to come from the private sector, mainly as PPPs. This type of public planning is seldom associated with privatization.

- ***PPPs and Outsourcing***

PPPs are more than a one-off engagement of a private contractor to provide goods or services under a normal commercial arrangement. Emphasis on long-term contracts and strict performance regimes, such as in Build-Operate-Transfer (BOT) or Design-Build-Finance-Operate-Transfer (DBFOT), with revenues, either from government or users, linked to performance are distinguishing characteristics of PPPs. The private sector partner is paid for the delivery of the services to specified levels and must provide all the managerial, financial and technical resources needed to achieve the required standards. Importantly, the private sector must also bear the risks of achieving the service specification. It would be seen that private sector assumes more risk in PPPs compared to outsourcing.

B. **Making PPPs Work**

The list of factors that determine the success of PPPs can be intimidatingly long and frustratingly project-specific. It is also the subject matter that much of this volume would be dealing with. However, in this section we shall use a three-level—Politics, Finance, Management (PFM)—structure to summarize a few of the key characteristics associated with most of the successful PPPs. It is worth reiterating that the list here is not a comprehensive fail-proof recipe for ensuring successful PPPs, but rather a description of "necessary" but not "sufficient" conditions. In other words, several forces and events can derail a project that fulfils this list, but one that does not fulfil these conditions would need a serious dose of luck to succeed.

In essence, the PFM framework emphasizes *political attractiveness* (P), *financial viability* (F) and *managerial structuring* (M) of a project to categorize success factors in a PPP.

(a) **Political Attractiveness**

(i) ***Do PPPs Make Political Sense?***

Only if PPPs make political sense will they be implemented. A significant, if unstated, goal of any policy initiative is to maintain political support (votes). However PPPs seem to work against political incentives. Traditional implementation of infrastructure projects through public procurement gives politicians power and other benefits. There is also a much larger scope of corruption in item-rate cost-plus contracts implemented by the public sector and therefore self-seeking politicians would not want a change to fixed-price PPP contracts in project procurement and maintenance. Since cost-plus contracts often deliver other political benefits such as new high wage jobs, giving suppliers incentives for cost minimization in PPP contracts only gets them to reduce these political benefits. Given these facts, the primary reason for politicians to let go of direct control on infrastructure projects and have them implemented as PPPs is the resource crunch facing governments—unmet infrastructure needs may lead to political backlash.

However, the very presence of the private sector in provision of "essential" services like water and power distribution raises political concerns. It is also quite easy to sensationalize issues in these politically sensitive sectors. If control over essential infrastructure services passes on to foreigners, there are further issues. In fact, it has been found that foreign control over essential infrastructure services like water and sewerage is a significant explanatory variable for private sector exit from these sectors.[6] However, it is also true that while privatization of essential services is politically difficult, it can be done. One of the most celebrated cases of PPPs in essential infrastructure sectors is the privatization of water services in Manila (Philippines). It is interesting how Manila Water Company, one of the two private concessionaires in Manila for water services, mobilized unserved communities to overcome resistance to tariff increases. In the public hearings on the tariff increases, people who represented non-governmental organizations (NGOs) and groups that were against tariff increases were often outnumbered by representatives of unserved communities that had been programmed for connection in the business plan justifying the tariff increase.

In the Smart Cities Mission of the Government of India, one of the major thrust areas is provision of adequate water supply in urban areas through PPPs. The most critical success factor that has been identified is that outcomes of PPP in water supply should be benign. There should be 24 * 7 water supply, improvement in quality of water supply, covering uncovered areas (mainly the poor) and reducing wastage and leakage (Non-Revenue Water).[7] If outcomes are benign, it is likely that PPPs in water supply would be successful.

Box 1 discusses some of the political models relevant for understanding the political motivations and machinations behind PPPs.

Box 1 ***Models of Political Behavior and PPP Implementation***

There are a few models of political behavior that explain the politics behind PPPs. The most important among these models are Rational Actor Model and Government Politics Model. We explain these models below.

---

[6]Pratap (2011).

[7]Presentation made by Kumar V Pratap on *Financing of Smart Cities in India* (http://smartcities.gov.in/upload/uploadfiles/files/Financing_for_Smart__Cities_Final.pdf).

Linear Model of PPP Implementation (Rational Actor Model)

A roughly linear model of the policy process is implicit in many proposals for reform (see Fig. 1). According to this view, a proposed reform gets on the agenda for government action, a decision is made on the proposal, and it is implemented either successfully or unsuccessfully. If implementation is unsuccessful, the usual remedy is to call for greater efforts to strengthen institutional capacity or to blame failure on lack of political will. In the absence of detailed knowledge about what goes on within the government and a capacity to analyze the decision process, lack of political will becomes a catch-all culprit, even though the term has little analytical content and its very vagueness expresses the lack of knowledge of specific detail.[8]

The Government Politics Model

A criticism of the traditional (RAM) model is that it is too simplistic. As seen above, RAM has little analytical content and is vague. In contrast to RAM, the Government Politics Model considers many actors as players as opposed to a unitary actor: players acting according to various conceptions of national, organizational, and personal goals rather than a consistent set of strategic objectives; focusing on many problems rather than a single strategic issue; players who make government decisions by tugging in various directions rather than by a single, rational choice.

According to this model, policy reform is a process and not a series of phases as the linear model would suggest. In current practice, governments focus extensively on the feasibility of making the reform decision. Decision makers should become more comfortable with going beyond the decision to question whether the reform has a fair chance of getting implemented, which brings us to the realm of political analysis. Failed reforms are worse than no reforms.

A state of equilibrium surrounds an established policy set. Efforts to alter existing policy upsets that equilibrium and will elicit some response from those affected by the change. The nature, intensity, and location of the response will determine whether the reform is implemented and sustained.

In PPP projects, costs are immediate (costs begin from day 1) and concentrated, for example, the requirement that beneficiaries will have to pay for better quality infrastructure services. On the other hand, benefits are long-term (lower fiscal deficit resulting from higher cost recovery through higher user charges) and diffused. It is true that "modest average real price declines thrill economists, but not voters". So, PPP projects need to show results in order to be politically sustainable. These results should be in terms of outcomes like 24 * 7 water and power supply,

---

[8]Grindle et al. (1991).

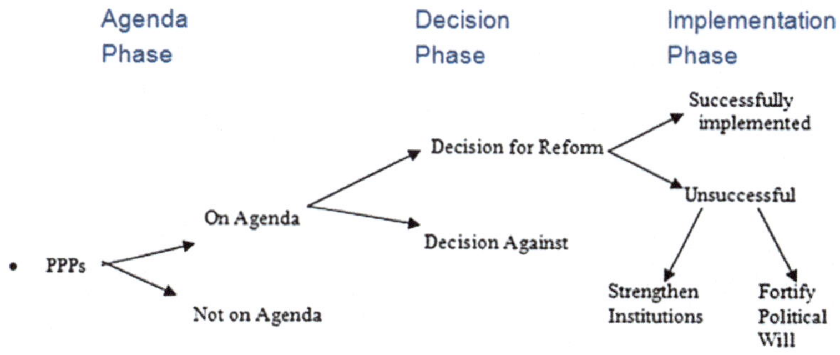

Fig. 1 Linear model of PPP implementation—Rational Actor Model (RAM) *Source* Adapted from Grindle and Thomas (1991)

spreading benefits to poor for long-term sustainability, and gradual cost changes through a transitional subsidy. In the case of Delhi Power Distribution PPP (arguably the most successful power distribution PPP in India), for example, there was a transitional subsidy of about Rs. 3500 crore in the first five years (2002–07) of PPP operations so that the retail tariff changes are gradual and politically feasible.

This brings us to the need for cultivating stakeholders like users and employees for PPPs to succeed. 'Stakeholder' strategies may not always be efficient from a pure financial perspective, but may be necessary to make PPPs politically feasible. In addition, for PPPs to be successful, outcomes should be benign and should produce value for money to the stakeholders. It is essential to examine whether PPP projects provide net benefits to government or they merely move liabilities to the future. Studies show that the average value for money to the government from PPP projects in UK was 17% as compared to 9% in Australia. However, no such value for money calculation is carried out in India and there is a need for carrying out this analysis for validating the use of PPPs in developing countries.

This also implies that public authorities should not give any reckless guarantees in terms of rate of return or revenues to make PPPs happen. Short-term incentives for political gain may adversely impact PPP implementation. Politicians may be tempted to offer excessive incentives to the private sector through reckless revenue guarantees and agree for pass through in tariffs on account of foreign exchange depreciation or domestic inflation to make the PPP project virtually risk-free to the private sector. However, in many cases, governments may find such projects too expensive to service when they become operational.

For example, excessive incentives to the private sector were the primary reason for the cancellation of the Dabhol Power Project in India. Since there is a gestation period of a few years in most infrastructure projects, the government at the helm may change by the time the project becomes operational. Thus, there may be an incentive for incumbent governments to indulge in reckless contracting with the private sector and show huge returns on paper without bearing the responsibility of seeing these projects come to fruition. Thus, in practice, there are many instances of improper contracts, frequent renegotiations, and regulatory capture by the private sector, raising apprehensions about returns to the government from private participation in infrastructure.[9]

(b) **Financial Viability**

Political attractiveness alone cannot ensure success of a PPP. An equally important element is the financial viability of the project at user costs that are politically feasible. The following aspects of the project can help indicate its financial viability.

- ***Bankability***

Government needs to ensure that the project design is "bankable"—that is, able to raise and service the project debt. For a project to be bankable, operating cash flows need to be high enough to cover debt service, plus an acceptable margin and risk of variation in cash flows should be small. Lenders carefully assess project risks, and their allocation among the parties to the contract, more so because PPP projects are financed on non-recourse basis.

It is important for the public sector to ensure that the financial viability of the project occurs without taking too many risks. While doling out revenue (or rate of return) guarantees may be politically attractive as they are contingent liabilities of the public sector (and the election cycle might incentivize such guarantees as the government would have changed by the time the contingent liabilities come to fruition), such guarantees reduce the value for money to the government and therefore should not be given.

A case in point is the Delhi-Noida Toll Bridge case where the contract provides for annual guaranteed rate of return of 20% on the total project cost and any shortfall in this return is added to the project cost to be serviced in the following year. The project opened to traffic in 2001 and by March 2016, the unpaid guaranteed returns were about Rs. 5000 crore (as against a project cost of about Rs. 400 crore). Similarly, other efforts to make a project bankable like the government participating as a minority shareholder may also be counter-productive as this may lead to conflict of interest between government as an operator wanting to sue the government as a grantor of the contract.

- ***Limiting the amount of debt allowed***

Higher leverage enables equity investors to achieve higher returns.[10] There is therefore an incentive to finance a PPP project with a high debt to equity ratio. Higher leverage is also incentivized as Governments often provide more protection

[9]Pratap (2011).

[10]Since higher debt implies a fixed share to the lenders, in a good state of the world (high revenues) the equity holders can get to keep more of the surplus to themselves. The exact opposite happens when revenues are low, however, and the net worth (equity) can get wiped out easily, making the venture more risky. The attractiveness of leverage also comes from the fact that debt provides tax cover—part of what is paid out as interest would have anyway had to be paid out to government as taxes if there was no debt. Hence cost of debt is typically lower than cost of equity.

to debtors than to equity investors. The case in point is the Indian Model Concession Agreement for the road sector where debt is protected to the extent of 90% even when there is termination of the contract due to default on the part of the concessionaire.

However, highly-leveraged projects also have greater default and bankruptcy risks. So, governments may prescribe a minimum equity ratio for PPPs. But, this can increase the cost of capital as cost of equity is higher than the cost of debt. Thus, restricting an investor's ability to choose his capital structure can increase the cost of capital.

- ***Refinancing of project debt***

The construction stage of a project is generally considered more risky than operation stage and therefore, initially the project may not be able to obtain financing with a long enough maturity to match the concession's length. After the beginning of commercial operations, project risks come down and the project may be able to obtain better terms of financing. Hence, the utility of refinancing of debt, which refers to taking on new debt to pay off existing loans.

The options for refinancing are:

- Take-out financing in which loan is handed over to another lender down the road. As we pointed out in the previous chapter, the Indian Infrastructure Finance Company Limited (IIFCL) has started a take-out financing scheme for infrastructure.
- Infrastructure Debt Funds (IDFs) through which lenders may offer better financing terms to projects with demonstrated track record.

The gains from refinancing (better credit terms) can be shared among the project sponsors, customers and the public authority. However, refinancing creates a refinancing risk, i.e., the risk that the shorter-term loan cannot be refinanced at the expected terms later on.

C. **Managerial Structuring**

A politically desirable, financially viable project can still get grounded unless certain key concerns are not adequately addressed in structuring it. We list a few of these here.

(i) ***Appropriate Risk Allocation***

Risk relates to uncertain outcomes that have a bearing on financial viability of firms. Risk allocation entails defining who, between the private and public partners, will bear which kind of risk. The objective here is balanced and cost-minimizing risk-sharing between the parties. For instance the private partner may charge a premium for accepting risks that are within the control of the government (e.g., political risks like expropriation, non-convertibility or non-transferability) reducing the value for money to the public sector. Similarly, if the government provides guarantees for commercial risks (e.g., rate of return guarantee for the Delhi-Noida Toll Bridge), the public sector may find it very expensive to service the project.

The guiding principle for risk allocation is that risk should be assigned to the agency that has greater control over the risk factor or which is best suited to manage its consequences on project outcomes,[11] by assessing and anticipating a risk properly and responding to it appropriately. For instance, while no party can control earthquake risk, since the party is responsible for project design, it could use techniques to minimize the damage, in an earthquake. So, while the risk of an earthquake is insurer's risk, if risk is insured, otherwise, this risk should be borne by the private partner. PPP contract (or Concession Agreement) will reflect the agreed allocation of risks and will include risk mitigation measures when deemed appropriate.

Based on this guiding principle for risk allocation, Table 1 provides a listing of various kinds of risk associated with infrastructure projects and the agency which should normatively bear them.

Most PPPs have an element of ***political risk*** about them. Given the public services produced by the project, the decision to adopt PPP is inevitably political. The government must consider the political and social implications of PPP and whether there is sufficient political will to implement PPP. In the water sector, it may be very difficult to implement a PPP. This is the reason why despite the overwhelming need for many well-structured PPPs in the water sector in India, there are a very small number of projects in the sector. Political risks like expropriation,[12] non-convertibility or non-transferability are within the control of the Government and so should be allocated to the Government.

Foreign sponsored and foreign financed projects are particularly prone to political risks. For example, the first entirely foreign funded Chinese infrastructure project, the $616 million Liabin B coal-fired plant, was marked by several government guarantees including clauses protecting the project from any significant changes in law, including tax and environmental regulations.

The pace at which a project is constructed is well within the control of the private sector and so the ***risk of construction cost overrun*** should be allocated to it through fixed price construction contracts plus liquidated damages. However, construction risk that is outside private partner's control like government action that delays the project like delays in obtaining environmental approvals may be allocated to the Government. In the same spirit, the Indian Model Concession Agreements classify environmental clearance as a condition precedent to be fulfilled by the Government.

Operation risks, including the risk of service interruption or asset availability, the risk of network non-functioning or poor functioning, or overshooting of estimates of the cost of operating and maintaining the asset, should be allocated to the

[11]The rationale only holds if the party is also given the right and responsibility to make decisions related to that risk.

[12]Government takeover of the project without (or with nominal) compensation.

Table 1 Normative risk allocation in a PPP project

Type of risk	Who should bear it
Political risk including expropriation, non-convertibility or non-transferability	Government should bear the risk. In case of contract termination on account of government default, compensation should be paid by the government
Construction risk *(within private partner's control)*	Takes the form of construction cost overrun. Private partner should bear the risk through fixed price construction contracts plus liquidated damages
Construction risk *(outside private partner's control: government action that delays the project like delays in obtaining environmental approvals)*	Government should bear the risk
Commercial risk *Operation and maintenance risk* *Demand risk* *Payment risk*	Private partner should bear the risk
Financial risk *Exchange rate risk* *Interest rate risk* *Inflation risk*	Governments may allow partial indexation of tariffs to inflation and exchange rate as this is beyond the control of private sector. Interest rate risk should be shouldered by the private sector as financial structure is within its control. Government can help through macroeconomic stability
Unexpected event risk *(Force Majeure: Acts of God like floods, earthquakes,* etc.*)*	Insurer's risk, if risk is insured. Otherwise, risk should be borne by private partner
Unexpected event risk (policy risk) *(Changes in legal or contractual framework directly affecting the project)*	Government should bear the risk
Regulatory risk (*Tariff risk* is the most common type, and refers to the risk that the regulator will not enforce cost-recovering level of tariffs)	Private partner bears this risk. Government should set up autonomous regulatory institutions to mitigate this risk

Source Adapted from Pratap (2011)

private sector as Operation & Maintenance (O&M) is within its control. Similarly, ***demand risk*** (lower than expected demand) and ***payment risk*** (customers do not pay the originally agreed tariffs) are also part of commercial risk and so should ideally be allocated to the private sector.

For mitigating ***financial risk***, Governments may allow partial indexation of tariffs to inflation and exchange rate as these macroeconomic factors are beyond the control of the private sector. Interest rate risk should be shouldered by the private sector as financial structure of the project company is within its control. Government can also help through macroeconomic stability, which should have a benign impact on price level, exchange rate and interest rates. Exchange rate risk is a significant factor in infrastructure projects. Seaport projects, with mostly foreign currency-denominated revenue, outnumber road projects, with local currency revenue in Sub-Saharan Africa, where local-currency long-term funding is not available in many countries.[13]

The most important regulatory risk is ***tariff risk***. Tariff risk refers to the risk that the regulator will not enforce cost-recovering level of tariffs. Thus, the average cost of supply of power in India is about Rs. 4.50 per unit of power and the average revenue realization is about Rs. 3.50 per unit of power, giving rise to tariff risk. Similarly, though the Delhi-Noida Toll Bridge contract mentions that tolls should move in tandem with the Consumer Price Index for Urban Non-Manual Employees [CPI (UNME)], the political ability of the Noida Authority to raise tariffs is suspect, giving rise to regulatory risk.

There is, however, nothing sacrosanct about the normative risk allocation shown in the above table. Much would also depend on factors like the level of private sector participation (PSP) in the country. For a country that is starting PSP from scratch, there may be a need for sharing even demand risk initially by the public sector (through minimum revenue guarantee, for example), otherwise PSP may not be forthcoming. As PPP arrangements mature, risk allocation to stakeholders including government may become more optimal. This is apparent from the evolution of PSP policy in the Indian road sector[14] where the Model Concession Agreement allocates revenue risk to the private sector in Build-Operate-Transfer (BOT, Toll) projects in contrast to the Delhi-Noida toll bridge, one of the earliest toll road PPP project in the country, where this risk has been allocated to the public authority through a rate of return guarantee. In power sector, fuel price and availability risk has been transferred from the private to the public sector in the new Standard Bidding Documents of the Ministry of Power. However, this may not be the right way to go when retail tariffs are politically capped as in India and any increase in the fuel (input) prices would be reflected in the increased losses of the largely public sector-owned power distribution segment.

The risk allocation among stakeholders may also depend on the type of contract. In a management contract, private party shares minimal risks with the public sector and gets paid a fee for operating and managing the project. In a lease contract, in addition, private parties take on operating and collection risks and pay a lease rent to the public sector. In Build-Operate-Transfer (BOT) contracts, private partners also take on investment and financing risks and therefore, the risk allocated to the private sector is higher.

Private partners may pass on some risks to other firms that can manage them better. Table 1 tells us that construction risk, that is within private partner's control, should be allocated to it. However, the private partner may transfer this risk to specialized Engineering, Procurement and Construction (EPC) contractors who take on construction risk through a fixed-cost contract with provision for liquidated damages for delay in construction attributable to the EPC contractor. When passing

[13]Farquharson et al. (2011).

[14]Pratap (2011).

on risks to the EPC contractor, it is important to ensure that the definitions and consequences of the risks in the PPP contract and the EPC contract are the same. Examples of areas where contract mismatches may arise include: difference between the scope of the works under the EPC Subcontract and the requirements of the PPP Contract[15]; different definition of completion between the two contracts; and a mismatch between the level of Delay Liquidated Damages under the EPC Subcontract and the PPP Contract. Similarly, the O&M risk may be transferred to a specialized operating and maintenance contractor as in the case of Delhi-Noida Toll Bridge where this risk has been transferred to the Indian subsidiary of Intertoll, Netherlands.

(ii) ***Competitive Bidding***

Infrastructure projects may enjoy monopoly in the delivery of services (e.g., airports[16] and energy transmission projects). Since *competition in the market* is ruled out in such infrastructure markets, competitive bidding would ensure *competition for the market* and thus value for money to the public sector,[17] besides ensuring transparency. Competitive bidding is expected to compete away the monopoly rent available to such service providers. Competitive bidding would assign provision of services to the party that is able to provide them most efficiently.

However, competitive bidding produces the most efficient outcome if there are sufficient number of bidders. It is, therefore, necessary to aim for a balance so that there is sufficient competition even as appropriate pre-qualification norms for bidders ensures that only credible and capable bidders are invited to submit financial bids.

Competitive bidding, by throwing up alternative suppliers, may also be instrumental in curbing market power of these suppliers. One method to manage market power may be through crossholding restrictions as was done in the two water contracts for Metro Manila, which were given to two separate companies even though Manila Water Company was the lowest bidder in both the service areas. Similarly, GMR-led consortium was the only technically qualified bidder (originally) for both the Delhi and the Mumbai airport concessions in India, but it was not awarded both the concessions to encourage innovation and allow for competitive benchmarking.[18]

---

[15]For example, there may be a different procedure for fixing the cost of variation in the project under the EPC Subcontract and for fixing the cost of the same variation in the PPP Contract, so that the cost of variation payable to the EPC Subcontractor may not be fully passed through to the public authority.

[16]As per Indian infrastructure policies, a competing airport may not be built within 150 km radius of an existing airport.

[17]It is said that the deal for projects like Delhi-Noida Toll Bridge or Dabhol Power Project may have been much better from the public sector perspective, if these projects had been competitively bid rather then negotiated.

[18]Pratap (2011).

Appropriate structuring of the bidding process is key to the effective design of a PPP. Box 2 discusses a few key issues in deciding a suitable bidding parameter.

Box 2 ***Deciding on the Bidding Parameter***

In general, *ceteris paribus*, there should be a single bidding parameter, lending transparency to the bidding process. All other important project parameters (including performance parameters) should be mentioned as 'Key Performance Indicators' in the Concession Agreement. For example, in the Model Concession Agreement (MCA) for the road sector in India, the bidding parameter is 'Viability Gap Funding' while the quality of roads, etc. are mentioned in the MCA.

This single bidding parameter could be:

- Lowest tariff to be charged to consumers: This is a very popular parameter for infrastructure projects and politically appealing too. This has been used in ports and airports in Chile, and federal roads in Brazil.
- Lowest subsidy that the government must provide: Many projects could have high economic returns, while the financial returns do not pass the standard thresholds of viability. To address this problem, the Viability Gap Funding (VGF) scheme has been devised in India and is designed to improve financial returns for such projects. Under this scheme, VGF is given as a grant up to 20% of the project cost by the federal government in India. Thus, for example, the private concessionaire bids for a road project on the basis of BOT (toll), where his investment is serviced by the toll revenue. However, if he finds that toll revenue would not suffice in terms of financial viability, then he can ask for a VGF from the federal government. If he finds that the toll revenue would provide a higher rate of return on his investment than his financial threshold, he may offer a premium to the government instead of asking for VGF.
- Highest price to be paid for the assets: Governments very often use this bidding parameter to insulate the PPP initiative from political challenges. This was used in the Orissa power distribution PPP in India.
- Shortest duration of the concession: In the first phase of the Mexican toll road program, the bidding parameter was the shortest duration of the concession. However, following the collapse of demand after the Mexican economic crisis of 1994, many of these projects reverted to the government as the concession period was too short to recoup the investment. For example, there were road projects with a concession period of 3.5 years for an asset that was going to last for 30 years. This resulted in unsustainably high user charges in an effort by the concessionaires to recover their investment in the short concession period. In 2007, Mexico re-privatized some of these roads employing an improved bidding

parameter (minimum public subsidy instead of minimum concession period[19]).

- Lowest annuity payment as in BOT—annuity projects: The main difference between BOT (toll) and BOT (annuity) projects is the allocation of traffic risk, which is allocated to the public sector in the case of BOT (annuity) projects as the government pays the annuity irrespective of the traffic on the road. The investment of the PPP operator is serviced through annuity payments over the concession period. This annuity payment is determined by competitive bidding and is paid on making available the asset of the required quality. Many road projects have been bid out in India using the BOT (annuity) bidding parameter. Government retains the right to toll such BOT (annuity) projects.
- Highest revenue offered to the state for existing infrastructure (either a share, or a flat offer). In the case of Delhi and Mumbai airports, the bidding parameter is revenue share to be paid to the public authority by the concessionaire, which is 45.99% in the case of Delhi airport.
- Least Present Value of Revenue (LPVR): One of the major issues in the case of BOT (toll) projects is the traffic, and therefore revenue, uncertainty. The LPVR bidding parameter addresses this problem. In this bidding parameter, user fees and discount rate are pre-determined and franchise is awarded to the firm that bids the least present value of toll revenue. Franchise ends when the PV of toll revenue is equal to the winning bid, mitigating traffic risk. Some roads in Colombia and Chile have been bid out using this bidding parameter.

The present value of future earnings can be found using the following formula:

$$\mathrm{PV} = \sum[\mathrm{CF_n}/(1+\mathrm{r})^{\mathrm{n}}]$$

where PV is Present Value; CF is Cash Flow in year n; r is the discount rate.

Cash flows are constituted by user fees and forecasted traffic. As already stated, user fees and discount rate are pre-determined in this bidding parameter. So, one is bidding the traffic and if the traffic turns out to be less than the forecasted traffic, the concession period is lengthened. In this way, LPVR mitigates traffic risk.

Santiago—Valparaíso—Viña del Mar Toll Road in Chile (Rutas del Pacifico) is one of the roads where this bidding parameter has been used. The project involves the engineering, construction, upgrade, operation, and maintenance of the existing 109 km toll road ("Ruta 68,") which connects the

[19]Pratap (2011).

capital city of Santiago with the Port of Valparaiso and the Viña del Mar region. The total project cost was about US$427 million. The sponsors, ACS and Sacyr, provided US$103 million of this amount. Under the arrangement, the regulator fixes user fees and discount rate, and the franchise goes to the firm that bids the least present value of toll revenue. The franchise ends when the present value of toll revenue is equal to the winning bid. If parties wish to terminate the concession early the LPVR mechanism allows for fair compensation. The concession started in August 1998 and the toll road was opened to traffic in 2001. The contract has a maximum term of 300 months (25 years).[20] Any issue that leads to a shortfall in revenues automatically results in extending the length of the concession—this mitigates traffic risk in road sector concessions. However, this uncertainty of the duration might affect the financing of the project.

(iii) ***Output Specification***

In a PPP, the requirements of the public sector need to be articulated in the form of an *output* requirement (for example, the availability of power or water of the required quality). In contrast, traditional project procurement has been *input*-focused specifying things like choice of building materials or a specific technology for a power plant. Output specification defines what is required, rather than how it is to be done. A useful thumb rule in developing output requirements is given by the acronym SMART—Specific, Measurable, Achievable, Realistic, and Timely.[21] An example of Output Specifications for a UK Housing PPP is shown in the table. The idea is that all performance parameters should be defined precisely (Table 2).

(iv) ***Watertight Contracting to Reduce Risk***

As in the more general project finance model, PPP projects are financed on a non-recourse basis. Lenders and investors to the project depend on the cash-flows generated by the project without having recourse to the sponsors' general assets or creditworthiness. The project implementing company is typically a Special Purpose Vehicle (SPV) specially created for implementing the project. Non-recourse financing increases the complexity of contracts as they have to be watertight so that the interests of various stakeholders are protected.[22]

The need to reconcile or harmonize the varying objectives of different actors with varying goals, objective functions and interests, necessitates a complex set of contracts in a PPP. Figure 2 illustrates the typical PPP contractual structure.

[20]Delmon (2010).

[21]Farquharson et al. (2011).

[22]Pratap (2011).

Table 2 Output specifications for a housing PPP

Characteristic	SMART	Not SMART
Specific	Refurbish or replace all dwellings on the estate to comply with the government's "decent homes" standard	Refurbish dwellings to a good standard
Measurable	Ensure that all dwellings are structurally sound, with adequate ventilation, lighting, and thermal comfort	Ensure that dwellings are fit for habitation
Achievable	Maintain internal temperature at X degrees when outside temperature is between Y and Z degrees	Ensure that internal temperature is always maintained at X degrees
Realistic	Ensure that faults with the temperature control system are rectified within 8 hours during business hours and 16 hours outside business hours	Ensure that faults with the temperature control system are repaired within 2 hours
Timely	Maintain a log of faults and report every month	Provide an annual report on performance

Source Farquharson et al. (2011)

Fig. 2 PPP contractual structure *Source* DeJongh (2009)

The Special Purpose Vehicle (SPV) implementing the project has an arms-length relationship with the project sponsors through a Shareholders' Agreement that restricts the financial exposure of the sponsors in the project to the amount of their equity.

The right of the SPV to undertake the project emanates from the Concession Agreement that the government signs with it that authorizes the PPP in the first place. It is indeed the umbilical cord of the SPV with the public side.

Very often, the SPV would like to transfer the construction risk to a specialized Engineering, Procurement and Construction (EPC) company and have an EPC contract with the entity. Similarly, the O&M risk could be transferred to a specialized O&M comapany through a separate O&M contract.

Supply risk is often dealt with a supplier agreement. In the case of a thermal power generation SPV, for instance, it would have a Fuel Supply Agreement with the fuel supplier (like Coal India Limited) so that it is assured of raw material supplies for generating power. Likewise the demand risk is dealt with using a Power Purchase Agreement (in the power sector) with the off-taker (customer; a power distribution company). More often than not, given the size of the contracts, these agreements will need the blessings of the government in the form of government guarantees.

Finally since the project is being financed on a non-recourse basis, and the lender has no guarantee other than project revenue, loan agreements would typically provide for an escrow account where all the project revenues are kept, with the lenders having first charge on these revenues. This implies that the lenders, and not the SPV, or its sponsors have the first right to dip into the revenues.

(v) ***Step-in Rights***

Step-in rights refer to the government or lender's power under the contract to take control of the project company in certain specified situations. Government may terminate the PPP contract and take over the project in the event the project company fails to meet service obligations or when the project poses significant health and safety risks, or is a threat to national security. Lenders' step-in rights get activated if the project company fails in its debt service obligations. Lenders would usually appoint new senior management or another firm to take over and operate the project company. It is important to have framework and timeline clarity in the Concession Agreement for invoking the step-in rights of both the government and lenders. This would also require that they are informed when problems begin to occur and can take remedial actions during the cure period.

So far we have discussed characteristics of designing PPPs in a fairly generic setting. The next section focuses on the role of PPPs in infrastructure provision.

2 How PPPs can Help in Infrastructure Provision

Good PPP contracts can help infrastructure provisioning in a number of ways, including augmenting resources and improving the delivery of infrastructure services. However, badly contacted PPPs can prove to be disastrous for public finances and may be extremely inefficient, producing results diametrically opposite to what they were supposed to achieve.

PPPs can bridge the infrastructure gap by catapulting scarce public resources and bringing in private sector technology and innovation for higher quality services and greater productivity. Figure 3 form The World Bank Reference Guide identifies a few key areas where PPPs can make a difference. We investigate these areas in greater detail in this section.

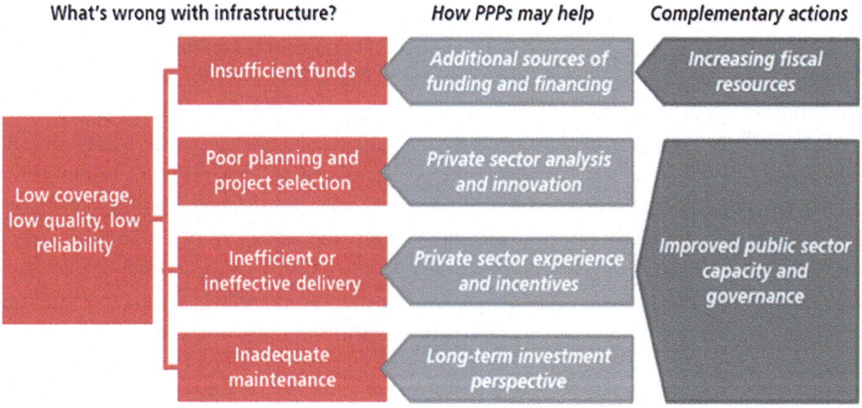

Fig. 3 What is wrong with infrastructure and how PPPs can help *Source* World Bank (2014)

2.1 Funds

Infrastructure is typically underfunded. McKinsey estimates that required global infrastructure investment would be about $57 trillion just to support projected economic growth between 2013 and 2030.[23] This is more than the estimated value of today's infrastructure worldwide. India's infrastructure deficit is large and the country expected to spend $1 trillion over the 12th Plan period (2012–17), but has fallen woefully short of that. In 2010, the World Bank's diagnostic study of infrastructure in Africa estimated that Sub-Saharan Africa needed to spend US$93 billion a year on infrastructure, of which only US$45 billion was already being met through existing sources like government spending, user charges, private sector investment, resulting in a total funding gap of US$48 billion per annum.[24]

PPPs can help increase infrastructure funding through, for example, charging users for services and improving asset utilization. Traditionally, water and sanitation services were provided free by the government. However, with a PPP, it is expected that reasonable user charges would be imposed for better quality infrastructure services. Thus, a new revenue stream is created when none existed before. By the same measure, the benefit of a PPP as a financing approach is less clear when the PPP is entirely funded by government payments (annuities).

Similarly, because PPPs incentivize increased asset utilization (for example, a school facility could be used for teaching children in the day time, but could generate additional resources when the same classrooms are used for adult education or coaching classes during the evening hours), increased efficiency in use of resources (resulting in increased revenues) may be achieved.

[23]McKinsey Global Institute (2013)

[24]World Bank (2014).

Governments can overcome short-term budget constraints by accessing private finance through a PPP, since the capital cost of a project is spread over its lifetime (through availability payments, for example), rather than being incurred upfront, allowing more investment within annual budget constraint.[25]

But, PPPs have been criticized for bypassing the budget process. Many impute the choice of PPPs to the fact that the government's commitments under these contracts are often not recognized as a part of public debt (like in India). Similarly, if PPPs have been incentivized by giving revenue and rate of return guarantees, they may prove to be a drain on public resources. In the case of Delhi-Noida Toll Bridge, for example, government gave a rate of return guarantee whose costs were not apparent immediately. These are contingent liabilities and not straight-forward to value as are explicit liabilities.

2.2 *Planning and Project Selection*

The process of making infrastructure investment decisions may not always lead to the selection of most optimal projects from economic-financial angle. In many cases, political economy of project selection leads to inappropriate projects being chosen.[26] Projects also tend to be carried out in isolation rather than as part of an overall system; therefore, we find ports with no rail connection to the hinterland or no transmission lines to evacuate wind energy. There is also optimism bias in publicly implemented projects, by over-estimating benefits and under-estimating costs. For example, in the early 1990s, when Mexico was on a major road-building spree, traffic demand was very often over-estimated.

With the private sector implementing projects, any given project is less likely to be selected only for political reasons as a business case would have to be built for the project to be able to attract commercial financing. For example, it is widely known that most parts of India, including Mumbai are water-stressed, with supply rationed to about 4–6 hours a day. In the specific case of Mumbai for instance, the corporation planned to bring water from faraway sources. When consultants engaged through one of the multilateral banks compared the cost of achieving a 24-hours water supply this way in one ward (K-East) with the cost of achieving 24-hours water supply through improving the distribution system to reduce leakage

[25]World Bank (2012).

[26]In early 2005, when one of the authors was working at the Indian Prime Minister's Office, Government of Japan (GoJ) had posed a project of a Bullet Train between Ahmedabad and Mumbai at a cost of Rs. 300 billion. GoJ saw this project as a way of reviving Mitsubishi which would have produced the hardware necessary for the project. However, it was felt that at the most what would happen with this project was that people who were traveling by air between these two cities would start taking the Bullet Train. Therefore, it was felt that there was no economic justification for the project given the huge expenditure and the meager benefits.

and theft, tha latter came to be one—sixth or less of the cost of bulk supply increments, for the same level of service improvements. The scale of the discrepancy indicates the bias toward large projects.[27]

If the revenue and cost risk sit with private sector sponsor and lenders in a PPP, a non-viable project is unlikely to generate private interest. As McKisney pointed out, many of the National Highways Authority of India's (NHAI) toll road projects have failed to attract bidders. Often demand forecasts were too high, or NHAI's cost estimates deemed too low, and the project not viable on more realistic cost assumptions.

South Korea established a Public and Private Infrastructure Investment Management Center (PIMAC) to eliminate the routine under-estimation of cost, over-estimation of benefit (optimism bias), and frequent fraud that had plagued the country's infrastructure planning. It rejected 46% of projects that it reviewed compared with the 3% rejection rate before its establishment, saving 35% of spending.

The High Occupancy Toll (HOT) lanes in Virginia, USA present an interesting example of the filtering ability of PPPs. The State of Virginia Department of Transportation's (VDOT) initial plan to decongest the stretch of I-495 involved a cost of US$3 billion, and displacement of over 300 businesses and homes that stalled the project. In 2002, an engineering and construction company named Fluor presented an unsolicited proposal to develop HOT lanes on the I-495—an innovative technology permitting drivers avoid traffic by paying a toll. The tolled lanes run alongside highway lanes, and are designed to be congestion free. Business can avoid paying toll on HOT lanes by having a minimum number of passengers in the vehicle. The total cost came down to US$1.9 billion, with VDOT paying US$400 million only. Businesses and homes displaced fell from 350 to 8. The HOT lanes project reached financial close in 2007 and opened to traffic in 2012.[28]

As we have seen, with a PPP, there is likely to be less optimism bias; but, not always. Engel, Fischer, and Galetovic[29] note that the government bearing revenue risk by issuing a demand guarantee, can make a non-viable project profitable for the private partner, reducing the "filtering ability" of PPPs. It is also true that in generating project ideas, private firms focus on those that are financially viable, but may not propose economically beneficial projects that do not meet the standard thresholds of financial viability like many projects in the social (health and education) sectors.

2.3 *Efficiency in Construction*

Public implementation of projects is often plagued with time and cost overruns in construction (see Table 3) and high cost and poor quality services in operations. World Bank's Africa infrastructure diagnostic study estimates US$6 billion to be

[27]World Bank (2014).

[28]World Bank (2014).

[29]Engel et al. (2014).

Table 3 Comparing PPP and traditional public procurement in the United Kingdom

Comparison	Proportion of projects over budget (%)		Proportion of projects with time over-run (%)	
	PPP	Public	PPP	Public
Contract award to final (2003)	22	73	24	70
Contract award to final (2008)	35	46	31	37

Source National Audit Office (UK), 2003 and 2008

the annual cost of inefficiencies in state-owned utilities and infrastructure providers in Sub-Saharan Africa.[30] Rightly contracted PPPs are more efficiently managed. However, for PPPs to be able to reduce time and cost overruns, it is necessary to transfer construction risk to the private sector through fixed price construction contracts plus liquidated damages.

As Table 3 shows, PPPs reduce construction time and cost over runs for new infrastructure assets, compared to traditional public procurement—although the difference was lower in 2008 than in 2003. Private companies' returns on a PPP depend on timeliness and cost control with stronger motivation than under public procurement, where changes to project cost are passed on to contracting authority. Improvements in public procurement and the demonstration effect of more efficient project implementation in PPPs in the United Kingdom may be narrowing the gap between these two methods of procurement as seen in the table.

A study comparing the performance of PPP projects with that of traditionally procured infrastructure projects in Australia[31] found that PPPs delivered projects for a price that is far closer to the expected cost than if the project was procured in traditional manner (less cost over-runs). (See Fig. 4, sample size: 67 projects—25 PPP projects and 42 traditionally-procured projects). The study also found that over the period from initial announcement of a project to when it is finally commissioned, PPPs and traditional projects are delivered with the same confidence in the likely overall time performance. One interesting observation in this study was that during the period prior to project execution, PPP projects are frequently delayed (average 15%). However, once PPP projects reach financial closure, there was only, on average, a further 2.6% delay to these projects. This indicates that PPP projects are well developed prior to release to market and changes after financial closure are minimal. This is in contrast to traditionally procured projects, where financial closure is faster than anticipated, but the project suffers from major time over-runs after that stage.

[30]World Bank (2014).

[31]Duffield (2008).

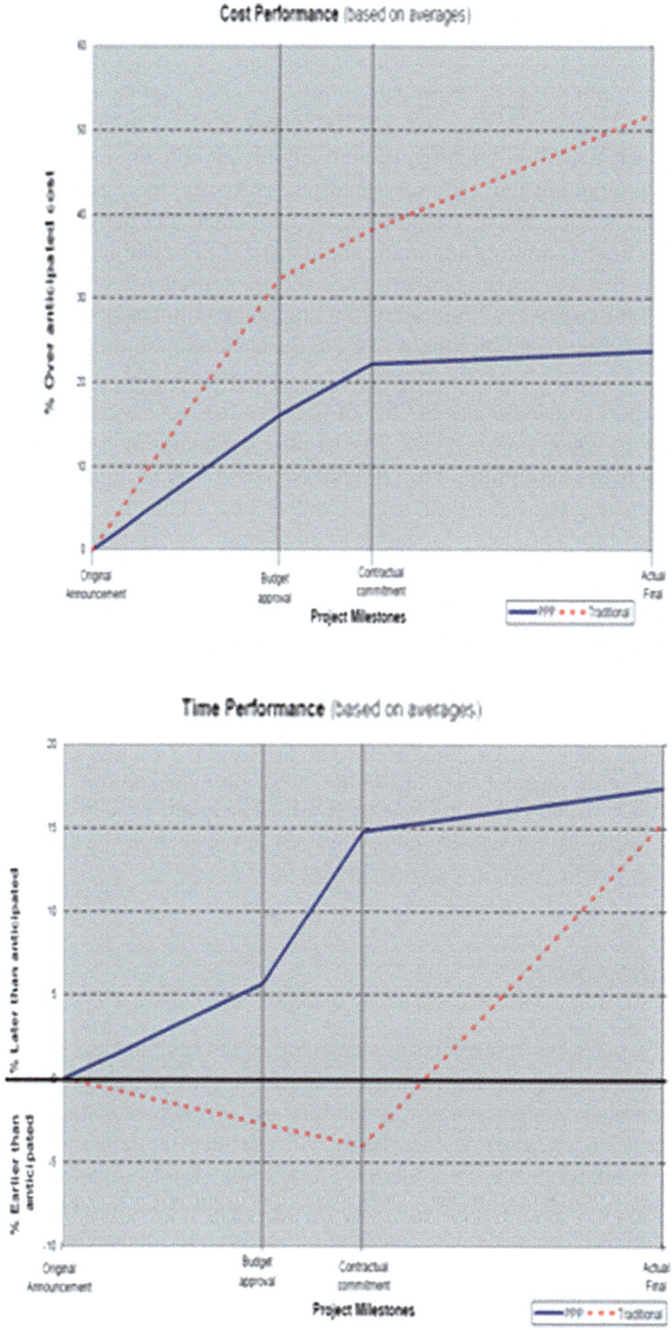

Fig. 4 Comparing PPP and traditional public procurement in Australia *Source* Duffield (2008)

2.4 Service Delivery and Management

A World Bank (2009) study on impact of private sector participation on power and water utilities[32] (sample size: over 1200 water and electricity utilities, in 71 developing and transition countries) found significant efficiency gains from private participation including reduced water and power losses, increased staff efficiency, and improved service delivery with increased coverage and daily hours of service.

However, there is nothing automatic about use of PPPs leading to improvement in service delivery and management. Guasch's comprehensive review of Latin American PPP experience[33] underscores a challenge with achieving the benefits of PPPs—the frequent renegotiation of PPP contracts. Guasch found, using a sample of over 1000 concessions between 1985 and 2000, that 10% of electricity concessions, 55% of transport concessions, and 75% of water concessions were renegotiated. The average time to renegotiation was 2.2 years after the award of concessions. Guasch suggests this high rate within a short time of concession award may indicate flaws in the initial tender processes, weak regulation, or opportunism in contracting. Most renegotiations ended up being favorable to the operator rather than the public sector.

2.5 Innovation and Design

In a typical PPP, at the outset of the tendering process, public authorities lay down a detailed output specification and bidders compete to provide the best cost proposal to deliver it. This is meant to encourage innovation and good design as in the Design-Build-Finance-Operate-Transfer (DBFOT) variant of a PPP. Occasionally, this brings value to the public sector through better technical solutions than the public sector would develop on its own.[34]

2.6 Maintenance

Traditionally, public assets undergo a vicious cycle of build, neglect and rebuild with maintenance of existing assets being accorded a low priority. This is exacerbated by a public expenditure system where capital funding is a separate line item, whereas maintenance is funded from revenue where it will lose out to the delivery of core services. Inadequate maintenance increases lifetime costs, while also decreasing benefits.

Some popular PPP types (for example, Build-Operate-Transfer contracts of a concession period of 30 years) bundle construction and on-going maintenance into a single contract, which incentivizes the private company to build the asset to a high quality

[32]Gassner et al. (2009).

[33]Guasch (2004).

[34]National Audit Office (2007).

upfront and carry out regular maintenance (may involve spending more on construction if it means spending less on maintenance, resulting in a lower "whole of life" cost of the asset). PPPs have a strong incentive to maintain properly as legitimacy of user charges depend on service quality. However, to ensure regular maintenance in PPPs, quality and service standards should be carefully specified, monitored, and enforced.

Regular maintenance is usually far cheaper than undertaking major rehabilitation. For example, it has been estimated that spending $1 on road maintenance provides a savings of $4 to the economy. In India, the Working Group on Roads for the National Transport Development Policy Committee (NTDPC) reports a 40–50% shortfall in the maintenance allocation for state highways and major district roads. The NTDPC estimates that poor road maintenance costs India about Rs. 350 billion annually. So some reallocation of resources from investment to maintenance may be warranted.

Similar estimates highlighting the importance of regular maintenance has been made for other countries. A review of road maintenance by the South African National Roads Agency indicates that a delay of road maintenance for three and five years results in a six-fold and eighteen-fold rise in the original costs of preventative maintenance respectively.

In some cases, like with user-pays PPPs with a monopoly provider, or for government-pays PPPs in weak regulatory environments, the maintenance incentive is weaker. Engel et al. (2014) note the criticality of monitoring to maintenance. Lack of equity or stake of the contractor also reduces the incentive to maintain. Maintenance may also suffer particularly towards the end of the contract, when the contractor knows he cannot internalize the full benefit of higher maintenance investments. Good contract design can avoid such situtaions.[35]

2.7 Customer Service Orientation

User fees often motivate private sector infrastructure providers to deliver better customer service. Because performance standards are set by the regulator or mentioned in the contract, minimum customer service levels are maintained in a PPP. But, there may be a need to enforce contracts through incentives and penalties for this outcome to follow.

2.8 Public Sector's Focus on Core Business

PPPs enable governments to focus on outcomes and core business. For example, PPPs in schools means that the private sector can take care of building, cleaning, security, grounds maintenance and information technology, leaving teachers free to actually teach children. PPPs also release governmental resources from commercial

[35]World Bank (2014).

sectors (like power generation, airports, roads and ports) to focus on non-commercial sectors like rural roads in which the private sector may not be interested.

2.9 Summing Up

While PPPs can help infrastructure building in several ways, the benefits from them are not automatic. In it eagerness to implement PPP projects, Governments may give rate of return guarantees to the private sector. This may, however, create problems as the Delhi-Noida Toll Bridge case study shows where initial Total Project Cost (TPC) has increased more than 10-fold because the contract gives a guaranteed rate of return of 20% per annum on the TPC and any shortfall in these returns get added to the TPC to be serviced in the following year. This clause in the contract has made the project virtually risk free for the private sector and highlights the need for balanced risk sharing among stakeholders for PPP projects to produce value for the government.

Renegotiations are also an issue that reduce the value that PPPs produce for the government. Examples abound where bidders engage in strategic bidding to win the contract, with a view to renegotiating later without competition as in the case of Tata Mundra UMPP Project and Delhi International Airport Limited. Renegotiations fritter away the value produced by a competitive auction as the principal parties to the contract engage in bilateral negotiations, which typically result in losses for the government.

For merit goods with high positive externalities, like education, government ownership may be a policy choice. But government delivery has its challenges of efficiency and quality. PPPs may thus help avoid the twin traps of market and government failures.[36]

In the following section we illustrate these concerns as well as the principles enumerated in the previous section through a short case study of a recent high profile PPP failure in India.

3 Delhi Airport Metro Express[37]: Anatomy of a PPP gone Wrong

The Delhi Airport Metro Express (DAME) was built to connect the heart of New Delhi to the glitzy and newly opened international terminal of Delhi International Airport. The 22.7 km long railroad, costing about Rs. 5700 crore[38] in capital

[36]World Bank (2015).

[37]Pratap (2013).

[38]Total Project Cost is Rs. 5697 crore (Rs. 2812 crore incurred by DMRC and Rs. 2885 crore by DAMEPL) [Source: CAG (2013)] (http://saiindia.gov.in/english/home/Our_Products/Audit_Report/Government_Wise/union_audit/recent_reports/union_compliance/2013/Commercial/Report_13/chap_15.pdf).

investment—was India's first PPP metro rail project. It was meant to catapult Delhi into the league of select aspirational cities with metro connectivity with the airport. Delhi Metro Rail Corporation (DMRC) was responsible for civil works (stations, tunnels and viaducts) while system works (track, signals, rolling stock) was the responsibility of the Delhi Airport Metro Express Private Limited (DAMEPL)—a special purpose vehicle consortium formed by Reliance Infrastructure Limited—part of India's giant Reliance group—owning 95% stake and Spain's Construcciones y Auxiliar de Ferrocarriles, SA (CAF).

DAME started operations in early 2011, after missing several deadlines including the critical Commonwealth Games. It was however completed within budget.

The partnership soon ran into problems, however. Problems kept occurring[39] till DAMEPL terminated the project in June 2013. Since then the project has been run by the public sector entity, DMRC. The separation has scarcely been amicable. DMRC encashed DAMEPL's bank guarantee of Rs. 55 crore.[40] DAMEPL filed and won an arbitration claim against DMRC amounting to several thousand crores.[41]

3.1 Salient Features of the Concession Agreement

The project started in 2008 with the signing of the concession agreement (CA) between the two parties (DMRC and DAMEPL) that gave DAMEPL the right of way, access and license to "develop, design, finance, construct, commission, operate and maintain" the railroad for 30 years. DAMEPL got the right to (a) Levy, demand, collect and appropriate the passenger fares; (b) Generate revenue from advertisement, retail, vending machines and property development. In return, DAMEPL must pay DMRC, throughout the life of the project, (a) Annual Concession Fee (starting at Rs. 51 crore from commencement of operation and rising 5% each year); (b) a rising share of Revenue: 1% of Gross Revenue up to 5th year of operations rising to 5% from 16th year onwards; and (c) a relatively nominal License fee of Rs. 10,000 per annum.

---

[39]DAMEPL suspended services for safety repairs on 8 July 2012. The joint inspection team found that a majority of the bearings in civil construction were defective. After repairs, services were resumed in January 2013.

[40]Source: Economic Times, 5 July 2013 (http://articles.economictimes.indiatimes.com/2013-07-05/news/40392194_1_bank-guarantee-metro-express-private-limited-airport-metro).

[41]DAMEPL has claimed from DMRC a Termination Payment equal to 130% of the Adjusted Equity and 100% of the Debt Due for the project. This is as per the Concession Agreement for DMRC's Event of Default.

3.2 What went Wrong and Who is to Blame: Post Mortem of a Failure

Project cancellations are relatively rare. Private Participation in Infrastructure database of the World Bank points out that about 5% of PPP projects in developing countries get canceled. The frequency was even lower in India, about 1% till 2012. This is primarily because of the keenness of governments to avoid cancelations.[42]

The project economics of DAME went awry almost from the beginning of operation with a massive shortfall in traffic realization—17,000 passengers per day compared to the projected 42,500[43]—leading to a far below expected revenue yield (both fare and non-fare).[44] Operational losses were estimated at Rs. 4 crore per month.[45] The project was proving seriously burdensome for the private party.

Inflated demand estimation is a common malaise for green-field projects around the world. To add to it, the CA appears, in hindsight, to have added to complications by sharing risks rather imprudently and encouraging aggressive bidding by the private sector.

Improper risk sharing: The CA, thrust responsibility for civil works to DMRC and system works to DAMEPL which seems to be at odds with general wisdom. Generally speaking, in designing a PPP, commercial, operational and maintenance risks is usually allocated to the private party while political risk including expropriation is assigned to the public party. This allocation stems from the idea that each party should be held responsible for managing risks that are relatively more directly under its control. In this case, the CA seems to have opened doors for mutual blame and dispute.

Aggressive bidding: In contrast to DAMEPL's winning bid of Rs. 51 crore per annum concession fee and a progressively increasing revenue share to be paid, the next highest bidder, a L&T-GE consortium had asked for an annual *subsidy* of Rs. 346 crore or an interest-free long-term loan of Rs. 1440 crore. In hindsight, this huge gap between the two bids ought to have set alarm bells ringing. Clearly the two bidders had very different views of the project, or potentially, different strategies in mind.

One can think of the decision making function of the concessionaire using the following equation[46]:

---

[42]Pratap (2011).

[43]The ridership of DAME was about 17,000 passengers per day as on the date of the initial shutdown of the project (8 July 2012; Source: Rajya Sabha Unstarred Question No. 1226, answered on 22 August 2012). The ridership during the peak of DAME's operations was recorded at 21,000 per day. Now, the ridership is 10,000–12,000 per day [from 1 July 2013, period after DMRC takeover]. Lately the ridership has increased following, among other factors, rationalization of fares.

[44]Only one-fourth of the total revenue was expected to come from fare collections (Source: Satish Mishra, director of DAMEPL, in a letter to DMRC). But, the other sources of revenue did not materialize due to inadequate traffic.

[45]Accumulated loss of DAMEPL as on 31 March 2012 was Rs. 341 crore [Source: CAG (2013)].

[46]Guasch (2004).

$$\text{Profits} = [\text{Price(or Tariffs)} \times \text{Quantity of service}] - \text{Operation \& Maintenance costs} \\ -\text{taxes} - \text{depreciation} = \text{Opportunity cost of capital} \times \text{Capital Outlay}$$

Opportunistic bidding can violate the second equality above in the hope of later renegotiation. One remedy of this situation is to rule out unrealistically aggressive bids from consideration. However this is difficult to implement in reality as it opens up government agencies to charges of favouritism and corruption.

3.3 The Way Out

In hindsight, DAME appears to have been a poorly contracted project with imperfect risk allocation between the public and the private sectors, marked by aggressive and unrealistic bidding possibly fueled by over-optimistic traffic projections.

Private sector is believed to have lesser agency problems and better property rights. Now with DAME becoming a brownfield project operated by a public agency, project risk has fallen, more realistic traffic projections are available, with greater transparency and data availability. Besides the really difficult problems of land acquisition and environmental clearances are behind DAME. For all these reasons, the project may he much more attractive to the private sector now than earlier.

It is important that the government learns its lessons in contracting, and ensures that these problems do not recur in future. The DAME case study, as part of a general introduction to PPPs, illustrates how common errors can lead to PPP project failures involving huge public liabilities. In the next chapter we look at different PPP models and the associated specific issues each of them entails.

Appendix: Value for Money to the Public Authority from PPPs[47]

The Concept of Value for Money (VfM)

For PPPs to be sustainable they should provide value to the government rather than being vehicles just for moving liabilities into the future, for example, through revenue or rate-of-return guarantees to the private sector. Such guarantees are contingent liabilities of the government and may not cost the government anything when they are given, but may prove quite expensive in the face of persistent revenue or rate of return shortfalls. Thus, Brazil had to nationalize the TermoCeara and Macae power projects because doing so turned out to be cheaper than servicing the revenue guarantees. In the case of the Delhi-Noida Toll Bridge in India, the public authorities would be well advised to terminate the PPP contract or at least renegotiate the contract, as the rate-of-return guarantee for the project has ensured that the project

[47]Partly based on Pratap (2011).

would become a huge public liability by 2031, when the original contract period ends, compared with a modest $100 million total project cost when the project became operational in 2001[48] (the courts have disallowed toll collection since then).

Value for money (VfM) to government, in this context, can be thought of as the best price for a given quantity and standard of output, measured in terms of relative financial benefit where the comparator is the cost of public sector provisioning. It is assessed through an analysis of the costs of similar outputs through a comparison between bidders' cash flows and those of the public sector alternative. More specifically, VfM is the financial comparison of the Net Present Value of the cash flows of the public sector option and the PPP option.

VfM analysis can be thought of as a project appraisal method—the question it answers is whether it is cheaper to implement the project as a PPP compared to traditional procurement. However, VfM analysis is only a part of a typical project appraisal process. Other project appraisal analyses could include the feasibility and economic viability of the project (that is, does the project provide VfM, irrespective of its implementation as a PPP or other procurement methods); its commercial viability (that is, whether the project is likely to provide adequate financial returns to attract good quality investors); and its affordability. VfM is manifested in similar services delivered at a lower cost than the public sector (cost-saving) and/or on-time delivery of services.

This evaluation is an integral component of all PPPs in the UK and Australia, some of the world's most developed markets in this type of contracting.[49] In India, however, no value-for-money analysis is generally done for PPPs. Given that PPPs are increasingly India's default option for investment in infrastructure, it is imperative that this analysis be done. We look at an example of the VfM calculation for the road sector in India later in this section.

Global Evidence on VfM of PPP Projects

This section surveys the experience of countries where PPPs have been extensively used to provide infrastructure. PPPs as a form of procurement began in the UK, where it was known as private finance initiative (PFI), in 1992. Since 1994, it became the preferred option for public procurement in that country. It now typically constitutes about 10% of the UK government's capital budget each year.[50] According to a pioneering UK study, the UK experience suggests that PPP projects deliver average

---

[48]Pratap et al. (2012).

[49]Construction of a Public Sector Comparator is (PSC) also a mandatory tool for assessing PPPs in Japan and South Africa [Source: Grimsey et al. (2005)].

[50]For example, in the UK, in the financial year 2011–12, Public Sector Net Investment (PSNI), the gross spending on investment less depreciation, totaled £26.7 billion. The capital cost of those PFI projects that reached financial close in 2011–12 was £2.1 billion. In the UK, total investment in 700 PFI projects was £55 billion. In Korea, PPP investment is 10–15% of total public investment. In India, the contribution of the private sector to total infrastructure investment in the Tenth Plan period (2002–07) was 25%. This percentage has gone up to 38% in the Eleventh Plan period (2007–12) and is projected to be 47% in the Twelfth Plan period (2012–17).

savings of 17% compared with traditional public sector delivery.[51] As per this study, the following six key drivers determine value for money in PPP projects:

- Risk transfer: Risk transfer can offer VfM if risk is transferred to the party best able to manage or mitigate it. The risk that attracted the highest valuation is that of construction cost overrun and this should be transferred to the PPP partner through a fixed price contract with liquidated damages.
- Long-term nature of contracts (including whole-life costing through combining construction, operation and maintenance in a single contract[52]): A long-term contract enables investment to be recovered over a reasonably long period thereby making the project affordable; long contract period also gives scope to invest in innovations in service delivery; long contracts incentivize service providers to focus on whole life costing—whole life costing can achieve optimization between capital costs and Operation & Maintenance (O&M) costs, and a realistic projection of total cost of the project. The study observes that while we would expect to drive on a PPP road in 20 years time and find a well-maintained asset still performing to the original specification, we would not have the same confidence if the asset had been conventionally procured.
- Use of outputs and outcomes for measuring performance: This is another best practice as monitoring expenditure is an input based performance measure and may not benefit the users. So, performance criteria should be specified in terms of outputs and outcomes and should be monitored rigorously.
- Competition: Competitive bidding for PPP projects should be preferred compared to negotiations. For delivering a successful PPP competition, engagement with the market place is required, as well as clear and thorough project documentation—bidders can only compete on price if they have a clear understanding of the procuring authority's requirements.
- Performance measurement and incentives: Operational information would be required on performance of individual contractors, including the level of penalties being incurred by concessionaires for poor performance. This information should be made known to other procuring authorities to improve procurement efficiency.
- Private sector management skills: The success of private sector managers is illustrated by the consistent record of PPP consortia in delivering projects within budget and on time. The within budget performance is facilitated by fixed price contracts while on-time performance is incentivized as faster completion of project makes it possible for the PPP operator to expedite returns.

---

[51] Arthur Andersen and Enterprise LSE. 2000. *Value for Money Drivers in the Private Finance Initiative*, a report commissioned by The Treasury Taskforce. The 17% Value-for-Money figure is the financial comparison of the Net Present Values (NPVs) of the cash flows of the public sector option compared to the PPP option. It was dominated by two large projects, with individual project savings varying between 0.7% and 45% across the sample of 29 projects.

[52] With public provision, a construction firm minimizes building costs subject to design characteristics. In a PPP, by contrast, the private firm minimizes life-cycle costs, which include building, operations, and maintenance costs. (See, for example, Engel et al. 2011).

The National Audit Office (UK) has found that in contrast to traditionally procured projects, PFI projects were largely being delivered on time (76% PFI projects delivered on time versus 30% traditionally procured projects delivered on time) and on budget (78% versus 27%).[53] Moreover, the public sector did not bear the costs of construction cost-overruns in the PFI projects, as that risk is generally transferred to the private sector through fixed-price construction contracts.

Another study reviewing large public procurement in the UK[54] found that 'optimism bias' for conventionally procured projects was higher than that for PFI projects. Optimism in project estimates arises from underestimating the costs and duration of a project or overestimating its benefits, and is accentuated in politically important projects. For projects to be delivered on time and cost, the optimism in project estimates should be minimised. According to the study, the reasons for lower optimism bias in PFI projects could be related to the high level of diligence demanded in PFI procurement to establish the business case, which was not observed for conventional procurement.

Australia has also used PPPs extensively. Department of Treasury and Finance (Government of Victoria, Australia) commissioned an independent external evaluation of eight PPP projects,[55] which concluded that the weighted average saving of a PPP project was 9% against the risk-adjusted public sector comparator (PSC[56]) using the then prevailing discount rate. Other positive aspects associated with PPP projects included timeliness of delivery, certainty of price, and a whole-of-life approach to maintenance. The methodology that was used to calculate the VfM was: Calculate the Net Present Cost (NPC) of the PSC; Calculate the NPC of the PPP option; Estimate the savings to the public sector in NPC terms of the PSC.

In contrast to better timeliness of delivery found for PPP projects in the above studies, another study for Australia[57] (sample size: 67 projects) found that over the period from initial announcement of a project to when it is finally commissioned, PPPs and traditional projects are delivered with the same time performance. However, in consonance with above studies, this Australian study finds that PPPs delivered projects for a price that is far closer to the expected cost than if the project was procured in traditional manner (less optimism bias in cost terms) (see Fig. 5, Panel A). One interesting observation in this study was that during the period prior

---

[53]Comptroller and Auditor General, UK (2003).

[54]Mott Macdonald (2002). In this study, a representative sample of projects (with costs exceeding £40 million at 2001 prices) procured traditionally and through the PFI route and implemented over the previous 20 years was compared.

[55]Fitzgerald (2004).

[56]The use of PSC for calculating VfM involves the following calculation: Estimation of the benchmark cost of providing the specified service under traditional procurement and a comparison of this benchmark cost with the cost of providing the specified service under a PPP scheme. This benchmark is known as the public sector comparator (PSC). A PSC, in other words, is the estimated cost of a conventionally procured project delivering the same output as the PPP project.

[57]Duffield (2008).

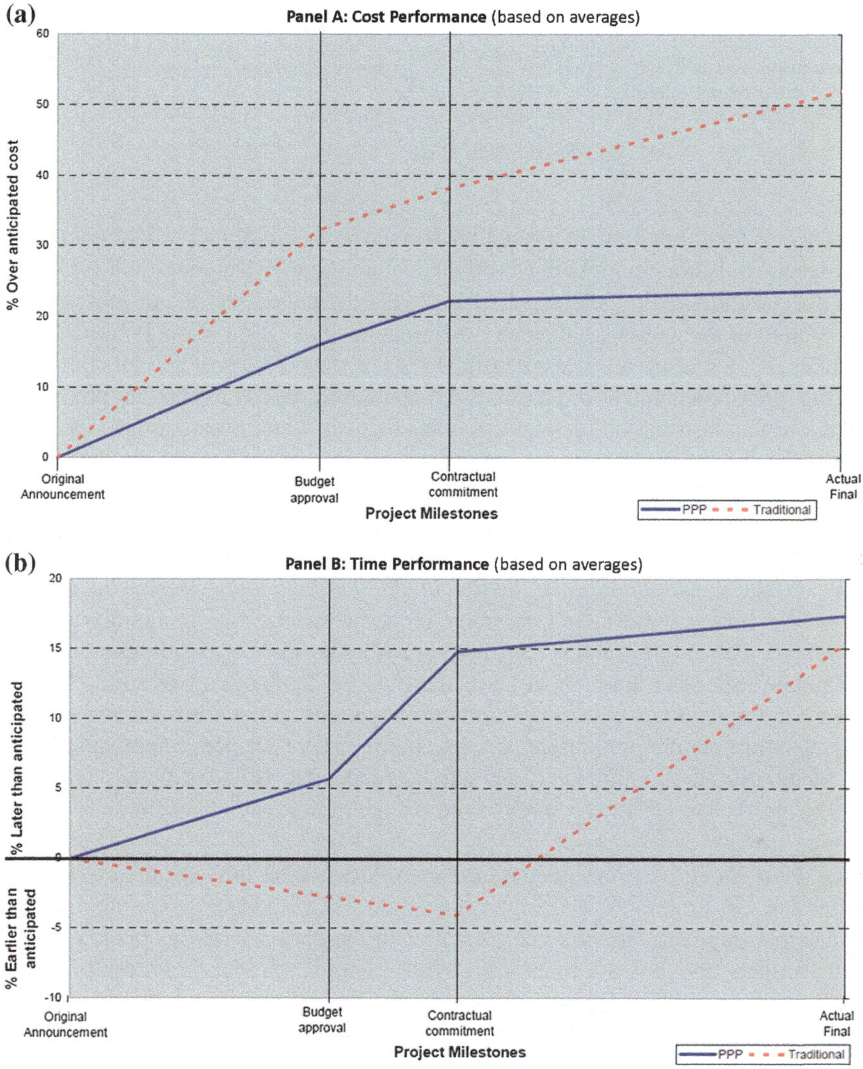

Fig. 5 Cost and time performance of PPP projects versus traditionally procured projects *Source* Duffield 2008

to project execution, PPP projects are frequently delayed (average 15% compared to traditionally procured projects). However, once PPP projects reach financial closure, there was only, on average, a further 2.6% delay to these projects. This indicates that PPP projects are well developed prior to release to market and changes after financial closure are minimal. This is in contrast to traditionally procured projects, where financial closure is faster, but projects suffer from major time over-run after that stage (see Fig. 5, Panel B).

Table 4 Construction cost overrun (conventional procurement versus PPPs) consolidated over 14 studies

	Conventional procurement (%)	PPPs (%)
Maximum	98	20
Average	25	13
Minimum	−9	−4

Source Bain (2010)

There is therefore logic in trying to reduce project development risks by carrying out land acquisition and taking environmental and forest clearances in the name of the Special Purpose Vehicle which is created in the public sector and subsequently transferred to the winning bidder as is being done in the Ultra Mega Power Projects in India. As found in the above Australian study, the public sector is more efficient in the pre-implementation phase as compared to the construction phase and therefore this distribution of responsibilities helps in faster project implementation. Since the public sector has a comparative advantage in the pre-implementation phase, the responsibility for this phase should be with the public sector for improving timeliness of delivery of projects.

Consolidating over 14 studies for UK, Australia, France, and Norway, Bain finds that average construction cost overrun in PPPs is half that observed in conventionally procured projects and the range of cost overruns is also significantly narrower (see Table 4). Even this construction cost overrun does not represent a risk to the public sector as Bain finds that experienced PPP contractors with strong balance sheets and reputations will complete their obligations as intended and at their own risk. To illustrate the point, Bain says that in the case of Spencer Street Station PPP in Melbourne, the contractor (Leighton) admitted that it had suffered significant losses, yet it completed the works with no additional payments from the public sector.

A 2002 study of some prisons in South Africa built and operated as PPPs[58] found that construction was completed on-time and on-budget; operating costs per inmate per day were broadly comparable with the public sector's operating costs; and facilities and levels of service in PPP prisons were of significantly higher quality than in public prisons. So, if one has a choice between occupying public or private prisons, one should opt for private prisons!

There is also the TINA (there is no alternative) factor at work—there is no realistic public alternative in the face of financial or implementation capacity constraints in many countries. PPPs have been used as a method of developing local private sector capabilities through joint ventures with large MNCs, as well as sub-contracting opportunities for local firms that such arrangements provide. PPPs have been instrumental in diversifying the economy by making the country more competitive through infrastructure creation as well as giving a boost to business and industry.

---

[58]Government of South Africa (Department of Correctional Services, National Treasury, Department of Public Works) (2002).

From the above brief survey, it is apparent that PPPs have emerged as a "third way", promising the advantages of privatization while avoiding its pitfalls.[59] First, PPPs are a means of resolving agency problems, which arise due to the divergence between ownership and control of assets, and are easier to manage in the private sector through managerial incentives and market discipline. Second, the transfer of risk to the private sector provides an incentive for private entities to maximize efficiency. Third, resources are more efficiently allocated in cases where a clear market for property rights can be established.[60] PPPs are also more politically acceptable than outright privatization in infrastructure sectors: given that user fees are generally low in infrastructure services (for example, in the water and sewerage sector) and there is a move towards cost-recovery charges following private sector participation, it is politically less problematic when governments are seen to be sharing risks and returns with the private sector as in a PPP, rather than outright privatization.

Overall, the literature suggests the following positives from PPPs:

- Value for money to the government is estimated at 17% for UK and 9% for Australia compared to traditional procurement;
- Off-balance sheet infrastructure financing,[61] augmentation of capital spending without increasing public debt, and thus reduced pressure on government budgets;
- Better defined and improved quality services through watertight contracts, improved efficiency, output-based service specifications, and strengthened monitoring and accountability;
- Public services provided more cost-effectively and quickly (without cost and time overruns);
- Transfer of design, construction, financing, and operation risks to the private sector, which promotes innovation in design, and improves incentives for adequate maintenance relative to traditionally procured projects;
- Business-friendly, which promotes investor confidence and can provide electoral dividends to government;
- To the extent that the public sector is benchmarked against private sector companies, PPPs are also likely to improve public sector efficiency.

However, PPPs have also been vociferously opposed on many counts. It has been alleged that with PPPs, government's role changes from traditional stewardship to mutually conflicting roles of policy advocacy, commercial signatory to a contract, and regulator over the contract life. Some have even castigated PPPs as "Problem, Problem, Problem" (Bowman, 2000). The reasons for this negative assessment of PPPs are:

[59]Engel et al. (2008).

[60]Grimsey and Lewis (2005).

[61]Around 85% of past PFI projects have been considered off-balance sheet in UK.

- Internationally, there have been many high-profile PPP project failures like some parts of the London Underground rail transportation project (UK), the Delhi Airport Metro Express project, the Aguas Argentinas project,[62] the Mexican toll road debacle,[63] and the Indian Dabhol power project,[64] exemplifying cases where PPPs, instead of providing fiscal help, turned out to being a drain on government resources.
- There is also a tendency for governments to be unwilling to "pull the plug" on PPP projects once they are underway because they fear that essential services may be disrupted, their reputation may be damaged, or they may be legally liable to pay the private provider if a contract is terminated. This reluctance increases the cost of a future consumer or taxpayer bailout of the project.
- Many PPPs are characterised by over-optimistic (and opportunistic) bids, subjecting governments to the risk of renegotiation after a private partner is awarded the contract. The outcome of renegotiations often favours the private sector vis-à-vis the public sector or consumers.[65]
- Ultimately the risk transfer to the private sector is limited, as government has the overriding obligation to provide public services—85% of the cancelled PPP projects revert to the government.[66]
- Because detailed information about PPP projects is rarely made public (leading to low transparency and the associated potential for corruption), such procurement has eroded democratic accountability.
- Annuity payments are a government liability, but do not appear in government accounts. Annuities also lock-in public resources for a long period as many PPP contracts are for 30 years or more (for the UK, total government commitments to future payments associated with about 670 PFI contracts are estimated at £141 billion over 26 years[67]), reducing flexibility in the face of changing needs and burdening future generations.
- Many PPPs are characterized by poor competition, time consuming bidding processes, high deal complexity and transaction costs.

---

[62]Aguas Argentinas was a $4 billion project awarded in 1993 for providing water and sewerage services to Buenos Aires, the capital of Argentina. However, in 2006, the project was canceled and the concession taken over by the government in the face of the Argentine Financial Crisis of 2002, on account of increasing water rates, and no commensurate performance improvements.

[63]23 Mexican toll roads were taken over by the government in 1997 as the financial condition of these projects bordered on bankruptcy after the Mexican peso crisis of 1994. The government paid over $7.7 billion to the creditors of these projects.

[64]In the case of the Dabhol power project (now known as Ratnagiri Gas and Power Private Limited), the government of India shelled out about $2 billion to buy out a PPP project of about 2000 MW capacity in 2005. Even now, the project is only partially operational owing to shortage of feedstock and high costs. Meanwhile, the project cost is increasing relentlessly imposing a substantial burden on the public sector.

[65]Guasch (2004).

[66]Harris and Pratap (2008).

[67]As quoted in Pollitt (2005).

- In terms of value-for-money calculations, there are problems associated with the PSC[68] and the associated discount rate.[69] Besides, commercial borrowing rates are higher than government borrowing rates, and there may be affordability issues because user charges may rise post-PPP thus negating the gains from VfM to the government.

Methodology of Computing VfM

Taking into account the methodology used for calculating value for money in PPPs in the UK, Australia, and South Africa, this section tries to establish the counterfactual by relying on the concept of Public Sector Comparator (PSC). The discounted incremental cost of the PPP option is compared to that of traditional public procurement based on PSC to arrive at the value for money to the government in such transactions.

To illustrate, the following methodology has been used to calculate the Value for Money to the government in BOT (Annuity) road projects:

$$\sum VfM_i = \sum [PVPC_i + PVOM_i - PVA_i)] \quad (1)$$

where

VfM_i is the Value for Money to the government from ith project,
$PVPC_i$ is the present value of the estimated Project Cost of the ith project,
$PVOM_i$ is the present value of the estimated Operation and Maintenance (O&M) expenditure over the life of the contract for the ith project, and
PVA_i is the present value of the Annuity payments over the life of the contract for the ith project.

More simply, the above equation can be written as: Value for Money to the government = Present Value of (estimated Project Cost + estimated O&M expenditure over the life of the contract−Annuity payments).

The methodology is illustrated in Fig. 6. The government, instead of making lumpy investments at the start of the project for constructing it (area A in Fig. 6) and subsequently making small Operation & Maintenance expenditures (area B), is making annuity payments for the duration of the contract (area C). Value for money to the government is given by the area (A + B − C).

Toll collection during the contract period and beyond is not accounted for, as the tolling option would be available to the government even with conventional

---

[68]Inaccuracy because of poor data availability, omitted risks like that of contract renegotiation, and inappropriate benchmark when the public sector does not have the resources to implement the project. (see, Leigland et al. 2006).

[69]In the Fitzgerald study (2004), when the discount rate was reduced from 8.65 to 5.7%, value for money declined from 9 to −6%.

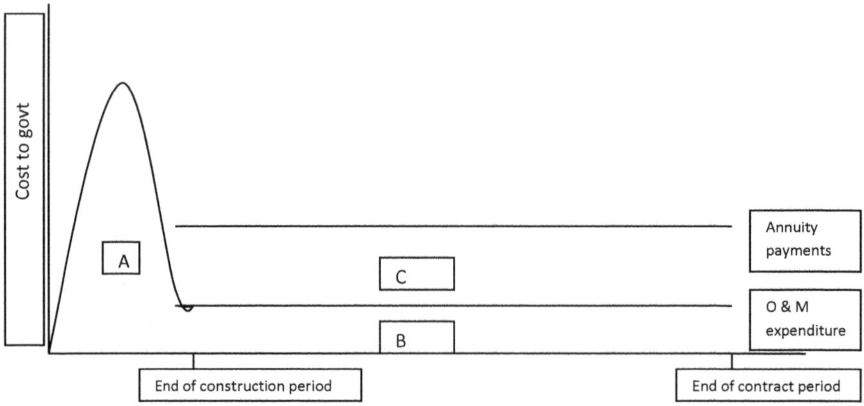

Fig. 6 Value for money in BOT (Annuity) road projects *Source* Author's conceptualization

procurement of the project. Asset residual value of PPP project is not taken into account because it is assumed to be the same as under the conventional procurement option to keep the VfM estimate conservative. Adjustment for differential taxation and transaction costs of the PPP projects is not made for simplification.

Obviously, the above estimation would be based on assumptions about the parameters used in the model such as project cost, operation and maintenance expenditure, discount rate, etc. The robustness of these assumptions would be examined through a sensitivity analysis by changing the important assumptions in the model.

There are obvious limitations in using PSCs[70]: inaccuracy because of poor data availability, subjectivity and dependence on assumptions (sometimes dealt with by using a range of estimates through sensitivity analysis rather than point estimates), omitted risks like that of contract renegotiation, no consensus on discount rate,[71] long-term nature of the contract and the associated uncertainty, and inappropriateness of the benchmark when the public sector does not have the resources to implement the project.

Therefore, overall, the PSC approach to calculating VfM, rather than being the best method, is simply a cost-effective compromise between a full cost-benefit analysis of all project options (the German way) and simply selecting the 'best' private bid (the French alternative) which at the same time ensures that all projects are treated in a analogous way and are subjected to a broadly similar and systematic test for VfM.[72] Thus, the value for money calculations using the PSC approach provide a useful, though incomplete, method to evaluate the utility of PPPs.

[70]Leigland et al. (2006).

[71]Opposite conclusions were reached in the Fitzgerald report when using a 8.65% discount rate (leading to the conclusion that the PPP mechanism was 9% cheaper than traditional delivery) compared to an evaluation adopting a 5.7% discount rate (when the PPP mechanism was apparently 6% more expensive).

[72]Grimsey et al. (2005).

Chapter 5
Models of PPP—Taxonomy and Issues

1 Introduction

PPP projects come with a vexing diversity on various aspects, and their contractual structures, as well as the associated challenges and drivers of success depend critically on their types. A standard terminology and taxonomy for classifying Public–Private Partnerships (PPP) according to various characteristics is therefore key to a better understanding of these projects. It is easier for both policymakers and practitioners across sectors and geographies to better understand and interact more fruitfully in the presence of such a standard terminology. This chapter seeks to create such a classification structure and develop the terminology.

In the next section, we discuss the three broad parameters along which PPPs can be classified:

A. The type of asset—New or Existing assets;
B. Functions that the PPP is responsible for—Design, Build, Finance, Operate, Maintain, and Transfer;
C. The mechanism of paying the private party—whether by the Government or users.

The third section takes a close look at the plethora of existing variations in contracting arrangements for creating a taxonomy of PPP arrangements based on contract specifications, mostly various combinations of B and C above.

We conclude the chapter by presenting a case study of a water supply and sewerage PPP in Tanzania. Though this case study is of a PPP outside India, it captures the contractual complexities and typical challenges of infrastructure operations in developing country contexts and demonstrates how contracting flaws and misjudged bids can undermine the success of these arrangements.

K.V. Pratap and R. Chakrabarti, *Public-Private Partnerships in Infrastructure*,
India Studies in Business and Economics, DOI 10.1007/978-981-10-3355-1_5

2 Parameters of Classification of PPPs

2.1 New or Existing Asset

Infrastructure PPP projects can be new—*Greenfield*—or existing—*Brownfield*. In India, for instance, examples of the former include the new 4000 MW power generation project in coastal Gujarat being implemented by the Special Purpose Vehicle (SPV), Coastal Gujarat Power Limited or the Delhi—Noida Toll Bridge, or the new international airports at Hyderabad or Bengaluru. In the second category, we have the several renovated airports like at Mumbai and Delhi. Another brownfield project is the Dar es Salaam Water and Sewerage Project in Tanzania, implemented by the City Water Services Limited, that we discuss in depth later in this chapter.

As Table 1 shows, investors around the world have generally tended to favor Greenfield projects over Brownfield projects.

As per the table, Greenfield projects constitute about 61% of the total number of PPP projects in the developing world and account for about 58% of the investment. The advantages of investing in a Greenfield project include the following:

- Defined capital expenditure implying greater certainty: This certainty may be lacking for brownfield projects. Thus, there would be a reasonably precise estimate of the total project cost for a new power project or a new airport. This may not be the case for an existing water supply system or a power distribution system where it may take a long time to assess the condition of the existing assets[1] and the associated capital expenditure for its rehabilitation.
- Ring-fenced operation: Most PPP projects in infrastructure are implemented through a new legal entity in the form of a Special Purpose Vehicle (SPV), which are created to implement the specific project like the Coastal Gujarat Power Limited implementing the power generation project in coastal Gujarat. This provides a more straightforward opportunity for segregation of the revenue stream, project assessment, due diligence, risk assessment, and forecast of financial viability. A new business, therefore, would be easier for project finance lenders to ring fence with security and step-in rights, and other control mechanisms.
- Need not be concerned with historical liabilities and employee issues: A new project would generally have no historical liabilities or employees compared to a brownfield project. Historical liabilities may be identified or unidentified leading to increased risk in estimating the total project cost. Existing employees may oppose a PPP contractual structure, which they may believe to be a precursor to full privatization, and therefore introduce new risks and costs to the project.

[1]There may not be even be an up-to-date asset register or any other record of the condition of existing assets for power distribution, like the authors have experienced in some of the jurisdictions in India.

Brownfield projects typically entail a project company taking over existing task or function with the possibility of expansion or refurbishing. It may relate to an entire task or business structure, or part thereof to manage the business. Thus, under the Indian Smart Cities Mission, the New Delhi Municipal Council is trying to bid out the operation and maintenance of the water supply system to a PPP operator. In general, common services allocated to PPPs in brownfield projects include the following:

- Management of distribution systems/assets, e.g., operation and maintenance contracts in power and water: In these sectors, operation and maintenance functions are transferred to the PPP with performance-based incentive mechanisms. The objective is usually to achieve efficiency improvement in managing assets, achieving better response to end-user complaints, new connection requests, and other asset-related services.
- Exploitation of commercial opportunities: Certain infrastructure sectors, like airports, present opportunities for affiliated commercial undertakings like duty-free shops and related businesses like hotels, using the available land, excess asset capacity, or selling additional goods and services to same end users. These are noncore services that may be operated efficiently by the private sector for added returns to the core activity. This is incentivized through lower agency problems in a PPP compared to a public sector managed enterprise.
- Billing and collection: Public sector providers are often poor performers when it comes to revenue collection either because of political implications or lack of incentives. Outsourcing the activity can shift collection risk as well as enforcement penalties, disconnection, etc. to the private sector. The franchise operations in Bhiwandi power distribution project, for instance, was able to achieve a large reduction in billing and collection losses and therefore aggregate technical and commercial (AT&C) losses as private sector efficiencies were brought in to improve the system. However, there is a risk of over aggressive collection and excess use of police power, which should be avoided through carefully planned incentive mechanisms.[2]

As Table 1 suggests, investors are generally more cautious about the risks associated with rehabilitating existing infrastructure assets (brownfield projects).

Table 1 Private participation in infrastructure—disproportionate incidence of greenfield projects (1990–2015)

PPI type	Number of projects	Total investment commitments (US$ billion)
Management and lease contract	287	8
Concession	1546	456
Greenfield project	3982 (61%)	1408 (58%)
Divestiture	732	546
Total	6547	2419

Source Private participation in infrastructure database (ppi.worldbank.org)

[2]Delmon (2010).

They are also more wary about sectors that involve political and regulatory risks, especially those that involve tariff increases for end users in socially sensitive sectors such as water or power. In the water and power sectors specifically, there is generally low-cost recovery and sustainable private operations would entail some degree of retail tariff increase, which is generally politically sensitive. Existing business also implies employees, contracts, undertakings, commitments, and other matters needing due diligence by prospective investors, as well as more complexity in the preparation required from the government.

Another disincentive for brownfield projects is path dependence. The existing design may make it difficult to carry out refurbishment, technology adoption, use optimal construction methods, and employ appropriate materials. This path dependence may put investments at a disadvantage, both technically and financially. In general, a brownfield project poses the risk of delay and cost increase simply owing to the nature of the legacy assets. Frequently, the project company would have inadequate opportunity to identify the sources of trouble. It is no surprise, therefore, that much of the private investment in these sectors has come into new power generation or water treatment plants rather than power or water distribution projects.

However, existing assets are also an opportunity as they exhibit a proven revenue source, cost, and demand information as well as reliable data on viability and sustainability. Thus, the greenfield Delhi Airport Metro Express project, that we studied in Chap. 4, continues to suffer from non-fruition of the estimated demand projections. As we saw, one of the important reasons for its failure was the aggressive bidding (in hindsight) on the part of the project sponsors. However, now that it is a brownfield project, there is an existing revenue stream, tested cost data, and historical demand data, which should preclude aggressive bidding, if DMRC decides to rebid the project.

2.2 Allocation of Functions to a PPP and their Implications

Apart from whether the project is new or existing, another way of categorizing PPP projects is in terms of the functions that the private party in the contract is responsible for. The two aspects are not mutually exclusive, though. The list of functions often depends upon the type of asset and service involved. For a new (Greenfield) project, the private party may be responsible for Design, Build, Finance, Operate, and Transfer (DBFOT) or a subset of these functions, as in many road projects in India. If it is an existing (Brownfield) project, the private party may instead be responsible for Rehabilitate, Operate, and Transfer (ROT) functions or only Operation and Maintenance (O&M) of assets. Before actually getting down to classifying the PPP types, it is instructive to find out what these responsibilities actually entail and what they may imply for the private party in the partnership.

- *Design*—also known as "engineering" work—refers to transforming the project from initial concept and output requirements to construction-ready design specifications. This process leaves considerable scope for innovation as the private sector is expected to do value engineering and achieve the objectives at a lower cost.
- *Build* or *Rehabilitate*—When PPPs are used for greenfield infrastructure projects, they typically require the private party to construct the asset and install all equipment. Where PPPs involve brownfield assets, the private party may be responsible for rehabilitating or extending the asset. Rehabilitation of existing assets increases project risks and, as we have seen, this is one of the reasons why greenfield projects are favored by PPP companies compared to brownfield projects.
  What does this imply for risk-sharing in the partnership? As we have seen earlier, optimal contracting suggests allocation of those risks to a PPP partner over which it has greater control than the other partner. In this vein, construction risk, which relates to 'Build' function, is best allocated to the PPP concessionaire through fixed price construction contracts and liquidated damages. The construction commitments add to the risks like managing contractors and coordinating funding. The revenue profile frequently changes and depends on several factors.[3] Construction cost overruns are a major bane of public implementation of projects and may be a source of major gain to the public sector, if this risk is transferred to the PPP.
- *Finance*—The private party is usually required to finance the necessary capital expenditure of a building or refurbishing of asset, either completely or at least partially. Financiers would want watertight contracts[4] and substitution rights (right to substitute the nonperforming PPP operator) as they bear huge risks in limited recourse or non-recourse financing[5] typically associated with PPP

[3]Delmon (2010).

[4]Watertight contracts: Commercial lenders will apply conditionality focused on improving revenues, managing costs, and protecting the lender's cushion.

[5]One of the most common, and often most efficient, financing arrangements for PPP projects is "project financing", often associated with "limited recourse" or "non-recourse" financing as we have seen in Chap. 4. Project financing normally takes the form of limited recourse lending to a specially created project vehicle (Special Purpose Vehicle, SPV) which has the right to carry out the construction and operation of the project. Limited recourse financing shifts some of the project risk to the lenders in exchange for which the lenders obtain a higher margin than for normal corporate lending. This motivates the lenders to require a detailed assessment of risk management and allocation before financing is committed to the project. Thus, major project challenges are identified and addressed early in the project in contrast to normal public procurement, in which risks may be discovered later, often when it is too late, or far more expensive to address.

projects. PPPs generally involve the construction of high value, long life assets with stable revenues, and therefore seek long-term, fixed interest debt. *Finance* obligations tend to extend the time for procurement in order to allow more robust risk assessment and allocation and for lenders to perform due diligence. Where private finance needs to be arranged (for concession fees, acquisition of assets, and/or construction costs), the risk profile of the project company will be high and will come down only with completion of construction.

Financing of PPP projects would have debt and equity components. On the equity side, the public authority granting the contract may require that the project company includes local investors (equity partners) in order to facilitate transfer of technology and provide jobs and training to local personnel. Local investors may also make the project more sustainable. In many countries, having a local partner in the consortium just makes more practical sense as the local partner is expected to help navigate the local politics and the associated political risks with relative ease. In the case study on Dar es Salaam water that we discuss later in this chapter, we will see that there is a local partner in the politically sensitive water sector.

In some cases, the public authority may want to control the PPP or may want to partake in the profits that the PPP project is expected to make through a public sector Joint Venture (JV) partner. Thus, in the case of Delhi International Airport PPP, though the private consortium has majority stake, the public sector Airports Authority of India is also a 26% equity partner. However, the key challenge with a public sector JV partner is the conflict of interest between the government as a shareholder and the government as a grantor of contract, for example, difficulties for the government as a shareholder to agree with the project company to sue the government as a grantor of contract.

On the debt side, the most important source of debt finance for infrastructure projects in India are commercial banks, in common with rest of the world. The nature of the lender, and their existing portfolio characteristics and plans determine bankability requirements and lender appetite. If the infrastructure projects as well as the lenders are in the public sector, the banks may have limited scope for savings on commercial considerations, contributing to the growing problem of non-performing assets as in India.

Infrastructure projects are generally associated with pronounced political risks, because of the essential nature of services that they provide. Lenders will react to political risks differently, with those more familiar with the setting possibly being less risk-averse. Multilateral lenders (like the World Bank, ADB, etc) may have better relationships with the relevant government, and will therefore view political risk as more manageable. Developing member countries also would take care that there is no loan default for these lenders, given their clout and associated country risk.

- *Operate*—the operating responsibilities of the PPP concessionaire can vary considerably, as per the PPP contract, the underlying asset, and the associated service. For example, the private party could be responsible for supplying to bulk consumers or retail consumers, technical operation of an asset, and providing a bulk service to a government offtaker—for instance, a power generation project or a bulk water treatment plant providing power or water to a public sector distribution company; technical operation of an asset, and providing services directly to users—for example, a PPP for a power or water distribution system supplying these services directly to retail consumers.

It would be considerably more risky to provide services directly to users compared to providing bulk services to a public sector offtaker. For a user-paying project company with diverse customer base, its consumer relationship can create specific complexities. The nature of this type of service delivery obligation is associated with specific risks collectively known as commercial risk:

- Demand risk: Demand for output and services, including demographic, technology, and usage changes. While there may be a power purchase agreement ensuring payment of fixed costs even when demand is suboptimal in the case of bulk power supply to power distribution companies, such risk mitigation may not be possible in retail supplies;
- Retail tariff levels, in particular where a regulator sets or adjusts or approves adjustment of tariffs: this is associated with regulatory risk[6];
- Billing, including identifying consumers, keeping track of consumption/metering, and delivering billing statements: The most important reason for lack of commercial viability of the water sector in India, for example, is the high percentage of water lost as Non-Revenue Water (NRW) owing partly to lack of water meters in majority of Indian households;
- Payment risk—consumers do not pay the agreed user fees. Collection of debts due, including the physical process of bill collection, the credit risk of consumers, and the design and implementation of penalty mechanisms of payment refusers are important here.

However, supply to retail consumers enables reaping of full benefits from PPP—reducing Aggregate Technical & Commercial (AT&C) losses, improving billing and collection, and thus improving the financial prospects of the PPP company.

[6]The most important regulatory risk is tariff risk and refers to the risk that the regulator would not allow full recovery of costs. Thus, in the power sector in India, the cost under-recovery is to the extent of Rs. 1 per unit of power (kilo Watt hour, kWh) sold in the country. One way to mitigate regulatory risk is to have autonomous regulatory institutions.

Box 5.1: Infrastructure pricing and regulation Many infrastructure firms operate in monopoly markets and there is a need, therefore, for independent regulation for setting tariffs, among others, to protect user interests. Natural monopolies are characterized by downward sloping average cost curves (see Fig. 1). The socially optimal price is at P_{pc}, where price equals marginal cost (P = MC), the long-run equilibrium condition under perfect competition. While the monopolist would want to set the price at the level of P_m, where marginal cost equals marginal revenue (MC = MR), the regulator[7] would want to set the price near P_{pc} or at the most where price equals average cost (P = AC) thus allowing a fair return to the monopolist provider of infrastructure services.[8] This will make the viability calculations harder with tariff risk. Regulatory assets, in the case of Delhi power distribution companies (discoms), are a manifestation of regulatory risks.

This, however, is a rather stylized analysis. Utility tariffs are a political issue. Infrastructure services have to be paid for either from the government budget or by the users. Historically, utility tariffs have been used to subsidize certain sections of society (poor), specific industries or public sector entities. More often, tariffs are not charged (power consumption in agriculture), charged at very low rates or not collected (arms of the government). PPPs will necessitate formal arrangements with the project company for government subsidies in lieu of supplies to these favored groups. In the long run, it is a positive change with enhanced transparency, but not without challenges on the way.[9] However, for this transition to happen, political will is needed from the highest level.

On the other hand, there may be a single utility buyer or a limited number of large offtakers, in which case the interface between the project company and its client is ostensibly easier to define and manage. Also, supplying to bulk consumers may be considerably less risky[10] than supplying to retail consumers—the experience of Indian power sector bears this out in that most private investment in the power sector has come into generation rather than distribution.

However, it is necessary to realize that bulk supplies may not be able to shield the PPP concessionaire for long from commercial risk if retail supplies

---

[7]The regulator would try to mimic the outcomes of a perfectly competitive market (Price = P_{pc}) in the absence of such markets.

[8]Pratap (2011).

[9]Delmon (2010).

[10]Risk is lower owing to lower revenue risk, including collection risk and credit risk of offtakers. Selling to bulk consumers also allows long-term, financially viable offtake arrangements (Power Purchase Agreements in the power sector) to protect investors from demand and market risks. Typically, there would be a capacity charge related to availability of the power project to compensate the power producer for the fixed costs. There would also be a fuel charge to compensate for the variable costs.

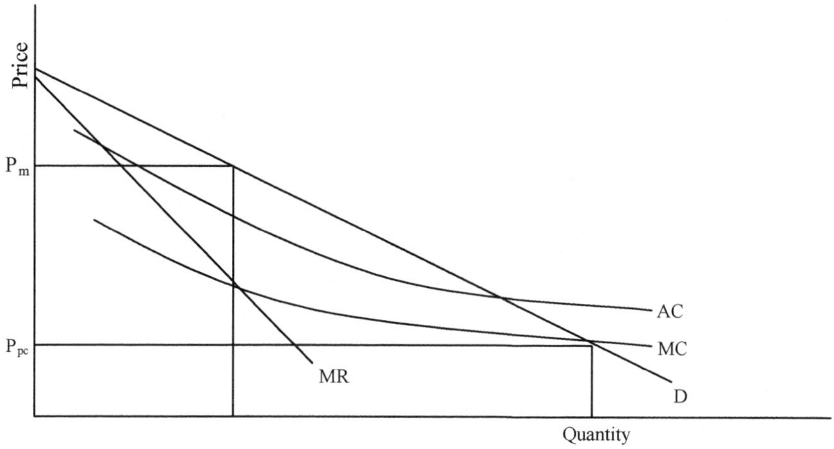

Fig. 1 Tariffs and regulatory risk. *Source* Author's conception

suffer from a high level of such risks. Again in the power sector, money comes into the system from power distribution segment and if this segment is bankrupt, which it is in India, then this will cast a shadow on the entire power value chain, from distribution to transmission to generation. Thus, fresh investments have dried up even in power generation because of bankruptcy of power distribution segment in India.

- *Maintain*—Many PPPs assign lifetime standard maintenance obligations to the private party. When building and maintaining are part of the same contract, it is likely that the incentives of the private sector are such that good inputs are used in building (or rehabilitating) the asset so that whole-of-life costs (including construction and maintenance costs) are optimized. One of the banes of plain vanilla construction contracts is that the contractors use substandard material for building the asset, which they know would not last very long after commissioning of the project. However, this failure would not affect them as they would have delivered on the contract and commensurate payments would have been made. However, building an asset and maintaining it for 30 years or so over the life of the asset would incentivize use of better construction material as the contractors would be expected to maintain the asset over its lifetime and by using better material, the whole-of-life costs would be optimized.
- *Transfer*—This refers to the transfer of assets back to the government at the end of the contract period. This raises a number of issues including maintenance of

the asset near the end of the concession period and the role of the Independent Engineer[11] often causing reluctance on the part of the private sector to accept this clause (as, for instance, in the case of the Standard Bidding Documents that were being developed for the power sector). If there is a "Transfer" clause in the concession agreement, the private sector may want to cut corners in maintenance near the end of the concession period that may have implications on the performance of the asset post-concession period. To ensure against this type of behavior, the Independent Engineer has a major role to play in certifying the condition of the asset near the end of the concession period.

2.3 *The Mode of Payment to the Private Party*

The final feature that can be used in distinguishing PPPs is the source of payment for the private party. For the private party to be able to enter into a PPP arrangement and deliver infrastructure services, there should be dedicated and sustainable revenue streams associated with the project. The revenue streams to the private party can come from the government or directly from users, or a combination of the two.

Examples of revenues coming from the Government budget are "availability" payments like annuities in the road sector depending on the asset or service being available of a contractually defined quality; or fixed charges paid as per the power purchase agreement by public sector power distribution companies (thus addressing demand risk). Then there could be output-based payments for services delivered to users—"shadow toll" road that is free for users, but for which the government pays a fee per user (thus addressing payment risk).

User tolls in toll roads, electricity tariffs for retail consumers, and tuition fees for educational institutions are examples of user fees servicing the private PPP investment.

Combining the two options of government pays and users pays, tolls (user fees) can be supplemented by subsidies paid by government thereby lowering the user charges, which may be performance-based (annuity payments conditional on the availability of service of a particular quality) or output-based (payments per user or shadow tolls).

The certainty, size, and nature of the revenue stream depend on its source. For instance, a government pays PPP will have lower collection risk. Shadow tolls may mitigate payment risk that may be associated with infrastructure provisioning in difficult law and order environments.

[11]A specialist firm who monitors construction and operation and approves completion of milestones, amongst other things.

3 Classifying PPPs in Terms of Contractual Agreements

The three broad parameters for classification of PPP contracts described above, i.e., type of asset—new or existing; functions that the PPP is responsible for—design, build, finance, operate, maintain, and transfer; and the mode of payment to the private party—whether by the Government or users, can be combined in various ways, to create a wide range of PPP contractual agreements. The figure below provides some examples.

As shown in Fig. 2, PPP contracts can be thought of as a continuum between purely public and purely private provisioning of infrastructure—transferring increasing responsibilities and risk to the private sector. Thus, PPPs fill the space between completely public sector-owned and operated projects and full privatization. PPPs are, however, not the only way the private sector can be involved in infrastructure—Fig. 2 also includes examples of arrangements (like full divestiture) that would usually not be considered a PPP.

3.1 *The Standard PPP Models*

As shown in Fig. 2, there can be a range of PPP contractual agreements. Figure 3 provides a schema to think of some of these arrangements in terms of the three parameters discussed.

We shall discuss each of them in turn.

3.1.1 Operation and Maintenance (O&M) or Management contract

As shown in Fig. 3, this is one of the most rudimentary forms of private sector participation (PSP) in infrastructure. This may be resorted to in the initial period when the business environment (read political environment) may not be conducive

Fig. 2 PPPs fill the space between purely public and purely private provisioning of infrastructure services. *Source* Delmon (2010). *Understanding options for public–private partnerships in infrastructure* (http://documents.worldbank.org/curated/en/999661468323693635/pdf/WPS5173.pdf)

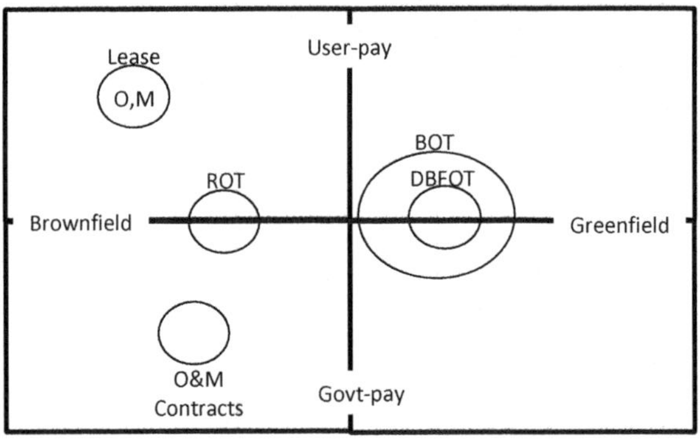

Fig. 3 A schema for understanding various PPP contractual agreement structures

for deeper forms of PSP. In this model, the private party manages a state-owned enterprise for a predetermined period, without having ownership and making investment decisions. In terms of the fundamental characteristics of PPP contracts discussed above:

- Type of Asset: Existing Infrastructure
- Functions Transferred: Operation & Maintenance—Typically most operational staff maintain their public sector employee status
- Payment mechanism: Government pays—usually a fixed component plus a performance-related payment.

What the typical O&M contract does is to enable private sector efficiencies in O&M functions thereby reducing AT&C losses in the power sector and decreasing non-revenue water in the water sector, for example.

O&M contracts for existing assets, like those associated with power and water distribution, may come under the definition of PPP where these are performance-based (failure to achieve performance parameters may entail penalties), and long-term (sometimes also called performance-based maintenance contracts). Thus, an O&M contract for 5 years for the water distribution system in the area served by New Delhi Municipal Council, as is being contemplated, would be classified as a PPP as it has penalties associated with failure to meet Non-Revenue Water (NRW) reduction targets.

3.1.2 Lease or Affermage or Franchise contract

Under this arrangement, Government leases the assets to a private operator for a fee. Private operator is responsible for O&M and therefore takes on the operational risk. In addition, the private sector is also responsible for revenue collection from users. So this model is similar to an "O&M contract" in that the government typically remains responsible for capital expenditure. In terms of the fundamental characteristics:

- Type of Asset: Existing Infrastructure;
- Functions Transferred: Operate and Maintain, providing services to users;
- Payment mechanism: User pays—private party usually passes on a part of user fees to government, to take care of capital spending.

One of the segments where franchise arrangements have been tried in India is in the power distribution sector. For instance, Bhiwandi, in the Indian state of Maharashtra, is the first large-scale franchise in the country and became operational in 2007. Torrent Power Limited is the private sector franchise operator. The billing efficiency[12] and collection efficiency[13] of the project improved dramatically after private sector participation—the former rose from 55 to 82% as shown in Fig. 4; while the latter improved from 68 to 99%. The net result was a sharp reduction in Aggregate Technical & Commercial (AT&C) losses[14] that came down dramatically from 62 to 18% in just 5 years. Customer service also improved through the setting up of a 24 * 7 control room and fault attendance center, and call center facility for

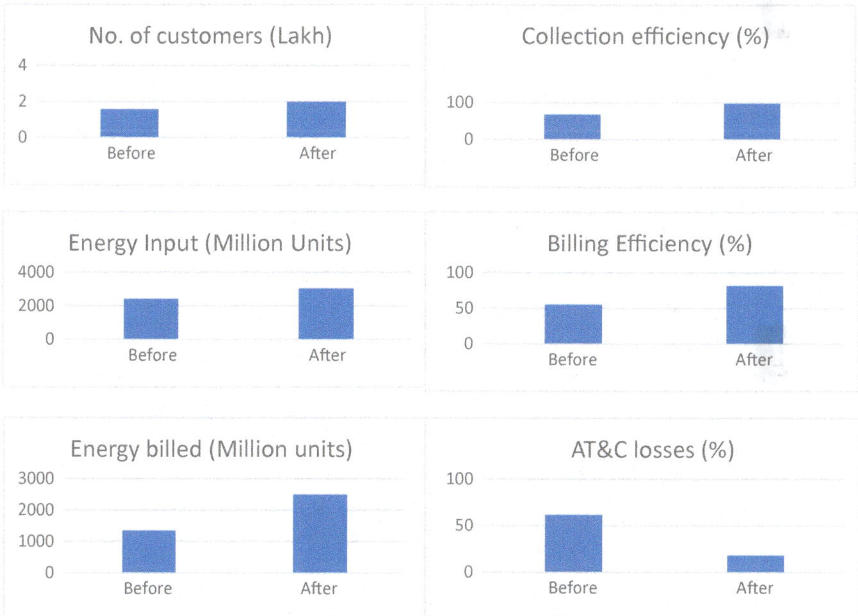

Fig. 4 Performance indicators for power distribution in Bhiwandi before (2005–2006) and after (2010–2011) private sector participation

[12]Billing Efficiency: Amount billed in kWh/ Energy Input into the system in kWh.

[13]Collection Efficiency: Amount realized in rupees/ Amount billed in rupees.

[14]Aggregate Technical & Commercial (AT&C) losses is the percent of electricity for which the utility does not receive payments and may be calculated as 1 − (Billing efficiency * Collection efficiency).

power-related complaints, as well as the introduction of mobile customer service vans and user-friendly electricity bills.

3.1.3 Build–Operate–Transfer (BOT) contract

The BOT contract is an advanced form of PSP where the private sector builds the asset, operates it for the concession period and transfers the asset back to the public authority at the end of the concession period. The contracting agency specifies the project requirements based on the Detailed Project Report (DPR). There may be risk-sharing between the public and the private sectors on the basis of a model concession agreement.

In terms of the fundamental characteristics of PPP contracts discussed above:

- Type of Asset: New Infrastructure
- Functions Transferred
  - Building the project (cost of construction)
  - Operating it for the concession period (expenditure on annual maintenance)
  - Transferring it back to the public authority at the end of the concession period
- Payment mechanism: User fee or government budget.

Under a BOT contract, the private company operates the project assets until they are transferred to the public authority at the end of the contract. Build–Own–Operate–Transfer (BOOT) is often used interchangeably with BOT.

- *Variants of Build–Operate–Transfer (BOT) Contract*

There could be variants of the BOT contract in terms of how the private investment is serviced. If it is serviced through user fees, it would be a *BOT (Toll)* contract. If it is serviced by government payments, it would be a *BOT (Annuity)* contract.

As would be apparent, in a BOT (Toll) contract, the traffic risk falls on the private partner as the investment is serviced through toll revenues. The quantum of toll revenues is determined through the traffic on the road. To mitigate the traffic risk falling on the private partner, a variation of the BOT project in the form of BOT (Annuity) may be used. This contract mitigates traffic risk falling on the private partner as the project revenues do not depend on the traffic volume but on the competitively bid annuity payments. Here also, the private sector meets the entire cost of construction and annual maintenance. In such contracts, no grant (Viability Gap Funding) is paid by the contracting agency, unlike BOT (Toll) contracts. The private sector recovers the investment through competitively bid availability-based annual annuity payments made by the contracting agency. The government retains the right to levy a user fee on the beneficiaries of the facility. BOT (Annuity) projects are similar to Private Finance Initiative (PFI) of the UK. Appropriate structuring of BOT (toll and annuity) projects can help capture the benefits arising out of allocation of construction and maintenance risks to the concessionaire.[15]

Often a combination of the two is used with a one-time capital grant provided by the contracting agency over and above toll collections to make the project viable (in India, the viability gap funding scheme determines the extent of capital grant). This capital grant may be made the bidding parameter to conserve fiscal resources.

Another combination of the user fee [BOT (Toll)] and availability-based PPP [BOT (Annuity)] is what is known as "shadow tolls" in PPP road projects, where the public sector pays, based on usage of road by drivers.

India, which has seen the second highest number of PPP projects and associated investments in the developing world,[16] with road sector projects being the primary constituent of the PPP program, has built its PPP program on the basis of standardized model concession agreements, with both variants of BOT contracts [BOT (Toll) and BOT (Annuity)] popular in the road sector.

3.1.4 Hybrid Annuity Model (HAM) contract

This model has recently been introduced in the Indian road sector for rejuvenating stalled projects. It is a combination of Engineering–Procurement–Construction (EPC) and BOT contracts, with government and private companies sharing total project cost in a 40:60 ratio (which gives the model its hybrid characteristic). Toll on the project would be collected by the government, and a fixed amount yearly (which gives the model its annuity characteristic, with a profit margin, will be given to the private concessionaire).

The objective of the model is to reduce the financial burden on the PPP concessionaire during project implementation. Projects bid out on the basis of HAM would have land acquisition and environmental/forest clearances (just like BOT projects). There is considerable risk mitigation for the private sector in HAM projects—payment risk, traffic risk, financing risk (40% of total project cost), and inflation and interest rate risks are borne by the public sector. HAM projects are expected to boost PPPs in the road sector.

The 14 lane Delhi–Dasna stretch of NH 24 (49 km) at a cost of Rs. 28.24 billion was Government of India's first project to be awarded under the HAM model. All the 21 HAM projects awarded since January 2016 have gone to small and mid-sized firms as the bigger firms are already highly leveraged and have little capacity to implement new projects. The firms that have bagged HAM projects include APCO Infratech, Sadbhav Infrastructure, MBL Infrastructure, and Welspun Enterprises.

---

[15]Pratap (2011).

[16]India is second to China in terms of number of projects and second to Brazil in terms of PPP investments as per the Private Participation in Infrastructure database of the World Bank (ppi.worldbank.org).

3.1.5 Build–Own–Operate (BOO) contract

In this model, government grants the right to design, build, finance, operate, and maintain a project to a private entity like in the BOT model. However, where this model differs from BOT is that the private entity is not required to transfer the facility back to the government at end of the concession period—private entity retains ownership of the project for an indefinite period (perpetuity). Many of the existing power generation projects have been bid out on BOO basis and there is resistance to the introduction of BOT model (with its 'Transfer' function) in the power sector.

From a project finance perspective, it makes little difference whether returns after about 30 years are considered while assessing BOO projects (discounted present value of returns after 30 years would be minuscule). However, the land on which the infrastructure facility is situated may become very valuable after 30 years and state governments may want it back after the concession period, especially if it is given free by the state government for setting up the infrastructure facility.

3.1.6 Design–Build–Finance–Operate–Transfer (DBFOT) contract

In this model, the contracting agency lays out the core project requirements based on a feasibility study. Bidders are encouraged to use innovative designs while remaining accountable for performance. In terms of the fundamental characteristics of PPP contracts discussed above:

- Type of Asset: New infrastructure as a brownfield project may not be amenable to new design, i.e., there is path dependence associated with brownfield projects.
- Functions Transferred: As suggested by name (DBFOT).
- Payment mechanism: User fee or government budget.

3.1.7 Rehabilitate–Operate–Transfer (ROT) contract

Brownfield projects like an existing water supply system would need to be rehabilitated (through capital expenditure) and would be operated over the concession period, at the end of which the system would have to be handed back to the public authority. As we have seen, brownfield projects are subject to legacy issues, employee issues, and the condition of the assets may be uncertain. These factors increase risks and therefore make such projects relatively unattractive for the private sector. In terms of the fundamental characteristics of PPP contracts discussed above:

- Type of Asset: Existing Infrastructure.
- Functions Transferred: The private party is responsible for rehabilitation, upgrading, or extension of existing assets; Other functions same as BOT.
- Payment mechanism: User fee or government budget.

3.1.8 Concession

"Concession" is used for a wide range of contracts. In the PPP setting, it generally refers to a "user pay" project. Brazilian law defines it that way. In contrast, Chile uses the term to include "government pays" projects as well.[17]

3.2 *Beyond Standard Models*[18]

Notwithstanding their significant range, the standard PPP models described above may not work in some situations and sectors. PPP procurement process is often long and expensive, making it unsuitable for small projects or those with a short lead time (like in an emergency). Standard PPP contracts are quite long-lived (a BOT (Toll) road contract in India is typically for 30 years) and relative uncertainty about costs implies that a contract should be negotiated upfront and some flexibility in costs may be provided for long-term sustainability of such contracts. Though there are "Change of Scope" clauses in standard PPP contracts, changing service requirements in a standard PPP project at a later stage often comes at a significant cost. For all these reasons, while the above contract types are widely used, many of the less commonly used models are described below.

The PPP models described below illustrate that no one model addresses all infrastructure issues and there is a need to accommodate differing extents of risk, transaction cost, and procurement time. With time, new hybrid models will continue to emerge to tackle the needs, as opposed to traditional pigeon-hole classifications.

3.2.1 Design–Build

Here government sets its requirements and contracts with a private partner to design and build a facility according to these requirements. After completion, government operates and maintains the facility. This is also called Build–Transfer (BT) model and is akin to the Engineering–Procurement–Construction (EPC) contract used in India. However, since the facility is neither operated nor maintained by the private sector, there are limited benefits to the government in terms of incentives for good workmanship by the private sector.

---

[17]World Bank (2014).

[18]Deloitte *Closing the Infrastructure Gap. The Role of Public–Private Partnerships* (http://www.cnrs.fr/aquitaine/IMG/pdf/closing_the_infrastructure_gap.pdf).

3.2.2 Design–Build–Maintain

This model is similar to Design–Build except that maintenance is a private sector responsibility here. Public sector retains responsibility for operations. Since 'Maintain' function has also been transferred to the private sector, it is expected that whole-of-life costs would be optimized by it by incentivizing the use of good material in the "Build" phase.

But there could be a possibility of blame game owing to divided responsibility between the public and the private sectors for operation and maintenance functions, respectively. This is not a remote possibility as apparent from the failed Delhi Airport Metro PPP where the private operator (Reliance Infra) and the public sector builder of some assets (DMRC) had a running feud about the quality of workmanship impacting the private sector operations function.

3.2.3 Hybrid PPP Models—Alliancing

In this model, designing, developing, and financing of the project is done jointly by the two parties. Sometimes, even building, maintaining, and operating are also done jointly. In cases where there are unknown technological risks, an alliancing model can allow projects to proceed. The goal here is collaboration rather than an adversarial relationship. This model works particularly well in defence with large and indivisible projects frequently with innovative outputs.

3.2.4 Hybrid PPP Models—Bundling

Bundling implies entering into multiple project contracts with one partner. This helps reduce the procurement and transaction costs which can be quite high, proportionally speaking, for small projects. It has been used in Ireland as well as in the school sector in India.

3.2.5 Hybrid PPP Models—Competitive Partnership

In this model, in some ways opposite to bundling, a project is broken down into different parts and these subprojects are contracted out among a set of private partners with the contract allowing for potential reallocation of projects among partners later by the public sector. Public partner can also set the cost and quality of other partners' output as a benchmark for all partners in the project (competitive benchmarking). This would impart some flexibility to the work assignment based on performance of individual contractors, which cannot happen in conventional PPP procurement based on standard models.

3.2.6 Hybrid PPP Models—Incremental Partnership

In this model, the public sector enters into a contract with a private partner, according to which certain parts of the project can be called off later if considered unnecessary. Analogously work can also be commissioned incrementally and possibly to alternative partners. This avoids the problems of irreversibility connected with a one-time commitment of large-scale project contract.

3.2.7 Hybrid PPP Models—Integrator

In this model, while the public sector contracts with a single private sector partner, the latter, the integrator, breaks up the project into subcomponents and contracts out to other private sector providers. The integrator remains responsible for overall project outcomes but plays a less direct role in project execution to avoid conflict of interest.

3.3 Using Appropriate PPP Models

The level of certainty and clarity that the public sector has about its requirements should essentially drive the choice of models. When one can define the project well (high level of certainty in the desired output), government can transfer substantial control and risk to the private sector using standard models, like BOT, DBFOT, etc. Hybrid models like alliancing or incremental partnership work better when a low level of certainty exists (e.g., social infrastructure, unknown technological risks).

In the next section, we take a close look at the travails of a PPP project (using lease contract) in a critical service in a developing country to develop an understanding of the complexities and challenges involved in such projects and contracts.

4 Case Study: Dar es Salaam Water and Sewerage Services Lease Contract

Project Description: In February 2003, the Government of Tanzania (GOT) awarded the provision of water and sewerage services in the area served by Dar es Salaam Water and Sewerage Authority (DAWASA) to City Water Services Ltd (CWS) under a 10-year lease contract.[19] DAWASA's service area included the city of Dar es Salaam, coastal towns of Kibaha and Bagamoyo, and settlements along the two transmission mains of Upper and Lower Ruvu (a river). DAWASA

[19]Pratap (2011).

had about 100,000 direct water customers and 22,000 sewerage customers. Biwater Gauff (Tanzania) Limited, BGT, an 80–20 joint venture between British Biwater International Limited and German HP Gauff Ingenieure GmbH and Co held 51% stake in CWS, the operating company. In February 2003, the Super Doll Trailer Manufacture Co. (T) Limited (STM) became the local partner in CWS with a 49% stake. CWS took over the provision of services in August 2003.

CWS had signed three contracts with DAWASA: the 10-year lease contract, the Supply and Installation of Plant and Equipment Contract (SIPE), and the Contract for the Procurement of Goods (POG). By the terms of the lease contract, City Water was to lease certain specified DAWASA assets and use them to provide water and sewerage services to DAWASA's pipeline network customers. Billing and tariff collections were the responsibility of City Water as well. Ownership of assets stayed with DAWASA and City Water was required to pay monthly rent to DAWASA for their use.

The lease contract explicitly fixed the customer tariff for the first 5-year contract in real terms, which comprised three components: Operator Tariff, Lessor Tariff, and the First Time New Domestic Water Supply Connection Tariff. The rates changed annually using an indexation formula to take into account inflation and exchange rate movements. On August 12, 2004, City Water was granted an adjustment on this basis by the Interim Regulator. There were also provisions for annual review, interim review, and major review of tariffs in the lease contract. In the long run, City Water's source of funds would be the Operator Tariff, which was a part of the customer tariff. Under this arrangement, City Water was to bear the commercial risk as its revenues were to come only from bills collected. GOT was to bear the foreign exchange risk.

The SIPE required capital improvements to the major elements of the water system, requiring City Water to install or refurbish pumps at the treatment plants, to draw more water from the upper and lower Ruvu River and, to pump it, after treatment, into the transmission mains to the reservoirs. Repairs and modernization of the transmission mains were also included, mostly in order to reduce leakage.

The POG governed the supply of customer meters to measure water consumption by a household or an institution. Universal metering was the objective. City Water subcontracted the SIPE and POG to BGT, which in turn subcontracted to a South African company Biwater Pty, an affiliate of Biwater Plc.

Initiation and award of contract: The water and sewerage services in Dar es Salaam were in a precarious state at the time the lease contract was signed with City Water Services (February 2003). The system was characterized by high levels of leakage, illegal connections, low billing and collection efficiency, and introduction of service was needed in several densely populated unplanned areas with difficult access. It was estimated that two-third of the piped water was lost to leakages and illegal tapping. Water was provided free till 1991 and low tariffs charged since then was inadequate to cover maintenance or capital expenditures leading to a continued worsening of the system. The water transmission lines had many weak points and could burst anytime. Water processed and distributed by DAWASA was not metered and bills were based on estimates, while only about half of the customers paid their water bills regularly. The situation regarding sewerage was even worse. Only about 10% of the population of Dar es Salaam (total population; 3.5 million) was served by sewerage system. The sewerage infrastructure built in the early 1980s was at various stages of collapse.

The state of the water and sewerage services in the city was having a number of ill-effects: women walked long distances, often more than two miles to fetch water, and sometimes became victims of domestic violence if they were unable to find it; communities waited all day near water taps in the hope of 1 or 2 hours of water supply; poor families spent high percentage of their income to buy water from private vendors; and water quality was suspect, with frequent cholera outbreaks and high infant mortality rate, especially in the city's low-income areas.

Tanzania had decided to address the poor health and economic outcomes of the deteriorating water and sanitation situation in the country by the 1990s. A new National Water Policy was adopted in 1991 with emphasis on decentralization and cost recovery with safety nets for the poor. In urban areas, the National Urban Water Authority (NUWA) was replaced by independent and autonomous local water authorities. In Dar es Salaam, DAWASA replaced NUWA in 1997 by an Act of Parliament, and merged NUWA's water operations with the sewerage operations of the former Dar es Salaam Sewerage and Sanitation Department.[20] Around the same time, Tanzania was also seeking funds from multilateral institutions and some form of private sector participation in DAWASA to bring about an improvement in services. This desire for private participation in water and sewerage sector was part of the wider program of economic reforms and liberalization in the country.

The total cost of rehabilitation and upgrade of the water and sanitation system in Dar es Salaam was pegged at $164.6 million and was funded, in 2003, by the World Bank ($61.5 million IDA credit), the African Development Bank ($48 million loan), and the European Investment Bank ($34 million loan) along with agreed contributions from CWS ($8.5 million) and DAWASA ($12.6 million).

As a condition of the funding from multilateral institutions, Tanzania was obliged to appoint an international private utility operator to operate and maintain the water and sewerage system, and carry out some of the works associated with the project (Dar es Salaam Water Supply and Sanitation Project). Tanzania, after an unsuccessful tender initiated in 1997, invited bids for the project in 2002. The lease contract was awarded through a competitive tender, with lowest tariff being the bidding criterion. Although there were three prequalified bidders [Biwater/Gauff joint venture, Générale des Eaux (France) and Saur International (France)], only one financial bid was ultimately received, that of the Biwater/Gauff joint venture.

In order to provide added comfort to the bidders and in recognition of the poor quality of the available information, the lease contract had an Enhanced Monitoring Period (EMP) that enabled the operating company to collect better data during the first year to year and a half of project implementation, in order to assess and if necessary change base values, and then, if needed, ask for a tariff adjustment.

[20]International Centre for Settlement of Investment Disputes (2008).

As a step towards private participation in the project, the Energy and Water Utilities Regulatory Authority (EWURA) was established in 2001 to regulate the provision of water supply and sanitation services on behalf of Government of Tanzania and audit the private operators in relation to their license. Due to a delay in appointment of its members, the Minister took on the role and functions of EWURA in respect of DAWASA and City Water as the "Interim Regulator", by amending the DAWASA Act in May 2003.[21]

Description of facts and process of cancellation: City Water began providing services in August 2003. However, right from the beginning, serious difficulties began to be experienced by both parties in performing their respective obligations of the lease contract. Overall, however, although City Water made improvements to the water system in difficult operating conditions, and repeatedly emphasized that improvements should not be expected overnight, its performance was viewed as "pretty poor[22]": cash collections deteriorated substantially over the course of the contract period and ended up being worse than that of DAWASA.

The problems arose because of a number of factors:

- CWS did not have monopoly rights over its service area. Before the contract was awarded, many private companies were already licensed to run water supply and sanitation business. Trucks owned by individuals and private companies were delivering clean water to city residents, while others were emptying sewerage tanks. This resulted in potential revenue losses for the water company.
- The performance of Biwater Pty in execution of POG contract (customer metering) was poor. This had an impact on revenue accrual to CWS.
- City Water had planned to introduce a new billing system within 6 months of the commencement to replace the outdated DAWASA system. The billing system was especially important given that revenues of CWS were to come from Operator Tariff. However, the system was replaced only by December 2004 (16 months into the lease contract).
- The Enhanced Monitoring Period allowed in the lease contract was for City Water to collect data, to address known data problems, and re-fix base values. But the data collection did not proceed as planned and City Water was not able to take benefit of the EMP.[23]
- The rapidly deteriorating relationship between BGT and STM added to City Water's woes. STM was refusing to put in more equity into City Water without a bigger say in management, which resulted in a shortfall of the equity that the company was expecting. The poor relationship with STM created management and operational problems for City Water.
- As per the World Bank, Biwater had a patchy record of operating smaller versions of such "lease contracts" in other countries—including South Africa,

[21]International Centre for Settlement of Investment Disputes (2008).

[22]Dr. Tony Ballance, the expert mediator in the 2005 renegotiation of the project.

[23]International Centre for Settlement of Investment Disputes (2008).

Mexico, and Britain—and had placed an inexperienced team to lead the Dar es Salaam operation.[24] The last point was acknowledged by Adrian White, the majority shareholder of Biwater, when he noted in early 2005 that "Our City Water staffing was totally with non-Biwater staff with a weak leader, no clear experience or qualified business plan."

In July 2004, after 11 months of operations, City Water was collecting considerably less than the projected revenue, which was also way below the performance by DAWASA just prior to awarding the lease contract. City Water concluded that financial viability required a review of the lease contract and a rise in the Operator Tariff. So the company pushed for a review pointing out that operating realities were at odds with the ones projected. In particular, CWS pointed out the following:

- The operating costs, especially those for local staff, exceeded those assumed in the economic evaluation of the project and the determination of the base Operator Tariff used in the contract.
- The failure of government agencies to pay their water/sewerage bills.
- The assumed volume of water available for distribution in Dar es Salaam was not in line with bid expectations.

Pricewaterhouse Coopers (PwC) was appointed auditor to determine "whether there are reasonable grounds for interim review of tariff as provided for in the lease contract." In its final report on November 26, 2004 PwC opined that no tariff adjustment was warranted after evaluating the nine possible events City Water had proposed. On water availability, PwC report concluded that there was insufficient data to make the case. On significant increase in staff costs and nonpayment by government agencies, it concluded that these matters were beyond the scope of the grounds for an interim review as per the lease contract.

DAWASA also had complaints against CWS: nonpayment of lease rent and Lessor Tariff; using collections of the First Time New Domestic Water Supply Connection Tariff that should have been held in trust for making connections to poor domestic customers; substantial delays in SIPE and POG; and lack of improvement in collection performance.

In January 2005, a formal request for renegotiation of the lease contract was made by City Water as it was suffering from financial distress and needed radical changes to the lease contract in order to survive and be financially viable. Given that, since January 2004, City Water had not been remitting the full collections of Lessor Tariff and had not been paying DAWASA the full monthly lease rent, DAWASA's financial position was also in a very precarious state. However, there was no compromise among the parties and the renegotiations failed. As had been announced by DAWASA at the beginning of the renegotiation process, this failure, in turn, necessarily implied the termination of the lease contract.

---

[24]The Guardian (2007).

Therefore, following the failure of renegotiations, in May 2005, the Tanzanian government terminated the 10-year contract with City Water, claiming the company had made less than half the required investment (US $4.1 million out of US $8.5 million), had failed to meet revenue collection targets or improve water supply services, and attain other performance conditions described in the contract. As per a newspaper report, "not only was the company unable to meet revenue collection targets agreed in the contract… At the same time, though, the people of the capital saw their water bills rising… yet there had been no discernible improvement in supply, reliability and quality."[25]

On May 16, 2005, the entire amount of the performance bond submitted by City Water in connection with the lease contract was called in. On June 1, 2005, City Water's senior management was deported, and representatives of the government and DAWASA seized the company's assets, installed a new management [Dar es Salaam Water and Sewerage Corporation (DAWASCO), the newly formed Government entity] and took over City Water's business.[26]

Post-cancellation status: Biwater filed for arbitration over the cancelled water contract contending that termination was illegal and demanded compensation for alleged expropriation of its investment. However, the Tribunal, International Centre for Settlement of Investment Disputes (ICSID), was of the opinion that "BGT had seriously underestimated the amplitude of the task. It had submitted a poorly structured bid, and then failed to perform as anticipated … with the consequence that it encountered serious financial problems at a very early stage."[27] ICSID opined that with a shareholders' equity of less than negative USD 8 million by May 2005, and not being capable of paying its bills, City Water was subject to winding up at the instance of any of its creditors. So "termination of the Lease Contract was inevitable."[28]

The opinion of ICSID was reflected in the nil "fair market value" of City Water assessed by ICSID at the date of the expropriation, June 1, 2005. Thus, while ICSID conceded that Tanzania acted in violation of the UK-Tanzania Bilateral Investment Treaty, it dismissed BGT's claims for damages in the final award dated July 24, 2008.[29]

In a separate case, the arbitration panel of the London-based United Nations Commission on International Trade Law (UNCITRAL), ruled in favor of the Tanzanian government in January 2008. City Water had to pay £3 million damages to Tanzania, and £500,000 toward legal costs.[30]

The new entity, the state-owned Dar es Salaam Water and Sewerage Corporation (DAWASCO), took over City Water's responsibilities in June 2005. The World

[25]The Guardian (2007).

[26]International Centre for Settlement of Investment Disputes (2008).

[27]International Centre for Settlement of Investment Disputes (2008).

[28]International Centre for Settlement of Investment Disputes (2008).

[29]International Centre for Settlement of Investment Disputes (2008).

[30]The Guardian (2008).

Bank continued its loan for the project despite the change in operator. Since the time DAWASCO has taken over operations, revenue collection is up, costs have been cut, and a new billing system has been put in place. However, problems of mismatch between collections and costs remain: DAWASCO collects only about 1.6 billion Tanzanian shillings a month, while its operations cost 2.2 billion, and this has forced the government to pick up the tab more than once.[31]

[31]Reuters (2008).

Chapter 6
Sectoral Distribution and Sector-Specific Issues for Infrastructure PPPs

In this chapter, we look at the distribution of infrastructure PPP projects across major sectors—both in India and around the world—in the first section. In the second section, we delve deeper into few of the sectors to develop an appreciation of some of the key sector-specific issues that are likely to affect projects in that sector. The third section will look at issues of infrastructure PPPs in the social sector. The fourth and final sector will provide a case study of the roller coaster experience of Mexico in trying out PPP in its road sector, to provide an understanding of the real-life challenges of a single sector in an emerging market country.

1 The Sectoral Distribution of Infrastructure PPP Projects Around the World

The Private Participation in Infrastructure (PPI) database (http://ppi.worldbank.org/), a World Bank product, highlights the contractual arrangements used to attract private investment, sources and destination of investment flows, and information on the main investors. It provides individual project information with PPI and summary information on the number of PPI Projects and their associated investments. The purpose of the database is to identify and disseminate information on PPI in low- and middle-income countries. The database helps the discussion on private infrastructure provision by supplying critical data and analysis to government policymakers, as well as other stakeholders. Figure 1 summarizes the sectoral distribution of the number of PPI projects and their associated investments in the quarter century since 1990 in developing countries.

As Fig. 1 shows, over 6500 PPI projects reached financial closure in developing countries in the period 1990–2015 accounting for an investment of about \$2.4 trillion. Telecommunication accounts for highest private investment among sectors ($\sim$43%) and water and sewerage accounts for the least ($\sim$3%). This is largely

K.V. Pratap and R. Chakrabarti, *Public-Private Partnerships in Infrastructure*,
India Studies in Business and Economics, DOI 10.1007/978-981-10-3355-1_6

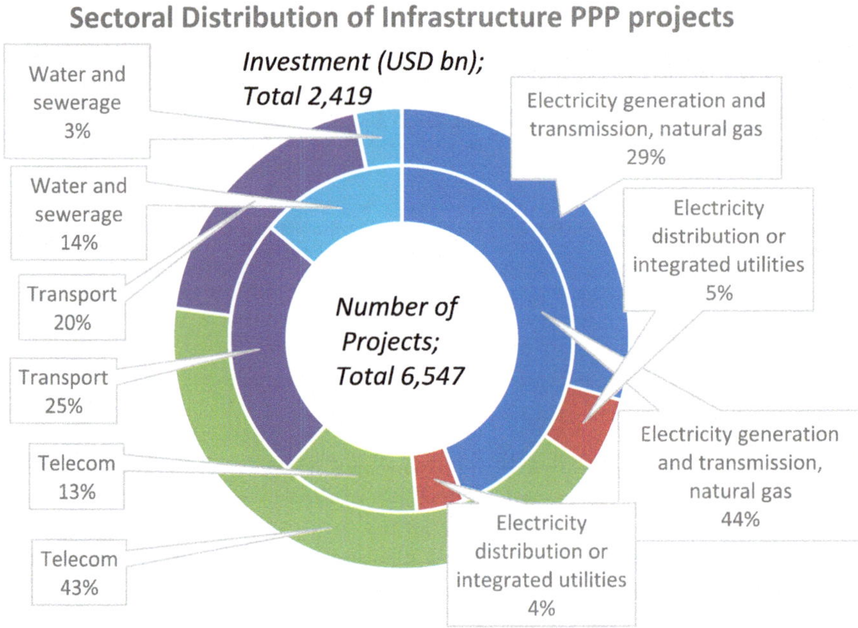

Fig. 1 Private participation in infrastructure (1990–2015) in developing countries. *Note* Only those projects have been considered that have reached financial closure. *Source* Private Participation in Infrastructure database (http://ppi.worldbank.org) (viewed on January 10, 2016)

attributed to sector viability (see Fig. 2) and the associated political sensitivity. In terms of the number of projects, the energy sector accounts for the highest number of projects (49%). Here also, most of the projects are in generation and not in distribution where political economy concerns are the highest.

As Fig. 2 shows, telecommunication tends to be an exception to the generally poor cost recovery in infrastructure. This, in many ways, determines sector attractiveness for the private sector. Private sector is more willing to invest in mobile telephones, power generation plants, and container terminals where the political economy issues relating to tariff increases are the lowest. Under recovery of costs impairs the financial health of utilities and slows the pace of their service expansion, creating problems for universal coverage and invariably it is the poorer segments of the population that gets rationed out.

1.1 PPP—Regional Spread and Key Sponsors

Figure 3 shows the regional distribution of Private Participation in Infrastructure by investment. Latin America and Caribbean (LAC) region has the highest investment among the six developing country regions identified by the World Bank.

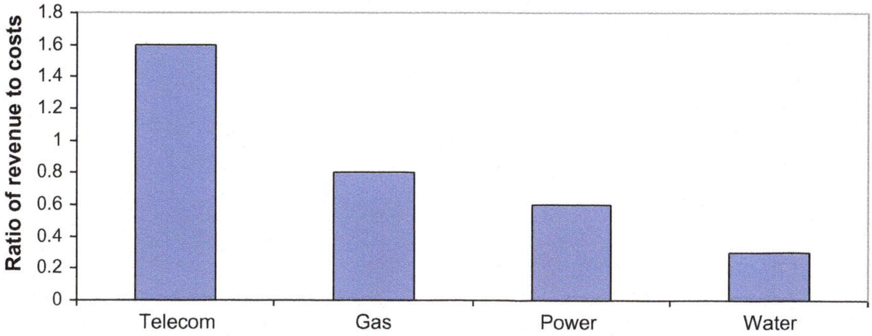

Fig. 2 Cost recovery in infrastructure sectors. *Source* World Bank (1994)

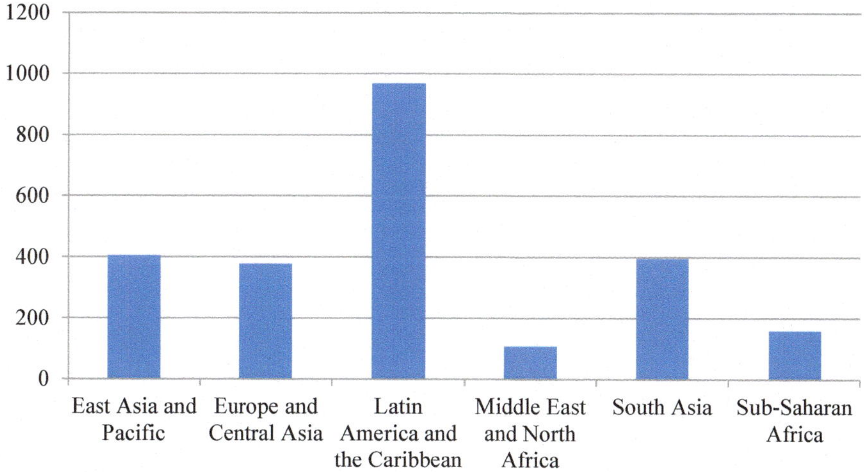

Fig. 3 PPI investment by region ($ billion). *Source* Private Participation in Infrastructure database (http://ppi.worldbank.org)

Sub-Saharan Africa (SSA) region has about the lowest investment because of low per capita income as well as other structural constraints of the region like political instability.

It is also relevant to note that the South Asia region is also an important player in the PPP market. The main contribution here is that of India that has the second highest number of PPP projects and investments among all developing countries (see Fig. 4).

Figure 4 shows Private Participation in Infrastructure (PPI) in selected countries in terms of investment and number of projects. As already stated, India is second both by investment and number of PPP projects among all developing countries. With regard to PPI investments, India is the second to Brazil and with regard to

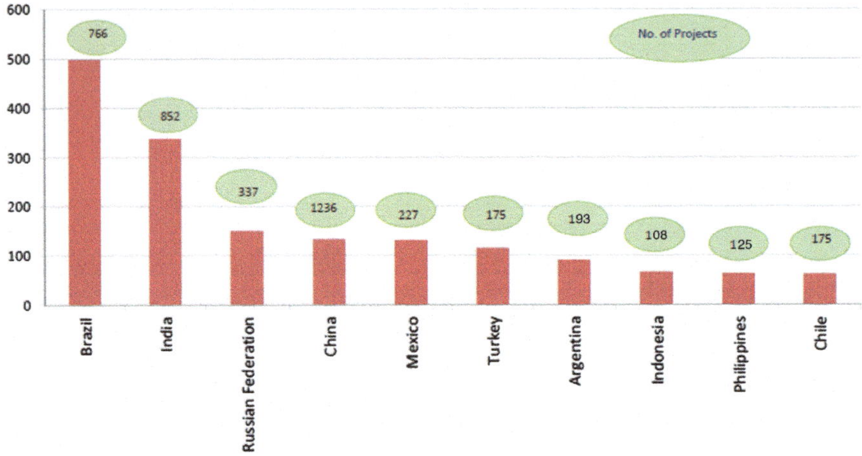

Fig. 4 PPI by country—investments ($ billion) and number of projects. *Source* Private Participation in Infrastructure database (http://ppi.worldbank.org)

Table 1 Top 10 sponsors by investment and primary sector (US$ million)

Sponsor	Total investment	Energy	Telecom	Transport	Water and sewerage
America Movil	104,202	0	104,202	0	0
Telefonica SA	97,434	0	97,434	0	0
Vodafone	44,942	0	44,942	0	0
SUEZ	41,491	26,762	0	280	14,449
Bharti Airtel Limited	39,581	0	39,581	0	0
Telecom Italia	39,578	0	39,578	0	0
TeliaSonera	39,313	0	39,313	0	0
Telenor	36,563	0	36,563	0	0
Reliance ADA Group	34,581	13,989	14,967	5,625	0
Telemar Participacoes SA	31,365	0	31,365	0	0

Source Private Participation in Infrastructure database (http://ppi.worldbank.org)

number of projects, India is the second to China. Significantly, the BRIC countries top of the developing world in PPI as well.

Tables 1 and 2 show the top project sponsors by investment and number of projects, respectively. As shown in Fig. 1, the telecom sector accounts for the highest private investment among all infrastructure sectors; so it is natural that telecom companies will dominate the list of private companies by investment: 9 of the top 10 project sponsors in Table 1 are telecom companies. These are mainly multinational telecom companies operating in a sector where political economy

Table 2 Top 10 sponsors by number of projects and primary sector

Sponsor	Total	Energy	Telecom	Transport	Water and sewerage
SUEZ	111	53	0	2	56
AES corporation	76	76	0	0	0
NWS Holdings Limited	69	5	0	45	19
Xinao Gas Holdings Limited	64	64	0	0	0
Veolia Environment	52	7	0	0	45
Odebrecht SA	42	7	0	13	22
Beijing Sound Environment Industry Group	36	2	0	0	34
Hutchison Whampoa Ltd	36	0	8	28	0
Hong Kong and China Gas Company	34	32	0	0	2
Reliance ADA Group	33	18	2	13	0

Source Private Participation in Infrastructure database (http://ppi.worldbank.org)

concerns are the least owing to the high-cost recovery in the sector (see Fig. 2). An important handicap that multinational companies face in provision of infrastructure is the perception that foreign investors are profiting from supplying these essential services. However, with high-cost recovery in the telecom sector that handicap does not play out too significantly. The sector where political economy concerns are the most pronounced is the water and sewerage sector and we find that there is only one company (Suez) figuring among the top ten that operates in the sector. The top 10 list includes two Indian companies: Bharti Airtel Limited and Reliance ADA Group. The former is in telecom, while the latter is a diversified group.

Table 2 provides the top 10 players in terms of number of projects. Given that energy has the highest number of projects (see Fig. 1), it is unsurprising that energy companies dominate the list of top sponsors by number of projects: 9 of the 10 top sponsors have projects in the energy sector. Only one Indian company makes the list (Reliance ADA Group).

1.2 *Emergence of Local Investors in Developing Countries*

As we have seen above, many of the top project sponsors are multinational companies from developed countries. But foreign investment in basic infrastructure services is not viewed too kindly especially in underpriced sectors like water—foreign investment in these sectors is subject to heightened political risks. Also foreign investors are more likely to use foreign financing where there would be foreign exchange risk as revenues in most infrastructure sectors are denominated in local currency. For these reasons and more, one recent feature of the private infrastructure markets in low- and middle-income countries has been the increased role of domestic investors—seen in countries such as India, Mexico, and Brazil.

Local and regional investors are starting to fill the gap created by large multinational companies from developed countries retreating from big infrastructure projects in emerging markets—especially when the economic environment deteriorates and becomes riskier like in the wake of the Global Financial Crisis of 2008. In 1998–2006, emerging market investors and operators (EMIOs) were responsible for 44% of private infrastructure investments. Major EMIO investment (32%) came from local companies investing in projects in their own country.[1]

Besides the push factors mentioned above, three possible reasons can explain this trend of growing importance of EMIOs in private participation in infrastructure. First, they build expertise through accumulating experience with infrastructure investments of these firms, frequently as minority partners with investors from developed countries. Second, these companies might be better positioned to understand, and, therefore, deal with issues related to the political economy in infrastructure projects in developing countries. Third, the broadening and deepening of capital markets in developing countries have enabled investors to mobilize more resources.[2]

In the next section, we explore key issues in major sectors of infrastructure PPPs.

2 Sector-Specific Issues in Infrastructure PPPs

2.1 Energy

As shown in Fig. 1, the energy sector accounts for the highest number of PPP projects among all infrastructure sectors. However, as shown in Fig. 1 also, most investment within the energy sector has gone to electricity generation rather than electricity distribution. Electricity generation poses less political economy problems than electricity distribution as generation is a typical business-to-business transaction. Cost under-recovery in distribution makes such investment difficult in this subsector. It has been estimated that there is a loss of about Rs. 1 per unit of electricity sold in India adding up to Rs. 600 billion loss per year.

This huge loss in electricity distribution segment casts its ugly shadow on the entire electricity value chain as money comes into the system through the distribution segment and if that segment is broke, there is no way that the generation segment would be entirely unaffected. Because of this, bank lending to even electricity generation slowed down in the 2012–15 period.

Clearly, the losses in electricity distribution segment are unsustainable. To address this problem, the UDAY (Ujwal Discom Assurance Yojana) scheme for

[1]World Bank (2008).

[2]World Bank (2008).

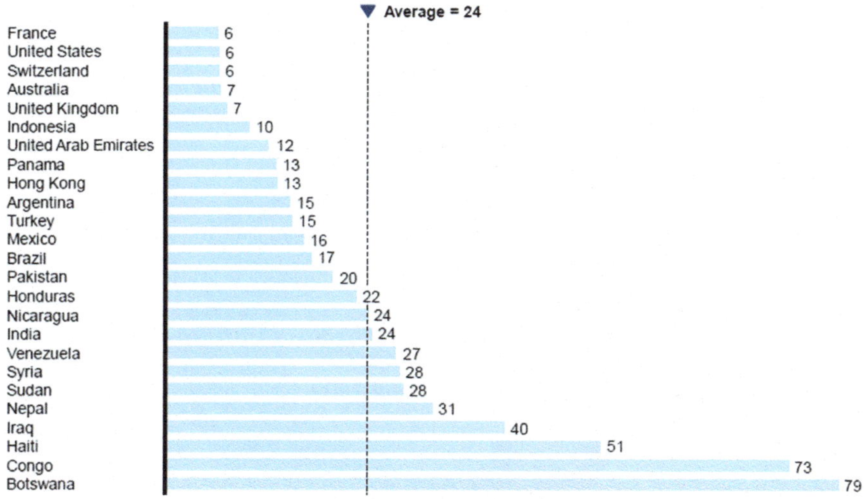

Fig. 5 AT&C losses across the world (%). *Source* Adapted from McKinsey Global Institute (2013)

financial turnaround of power distribution companies has been formulated and launched by the government in November 2015. The scheme envisages reducing interest burden, cost of power, and Aggregate Technical and Commercial (AT&C) losses. Under the UDAY scheme, discoms (distribution companies) and participating states would enter into a tripartite agreement with the Government of India to achieve operational and financial targets as per agreed trajectory.[3]

Another problem area in the electricity sector is the high level of AT&C losses, which has been estimated at 24% for India in Fig. 5. As the figure shows, there are high AT&C losses (>50%) in some developing economies while developed countries like USA, Australia, and UK have single-digit AT&C losses.

Figure 5 also shows that Indonesia has AT&C losses of 10%. India produced 1049 billion units of electricity during 2014–15 out of which the distribution segment received payment for only 0.76 * 1049 billion units. If we are able to reduce AT&C losses to the level of Indonesia, there would be extra revenues of Rs. 0.14 * 1049 billion * Rs. 4 per unit or about Rs. 587 billion, which should be enough to wipe off most of the annual losses of the entire Indian power sector!

There is also the issue of inadequate transmission capacity leading to high AT&C losses in India. Symptoms of inadequate transmission capacity are apparent from the fact that there are no transmission lines to carry about 800 MW wind power from Tamil Nadu, and 7000 MW surplus power from west to south India.

[3]Government of India (Ministry of Finance) (2016).

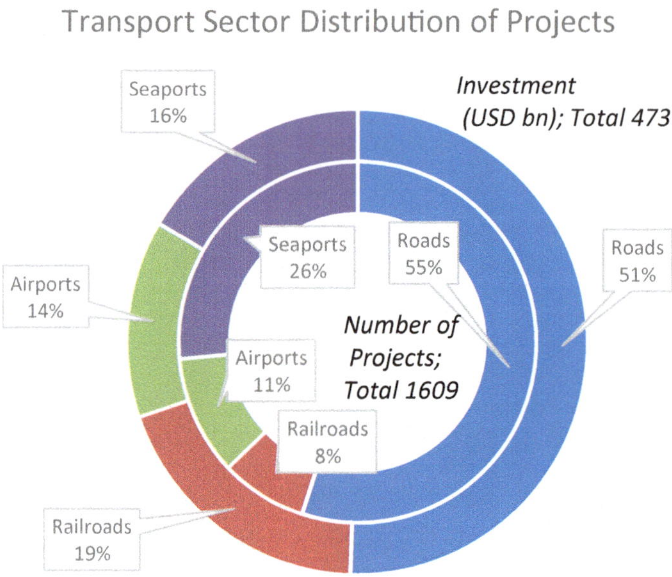

Fig. 6 Private participation in transport infrastructure (1990–2015) in developing countries. *Source* Private Participation in Infrastructure database (http://ppi.worldbank.org)

2.2 *Transport*

(i) *Roads*

Australia's transport sector was among the first to use infrastructure PPPs, with the states of Victoria and New South Wales showing the way with road projects. As shown in Fig. 6, roads account for the highest number of projects (55%) and investments ($\sim$50%) so far as transport infrastructure is concerned. The popularity of PPP in roads is primarily from the growing (but far from universal) public acceptance of associated user fees around the world enabling private financing here than in sectors where the government often has to pay the private sector for the service.[4]

With about 5.2 million km of road network, India has the second largest road network in the world, comprising National Highways, State Highways, and other roads. As of 2015–16, the National Highways (NH) covered 1,00,475 km and carried about 40% of the national road traffic. India has launched a major road development project in the form of the National Highways Development Project (NHDP) connecting the four metros [Delhi–Mumbai–Chennai–Kolkata, called the Golden Quadrilateral Project (NHDP Phase I)], connecting the North–South and East–West extremities of the country (NHDP Phase II) and other phases.

[4]Deloitte. *Closing the Infrastructure Gap: The Role of Public-Private Partnerships* (http://www.cnrs.fr/aquitaine/IMG/pdf/closing_the_infrastructure_gap.pdf).

The objective of the NHDP is capacity upgradation and the requirement that these highways meet minimum standards.[5] PPPs are being actively encouraged in the NHDP.

PPPs in the road sector have encountered a number of hurdles including inadequate land acquisition, and environmental and forest clearances impacting the timeliness in awarding of contracts with the result that the pace of road construction has slowed down considerably in recent years. These factors also adversely affected timely completion of road projects. An example is the Delhi–Jaipur highway project described in the box below.

Box 1: Delhi–Jaipur Highway

The Concession Agreement (CA) for Delhi–Jaipur highway was signed between National Highway Authority of India (NHAI) and Pink City Expressway Private Limited[6] (PCEL) on June 6, 2008. The CA is for construction, operation, and maintenance of the project for a concession period of 12 years (including construction period of 2.5 years). The total project cost was estimated at Rs. 1896 crore.

The project is for six laning (from existing four lanes) of Gurgaon–Kotputli–Jaipur section of National Highway—8 (NH-8) from km 42.70 to km 268.00 (length: 225.30 km) in the states of Haryana (64 km) and Rajasthan (161 km) under National Highways Development Programme (NHDP) Phase V as Build–Operate–Transfer (Toll) on Design–Build–Finance–Operate pattern. The road passes through the important towns of Manesar (km 48), Dharuhera (km 68), and Bawal (km 96), all important industrial hubs in the state of Haryana, and through Behror (km 132), Kotputli (km 155), Paota (km 175), Shahpura (km 200), and Manoharpura (km 211.5) in Rajasthan. Toll plazas exist at three locations: at Bilaspur (km 61), Manoharpur (km 211), and Daulatpur (km 241). The entire project construction work has been divided into six Engineering, Procurement, and Construction (EPC) packages.

The conditions precedent required to be satisfied by NHAI prior to the appointed date (i.e., April 3, 2009) includes the right of way to the site to be provided to the concessionaire, procurement of approval of the railway

[5]On the other hand, the objective of improvement of rural roads, where there are minimal PPPs, is to improve connectivity rather than capacity.

[6]Pink City Expressway Private Limited (PCEL) is a Special Purpose Vehicle company incorporated by M/s Emirates Trading Agency LLC (ETA) and M/s KMC Constructions Ltd (KMC). ETA is the lead member of the consortium with an equity stake of 51%, whereas KMC has 49% equity stake in the SPV. ETA is a part of ETA-ASCON-STAR group, a multinational organization with headquarters in Dubai. The group network encompasses 140 entities and associate offices in 28 countries. The group's consolidated revenue for the year ending 2007 was more than US$5 billion. KMC has been among the leading Indian contractors for the past 36 years in the construction of major highway projects, airport runways, major bridges, and other civil engineering works.

authorities in the form of a general arrangement to construct road overbridges/under bridges at level crossings on the project highway in accordance with the specifications and standards provided in the CA, and procurement of all applicable permits relating to environmental protection and conservation of the site. As per the CA, upon procurement of environmental clearance, the concessionaire shall be entitled to a 12-month period for completion of the overbridges. As per the CA, NHAI shall also grant vacant access to 60% of the land required for the six-lane project highway prior to the appointed date.

There are many issues with the project:

Design issues: There are excessive numbers of flyovers on the highway. As per the CA, the number of flyovers had to be 44, which was later increased to 52, or a flyover every 4 km or so. The completed flyovers, however, are only 33 while the balance 19 flyovers are under various stages of construction. The main problems that are preventing the balance flyovers from being completed are inadequate land acquisition and lack of finances. The average cost of the flyover on the Gurgaon–Jaipur highway is Rs. 16 crore. Hence, construction of these flyovers at locations where they are not required as per the Manual of Specifications and Standards in the road sector leads to wasteful expenditure.

Land acquisition: One of the major problems faced by the project is that of land acquisition. It is estimated that the total land required for the project is 1477 hectare (ha) out of which the concessionaire has been made available only 1066 ha (including 308 ha of forest land). Out of the balance required 411 ha, payment has been disbursed for 169 ha giving a total of 84% of the total land required even after more than four and a half years of the appointed date (till September 2013). However, it is important to note that 99% of the land requirement for the main carriageway is available.

There are poor land records for certain pockets of the land. Due to the thickly populated surrounding areas of the highway, these pockets of land are difficult to acquire. Moreover, in some cases, NHAI could not get clear land even after full payment to the owners.

NHAI needs to expedite land acquisition at Gurgaon, Behror, and Kotputli, where work is pending and affecting construction of flyovers, PUPs, and service roads.[7] In addition, about 4.55 ha of land for approach to major bridge[8] at km 76 + 980 is yet to be transferred by irrigation department of Government of Haryana.

---

[7]Due to problems of land acquisition and forest clearance, it has been observed that inventory worth Rs. 60 crore is lying unused in the yard of the concessionaire. There is a need to immediately address the issue so that 19 pending structures can be completed at the earliest and the unused inventory utilized.

[8]The bridge was completed in 2010–11.

Forest clearance is also a major issue in the following cases:

- Manesar Forest: 8.6 ha of forest land (km 46 + 650 to km 47 + 900) has not yet been handed over to PCEL for construction work.
- Bawal Forest: 10.9 ha of forest land (km 94 + 340 to km 97) required for construction of service road has not yet been handed over to PCEL.
- Sanjay Van: Although NHAI has obtained permission for tree cutting from Ministry of Environment and Forests (MOEF), permission is pending from District Forest Officer (DFO), Jaipur, which needs to be expedited.

One of the important learnings from the case is that land acquisition of at least 80% should be a condition precedent for the authority. Projects would not be expedited by bringing half-baked projects (with insufficient land acquisition) to the market.

Time overrun. The appointed date was April 3, 2009. The scheduled date for completion of six lanes is 912th day (two and half years) from the appointed date, which makes it October 2, 2011. The revised deadline was June 2014, which has also been missed. The reasons for delay are as follows: slow construction progress by concessionaire owing partly to banks stopping release of loans, delay in land acquisition, delay in Forest Clearance, delay in removal of religious and other structures,[9] and additional works in the project scope owing to public representations.

Cost overrun. The original total project cost was Rs. 1896 crore, while the current cost is estimated at Rs. 3009 crore out of which expenditure of Rs. 2617 crore (87%) has been incurred. The physical progress of the highway is 84%, which also points toward cost overrun in the project. The average cost of the six laning projects per km works out to Rs. 13.37 crore as against an estimated Rs. 8.43 crore originally.

The project, as it stands today, is suffering from considerable problems ranging from time overrun, cost overrun, high user fees even in construction period, poor road quality, and severe congestion causing considerable pain to the users. The diversions, whose number is at least 40, are full of potholes. Problem is acute on a 100-km stretch between Gurgaon and Behror, particularly at Manesar, Dharuhera, and Bilaspur. At places like Manesar, Kausala,

[9]At km 256 + 140 and km 267 + 255, NHAI has to approve estimate for lifting/ shifting of existing 132 KVA high-tension (HT) electricity line. The Vehicular Under Pass (VUP) at km 267 + 255 is complete, but traffic could not be allowed due to inadequate vertical clearance from the existing 132 KVA line. The substructure of the flyover at km 256 + 140 is complete, but work is currently suspended due to the inadequate vertical clearance of the existing 132 KVA HT line. At km 60 + 647, permission to dismantle the Bilaspur old toll plaza building has not been received from NHAI. Similarly at km 105 + 444, a temple and toll collection building was to be relocated but the decision has been pending with NHAI despite repeated reminders.

Kalyanpur, and Pragpura, skeletons of structures are lying idle since land is yet to be acquired. Diversions are at regular intervals and the condition of the road is bad due to rain[10] and plying of overloaded trucks, which damages the road. NHAI has refused to allow thickening of the bituminous layer on such stretches. On the main highway stretch, the bituminous layer is 250 mm deep, while at the diversions it is only 90 mm, according to norms. The concessionaire had requested NHAI to go for the highway norm in the diversions but NHAI has not agreed because of cost implications. NHAI, in addition, feels that to increase the bituminous layer, one has to go for complete reconstruction of the road which would mean blocking traffic, causing difficulty to the users.

NHAI issued a default notice to the concessionaire of the Gurgaon–Jaipur highway in September 2013 for its failure to complete work on-time and for poor maintenance even after the end of the 60-day deadline for remedial measures. The concessionaire's failure to remedy the defaults within the cure period gave the authority the freedom to take action as per the contract norms, including taking over the toll collection for at least 180 days.

The economic slowdown during 2012–14 caused a reduction in traffic growth and consequently lower revenue realization for Build–Operate–Transfer (BOT) road projects. This, in turn, adversely affected debt servicing by concessionaires causing widespread default and seeking of loan restructuring. As debt repayment deferments raised debt obligations, the sector exposure increased, reaching the sectoral ceiling norms. As a result, the preference for BOT PPP projects fell sharply as developers were strapped for equity and lenders were not forthcoming with debt. The government had to step in with multiple confidence-building initiatives. To avoid cash flow constraints affecting project execution, rescheduling of premium payment in BOT projects with revenue shortfall has been granted.[11]

A few other recent initiatives include the following:

- Introduction of Hybrid Annuity Model (HAM): As we have seen in Chap. 5, this model is a combination of Engineering–Procurement–Construction (EPC) and BOT contracts, with government and private companies sharing total project cost in a 40 : 60 ratio (which gives the model its hybrid characteristic). Toll on the project would be collected by the Government, and a fixed amount yearly, with a profit margin, will be given to the private partner (which gives the model its annuity characteristic). The objective of the model is to reduce the financial

[10]There are choked drains throughout the length of the highway. This problem becomes acute during the rainy season when overflowing drains flood several areas along the highway. The poor drainage is also because truck drivers and dhabawallahs park their vehicles/ block the service lane permanently.

[11]Government of India (Ministry of Finance) (2015).

burden on PPP concessionaire during project implementation. In all, 21 HAM projects have been awarded in the first 6 months of 2016.

- Exit policy permitting 100% equity divestment 2 years after Commercial Operation Date (COD) has been introduced. Earlier, exit of the lead sponsor was not allowed during the concession period. However, this has been changed now and it is expected that equity locked in projects estimated at Rs. 4500 crore would be available. Some transactions have already taken place.
- Fund infusion by NHAI to salvage physically incomplete and languishing BOT (Toll) and BOT (Annuity) projects. It is estimated that 12 projects with estimated fund requirement of Rs. 3235 crore fall in this category.
- NHAI to compensate road developers for delays not attributable to them. It is estimated that compensating road developers would potentially unlock investment of nearly Rs. 35,000 crore in 34 stalled projects.
- NHAI can extend the toll period for delayed projects.
- Land cost has been removed from total cost for approval purposes. Ministry of Road Transport and Highways is empowered now to approve projects with total project cost up to Rs. 1000 crore. With land costs removed, which can constitute as much as 40% of project costs, delays in approvals would be reduced.

The case study at the end of this chapter details the challenges of the road sector PPPs in Mexico.

(ii) ***Railroads***

PPPs in railroads are a major challenge and Fig. 6 bears this out with the least number of projects in this subsector when compared to other transport subsectors. The Indian Railways is among the world's largest, spread over 7146 stations. However, only 4% of the investment in Indian railways has come from the private sector (only in container trains). PPPs in railroads would relieve congestion in road and rail segments, cater to a growing economy, and help decarbonize the economy. However, the major negative is huge scale of investment required in some of the projects (e.g., the proposed Mumbai–Ahmedabad bullet train would cost about Rs. 1 trillion, see Box 2).

Box 2: PPP in High-Speed Rail Projects

The Government of India approved the Mumbai–Ahmedabad High-Speed Rail (MA HSR) project in December 2015, to be implemented with Japanese technical and financial assistance using Japanese Shinkansen technology.[12] The Total Project Cost (TPC) of MA HSR (508 km[13]) is about Rs. 98,000

[12]Japan's bullet trains have the best safety record with no fatalities since its inception in 1964 and delays are less than 1 minute.

[13]A distance of about 500 km between two major cities spanning a corridor with good economic development was the attribute of the first route in many countries including Japan, France, and Korea.

crore, which works out to about Rs. 200 crore per km. Of the total project cost, around Rs. 17,000–18,000 crore would be the cost of land. The construction period is 7 years from 2017 to 2023. The MA HSR will have 12 stations and the operating speed of the train would be 320 km per hour. This would bring down the journey time between Mumbai and Ahmedabad from 8 to 2 hours. In this way, the train would compete mainly with air travel. On February 12, 2016, a company called National High-Speed Rail Corporation was incorporated by the Ministry of Railways to implement the Mumbai–Ahmedabad HSR.

The benefits of HSR that are often cited are in terms of increasing capacity and speed, improved journey time reliability, economic development through agglomeration economies, political integration, and environmentally benign outcomes. However, it has also been opined that environmental benefits of HSR over conventional rail are marginal. It takes decades for HSR to compensate for the significantly higher emissions during the construction phase and higher energy costs during operation.[14]

The terms of the Agreement with Japan to build MA HSR are as follows: Japanese Official Development Assistance (ODA) would fund 81% of the TPC; low-cost funding by Japan International Cooperation Agency (JICA) at about 0.1% interest rate; loan would have 50-year tenure with a moratorium of 15 years; certain packages/goods would be procured from Japan; and there is a provision for technology transfer and local manufacturing for a specified period.

According to the feasibility report submitted by JICA, the IRR for MA HSR project would be about 3% while the economic rate of return would be 11.9%. It will have 36,000 daily users (both ways) or 13 million passengers per annum by 2023.[15] The daily users are expected to go up to 1,86,000 per day or 68 million per annum by 2053. Thirty-five trains per day each way will operate by 2023, which will go up to 105 trains per day each way in 2053.[16]

The Ministry of Railways intends to create a diamond quadrilateral of high-speed train links with the cities of Chennai, Delhi, Mumbai, Ahmedabad, and Kolkata as the nodes. The Ministry of Railways has selected seven corridors for carrying out pre-feasibility studies for the introduction of high-speed passenger trains. Feasibility studies for the Delhi–Mumbai, Mumbai–Chennai, and Delhi–Kolkata corridors are underway.

---

[14]Other nonfinancial negatives that have been pointed out include suicides by jumping onto railway tracks in front of trains and safety issues in the event of earthquakes. Noise pollution, especially the tunnel boom phenomenon, has also been a concern [Source: Raghuram and Prashanth (2016)].

[15]The total traffic across all modes in the MA sector was estimated at 62 million for 2010–11.

[16]Government of India (Ministry of Finance) (2016).

International experience

The main issue with the project is its financial viability. HSR projects are highly capital intensive, requiring high passenger volumes and high tariff to justify the investment. Few HSR schemes like the Tokaido (Tokyo-Osaka) and Sanyo Shinkansen (which combined had 207 million passengers in 2011), and the TGV Sud-Est (Paris-Lyon) have generated reasonable financial returns. In China, of four recent openings studied, only the Jinan–Qingdao line is covering financial costs. These have first-year usage in excess of 20 million passengers per annum.[17]

Ex-post evaluations of HSR lines in France have shown that except for the Sud-Est, financial and socio-economic internal rates of return have been much lower than the expected figures. The same applies for the Madrid–Seville and Madrid–Barcelona lines in Spain.

Taiwan, which has been running HSR based on Japan's Shinkansen Bullet Train system since 2007,[18] has seen massive losses owing to high depreciation and interest payments as well as low ridership and the operator has sought bailout from Government; about $1 billion has already been given. Under the terms of the 35-year BOT concession, Taiwan High-Speed Rail Corporation (THSRC) had to pay the government 10% of its pre-tax profits each year, and a minimum of Taiwan Dollar (TWD) 108 billion in aggregate. THSRC also had a 50-year concession for commercial development of land around its stations. Both the concessions were terminated in July 2015 after continued "long-term losses". THSRC, however, was to continue to operate the services, but with enhanced shareholding of government institutions from 22.1 to 63.9% and reduced holdings of private investors (down from 37.4 to 17.4%).[19]

The ticket prices for Beijing–Shanghai HSR is Rs. 4.4 per km. Assuming the same rate for the Mumbai–Ahmedabad HSR, the ticket price works out to about Rs. 2300 for second-class ticket compared to Rs. 3000 for air travel. The MA route is well connected by air, rail, and expressway and HSR is expected to attract passengers from all these modes. In view of these factors, it is expected that MA HSR would require substantial public investment (>50% of the TPC) to be run as a viable PPP. Thus, the play seems to be between long-term economic benefits and financial returns.

As of 2015, 15 countries have HSR of about 30,000 km carrying 1.6 billion passengers annually with China alone accounting for 0.8 billion

---

[17]Raghuram and Prashanth (2016).

[18]The cost of the Taiwan HSR system is considered high at about $15 billion. By comparison, the MA HSR is expected to cost about $16 billion at current exchange rates.

[19]Raghuram and Prashanth (2016).

passengers. China[20] has more than 19,000 km of HS tracks—the longest in the world constituting two-thirds of the world total. Spain (3100 km), Japan (2664 km), France (2036 km), Turkey (1420 km), and Germany (1334 km) are the only other countries where tracks dedicated for high-speed trains are more than 1000 km long. Japan was the first to have an HSR line [Tokyo to Osaka, 515 km (1964)], followed by Italy [Rome to Florence, 252 km (1978)] and France [Paris to Lyons, 460 km (1981)].

At $17–21 million per km in infrastructure costs, Chinese rail is cheaper as compared to $25–39 million per km for traditional exporters of high-speed rail like Japan and Germany, according to World Bank estimates. By comparison, the MA leg costs $28.8 million per km. China's expertise has largely been developed in the last decade, as China built the world's largest network of high-speed rail. Moreover, the Chinese companies have a higher threshold for building in risky areas and willingness to finance their projects—Export–Import Bank of China will be funding 85% of the Mexico rail project.

The Government is very keen on having more PPPs in the railroad sector. For example, the Railway Minister's Budget Speech 2014–15 stated that:

- Future projects will be financed through PPP mode, including the high-speed rail;
- PPP investment through BOT and Annuity route would be attracted and 8–10 capacity augmentation projects on congested routes will be identified;
- Indian Railways has taken up port connectivity on a priority through PPP mode of funding;
- Development of identified stations to international standards will be through PPP mode. The first such contract has been signed (see Box 3).

Box 3: Development of Habibganj Railway Station in PPP Mode

The first contract, for redevelopment and modernization of Habibganj railway station in Madhya Pradesh, through PPP has been signed. The total project cost is estimated at Rs. 450 crore divided between station redevelopment (Rs. 100 crore) and commercial development (Rs. 350 crore). The PPP agreement was signed between Indian Railway Station Development Corporation (IRSDC) and Bansal Group. The SPV is called Bansal Pathways Habibganj Private Limited. After meeting the conditions precedent by IRSDC and Developer, the operation and maintenance of the Habibganj station have been

[20]China introduced its first HSR line in 2004 that uses magnetic levitation (maglev) technology—the 30 km Shanghai Transrapid from the Shanghai International Airport to the Longyang Road station of the Shanghai Metro. The Harbin-Wuhan train (covering 2421 km in 14.5 hours), which began service in December 2014, became the then longest HSR service in the world.

taken over by the developer on March 1, 2017, which has been reckoned as the appointed date.

Habibganj railway station will have dedicated pick-up and drop off parking facilities for users, as in airports. Other facilities featuring in the redeveloped "world-class" station will include environment-friendly practices like solar energy generation, catering and food stalls, public conveniences at affordable rates and accessibility to differently abled people.[21]

Indian Railways plans to redevelop 400 such stations, apart from Habibganj. The list includes Chandigarh, Surat, Shivaji Nagar, Brijwasan, Anand Vihar, Mohali, and Gandhinagar stations.

(iii) ***Airports***

The civil aviation industry in India is undergoing rapid change, with private participation in PPP mode, development of greenfield airports, as well as restructuring and modernization of old airports, Foreign Direct Investment (FDI) in domestic airlines, entry of Low-Cost Carriers (LCCs) and an emphasis on regional connectivity, with technological upgradation using IT interventions.[22]

169 million passengers were handled at Indian airports in 2013–14. Projections indicate that 1150 million passengers per annum would be handled at Indian airports by 2031–32. The investment required to handle this growth rate is Rs. 5.9 lac crore ($100 billion), most of which should come from the private sector through PPPs given the fiscal resource crunch.

In India, the airports at Delhi, Mumbai, Bengaluru, and Hyderabad have come up as PPPs. Following this development, many of the Indian airports, including Delhi and Mumbai, have been rated amongst the best airports in the world from being among the worst. The quality of services has also improved even in the public sector (Airports Authority of India) operated airports because of the demonstration effect of the PPP airports. One recent development has been the signing of Memorandum of Understanding for engaging Changi airport, Singapore, for implementing Operation and Maintenance (O&M) contracts at Ahmedabad and Jaipur airports.[23]

(iv) ***Inland Waterways***

Fuel-efficient, cost-effective, and environment-friendly water highways are cheaper than road and rail, both to develop and maintain. A single horsepower of energy can move 4 tons by water, compared to 150 kg by road and 500 kg by rail.

[21]Financial Express. 15 July 2016. *Habibganj to have India's first "world-class" railway station; here's what it will look like.*

[22]Government of India (Ministry of Finance) (2016).

[23]Government of India (Ministry of Finance) (2016).

While several countries carry as much as over 40% of their passenger and freight traffic through waterways, the comparative figure for India is a measly 3.5%.

The National Waterways Bill, 2015, passed by the Parliament in 2015 seeks to create 101 national water highways, in addition to the existing five national corridors and a few other smaller waterways. The law, including an entry in the Union List to avoid inter-state disputes, had no resistance in Parliament indicating political consensus over the matter.

Though cheaper to develop, to be operational year-round and able to carry heavy loads, water channels need to have enough width and depth. Navigating India's many seasonal rivers in the lean season will require regular and extensive dredging and desilting. Moreover, water highways will also require more river ports and their supporting facilities for road and rail connections, warehouses, and related services. Procuring equipment, including dredgers, shipping vessel, and barges of different sizes, will also need sizeable investment.

Private participation in waterways will be possible only if such ventures show financial viability, which requires enough and guaranteed two-way traffic. But the traffic in bulk goods, such as coal, minerals, foodgrains, fertilizer, and similar other commodities, is mostly one way, compelling the vessels to return empty or under-loaded, raising costs.[24]

Transportation PPPs—Sector-Specific Challenges and Solutions

Taking the transport sector as a whole, including roads, railroads, airports, and waterways, there are certain common challenges:

- ***Demand forecasting***. Accurate traffic demand forecasting is extremely difficult for new roads and other forms of transport, making financing arrangements difficult.
- ***Competitive markets***. In developing country PPP markets, only a small group of companies may have the technical and financial capabilities to deliver cost-effective PPP projects.[25] Therefore, they may be the only ones who would qualify for bidding, thus limiting competition.

However, there exist mechanisms to address at least some of these challenges. For example, payment mechanisms like annuities have been used to address demand uncertainty. Under this mechanism, as we have already seen, public sector pays "annuity" to the private partner based on the availability of the asset to users and on service quality levels, like the condition of the roads, thus effectively taking on itself the demand risk. "Shadow tolls" have been used to address payment risk. Under this mechanism, the public sector pays the private concessionaire on the basis of the number of users of an asset. This should take care of payment risk or the unwillingness of users to pay for the use of the facility. Then there is the Least

[24]Business Standard (2016).

[25]Deloitte. *Closing the Infrastructure Gap: The Role of Public-Private Partnerships* (http://www.cnrs.fr/aquitaine/IMG/pdf/closing_the_infrastructure_gap.pdf).

Present Value of Revenues (LPVR) bidding parameter that endogenously adjusts the concession period to traffic fluctuations.

2.3 Water and Sewerage

Water is unique among infrastructure sectors in that it is essential to life. One can survive without power, telecom, or transport facilities for days and weeks, but not without water. Because of this, private investment in the sector may be subjected to unmanageable political risks[26] and therefore, 85% of water utilities worldwide are publicly owned and controlled.

Water is an inherently difficult sector to enter for the private sector and there is a high failure rate of PPP projects in the sector. As shown in Fig. 1, water and sewerage sector accounts for the least private investment among all infrastructure sectors in developing countries. It is very difficult to get the private sector interested in provision of water mainly because of poor cost recovery (see Fig. 2) and any effort to raise tariffs is subject to heightened political risk.[27] (If it is a foreign company providing water, the risk of project cancelation increases further. Once private companies start providing water, the risk of project cancelation is disproportionately high in terms of both numbers and more so, investments. As shown in Fig. 7, the project cancelation rate for water and sewerage sector, especially in terms of investment, is the highest among all infrastructure sectors).

However, there are many PPP water and sewerage projects in developed countries like Australia, Canada, Ireland, and Netherlands. One of the most celebrated successful water projects in developing countries is in Manila, Philippines.

Political and Regulatory Risk in Water Sector

The main regulatory risk in the water sector is Tariff Risk, which is the risk that regulators would not set the tariffs at cost recovery levels. Thus, on an average, the cost recovery in the water sector could be as low as 10–20% of even the operation and maintenance expenditures. Regulatory risk could also be manifested in regulators disallowing some expenditures. However, the water sector in India has no independent regulators and the regulatory role is performed by contracts and the public authority.

Water Sector is Subject to High Non-revenue Water Losses

The volume of water entering the distribution system minus the volume billed to customers is termed Non-Revenue Water (NRW). It has three major components:

---

[26]Two water and sewerage contracts in Uruguay reverted to the public sector in 2004 when the electorate approved a constitutional amendment that made access to water a fundamental human right and transferred water and sanitation services to the public sector.

[27]Any effort to raise tariffs may cause law and order problems (a form of political risk).

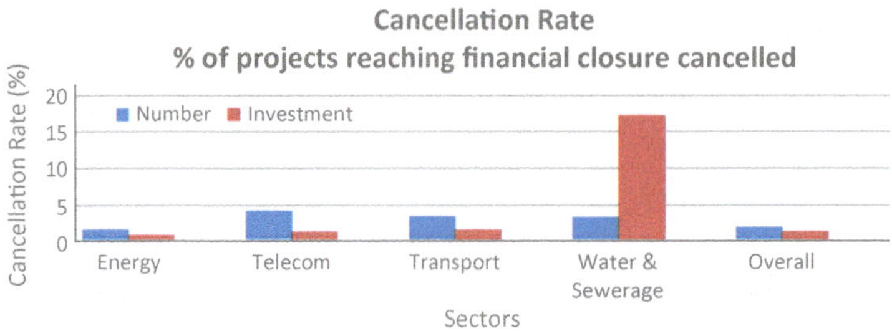

Fig. 7 Water and sewerage is difficult for the private sector to enter and PPPs to be sustainable. *Source* Author's tabulation from the Private Participation in Infrastructure database of the World Bank (http://ppi.worldbank.org) (viewed on 31 January 2016)

physical water loss, commercial loss (theft), and unbilled authorized consumption (free water).

- Poor operational practices and maintenance of tanks, pipes, and underground assets usually cause most of the physical losses;
- Faulty metering and data handling and general water theft lead to commercial losses;
- Unbilled water is a policy choice for public purpose like firefighting or as subsidy to some citizen groups.[28]

An important characteristic of the water sector is the high levels of NRW[29] losses (see Fig. 8). The developed countries like Germany and Japan have NRW losses in single digits while the developing world including India has much higher losses. In India especially, about half of the water supply is lost to NRW, the major constituent of which is water theft.

A performance assessment of water utilities in 20 Indian cities reported that water was available only for 4.3 hours per day on average (Asian Development Bank, 2007). 32% was unaccounted-for water,[30] while 75% of connections were unmetered. Utilities were generally unable to recover operating costs through tariffs. Six of those 20 cities provided less than 2 hours of water supply per day. Shockingly, some provided well below 100 litres per capita per day, the minimum amount required for healthy and sanitary living as recommended by the World Health Organization.

[28]Bill Kingdom et al. (2006).

[29]NRW is a measure of efficiency in the water sector and is similar to Aggregate Technical & Commercial losses in the power sector.

[30]NRW is sometimes also referred to as unaccounted-for water (UFW). While the two terms are similar, they are not identical, since non-revenue water includes authorized unbilled consumption (e.g., for firefighting or, in some countries, for use by religious institutions) while unaccounted-for water excludes it.

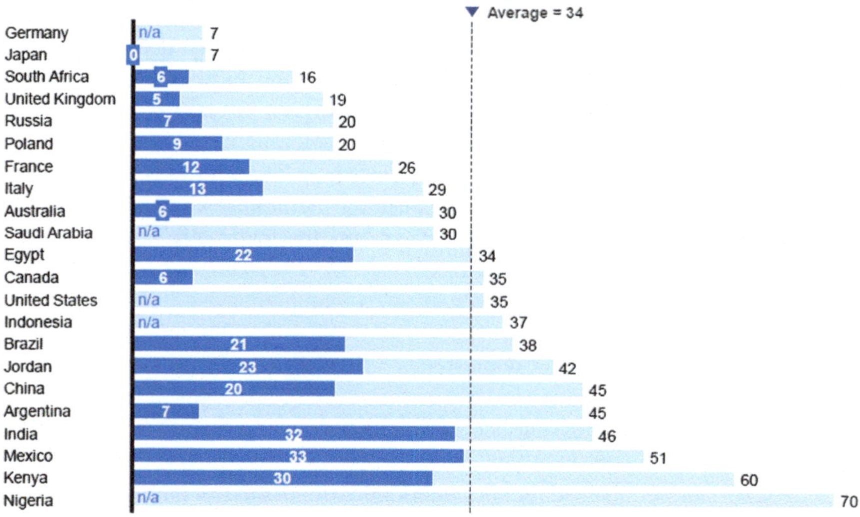

Fig. 8 High proportion (%) of non-revenue water (NRW) result from high rates of theft in most countries. *Note dark* portion in the above figure shows the percentage of water lost to theft. *Source* McKinsey Global Institute (2013)

Water and Sewerage—Challenges and Solutions

As we have seen, the water and sewerage sector is prone to several risks (heightened political and regulatory risks, high level of NRW losses, etc.) which deter the participation of the private sector. Add to the list, the uncertainty about the condition of assets (water pipelines, etc.) as they are mostly underground and may have been there for decades. This adds to risks, may increase project costs, and lead to path dependence preventing the use of better technology. One of the ways to reduce uncertainty arising from the condition of assets is to allow an enhanced monitoring period (EMP) during which the private sector may monitor the system after contract award, in the process of which it may get to know more about the condition of assets. If the condition of these assets is worse than assumed, private sector may be given the liberty to ask for a re-calibration of tariffs. However, this is politically sensitive and the public sector may be subjected to the charge of changing the rules of the game after contract award. Nevertheless, an EMP was allowed in the case of Dar-es-Salaam Water and Sewerage Services as we have seen in the last chapter.

In common with majority of brownfield projects, employee resistance could be another challenge for the water sector. Handling this challenge is important and one way to do so is to give liberty to the employees that do not want to join the PPP to be deployed elsewhere (as was done by the Airports Authority of India in the case of Delhi Airport when it was contracted out to GMR Group as a PPP). In addition, a monetary incentive can also be considered and the conditions of service of employees not allowed to worsen after the project has been contracted out to the private sector (as was done in the Delhi power sector PPP).

As we have seen, the high level of NRW in the sector is a major challenge for sustainable operations, whether public or private. If the utility does not receive payment for about half of the water supplied, it obviously creates problems for financial sustainability, which could be reflected in poor coverage of piped water supply. But this high level of NRW seen in the developing world could also be an opportunity as decrease in NRW could be a win-win solution for most stakeholders. Decrease in NRW would mean extra revenues for the utility, which should reduce the need for tariff increases that may be required for financially sustainable and qualitatively improved private operations.

Making the reduction of NRW part of a comprehensive reform program including increasing access often yields good outcomes. Phnom Penh's Water Supply Authority in Cambodia witnessed a sevenfold rise in its number of connections while reducing non-revenue water from 72% to below 6%. Part of the financing required for increasing access would have come from NRW reduction. Reducing technical losses in water can cost less than 3% of the cost of adding capacity and can be attained much faster. In Latin America and India, similar programs in electric power have produced savings of 7–38%. In the case of Delhi Power Distribution PPP, the AT&C losses came down from around 50% to about 15% following contracting out the services to PPPs. According to the World Bank $1 million spent to reduce line losses in Africa could have yielded the benefit equivalent of $12 million in power generation capacity.[31]

Because of low-cost recovery in the water sector, tariff increases may be required for financially sustainable private operations. This is obviously disliked by voters. If it is desired that subsidies need to be given to deserving groups, this may require connection subsidies instead of consumption subsidies. It is estimated that about $1000 per household is required to increase coverage, which may not be affordable to the poor households that are rationed out of piped water supply. Therefore, connection subsidies may be more desirable than consumption subsidies (low per unit cost of water) on both efficiency and equity considerations.

Figure 9 shows the false premise of keeping user charges low to benefit the poor for both piped water supply and grid-based electricity. The poorest households are generally not connected to public services (the coverage of piped water supply and grid-based electricity is less than 20% in lowest quintile, Q1). So these households cannot benefit from low unit charges made possible through consumption subsidies, typical of these public services. The primary beneficiaries of consumption subsidies are the richer households that are connected to these public services (Q5) (Fig. 9).

In other words, the poor do not benefit from low user charges. They end up paying much more to vendors (see Fig. 10). It is the lower income households without access to public networks that typically have to pay higher market prices for water. Thus, water from public connections is the cheapest while water from

[31]McKinsey Global Institute (2013).

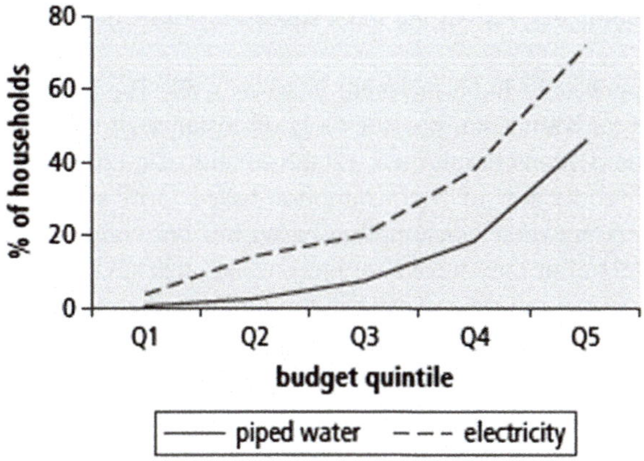

Fig. 9 Piped water supply and grid-based electricity, access by quintile. *Source* As quoted in Foster and Briceño-Garmendia (2009)

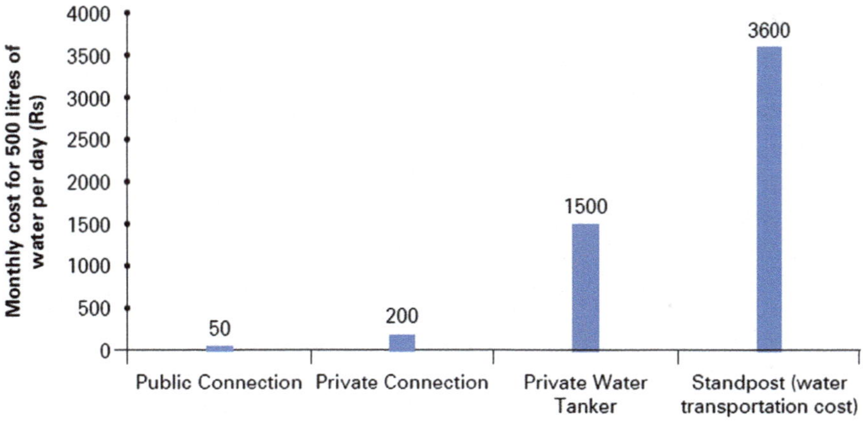

Fig. 10 The poor end up paying much more for water than the rich. *Source* Report on Indian Urban Infrastructure and Services (2011)

standposts[32] is the most expensive. So operational cost recovery of public services should be a feasible objective. But any such move would have political resistance. Necessary user charge revisions must have some perceptible delivery improvements to make the hike palatable to users. Improvement in service coverage would also help in building political support for any such move (as was done in the case of

[32]Water from standposts is actually free, but it turns out to be the most expensive as private operators collect water in containers provided by households and deliver it to their doorstep at a transportation charge of Rs. 6 for 25 litres.

Manila Water Company, one of the most successful PPPs in the water sector in the world).

This has happened in India in recent years as well. The pilot project of 24 * 7 water in Gulbarga, Karnataka, provides a good instance of tariff hike, metering of all houses in the demonstration area, establishment of a continuous water supply network, and introduction of a consumption-based tariff system. For the first 6 months, the users got their consumption-based bill but continued to pay their old fixed charge. Only after they were convinced of the cost saving in the new scheme, as well as the service improvement of a continuous water supply system, that the customers willingly accepted the new system of consumption-based payments. Similarly, the city bus service in Indore raised the bus charges three times in 4 years after completely upgrading the public transport with good-quality bus service.[33]

3 PPPs in Social Infrastructure

Changes in age structure of population require new investment in social infrastructure in many parts of the world by large young populations in rapidly urbanized settings. Emerging markets are driving investment in schools while aging populations in industrialized economies are causing investment in health infrastructure.[34]

There is an immense need for tapping private resources and efficiencies for improving health and education services. Like PPPs in economic infrastructure, PPPs in social infrastructure are expected to improve on-time and within-cost delivery of services, provide value for money to the government, and supply better quality services, leading to inclusive growth. Better quality education and health services could be reflected in increased rate of educational attainment for students[35] and improved health and longevity for the people. In terms of outcomes, this could facilitate better quality of life for the population.

However, PPP projects in social infrastructure pose hurdles as they are generally smaller and also tend to be more complex and politically sensitive (affordability could be a major issue) than economic infrastructure projects. The private sector often finds social infrastructure projects more challenging as financial rewards are smaller and the operational demands are more complex.

[33]Report on Indian Urban Infrastructure and Services (2011).

[34]PwC. Capital Project and Infrastructure Spending Outlook to 2025 (https://www.pwc.com/gx/en/capital-projects-infrastructure/publications/cpi-outlook/assets/cpi-outlook-to-2025.pdf).

[35]In a series of research reports, KPMG has found that students attending classes in new buildings that were procured, built and operated under a PPP structure, achieve a faster rate of improvement in educational attainment than those that attend schools that were conventionally procured (KPMG. 2010. *Infrastructure 100*).

3.1 Education

PPPs in education are common in many developed countries like UK, Australia, and Canada. UK is home to the world's largest and most sophisticated PPP schools program based on Design–Build–Finance–Operate–Transfer (DBFOT) model. Under this model, while the government continues to provide core services (teaching), private sector invests in the school infrastructure and provides related non-core services (school transport, food services, cleaning) under contract. Thus, PPPs enable the government to concentrate on the core teaching function while non-core activities are provided by the private sector. UK has signed nearly 100 education Private Finance Initiative (PFI) deals valued at £3.5 billion. There is increasing investor interest in education PPPs in Australia, with projects valued at $3.7 billion in the pipeline.

Scheme for PPP in School Education in India: India has introduced a scheme for setting up of 2500 Model Schools under PPP mode, with every block having at least one such school. School infrastructure will be provided by the private entity like in UK. The PPP will be governed by an initial 10-year contract, extendable on mutual agreement, and have classes from Grade VI to Grade XII.

In these schools, the government would pay for the students it sponsors. In addition, the school management can admit fee-paying students as appropriate without exceeding the cap on total students at 2500. Government-sponsored students study free till class VIII, and after that at a nominal monthly charge of Rs. 50, further halved for students from deprived sections of society. The nongovernment-sponsored students would pay regular fees.[36]

For a single private entity, there is a ceiling of 20 schools per state and 50 schools overall in the country. Private partner will enter into a concession agreement with central government. Since payment to the private entity will be based on output parameters, close monitoring would be enforced as per the concession agreement. Pilot phase for 50 schools has been launched. 65 potential bidders have been shortlisted on the basis of Request for Qualification (RFQ).

Challenges in Education PPPs: Budgeting is a challenge because of high procurement costs for small projects and the uncertainty of revenue streams. User fees (tuitions) may be too high, not taking into account externalities.[37] Future demographic and policy changes make rigid, long-term contracts less suitable for schools.

One way to address the issue of small size of projects with associated high transaction costs in the education sector is bundling, in which the concessionaire would be handed over the responsibility of a number of schools. In education, the

[36]Model School under Public-Private Partnership (PPP) Mode (http://pibmumbai.gov.in/English/PDF/E0000_H114.PDF).

[37]Positive externalities in primary education are more than tertiary education. Positive externalities in girl education are more than that of boys.

financial viability of a PPP increases with the number of schools covered by the contract, especially for primary schools, where projects are limited in both size and scope.

3.2 Health

India is typical of a developing country in many ways. Approximately, 45% of the Indian population has to travel 100 km or more for access to quality health care. Health access is especially poor in rural areas. For example, India's bed density is still the lowest among BRICS nations and about 70% of the available beds are concentrated in top 20 cities of the country. Average spending by OECD countries on health care is 9.9% of GDP compared to 3.9% of GDP (both public and private spending on health care) in India.

Like economic infrastructure and other sectors in social infrastructure, the PPP objective in health sector is to improve access to quality and affordable healthcare facilities and address resource constraints. PPPs may be used for new infrastructure (new hospitals) or management of existing infrastructure (primary healthcare centers).

Like its social infrastructure twin (education), PPPs in the health sector are quite challenging owing to the need for standardization of risk-return framework and key performance indicators through model concession agreement, and the need for a strong monitoring mechanism, especially as it has direct interface with users. Public sector capability to procure PPP health projects is also suspect in India.

In the UK, 130 PFI hospitals have been built since 1997 compared to 12 publicly funded hospitals. Medical services usually remain the responsibility of the public sector, while the private sector builds and operates the facilities. Contract term is generally 30–35 years.

PPP in Health care in India

Government of India has rolled out the National Rural Health Mission (NRHM) to address healthcare gaps. PPPs are expected to play an important role under NRHM. It is estimated that India has eight healthcare PPPs with investment of Rs. 1833 crore (across all segments of healthcare). This includes super speciality hospitals and medical colleges (Punjab Institute of Medical Sciences—750 beds), diagnostics [Magnetic resonance imaging (MRI) in Sawai Mansingh Hospital, Jaipur], dialysis centers (B Braun Dialysis Centers in Andhra Pradesh[38]; 11 centers

[38]Government of Andhra Pradesh has selected Braun to establish and operate dialysis centers in 11 tertiary-care state-run hospitals on a Build–Operate–Transfer (BOT) basis for 7 years. Government pays the private operator an agreed price for each dialysis (shadow pricing). Dialysis is provided to the Below Poverty Line population through the state-sponsored health insurance scheme. The scheme's robust payment mechanism ensures timely payment to the private operator and seamless service to the people.

are in operation housing 111 haemodialysis machines), and mobile medical units in Odisha and Uttarakhand under NRHM.

3.3 *Prisons*

PPPs have also been used in the construction, operation, and maintenance of prisons. The figure below shows prisoners held privately across countries. In the US, private facilities house eight percent of prisoners, the highest number anywhere in the world. Australia has the highest proportion of prisoners in private prisons (19%) followed closely by Scotland, England & Wales, and New Zealand (Fig. 11).

For the two leading US private players in the prison PPP space, Corrections Corporation of America and GEO Group, average annualized returns have been in excess of 15% since 2004, primarily owing to the USA's penchant for higher incarceration rates. They are, however, also accused of funding groups that lobby for harsh sentencing. But because they build their own prions, they have also enjoyed strong competitive positions given few alternatives for the public authorities.[39]

A 2002 study of PPP prisons in South Africa[40] found that construction was completed on-time and on-budget; operating costs per inmate per day were similar to the public sector's operating costs; and the quality of facilities and levels of

Fig. 11 Prisoners held privately, 2012 or latest (% of total). *Source* The Economist (2014)

service was better in PPP prisons. The implication is that if one has a choice between public and private prisons, one should opt for private prisons!

[39] The Economist (2014).

[40] Government of South Africa (Department of Correctional Services, National Treasury, Department of Public Works). 2002.

4 Case Study: Mexican Toll Roads—Concession, Cancelation, and Re-privatization

Project description: In the period 1989–94, the Government of Mexico undertook an ambitious program of constructing about 5500 km of private greenfield toll roads. By 1995, about 53 contracts had been awarded. The investment for constructing the toll roads was around $13 billion (constituting roughly 5% of the then GDP of Mexico), financed through the domestic banking sector (50%); concessionaire equity (30%), funded through expensive, limited tenor, floating rate commercial loans, and/or "sweat equity" (an arrangement whereby a construction company builds a facility on behalf of a concessionaire, to be compensated later through an equity stake in the concession); and the remaining mix of public sector grants/equity contributions (20%).[41] The project companies were typically highly leveraged and the debt provided by domestic banks was mainly at floating rate. Ruster (1997) has noted that indirect guarantees from the government to the investors and lenders funding the projects might have reduced the extent of due diligence on these projects, leading to higher leverage. As noted earlier, toll roads were partly financed using floating rate short-term paper,[42] which led to an asset–liability mismatch, besides increasing the toll rates to unsustainable levels to be able to service these debts.

Concession terms contained some estimate of usage volume on which projected revenues were based. If usage did not meet projections, the government could extend the length of the concession; if usage exceeded projections, the government could terminate the concession once the concessionaire had recouped its investment. Government also subsidized cost overruns by extending concession periods of toll road companies.[43]

Initiation and award of contract: The market-oriented government of President Carlos Salinas hoped to have more than 5500 km of four-lane toll roads either built or in construction by the end of 1994. Better roads were crucial for Mexico's economy. Roads in the undeveloped southern part of Mexico needed to be improved to allow traffic to flow into the economically strong north and thus promote intra-country integration and improve the economies of both regions. The country could reap the benefits of the North American Free Trade Agreement, which took effect from beginning 1994, through better infrastructure of which road infrastructure was an important constituent. Increased trade as a result of NAFTA (US–Mexico trade grew at an average rate of 16% per annum between 1994 and 2000) and globalization would require more ways for trains and trucks to cross between the US and Mexico, particularly in Texas and Mexico's four northern states.

---

[41]Standard & Poor's (2006).

[42]Project Finance International (1992).

[43]New York Times (1993).

The government pursued the BOT route, under which a private consortium builds the road and then operates it for a fixed concession period using toll revenue to repay the construction loans. At the end of the concession period (the maximum period was extended to 30 years), the concessionaire was to hand over the road to the government. Under the program, the government, through the Ministry of Communications and Transport (SCT), awarded concessions for particular routes following a competitive bidding process. In following this process, the government's intent was to move road construction off its balance sheet.

Description of Facts and Process of Cancellation: The projects ran into trouble pretty soon. Construction costs were way higher than estimated and the projected traffic never materialized (averaging between 25 and 65% with three-quarters of projects having had over-optimistic forecasts). Mexican laws required a free road to run parallel to the toll roads, making demand estimation even more uncertain. Given concession periods as short as 30 months, the tariffs imposed were some of the highest in the world, with toll rates at over 16 US cents per km (US had 2–9 cents/km).[44] The Mexico city–Acapulco road charged 30 cents/km, ten times more than the New Jersey Turnpike.[45]

The problems were further exacerbated after the macroeconomic crisis of 1994 when traffic declined by 12% (see Fig. 12) and foreign currency-denominated loans became huge liabilities. The floating rate debt also became expensive to service when short-term interest rates increased to over 71% in April 1995. Most toll road companies became technically insolvent. To be sure, investors wondered how GrupoTribasa, GrupoMexicano de Desarollo (GMD), and Empresas ICA (the three main concessionaire companies) would service the estimated Ps 24 billion toll road debts with a severe drop in traffic on the highways and fewer construction contracts. In fact, GMD was on the brink of bankruptcy after the Mexican peso crisis as the firm defaulted on a US $10.4 million interest payment on a 1994 Eurobond and said it was laying off 80% of its staff on the next business day after the government's bailout announcement (August 22, 1997).

Overruns of 30% were reported for construction costs, with at least one project (CuernavacA-Acapulco toll road) showing a 200% increase. Additionally, concessions awarded before securing all necessary permits, approvals, and the right-of-way, introduced further delays and exposed concessionaires to public pressures for route realignment further enhancing costs.[46]

The technical and administrative capability of the government was stretched in this large-scale road construction program. There were also allegations of corruption, lack of transparency, and impropriety. Ruster has emphasized the problems in bid selection criteria as well as choice of operators. He writes "In addition to the problems relating to bid selection criteria, there was no efficient pre-selection process to screen out potential bidders that lacked the capacity to assume the

[44]Standard & Poor's (2006).

[45]Project Finance International (1997).

[46]Standard & Poor's (2006).

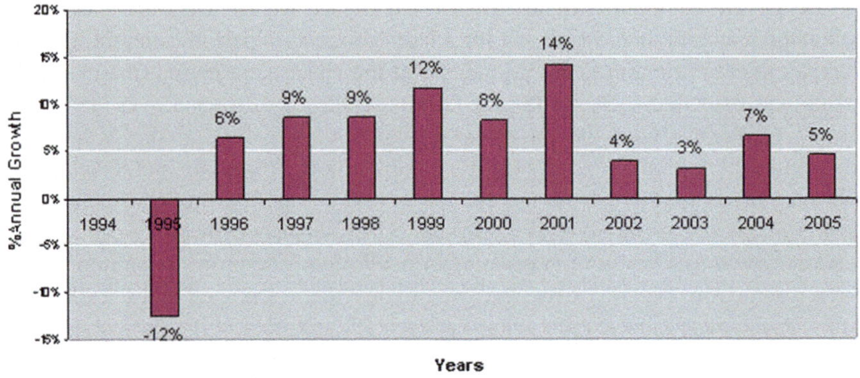

Fig. 12 Toll road traffic growth in Mexico, by years. *Source* Standard & Poor's (2006)

essential risks of construction design and management, completion of large projects, and commercial management of toll road operations…The lack of a good screening process led to the selection of medium-size concessionaires that financed their equity contributions through commercial loans." The initial Mexican toll road program, thus, was poorly designed and gave the impression of being rushed[47] so that the targets may be achieved.

Though the companies went in for renegotiations and some of the problems were addressed, that did not help in sustaining the projects, ICA, for example, renegotiated four of its nine concessions (Guadalajara–Tepic, Leon–Lagos–Aguascalientes, Mazatlan–Culiacan, and San Martin–Tlaxcala) at the end of November 1994. Toll rates were cut by about 30%. In the case of Mazatlan–Culiacan toll road, the government extended the term of the concession from 17.5 to 30 years and contributed money to reduce debt and establish a reserve fund. Total equity increased from 56% to 80% and total debt fell from 44 to 20%. The concessionaire's principal debt fell from 17% to zero. But most of these contracts had to be cancelled as we see below.

The Mexican government (through its entity called Fideicomiso de Apoyo al Rescate de Autopistas Concesionadas, FARAC) took over the 23 most troubled federal highways operated by private concessionaires. As per the PPI database of the World Bank, a total of 16 private toll road projects were cancelled (constituting half of the road sector projects that had been cancelled till 2010 across the developing world[48]) in the wake of the Mexican macroeconomic crisis of 1994. These were (i) Aguascalientes–Leon toll road; (ii) Arriaga–Huixtla toll road; (iii) Cadereyta–Reynosa toll road; (iv) Chamapa–Lecheria toll road; (v) Champoton–Campeche toll road; (vi) Cordoba–Veracruz and La Tinaja–

[47]Ruster (1997).

[48]Private Participation in Infrastructure Projects database of the World Bank (http://ppi.worldbank.org).

Cosoleacaque toll roads; (vii) Guadalajara–Tepic toll road; (viii) Guadalajara–Zapotlanejo toll road; (ix) Lagos de Moreno–Zapotlanejo toll road; (x) Libramiento de Tampico toll road; (xi) Maravatio–Zapotlanejo toll road; (xii) Mazatlan–Culiacan toll road; (xiii) Monterrey–Nuevo Laredo toll road; (xiv) Puente El Zacatal toll road; (xv) Toluca–Atlacomulco toll road; and (xvi) Torreon–Saltillo toll road.[49]

Post-cancelation status: These concessions were taken over by the federal government because of concerns about the health of the construction and the banking industry. The typical deal (1997) was that the government agreed to pay the sponsor's debt in exchange for the concession rights in view of sponsor difficulties in honoring the project related debt. The projects were turned over to the government in 1999. In the bailout, the government took on about $7.7 billion in debt, two-thirds owed to Mexican banks and one-third to construction companies. The equity holders are estimated to have lost about $3 billion[50] as government offered them no compensation. The outstanding bank loans were assumed by the new government entity, FARAC. There were no cash payouts. The compensation came in inflation-adjusted zero-coupon peso-bonds that the government issued directly to the debt holders—25% of it at 5-year maturities, and the remainder divided between previously unknown 10- and 15-year paper. Once under government control, tariffs on these toll roads were significantly reduced (by 40% for trucks) and commercial users were offered substantial tax discount incentives to promote asset usage and revenue generation.

The FARAC roads are now part of government umbrella agency for toll roads and bridges, CAPUFE (Caminos y PuentesFederales de Ingresos y ServiciosConexos)—which, along with BANOBRAS, the national development bank, controls 74 toll roads and 48 bridges covering 5900 km.

The re-privatization: As per SCT, Mexico needs about $5.5 billion every year for road construction and maintenance. Given the competing demands on resources, the government can provide only about half the resource requirements for the road sector. Therefore, re-privatization of the existing PPP projects had become very important.

In August 2007, ICA, Mexico's largest construction company, and its partner Goldman Sachs Infrastructure Partners were awarded four toll road concessions [Aguascalientes–Leon toll road (104 km), Guadalajara–Zapotlanejo toll road (26 km), Lagos de Moreno–Zapotlanejo toll road (119 km), and Maravatio–Zapotlanejo toll road (309 km)] totaling 558 km as the consortium made the highest bid of Ps 44.1 billion (US$ 4.0 billion). This was financed with the help of a peso-denominated US$3.7 billion loan (which included funds for liquidity) via lead bank, Santander. The debt–equity ratio for the project was 66 : 34. This was a 30-year concession to build, operate, exploit, conserve, and maintain the four toll

[49]Pratap (2011).

[50]Ehrhardt and Irwin (2004).

roads. The roads are being acquired from FARAC and the sale has been christened FARAC I. To collect proceeds from the sale of toll roads, the government has launched an infrastructure fund (El FondoNacional de Infrastuctura) that it hopes will grow to around Ps 270 billion (US$25 billion) over the next 5 years.[51] The fund will look at potential investments in roads, railroads, ports, airports, water management, and environmental projects. Analysts said that the Mexican government is planning to divest the toll roads in 8–13 packages over the next 6 years, totaling several billion dollars.

The outcome of FARAC I (in which 36 parties acquired bidding documents, 9 formed consortia, and 6 finally bid) was very successful for Mexico and for future transport infrastructure financing in the country as utilization of existing highway assets would support new project development. Some of the money raised through re-privatization was earmarked for retiring debt raised when these assets were taken over by the government in the late 1990s. The re-privatizations after a decade long hiatus "reflects an uplift in sector credit quality"[52] and commensurate reduction in risk perception among private participants. Four of the ten toll roads in Mexico rated by Standard & Poor's recently were rated at the top of the global scale (AAA).

The FARAC II project in 2008, however, ran into problems as the bids received were way below the government's expectations partly because of the onset of the global financial crisis and partly because FARAC II had several greenfield projects as opposed to the almost exclusively brownfield offering of FARAC I.

Closing Thoughts

This chapter has scanned the global infrastructure PPP space to survey the sectoral distribution of PPP projects and has delved into a few of the typical sector-specific issues particularly in India to develop an understanding of the challenges that infrastructure PPPs experience in India as well as around the world.

Armed with this context of sectoral realities, the next chapter will focus on the critical issue of optimally designing and managing PPP transactions, to best avoid, as much as possible, the minefield of challenges that threaten to derail such projects. It will provide a close-up view of some of the challenges, and the rationale behind, as well as shortcomings of, common practices that have evolved from experience in various PPP contexts.

---

[51]Project Finance International (2008).

[52]Standard & Poor's (2006).

Chapter 7
Designing and Structuring PPP Transactions

As we have seen in previous chapters, PPP transactions are multiparty, complex, and subject to considerable sector-specific and context-specific risks. Proper structuring therefore lies at the heart of successful PPP projects. This chapter takes a deep dive into the various aspects of structuring multiparty PPP projects and provides an overview of the standard processes in this area. It also offers a close look at Model Concession Agreements going through their various key elements like performance requirements, payment mechanism, dispute resolution mechanism, and termination provisions.

1 PPP Design—Key Steps and Issues

Rightly structured Public–Private Partnership (PPP) projects are expected to promote on-time and within-cost delivery of projects and provide improved quality services at reasonable costs. For all these reasons, private capital has been courted by countries all over the world to fund public projects and provide public services like water and electricity supply, various modes of transport including roads, railways, and metro rail, etc. Traditionally provided by the public sector, the expanding demand for services, combined with the fiscal resource crunch and concern for quality of public services has often compelled governments to turn to the private sector for provision of these services.

Private provision of public services has meant that the selection process of these providers is extremely rigorous, at least on paper, because the ultimate responsibility for provision of these services rests with the government and any poorly performing private provider can cause considerable grief to the government, both financially and in terms of votes. Also given the size of the projects and the sums involved, appearance of integrity and "due process" is critical for political viability of the governments initiating or administering them.

K.V. Pratap and R. Chakrabarti, *Public-Private Partnerships in Infrastructure*, India Studies in Business and Economics, DOI 10.1007/978-981-10-3355-1_7

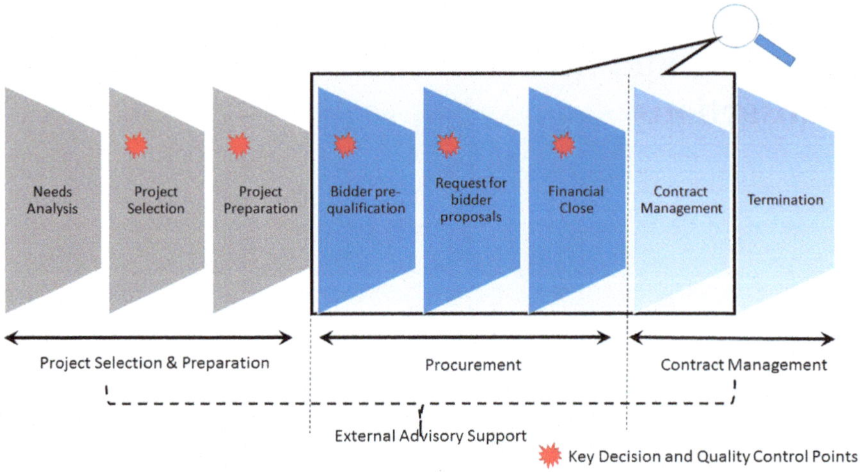

Fig. 1 Key stages of PPP transaction process

It is in this context that selection of credible project sponsors is important, as such projects frequently involve *large capital outlays* for providing *essential infrastructure services* to users for a *long term.* A typical coal-fed Ultra Mega Power Project (UMPP) for example, has a capacity of 4000 MW and costs about $4 billion to build. Not many private operators have the technical and financial capacity to implement such large projects. The criticality of reliable power supply in today's world can hardly be overstated. These projects also take a long time to be built (at least 4 years for an UMPP) and given the huge investment required and its sunk nature, the private sector has to be assured of a long-term contract for supply of power to be able to finance and build the project in the first place. Without a long-term contract for power supply and the associated demand risk mitigation, it would be difficult to accomplish financial closure[1] of a project of this scale.

Returning to PPP procurement, a bidder with inadequate technical and financial capacity can bring serious risks to the project and fail to ensure the quality of services committed by the government. We saw this in the case of Dar-es-Salaam Water and Sewerage Services, where the PPP provider (City Water Services) could not improve water services and the Tanzanian government had to terminate the contract and provision of these services reverted to the public sector.

Figure 1 shows the key stages of the PPP procurement process. In this chapter, we would be concentrating on stages 4, 5, 6, and 7, namely bidder prequalification, request for bidder proposal, financial close, and contract management.

[1]Financial closure means that adequate financing for the project has been arranged, both the contract as well as the financing documentation have been signed, and the specified condition precedents required of the public authority and the concessionaire have been met.

The objective of the PPP procurement transaction is to select a capable firm who delivers the project functions while offering value for money to government and users. Infrastructure projects are characterized by large investments, long payback period, and the need for reliable and quality infrastructure services, characteristics that subject providers to considerable risks—so, public authority would only want serious players to supply these services. Including firms with a considerably poorer track record tantamounts to allowing for unfair competition. Lower qualified firms can often undercut and quote lower bids as compared to better qualified counterparts. Since a capacity-constrained firm is likely to deliver poorer service level, this compromises public interest.

1.1 Bidder Prequalification (Request for Qualification, RfQ)

One of the first decisions to take is whether it would be a single-stage bidding or a two-stage bidding process. ***Single stage bidding*** refers to the process whereby bidders present both technical and financial proposals at the same time, which are evaluated together to select the preferred bidder. In the ***two-stage bidding process***, the technical and financial strength of the applicants is evaluated in the first stage using predetermined eligibility criteria (Request for Qualification, RfQ stage) and only qualifying firms are allowed for the second stage of bidding (Request for Proposal, RfP stage), usually involving only financial bids. In order to lend further transparency to the procurement process, there is generally a single bidding parameter at the Request for Proposal (RfP) stage. All key performance indicators, risk allocation clauses, etc. are mentioned in the Draft Concession Agreement, which is shared with the qualified bidders at the RfP stage.

The small non-complex contracts involving easily identifiable quality standards usually follow single-stage bidding while two-stage bidding is generally adopted for larger, quality-sensitive and complex contracts.

The Government of India requires a two-stage bidding process comprising of RfQ and RfP stages in a typical infrastructure project procurement on PPP basis or otherwise. The Draft Concession Agreement is provided as part of the bidding documents at the RfP stage. As the procurement process is capacity intensive, best procurement process depends on the country context, nature and capacity of the government institutions involved, and characteristics of the particular project.

In India, there is a requirement of competitive bidding at the prequalification or RfQ stage and the financial bidding or RfP stage. Competitive bidding ensures that the most efficient service provider is chosen, especially in markets where there can be only monopoly supplier of services[2] (e.g., airports in India, where there cannot

[2]In monopoly markets, competition *in* the market is precluded. Competitive bidding for provision of services in such markets ensures that there is competition *for* the market, thus competing away the monopoly rents that could be available to such monopoly service providers.

be another airport within 150 km radius of the first airport). Using competition to select the best proposal is also likely to result in value for money to the Government, besides ensuring transparency. To enable competitive bidding and participation of a large number of players in the bidding process, the approach and criteria for PPP transactions should be set out in advance, and clearly communicated to potential bidders.

Direct negotiation with a private firm is the alternative to a competitive process. This can deprive the public exchequer and users of the guarantee of paying a "fair" or competitive price. This would eat into the value for money that competitive arrangements produce for the government. However, there could be few reasons for procurement through direct negotiations: small projects (say individual primary schools), where transaction costs of a competitive process would be prohibitively expensive compared to the level of expected returns; instances like extension of an asset for which a contract is already in place and where competitive interest is likely to be limited; and need for speed in procurement in the case of emergencies and natural disasters. However, challenges in and to the procurement process can make time gains illusory. Given that these are special cases, the gold standard in procurement in general, and PPPs in particular, is competitive bidding.

Box 1: Importance of Standardization of PPP Transaction Process

Standard PPP procurement documents, also called model documents, usually lay down the norms, principles and parameters needed for procuring PPP projects. Model documents are fairly generic with the goal of imparting *transparency, consistency* and *predictability* to the procurement process, ensuring *objective* and *expeditious* decision-making.

Transparency of the selection process is a key success factor for a PPP project. It is critical to select the private partner through a competitive process (as opposed to selection based on negotiations). Otherwise, the perception that the PPP procurement is not above board can prove to be quite challenging, sometimes leading to project failure as in the case of Dabhol Power Project of India.

Standard or model contracts are expected to incorporate best practices in procurement. They also place several provisions within square brackets providing for project-specific flexibility. The project authority is expected to fill in project-specific data before the standard documents are released for bidding. Standard or model documents save on time and costs in structuring complex projects. For example, it is estimated that about 300 road projects, both at the federal and the state level, have been bid out on the basis of the Model Concession Agreement for the road sector. The use of standardized documents also saves individuals with responsibility for procurement from making mistakes and being liable for them.

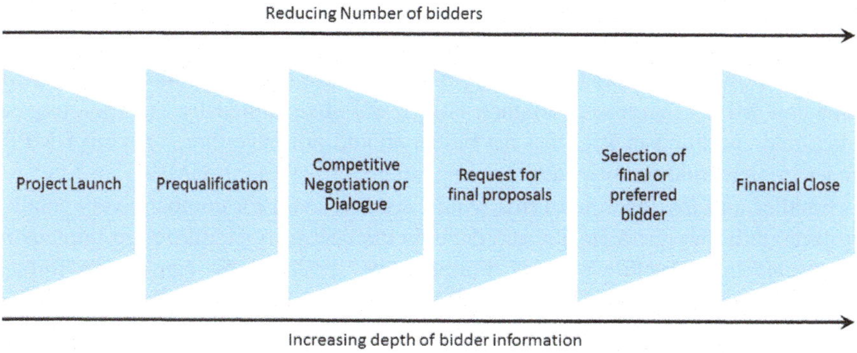

Fig. 2 Typical PPP procurement process

The typical transaction process is shown in Fig. 2. After it is decided that a particular project providing public services (like power or water, etc.) would be bid out on PPP basis, the project procurement process starts with pre-qualification (or expression of interest or Request for Qualification) of the bidders during which the technical and financial capacity of the bidders is evaluated to be able to implement the project. The bidders who qualify this stage proceed to the financial bidding or Request for Proposal stage. Generally, a single bidding parameter (like Viability Gap Funding, VGF) is used to decide on the selected bidder. The competitive PPP procurement process ensures that the selected bidder not only possesses the required technical and financial capacity to implement the project, but also is the most efficient supplier of these services as it is providing these services at the least cost (least VGF, for example) to the public exchequer.

As already stated, the first stage of procurement process is generally referred to as the Prequalification, Request for Qualification or Expression of Interest stage. The objective of this stage is to select competent bidders who have the requisite technical and financial capacity to implement the project. The end-result would be to short-list prequalified applicants who will participate in the second stage of the bidding process, so that only well-qualified firms are invited to submit financial bids.

The advantage of this stage is that it reduces the risk that the bid process will be compromised through unrealistically low financial bids from low-capability firms. The disadvantage is that the same top players are generally invited to bid for large projects, which may encourage collusive behavior. This stage also adds a few months to the procurement process and thus may be time-consuming. However, once the procurement process is completed, it may be time well spent as objective criteria are used to prequalify firms and only well-qualified firms are given the opportunity to graduate to the next stage of the bidding process. The disadvantage of selecting the same large firm can often be addressed by specifying quantitative restrictions. For example, Reliance Power was implementing three Ultra Mega Power Projects (UMPPs) at one stage with none completed, and it was felt that Reliance Power may spread itself too thin if it were given opportunity to bid for another UMPP. Therefore, Reliance Power was disqualified by incorporating an additional condition in RfQ that the bidder should not have three or more UMPPs under implementation to qualify for implementing the fourth UMPP.

Smaller and less qualified firms would need to settle for comparatively smaller projects until they grow in size and develop the necessary credibility to implement large-scale infrastructure projects. Furthermore, smaller firms can always form a consortium to bid for larger projects and learn in the process to be able to bid on their own later. This may be desirable as the public authority needs to be sure that the selected bidder would be able to deliver services. Any failure on this front would devolve this responsibility on to the public authority with immense financial and reputational implications.

Guidelines for RFQ: RfQ document should not require respondents to incur significant expenses in preparing a response. This would encourage greater participation from credible investors and enable casting of the net as wide as possible. Information sought should be precise and quantifiable so that the process of short-listing is fair and transparent, and does not lead to disputes. Conflict of interest should be eliminated to prevent potential collusion or cartelization among bidders. A generic Model RFQ should provide sufficient flexibility to adapt its provisions for meeting sector-specific and project-specific needs. This may be enabled by putting project-sector-specific provisions in square parentheses that can be modified by the project authorities to suit their respective requirements. It is also an international best practice to short-list 3–6 bidders for the second and final stage of bidding.

Approaches to prequalifying bidders: There are two approaches to prequalify bidders.

- Set a threshold in terms of technical and financial capacity and invite financial bids from all firms that pass the threshold. This is akin to a pass/fail qualification criteria and the bidders who pass the threshold are eligible to go to the next stage of the bidding process and vice versa.
- Short-listing: Under this method, potential bidders are ranked according to specified technical and financial qualification criteria, and the top ranking bidders—typically 3 to 6—are invited to submit financial proposals. Using this method, one can be sure that the desired number of prequalified firms would cross over to the next bidding stage.

It is sometimes said that the desired number of bidders may also be short-listed by raising the threshold. This is actually not true because of the difficulty in anticipating the bidder response for a particular project, and the threshold criterion used could well be off-the-mark with hindsight. There can be significant case-to-case variation. In the case of regional airports, for instance, the lowest short-listed bidder for Amritsar airport scored about 28,000 points. For the Udaipur airport, the corresponding score was only 11,000 points. This level of variation is simply unforeseeable. If threshold alone decided prequalification, the Airport Authority could have either ended up with a large number of prequalified bidders or barely one or two bidders, (as was the case in Delhi and Mumbai airports where the threshold was 80%).

Thus, prequalification based on threshold would not only be subjective, it could very well produce too few or too many bidders. Setting a minimum eligibility criteria and then short-listing 3–6 best qualifying bidders, on the contrary, appears to yield more desirable results—it selects the best available firms and gives some control over getting an adequate number of eligible bidders. This outcome is likely to be far better than a pure threshold-driven process which may throw up unanticipated results.

How many bidders to be short-listed? While we have answered that question above in that the bidders to be short-listed should be 3–6, the number of prequalified bidders should be sufficient for ensuring adequate competition in financial bidding, i.e., the second stage of the bidding process. Large number of short-listed bidders may reduce participation by serious bidders, because investors are likely to stay away from overcrowded fields. The aim should be to minimize errors of inclusion and exclusion[3]—inclusion of low-quality bidders in the short-list and exclusion of high-quality bidders from the short-list.

There are differences in national approaches as well. The Infrastructure Australia Practitioner's Guide suggests prequalification to select at least three bidders, while the Singapore PPP Handbook forbids predetermining the number of qualified bidders, lest it reduces competition. The public authorities in India may be restricting the number of qualified bidders to about half a dozen because putting in a financial bid is often expensive and the better qualified firms would sometimes not put in the money and energy for putting in a competitive bid if they are not sure that they would be undercut by a poorly qualified bidder submitting a low bid.

Past experience in India regarding prequalification: In several PPP projects, fairly tough RfQ criteria have led to a small number of firms being prequalified, removing the need for further short-listing and all the prequalified firms were invited to bid. Some examples are in the Table 1.

For selecting a preferred bidder for Delhi and Mumbai airports, 80% was the pass mark and the eligibility criteria included a large number of subjective items, such as long-term vision; development path; quality of business plan; and Human Resource approach. Bid responses for these two airports ran into 41,000 pages! It took over 6 weeks to evaluate. Only two firms prequalified. To ensure some competition, the threshold of 80% was lowered after evaluation and four firms were prequalified for each airport. Ultimately, GMR-led consortium won the Delhi airport while the GVK-led consortium got the Mumbai airport, though GMR was the winner on both the bids.

[3]Careful selection of qualification criteria is important to avoid including firms that are poorly qualified and excluding firms that could make good partners (e.g., smaller firms).

Table 1 Prequalification examples in India

	Project/Project company	Number of firms that prequalified
1.	Delhi Airport/Delhi International Airport Limited	2 (later increased to 4)
2.	Mumbai Airport/Mumbai International Airport Limited	2 (later increased to 4)
3.	Mumbai Metro Line-1	3
4.	Hyderabad Metro Project	5
5.	Delhi Metro (Airport Line)/Delhi Airport Metro Express	5

Source Planning Commission, Government of India (2009)

1.1.1 Contents of RFQ

Eligibility criteria for bidding should be aimed at getting an optimum number of bidders (typically 3–6). There should be a balance between too few and too many bidders for serving the objective of prequalifying a reasonable number of suitable bidders for the next (Request for Proposal) stage. The information sought for prequalification should generally be confined to project-relevant *technical* and *financial* capabilities. The eligibility criteria like technical and financial capacity should be defined with the intent of prequalifying an optimum number of bidders. The response should be amenable to *precise quantification* so that the process of short-listing is seen to be fair and transparent. Transparency is a great virtue in public procurement, like everywhere else, and should be practiced to preclude challenges on this account.

- Eligibility criteria
  - ***Technical Capacity***: Applicant should have enough experience and capacity in implementing infrastructure projects.

    Project/Construction Experience: Experience in the same or related sector is the key. More weightage should be given to project experience compared to construction experience because of the higher risk assumed under project experience. Similarly, if the project is say a water project, more weightage should be given to experience in water sector like water treatment or distribution vis-à-vis experience in other core sectors like road, ports, etc. Bidders should have experience in projects of a minimum size (typically 20% of the total project cost) to be eligible. The total experience should also typically be of minimum twice the total project cost to be an eligible bidder.

    O&M experience: Many PPP projects are of BOT variant. Since “operate” function is for the longest duration compared to other functions, that function is responsible for revenue accrual to the project, and specialized operations require a specialized firm, many RfQs require a specialized O&M firm to be a part of the consortium or seek a commitment from the bidder that such a firm would be made a part of the consortium in case the bidder is the selected bidder. Thus, the consortium must include a member with relevant experience in operation and maintenance (O&M). Alternatively, the successful bidder should enter into an O&M agreement with a similarly experienced entity.

- ***Financial Capacity***: Minimum net worth of applicants should be 25% of the estimated capital cost of the project, e.g., if the estimated capital cost of the project is Rs. 5 billion, then the net worth of the bidder should be at least Rs. 1.25 billion. Net worth criteria would ensure that prequalified applicants have sufficient financial strength to undertake the project. In exceptional cases, the Authority may also prescribe other indicators—like minimum annual turnover (sales) and/or net cash accruals—as measures of the applicant's financial health.[4]

It is an international best practice to have technical evaluation in the Prequalification (RfQ) stage. Technical evaluation at the RfP stage would become an elaborate and costly process with hard to compare proposals with a wide range. It would also lead to proposal-led evaluation rather than a parameter-led evaluation. With the government setting the technical parameters and asking for financial bids only, it leaves enough flexibility for bidders to design and engineer the project so as to conform to predetermined standards and specifications.

Some other caveats for prequalification are:

- Only recent experience is counted, typically 5 years preceding the bid due date. The logic is obvious that since the project for which the RfQ has been floated would be implemented in the next few months, the relevant experience that should matter is the one which is nearer to the project implementation date.
- The experience and net worth of consortium members who have a substantial stake (minimum 26% in consortium's equity) is to be considered. This ensures that only the experience of members with a substantial stake, and hence commitment, is counted for the purposes of prequalification, avoiding the tendency to add members with a small equity holding to "window-dress" proposals to gain in ranking in prequalification.
- The RfQ document also contains format in which information should be presented (for making the submissions uniform, which contributes to transparency), timeline and process of evaluation.

Box 2 illustrates the broad contours of RfQ for a power generation project.

Box 2—Request for Qualification (RfQ) for a Power Generation Project

- Scope of work will include design, build, finance, operate, and transfer (DBFOT) the power station and supply of power in accordance with the terms of the power purchase agreement.

[4]Government of India (2009).

- Indicative capital cost of the project will be stated in the RfQ. Applicants must carry out assessment of actual costs. This is very important as the public authority cannot be subjected to any claims on account of faulty data, which has been provided on a "best effort" basis.
- Applicants shall bear all costs related to the preparation of their applications and their participation in the bid process.
- Applicants are encouraged to apply after visiting the project site and checking out the site conditions.
- Cost of RFQ document: Rs. 10,000 for every Rs. 5 billion or part thereof comprising the estimated project cost.
- Instruction to Applicants
  - Eligibility of applicants: A single entity or a group of entities (consortium), joining hands to implement the project.
  - Applicant shall not have a conflict of interest that affects the Bidding Process. This includes the requirement that no applicant can overlap with another applicant, either individually or as a member of a consortium.
- Eligibility criteria
  - Project/Construction Experience: Such that the sum total of these is more than [Rs. 10 billion]. This should be equivalent to twice the estimated project cost for which bids are being invited. Information in square brackets should be appropriately modified by the project authority before floating the RfQ.
  - Financial Capacity: Applicant shall have a minimum net worth of [Rs. 1.25 billion] at the close of the preceding financial year. This amount should be 25% of the estimated project cost for which bids are being invited. Financial capacity would ensure that prequalified applicants have sufficient financial strength to raise the equity and debt necessary for undertaking the project. In exceptional cases, the authority may also prescribe minimum annual turnover (sales) and/or net cash accruals as an indication of the applicant's financial health and cash flows.
- Criteria for Evaluation
  - Applicant's capability to be established by the following parameters:

    Technical Capacity—Project/construction experience on eligible projects in power/core sectors. Power sector would include generation, transmission, and distribution of electricity; and core sector would include telecom, ports, airports, railways, metro rail, highways and bridges, industrial parks/estates, logistic parks, pipelines, irrigation, water supply, sewerage, and real estate development.

Eligible Project: Project implementation on BOT, BOO, BOOT or other similar basis; entity claiming experience should have held a minimum of 26% equity; capital cost of the project should be more than [Rs. 1 billion]; entity claiming experience shall, during the last 5 financial years preceding the application due date, have (i) paid for development of the project (excluding the cost of land), or (ii) collected and appropriated the revenues from users.

- Weightages can be 1.25 for project experience for power sector; 1 for project experience for other core sector; 0.75 for construction experience for power sector; and 0.5 for construction experience for other core sector.
  - **Financial Capacity**—Minimum Net Worth of 1.25 billion reflected in audited annual accounts for last five years.
- Credentials of eligible applicants shall be measured in terms of their experience score with weightages for category of projects.
- In case of a consortium, the experience score of each of its embers, who have an equity share of at least 26% in such consortium, shall be summed up for arriving at the combined aggregate experience score of the consortium. This would ensure that members with small equity holdings are not included for the sole purpose of achieving prequalification. In other words, only the experience and net worth of consortium members with a substantial stake are to be counted as they alone can be expected to implement the project successfully and bear the project risks. Prequalifying a consortium on the strength of a member who has a small equity holding can lead to unintended outcomes and jeopardize the project.
- Applicants shall be ranked on the basis of their respective experience scores and short-listed for submission of bids.
- Utility may short-list up to six applicants for participation in the second stage of the bid process.

Source Compiled from Ministry of Power, Government of India website (www.powermin.gov.in) and other Government of India sources.

1.2 Request for Proposal (RfP)

This is the second and generally the final stage of the PPP procurement process. Technical proposals are evaluated first at the RfQ stage, on a pass–fail or short-list basis and only bidders who pass the technical evaluation proceed to financial evaluation at the RfP stage. At this RfP stage (or invitation of financial bids stage), the selection is based on the financial bid using generally a single bidding parameter like viability gap funding (VGF). In this stage, the bidders engage in a comprehensive scrutiny of the project before submitting their financial offers. Objective selection at RfP stage ensures that the public authority gets the best financial proposal, which is at the lowest cost to public exchequer and, therefore, provides the most value for money (VfM) to the public authority.

Short-listing is needed at the RfQ stage, as bidders carry out a complete inspection of the project before submitting their financial proposals. This study includes a careful calculation of the capital and operating costs of executing the project as well as the likely revenue streams over the concession period. It also involves figuring out the potential risks in the construction and operation of the project. All this feeds into the bidders' financial model and should throw up a single number corresponding to the bidding parameter like VGF.

In the RfP stage, the key requirements of a fair and competitive bidding process must be laid down. The Model RfP document, like the Model RfQ document, would be fairly generic with the goal of imparting *transparency, consistency,* and *predictability* to the procurement process, ensuring *objective* and *expeditious* decision-making. Project-specific flexibility is built-in by keeping a number of clauses in square brackets which the project authorities are expected to populate.

1.2.1 Contents of RfP

The RfP should optimally seek information related to the financial offers only. It is desirable that it be simple and transparent requiring the bidder to quote only the value of a single bidding parameter, e.g., viability gap funding, annuity payment, premium, revenue share, fixed charge, etc. Draft Concession Agreement (Power Purchase Agreement—PPA—in the power sector) should form an integral part of the bid documents provided to the bidders along with the RfP. The draft concession agreement[5] lays down, in detail, the terms and conditions for grant of the concession, the scope of the concessionaire's services and obligations on both sides. It should also mention the concession period and other terms and conditions of the project.

A Feasibility Report/Detailed Project Report would also be provided to the bidders at the RfP stage to help them, rather than bind them to its contents. It should be made doubly clear to prospective bidders that the public authority would not entertain any claims or damages on account of deficient data in the feasibility report or the DPR, etc., that have been prepared on a "best effort" basis. It is the bidders' responsibility to carry out the necessary due diligence and not rely solely on the documents supplied by the authority before submitting a financial bid.

The RfP would have ***project-specific information*** like key features, PPP commercial terms, copies of any permits or approvals for the project, provision that detailed technical information will be provided by the project authority on best effort basis, etc.

[5]The final concession agreement would be signed between the public authority and the winning bidder at the award of contract stage.

RfP would also have ***instructions to bidders*** like no bidder shall submit more than one bid for the project; bidder may have no conflict of interest; cost of bidding to be borne by bidder; bidders are encouraged to submit their respective bids after visiting the project site and ascertaining facts for themselves, etc. There will be a cost of the RfP document, proportional to the estimated project cost.[6]

RFP would also have ***information on the bid process*** like bid validity [120 days from bid due date]; evaluation criteria, e.g., lowest grant (VGF)/highest premium[7]; bid security requirements (1% of the estimated project cost—to prevent frivolous bids) as bank guarantee/demand draft[8]; formats of various documents to be submitted—letter comprising the bid, bank guarantee for bid security, and schedule of bidding process. In the Government of India Model RfP document, there is no provision of "most economically advantageous offer[9]" or "variant bids[10]".

It is important for the RFP submission timetable be realistic. The bidders have a lot of work to do: make their bid teams and appoint advisers; carry out their own due diligence of the project information; firm up detailed arrangements between consortium members and often several subcontractors; obtain necessary management and other approvals; develop detailed financial models; negotiate pricing arrangement and terms, across the various subcontractors; and, in some cases, seek firm commitments of long-term funding from lenders. A frequent private sector complaint is that the timetable for all this is too short. An illustrative schedule of bidding process is stated in Table 2.

Bidders may seek clarifications on the RfP in writing through fax or e-mail. The authority shall try to respond to the queries at the earliest, but no later than 15 days prior to the bid due date. The authority will share all such communication with all bidders, without identifying the source of queries.

Negotiating can reduce the transparency of the bid process. For this reason, some governments forbid negotiations on the contract at any stage of the process. But communication can help resolve critical doubts. In 2004, the European Commission introduced the "competitive dialogue" procedure for procuring PPPs in the European Union, creating a dialogue window. Here, after getting initial bids, the government can communicate with bidders on any aspect of the RfP. It then

[6]Government of India recommends that this cost be fixed at the rate of Rs. 20,000 for every Rs. 1 billion of the estimated project cost. The authority may, in its discretion, raise this to up to Rs. 50,000 per Rs. 1 billion of the estimated project cost.

[7]Grant shall be payable by the authority to the concessionaire and the premium shall be payable by the concessionaire to the authority, as the case may be. These are examples of a single bidding parameter. Other examples of bidding parameters could be the highest price of the assets, the highest share of revenue, etc.

[8]For example, it may be stated that the bid shall be summarily rejected if it is not accompanied by the bid security to be provided as a demand draft or an acceptable bank guarantee. The bid security shall be refundable no later than 60 days from the bid due date except for the selected bidder.

[9]"Most economically advantageous offer" is a bidding parameter formed by combining quality as well as price in some proportion

[10]"Variant bids" are alternative and improved solutions proposed by bidders.

Table 2 Illustrative schedule of bidding process

	Event description	Date
1.	Last date for receiving queries	[25 days from the date of issue of RfP]
2.	Pre-Bid meeting-1	[To be specified]
3.	Authority response to queries latest by	[35 days from the date of issue of RfP]
4.	[Pre-Bid meeting-2]	[To be specified]
5.	Bid Due Date	[To be specified]
6.	Opening of Bids	On Bid Due Date [at least 50 days from the date of issue of RfP]
7.	Letter of Award (LOA)	Within 30 days of Bid Due Date
8.	Validity of Bids	120 days of Bid Due Date
9.	Signing of Concession Agreement	Within 30 days of LOA

Source Government of India (2009)

re-issues a final version of the RfP documents and invites final bids. A clear and comprehensive RfP and draft concession agreement avoids the need for post-bid renegotiations. Figuring out investor interest is a challenge. Pre-RfP consultation with bidders, as well as hiring experienced advisors, can improve the acceptability of the contract structure to investors. For particularly complex contracts, the competitive negotiation procedure described above could well be unavoidable.

1.3 Model Concession Agreement

PPP is a long-term contractual relationship between the public and the private party for performing functions traditionally performed by the public sector. There should be transfer of risk to the private party (e.g., commercial risk) for the relationship to be beneficial to the public party. There should also be sustainable revenue streams for the private party. All these requirements should be reflected in the concession agreement. Thus, a typical concession agreement would have provisions in five key areas.

- **Performance requirements**—The public sector is delegating some of its responsibilities to the private sector in a PPP. Therefore, the public sector needs to be certain that the quality of delegated services provided by the private party would be satisfactory. In this context, the key performance indicators need to be stated in the concession agreement. They could relate to defining the required quality and quantity of assets (like roads) and services, along with monitoring and enforcement mechanisms, including incentives and penalties, like defining required maintenance standards for a road, or the required service quality for power or water services provided directly to users. A key feature of a PPP as opposed to conventional procurement is that usually performance is specified in terms of required outputs rather than inputs. This enables the private PPP company to innovate in responding to output requirements and is the essence of a DBFOT model, which leaves the "design" function to the private sector while specifying the output requirements of the public sector.

- **Payment mechanisms**—Private sector would not invest if it is not assured of sustainable revenue streams providing it with the required return on investment. So, it is necessary to define how the private party will be paid, through user charges (road tolls), government payments based on usage or availability (fixed charges paid by the public authority based on availability of the power generation project), or a combination, including incentives and penalties. If it is the user fees that would service the private investment, the key question for risk mitigation is how tariffs would be allowed to change on account of changes in price level (inflation) or foreign exchange rate. Tariffs can be regulated by establishing tariff formulae in the PPP contract or by independent regulatory agencies, or a combination of the two. For instance, the contract may define initial tariff levels, and a formula may index it to inflation.[11]
- **Adjustment mechanisms**—PPP contracts are necessarily incomplete—that is, they cannot fully specify all future possibilities and how they should be resolved. The PPP contract therefore needs to have built-in flexibility to deal with changing circumstances within the contract, rather than through renegotiation or termination.

  In the water sector, for example, the condition of the assets may not be known with the required certainty. Therefore, an "Enhanced Monitoring Period" of a year or so may be allowed in the contract so that the PPP partner may assess the condition of underground assets and may request recalibration of tariffs if it is found that the asset condition is worse than initially assumed. Similarly, mechanisms for handling changes, such as extraordinary review of tariffs on account of changing service requirements, may also be built-in the concession contract.
- **Dispute resolution procedures**—Because PPP contracts are necessarily incomplete, defining institutional mechanism for resolution of contractual disputes should be included in the concession agreement. The Indian Model Concession Agreement (MCA) prescribes a dispute resolution procedure consisting of conciliation, arbitration, and adjudication.

  The relevant clause in the Indian MCA states that if a dispute arises between the two parties, either party may call upon the Independent Engineer to mediate and help resolve the matter amicably. If that fails, the Chairman of the Authority and the Chairman of the Board of Directors of the Concessionaire maybe the next

[11]For example, road tolls have been linked to inflation to the extent of 40% of Wholesale Price Index in India in the Model Concession Agreement owing to the fixed interest rate charged for debt, which is the major source of financing in project financed PPP projects.

stop for amicable settlement through conciliation. When conciliation fails, the dispute shall be decided by reference to arbitration by an arbitral tribunal comprising of three arbitrators, one each selected by either party, and the third by these two arbitrators. The award of the arbitration tribunal, shall be final and binding on the Parties.

If a statutory tribunal or other fora with powers to adjudicate upon disputes between the concessionaire and the authority are constituted, then it shall naturally adjudicate upon all disputes arising after its constitution. Such tribunal was mooted in India through the Public Contracts (Resolution of Disputes) Bill, 2016. This Bill would establish a mechanism to address disputes among contracting parties in public contracts including PPPs.

Together, the adjustment and dispute resolution provisions in the concession agreement may play a major role in risk mitigation for the private sector. These provisions allow for changes, and resolve problems, within the framework of the contract and thus preclude renegotiations.

- **Termination provisions**—The concession agreement should state the contract term, handover provisions, and circumstances of early termination of the PPP contract. Since the investment in a PPP project is largely sunk, there should be premature termination provisions for the comfort of the sponsors and the lenders. Otherwise, there are chances for the public party to behave opportunistically once the assets have been built, and likely difficulty in financial closure of the project.

  Early termination can arise out of three broad causes: default by the private party,[12] termination by the public party, and some external reason (force majeure). In each case, the government typically takes over control of the project assets after making a payment to the private party. These assets may be re-tendered under a new PPP contract. Termination payments defined in the contract usually vary depending on the reason for termination.

  Lenders are typically given "step-in rights" to empower them to solve problems due to an under-performing contractor, with termination only occurring if this proves to be ineffective, or if lenders choose not to exercise such rights. Termination payments are typically defined to ensure that equity-holders bear some risk and burden of default. Lenders may also have some exposure (skin in the game) so that they carry out their due diligence.

PPA is an example of a concession agreement between the power generator and distribution companies. PPA takes care of demand risk (or the risk that there would be insufficient demand for the power produced by the generator). By mitigating demand risk, a PPA helps in financial closure of the power generation project. Draft PPA should be given as a part of the bidding documents for a power generation project.

---

[12]Private party default triggers include failure to complete construction, persistent failure to meet performance standards, and insolvency of the project company.

1.4 Contract Management

Financial close in itself does not constitute success for a PPP project. Success implies completion of construction and the sustained delivery at a satisfactory level of the contracted services. So, managing contracts matters throughout the life of the PPP and not till only the commercial operation date of the project. Nevertheless, frequently, even in mature PPP programs, closing the deal, rather than fulfilling the contract, acquires primacy. Managing PPP contracts well essentially involves monitoring and enforcing the contract requirements, as well as managing the relationship between the public and private partners. The stage spans the entire life of the project.

The four key aspects of ensuring contract management are: establishing contract management institutions; monitoring PPP delivery and risk; dealing with change; and managing contract expiry and asset handover.

Establishing contract management institutions implies laying down and putting to practice the responsibilities and communication protocols to enable an effective relationship between the public and private partners to the contract. The implementing agency (like NHAI in the Indian road sector) typically has primary responsibility for contract management. This responsibility is typically handled within the agency by a designated "PPP contract manager"—its chief point of contact for everything relating to that PPP.

Monitoring PPP delivery implies ensuring contract compliance and service performance by the private party, ensuring the government delivers on its responsibilities under the contract efficiently, and risk monitoring and mitigation. For PPPs in sectors that are regulated (like power, telecom, ports, and airports in India), the sector regulator may also undertake partial or complete monitoring responsibility.

For user-fee PPPs, a regulatory framework (regulation by the concession contract or independent regulator) may be needed to guarantee that the terms of the contract are followed, key performance indicators are achieved, and the interests of the users are protected. The public authority may have an even greater role in managing the contract for an availability-based PPP project, as it assumes direct responsibility for the periodic performance-based payments as per the contract.

Generally, the PPP operator would be reluctant to part with performance data. PPP contract should, therefore, require the private partner to provide regular information on the performance of the project. The concession contract should vest in the public sector the right to inspect and audit as necessary and require the private party to implement and submit periodic user surveys. The contract should therefore clearly lay down the data requirements for post-signature monitoring by the regulator or other monitoring entity. The content, format and frequency of performance reports should also be specified in the contract.

It is the task of the implementing agency to ensure that enforcement mechanisms are implemented as needed, on the basis of the monitoring information received. This could include adjusting payments (for government pays PPPs) as per the contract, or in extreme cases, calling the performance bond. Communicating with the contractor, monitoring the trigger points for default, monitoring attempts to rectify performance shortfalls, step-in by the lenders or the public party, and termination also come within its ambit.

Generally, there is a provision of Independent Engineer (IE, a qualified firm) for monitoring and supervision of construction and operation and maintenance who will be jointly selected by the public authority and concessionaire through a transparent process. Independence of IE would add to confidence of all stakeholders and improve the project implementation efficiency. Independent Engineer may be called upon to carry out checks on construction (during construction phase), maintenance, and service standards (during operation phase), while avoiding concerns of bias in results. The IE is expected to provide an independent opinion on the progress and achievement of prespecified objectives and to regularly inspect the development of the project, reporting on progress, safety, and environmental issues to the public authority.

Dealing with change, as we have discussed, is very important and necessary mechanisms need to be put into practice to deal with contract adjustments, dispute resolution, and contract termination, and the terms and conditions of renegotiations, if that becomes necessary.

The last aspect, managing contract expiry and asset handover relates to managing the transition of assets and operations on expiry of the contract term. As we have discussed, these need to be included as termination provisions in the concession contract.

1.5 Some nuances in Project Procurement

We have seen above that there should generally be a two-stage PPP transaction process consisting of the RfQ and the RfP stages and that the procurement process should not have any provision of negotiations. However, there may be situations in which both these conditions may have to be relaxed. Let us examine them in succession.

1.5.1 Selection Based on Combined Technical and Financial Criteria

For smaller projects, proposals may be evaluated based on weighted combination of technical and financial criteria, very often captured as quality cum cost-based system (QCBS). Examples could be selection of a technical consultant for preparation of a feasibility report for PPP in power distribution where the weightage of technical score is 70% and financial score is 30%. However, defining appropriate quantitative technical criteria and how they are weighted can be subjective, which may impact transparency of the selection process.

1.5.2 Negotiation with Bidders

Provision relating to negotiation may impact transparency as it may be seen as providing clarity selectively thus precluding benefits to other possible bidders. However, negotiations with bidders are allowed in the pioneer PPP countries like UK and Australia. These countries negotiate with multiple bidders—a process sometimes referred to as "competitive negotiations". Governments may also sometimes enter into negotiations with a single preferred bidder. The advantage is that it helps clarify aspects of the RfQ, draft CA, and RfP that more closely meet government requirements. However, the disadvantage is that it reduces the transparency of the bid. The best way to avoid the need for negotiations is to prepare clear and comprehensive bidding documents—RfQ, RfP, and draft CA. However, for complex projects, competitive negotiations could be the best method for proposals to meet government requirements.

Negotiation with bidders has been tried in India too in Delhi Power Distribution Privatization. In April 2002, only two companies, BSES and Tata Power, submitted bids in response to the RfP. These are among the largest private power providers in India and are almost fully domestically owned. The Delhi Government Cabinet considered the bids unacceptable "in the present form" and constituted a Core Committee of senior officers to explore alternatives including negotiations. On May 31, 2002, the Delhi Government Cabinet met and approved the report of the Core Committee, which had managed to obtain acceptable bids following long and hard negotiations (see Table 3).

Table 3 AT&C loss reduction targets (%)—original and final

Region	Opening loss level	Original—minimum stipulated by government in RfP					AT&C losses at end of period
		2002–2003	2003–2004	2004–2005	2005–2006	2006–2007	
South/West (BRPL)	48.1	1.25	5.00	4.50	4.50	4.00	28.85
Central/East (BYPL)	57.2	1.50	5.00	5.00	5.00	4.25	36.45
North/North West (NDPL)	48.1	1.50	5.00	4.50	4.25	4.00	28.85
		Final—agreed after negotiation					
South/West (BRPL)	48.1	0.55	1.55	3.30	6.00	5.60	31.10
Central/East (BYPL)	57.2	0.75	1.75	4.00	5.65	5.10	39.95
North/North West (NDPL)	48.1	0.50	2.25	4.50	5.50	4.25	31.10

Source Adapted from Sagar (2003)

Needless to point out, the multiple steps in the journey of a PPP partially sketched above is akin to a trek down a veritable minefield. The landscape of infrastructure PPPs is strewn with scraps of failed projects that have taken one or more mis-steps in their journey.

Chapter 8
Infrastructure Regulation

One of the fundamental theorems of Economics demonstrates how perfectly competitive markets produce welfare maximizing outcomes. However, concerns about market failures that can lead outcomes away from the ideal state of affairs occupy an equally prominent place in Economics. The concerns are far more pronounced when the sector in question involves mammoth chunky investments, frequently has monopoly as the most efficient market structure and, owing to its prominence and criticality to the heart of governance through the provision of public goods, is prone to political interference.

Naturally, then, infrastructure requires an elaborate regulatory structure and mechanism to ensure that the sector provides the much needed services in an efficient and fair manner, and avoids, or at least resolves quickly, the myriad disputes that are bound to arise when multiple players cooperate on technologically complex, massively investment-heavy projects. This chapter looks at the objectives, principles and nature of infrastructure regulation, with particular focus on regulations and regulatory institutions in India.

The chapter is divided into four sections. The first section, after this introduction, provides an overview of the objectives, broad principles, and challenges of regulation in the infrastructure space. The second section provides a quick taxonomy of the various kinds of infrastructure regulatory systems prevalent around the world. The third section focuses on the infrastructure regulatory structure and institutions in India and the fourth section concludes with a pointer towards regulatory reforms in the infrastructure space.

K.V. Pratap and R. Chakrabarti, *Public-Private Partnerships in Infrastructure*,
India Studies in Business and Economics, DOI 10.1007/978-981-10-3355-1_8

1 Infrastructure Regulation—Objectives, Principles, Challenges

Regulation usually denotes controls on business activity imposed by governments. A regulatory system refers to the panoply of institutions, laws, and processes that collectively enable a government to exercise control—whether formally or indirectly—over the operation and investment choices of infrastructure businesses. At the same time, regulation can tie the government's hands in taking ex-post actions by delimiting powers and responsibilities clearly.

More than 200 infrastructure regulators have been created worldwide since 1995, primarily for telecommunications and electricity (and/or natural gas), with a smaller number in water and transport. Telecommunication is typically the first sector for which countries establish a regulatory entity. India too has witnessed setting up of independent regulatory agencies following the induction of private sector in these infrastructure sectors.

A sound regulatory architecture is a prerequisite for private investment in infrastructure. There is a clamor for independent regulation once the private sector enters the infrastructure industry, be it telecom, electricity, ports, and airports.

1.1 Objectives of Infrastructure Regulation

A key issue that infrastructure regulation should address is the fear of a *predatory state*. Infrastructure investment is highly project-specific, (think, for example, transmission lines), and hence "sunk" once installed. Sunk costs cannot be recovered, at least without significant effort, if the economic environment worsens or if the operator ceases operations and the investment is not useful elsewhere. These high irrecoverable costs tend to lure governments into opportunistic behavior, acting to expropriate assets after irrecoverable investments have been made. A typical scenario is a populist government after taking office deciding to cut tariffs or choose not to honor agreed-upon tariff increases.[1]

Investors, conscious of such risks, might hold back investments till such issues are adequately addressed, or they may demand additional compensation (enhanced tariffs, lower transfer fees, etc.) to address the risk. Such regulatory risks can raise cost of capital by as much as 2–6% points depending upon the country and sector in question. These higher costs, in turn, necessitate higher tariffs or reduced transfer fees or sale prices. This may also impact access to infrastructure services. So, independent regulation is necessary for the protection of investors from such politically inspired government intervention.

[1]This is the case of a state government in India, which has come to power on the plank of cheaper electricity and is adamant at compromising regulatory processes to honor its promise.

Often private players enter the infrastructure space dominated by one or more public sector incumbents in a developing country. For instance, when private sector was inducted for telecom service provision in India, the dominant player was the public sector incumbent, Department of Telecommunications (DOT) and later the public sector players, Mahanagar Telecom Nigam Limited (MTNL) and Bharat Sanchar Nigam Limited (BSNL). It was necessary, under these circumstances, for the private sector to be provided *a level playing field*, as the incubent public sector players may very well have refused interconnection services in telecom,[2] which would have made private sector participation in telecom stillborn. Ensuring a level playing field is again the role of the regulator.

Independent regulation is also important for *promoting competition*. However, only the inevitably "natural monopoly" segments need to be regulated to produce competitive outcomes. Rest of the segments where there is widespread competition may be left to market forces. The classic case is that of telecom sector in India where there is sufficient competition among players as not to require any regulatory role for setting telecom tariffs. On the other hand, there is role of regulation for setting tariffs and user charges in power transmission or airports that are natural monopolies.

Related to this is the role of regulation to safeguard *user interests*. The incumbent monopolist in provision of infrastructure services may have an incentive to abuse its monopoly power in terms of high user fees, low service quality and safety, etc. Regulation, whether by contract or independent regulatory agencies, may be able to prevent this. Even when government is the only provider, there may be a need for independent regulation to ensure good quality services.

Box 1: The Monopoly Pricing Problem in Infrastructure

Infrastructure players often function in monopoly environments. Downward sloping marginal cost curves characterize a natural monopoly. The socially optimal price is at P_{pc}, where Price is equal to Marginal Costs (P = MC) (please see Fig. 1 on page 195). The monopolist, however, would like to set the price at P_m, where Marginal Cost is equal to Marginal Revenue (MC = MR), but the regulator would prefer to set the price near P_{pc} or at the most where P = AC thus allowing a fair return to the monopolist provider of infrastructure services, and preventing the monopolistic exploitation of users. We also see that in the instant case, economic regulation aims to achieve competitive outcomes in the absence of such markets (Price = AC).

[2]The incentives of the new entrant and the monopolist are likely to differ. For instance, the Department of Telecommunications had little incentive to give access to its infrastructure to new entrants who would compete with it in the downstream market. The absence of an independent and neutral regulatory body worsened the problem.

Inclusion is also a major objective of regulation. Private service providers, being profit maximizers, may not have any incentive to provide services to low-income households and remote areas. Regulators, with a part of their mandate to provide universal access to public services, have an obligation towards these deprived sections of the society and encourage infrastructure access to low-income households and remote areas.

1.2 Principles of Sound Regulation

The first principle of regulatory governance by an effective agency is *autonomy*. This can be viewed as having three elements to it. *Political autonomy*, the functional independence of the agency from political authorities, measured by the autonomy of its decision-making processes, comes from procedures, mechanisms, and instruments alike. *Managerial autonomy* refers to the autonomous management of its resources and is reflected in its powers to determine its organizational structure and use its budget. Finally *regulatory autonomy* denotes its ability to regulate the sector in question. It is indicated by the criticality of the agency's responsibilities in infrastructure regulation.

Accountability is the second aspect of an agency's governance that gives an adequate level of control of the agency's budget and performance to political authority like the Parliament. Parliamentary accountability matters for two reasons. The "independent commission with congressional oversight" model of the US inspires the institutional design model adopted in several countries like India particularly with strong history of political interference of the executive in utilities underlining the criticality of including broader political stakeholders like legislature and the concurrent transparency in the regulatory process.

Transparency, the third aspect, includes disclosure and publication of relevant regulatory and institutional information, involvement of stakeholders in the agency's decision-making, and ensuring compliance to rules by agency officials. *Social transparency* refers to the involvement of non-institutional actors in the agency's policy making such as public hearings. *Institutional transparency* focuses on the transparent management of the agency not necessarily connected to stakeholder involvement. Publication of the agency's annual report, the use of norms of ethics, and the existence of public processes for hiring employees fall within this element.

Finally, *predictable* regulators and regimes helps in facilitating capital investment designed to improve the quantity and quality of infrastructure services as the PPP players would be assured that these sunk costs would be allowable expenditures for cost recovery and would be reflected in user fees. In this context, a multi-year tariff regime with predictable changes facilitates private participation in infrastructure.

1.3 Key Areas of Regulation, Regulatory Challenges, and Some Solutions

Main Regulatory Tasks: Greater access to affordable and quality utility services is an important objective in many developing countries. Regulators play an important role here in setting and monitoring connection and investment targets, overseeing appropriate cross-subsidies, and designing and implementing tariffs in order to achieve this. There are two universal tasks of economic regulation.

- Tariff determination and enforcement. Associated roles are depoliticizing the tariff-setting process and addressing issues of subsidies and cross-subsidies. Most infrastructure is still a natural monopoly (transmission lines and airports, for example) and may lead to high tariffs and monopolistic exploitation of users if pricing is not regulated as we see in Fig. 1. In addition, much of infrastructure investment is also sunk costs because of its specificity and therefore prone to opportunistic behavior from both public and private sectors. If opportunistic politicians talk about not following the signed concession contracts, the private sector would have nowhere to go because of the sunk costs. In such instances, regulators may play a sobering role by depoliticizing the tariff-setting process. If the politicians want certain sections of the society to be subsidized, then money has to come to service providers through explicit subsidies or the regulators have to allow cross-subsidization to address this issue.
- Achieving key performance targets. The government is delegating its responsibility of provision of public services to the private sector in a PPP. The private sector has to achieve the key performance indicators mentioned in the concession contract. Enforcing key performance standards related to consumer protection, maintaining health and safety standards, and ensuring universal and equitable access are the responsibilities of the regulator.

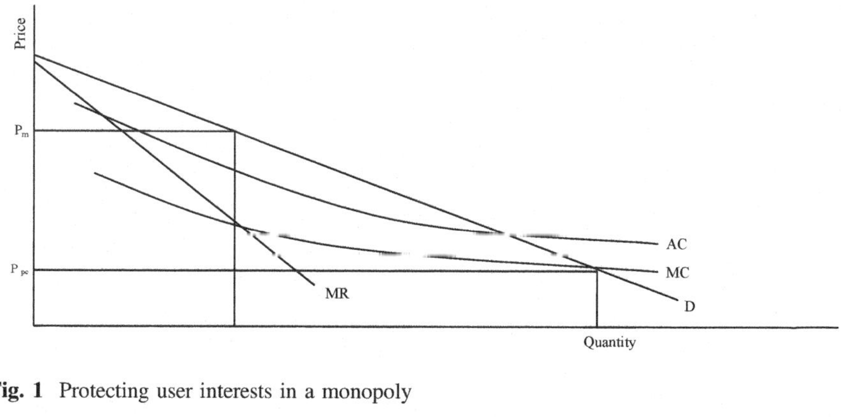

Fig. 1 Protecting user interests in a monopoly

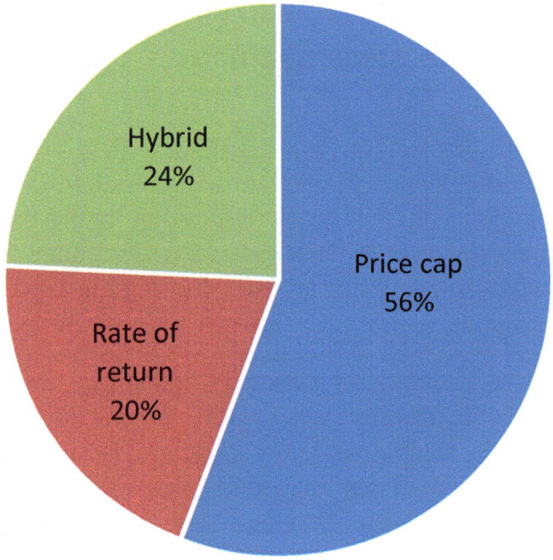

Fig. 2 Evidence on type of tariff regulation. *Note* Concession contracts in Latin America and Caribbean region in the period 1985–2000 by type of tariff regulation. *Source* Guasch (2004)

Types of tariff regulation: As we have seen, setting tariffs is among the most important of the regulatory tasks. Guasch (2004) studied over a thousand concessions granted in Latin America and Caribbean region in the period 1985–2000 and found that price cap regulation is the most popular followed by hybrid regulation and rate of return regulation, in that order (Fig. 2).

Let us study the major types of tariff regulation.

Rate-of-Return Regulation: This is also called cost-plus regulation in which costs allowed by the regulator (capital costs and operating costs) are passed through to tariffs. Regulators estimate the prudent level of operating and capital costs and add a reasonable rate of return on the invested capital to set the tariffs. Regulators in some jurisdictions use advance scheduling of price reviews to enforce rate of return regulation. For instance, private providers may present their annual revenue requirement to the regulators in an annual price review. This type of regulation is business-friendly as it provides the greatest predictability of earnings and aligns with the objective of business that requires a rate of return. In this way, this type of regulation poses less risk for the private sector and we find that the system is associated with a lower incidence of renegotiation of contracts. This type of tariff regulation is prevalent in USA.

However, the disadvantage with this type of regulation is the lack of incentives for cost control as all allowable costs are passed through to tariffs. This could promote unnecessary investments (gold plating[3] and higher capital intensity) that increase the asset base on which providers earn a return.[4] The cause of this type of

[3]This is also called the Averch–Johnson effect, or padding the rate base, and is a common criticism of rate of return regulation.

[4]This is the Aam Aadmi Party allegation against PPP power distribution companies in Delhi.

behavior is information asymmetry as regulators will always know less than managers about the "true" costs of enterprises.

Price Cap Regulation: In this system, a forecast of efficient cost levels over the future price control period serves as the basis for tariffs. Price control is set for a multi-year period, within which the regulator commits to price stability regardless of movements of actual costs. During that period, allowed prices are indexed to measures of expected cost changes like inflation plus an efficiency improvement factor. This type of tariff regulation is prevalent in UK and Australia, the pioneer countries for PPPs.

Traditionally, price change in a price control period is determined by the difference between inflation and efficiency gains, RPI-X, where RPI is the Retail Price Index and the factor X is a measure of the "productivity offset." In this way, this type of regulation addresses inflation risk, which is a major risk mitigating factor for the private operator, while taking into account efficiency improvements to the benefit of users.

In terms of implications, the Price-Cap Regulation incentivizes managers to cut costs through efficiency improvements as the price is not adjusted during the price control period if there is increased efficiency and any cost reductions below forecast levels are reflected in higher profits for the private operator. This type of regulation also lessens information asymmetry as it allows regulators to estimate the "true" costs by observing the extent of cost reduction from forecast levels. This information can then be used to set forecast costs for the next price control period, thereby gradually bringing prices closer to the efficient cost level. However, the private partner's risk is higher in case the expected cost efficiencies do not materialize. So, this type of regulation is more risky for the private sector and is associated with higher incidence of renegotiation compared to rate of return regulation.

Hybrid regulation: Generally regulators use what may be called hybrid regulation, a combination of the above methods. For example, in UK, regulators often add rate of return regulation to price cap regulation and end up with a version of RPI-X regulation. The optimal combination of parameters—rate of return tools, price or revenue caps, benchmarking, and length of time between price reviews—depends on country-specific contexts including national goals, institutional sophistication, level of competition, and economic maturity.

Regulatory risk: Tariff risk is the most common type of regulatory risk and refers to the risk that the regulator will not enforce cost-recovering level of tariffs. This risk is important as most infrastructure PPP projects are implemented on a non-recourse basis and project revenue streams remain the main source of comfort for lenders. As we have seen, setting and enforcing tariffs is among the most important functions of regulatory institutions in the country. However, tariff-setting remains highly politicized even though there are electricity regulatory institutions both at the federal and the state level. The average cost per unit of electricity is about Rs. 4.50 while the average revenue realization is only about Rs. 3.50 per unit leaving a gap of about Rs. 1 ($0.015 at the current exchange rate) per unit of electricity sold in India. This loss adds up to Rs. 600 billion at electricity distribution level in the country.

Regulatory risk can also arise due to arbitrary changes in tariff-setting regimes (a particular state government in India wanted to bypass the regulatory institutions in setting tariffs in the electricity sector), the method of calculation, or parameters, or in various performance requirements like investment obligations, indicators of service quality, environmental and safety performance, all of which usually with financial implications.

Other Regulatory Challenges: There are many other regulatory challenges like institutional fragility—appointments in regulatory agencies take a long time to be made and are suspect, leading to usurping of regulatory powers by the political executive as we saw in the Dar-es-Salaam Water and Sewerage case study where a government Minister became the regulator, thus increasing regulatory risk for the PPP operator, City Water Services.

There is no dedicated source of funding for the regulator in many cases and they depend on the government ministry for their funding, which could impact their independence and autonomy. Tariff risk could be a manifestation of government capture of regulatory institutions. Similarly, there could be private sector capture of regulatory institutions when these institutions favor the private sector rather than be neutral.

Another major concern is that regulatory agencies are staffed with retired officials too eager to tow the official line and thus have little credibility. The tariff risk that we discussed earlier could be related to this factor in that the regulators cannot run an independent course when they have been appointed by the political executive that wants low retail tariffs for infrastructure services including electricity. It may not be a coincidence that all four infrastructure regulators in India are headed by ex-bureaucrats. In this context, it has been said that "quality human resources are scarcer than money,"[5] as far as regulation is concerned. The result is that regulatory substance is compromised because of lack of capacity and competence among regulators that affects the quality, credibility, and impact of regulatory decisions. In the case of Nhava Sheva International Container Terminal (NSICT), the bid parameter (revenue share to government per container) was permitted as an allowable expense to be reflected in container charges to users, thus giving rise to the bizarre proposition that the bid was won by the firm that promised to charge the highest amount per container to users.

Even with non-partisan regulators with legal mandates for tariff setting and other regulatory decisions, government can still try to influence them to modify or overturn decisions. Tariff setting remains a highly politicized area and governments are usually sensitive to public angst against price increases (that are often necessary to cover costs as in the electricity sector in India).

There is also lack of transparency and public participation in regulatory decisions. Regulatory contracts like concession agreements or power purchase agreements frequently compromise transparency. More often than not, they evade public scrutiny on account of commercial secrecy. But, when taxpayers and customers

[5]Tremolet and Shah (2005). As quoted in Eberhard (2007a).

bear the burden of bad PPP contracts (e.g., the Delhi-Noida Toll Bridge contract), they should be in public domain. Transparency is essential for building legitimacy. Participation implies public hearings where stakeholders can provide inputs relevant for making regulatory decisions. This is often not done. Accountability through appeal mechanisms is not prevalent in many sectors like in the port sector in India.

For all these reasons, regulatory contracts are under stress and seeing increasing incidence of renegotiations—Guasch[6] finds that the incidence of renegotiations has increased from 30% (using dataset for 1985–2000) to 68% (using dataset for 1988–2010) in Latin America.

This brings us to the question of the *mitigation of regulatory risk*. We need autonomous, accountable, transparent, predictable regulators and regimes as discussed above. An institutional design model promoting an agency taking decisions independent of the executive branch (autonomy), subject to accountability to Parliament, having transparent decision-making procedures emphasizing public hearings, and having budgetary autonomy therefore provides an ideal paradigm of an infrastructure regulator.

However, it has been found that independent regulatory agencies are also not enough as they could use regulatory discretion in a way that could stymie private investment. So, it has been suggested that regulatory discretion may be reduced, for example, by incorporating tariff regimes in the concession agreement itself (regulation by contract). This system has been used in the Indian model concession agreements extensively in that the first year tariff needs to be bid by the private PPP players and the tariffs in subsequent years are determined by linking it to wholesale price index. But, if concession agreements are over-specified to reduce regulatory discretion, there is a risk of frequent renegotiations when the financial architecture included in the concession agreement may have to be changed because of unforeseen developments. So, there is a need for balance between over-specified contracts and unimpeded regulatory discretion for facilitating private investment.

Additional mechanisms for reducing regulatory risk are: partial risk guarantee (PRG) for regulatory performance, indexation of contracts, and appeal, arbitration, and other dispute resolution mechanisms. Uganda, in 2004, effected the first application in the world of a World Bank PRG for utility regulatory systems. The PRG sought to protect the investors in the electricity distribution concession from the regulator making decisions in conflict with tariff-setting provisions of the concession agreement. It provided support for potential loss of regulated revenues emanating from a "guaranteed event," using a predefined calculation process. Such events include non-compliance by the regulator to the agreed tariff framework, and other agreed-upon arrangements (like, in the case of Uganda, complete pass-through of the bulk electricity tariff supply from the state-owned Uganda Electricity Transmission Company (UETCL), and timely adjustments of tariffs).

---

[6]Guasch (2004).

Such guarantees provide comparatively low-cost instruments to cut cost of capital and facilitate deal closure.

Very often, the private partner insists on tariff indexation on account of exchange rate depreciation (to cover foreign exchange risk) and inflation (to cover inflation risk). These may be allowed in concession contracts, as we have described above, to provide comfort to the private partners and reduce regulatory discretion. A three-step dispute resolution mechanism, consisting of conciliation, arbitration, and adjudication, has also been specified in Indian model concession contracts.

2 Types of Regulatory Systems

Broadly speaking, there are at least *five* distinct types of infrastructure regulatory systems. Figure 3 provides an overview

- **Regulation by Government**: Traditionally, governments regulate where there is market failure[7] and where they seek to achieve specific socio-economic and environmental objectives. The latter concern is most evident in government actions like provision of free power to farmers. However, when the Government acts as regulator, its conflicting roles become evident: Governments often represent specific political constituencies and wish to offer low-cost or free services to these constituencies. When governments also play a regulatory role, it has to balance financial viability of the project with customer protection. These different and at times conflicting roles are seldom separated explicitly, leading to one or more functions being compromised. Therefore, government's conflicting roles of grantor of concession and regulator should be separated and government's political role in relation to utility services should be made explicit through transparent policies and public funding streams. In other words, if governments want to cultivate political constituencies by giving them access to public services below costs, there have to be commensurate revenue streams available from the budget for private providers.
- **Regulation by Contract**: Many infrastructure sectors like the road sector in India do not have independent sectoral regulators. In such sectors, regulatory certainty is provided by the concession contract, which has the current toll rates set by the Government Order on National Highway Fee (Determination of Rates and Collection) Rules, 2008 and the tariff-setting formula for future years stated upfront in the concession contract with its linkage to the Wholesale Price Index to the extent of 40%. Government of India is also trying to bring in private investment in the water sector and in the absence of a sectoral regulator,

[7]A market failure is a situation where free markets fail to allocate resources efficiently. It is apparent in many real-life situations including failure to produce enough merit goods, such as education and health care, failure to control the manufacture and sale of sin goods like cigarettes and alcohol, etc.

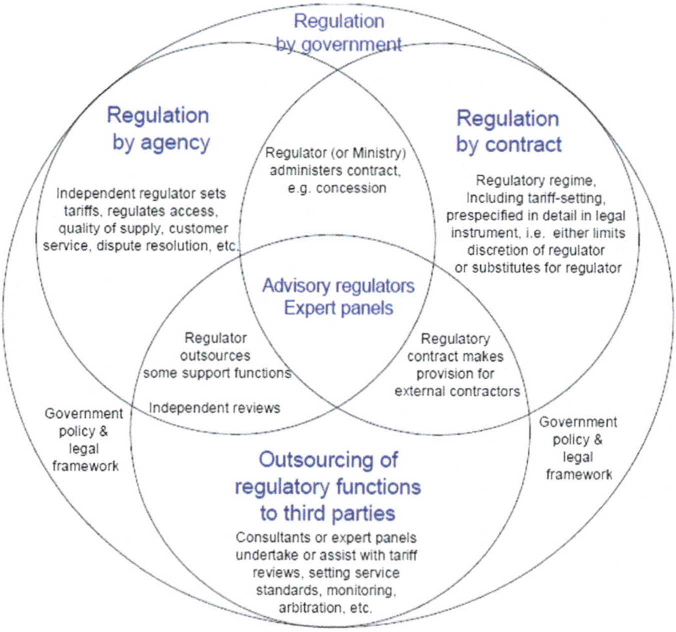

Fig. 3 Types of regulatory systems. *Source* Eberhard (2007b)

regulatory certainty would be provided by contract. Regulation by contract is prevalent in countries with previous colonial ties to France and Spain like Gabon.[8]

- **Independent Sectoral Regulators**: Because of high asset specificity in infrastructure sectors, much of the investment in such sectors is sunk costs, giving rise to regulatory risk that government would not set cost recovery level of tariffs. So, the private sector insists on independent sectoral regulators to de-politicize the tariff-setting process. The facets of independence for the regulator could be in terms of decision-making, institutional, and financial independence. *Decision-making independence* could be through a clear mandate existing in law to make regulatory decisions without prior government approval, with no entity short of a court or pre-designated arbitrator having the right to overrule it. *Institutional and management independence* could be in terms of the regulatory institution existing separately from a government ministry or department and having control over internal administration as well as security of tenure protecting from removal for political reasons. *Financial independence* could be in terms of the regulator having an earmarked, adequate, and secure

[8]France is a written law (civil law) country. Everything should be specified in detail in the law there.

source of funding. Regulation through independent sectoral regulators is prevalent in countries with previous colonial ties to UK like Kenya and Zambia.
- **Outsourced regulatory functions**: This entails use of external contractors to perform certain regulatory functions such as tariff reviews, monitoring of compliance with the concession contract, or dispute resolution. The recommendations of these contractors could be binding or advisory.
- **Hybrids**: Many countries could have sectors where the above types of regulation coexist. For example, in the airport sector of India there is coexistence of the above models—regulation by contract as well as the existence of an independent regulator (Airport Economic Regulatory Authority, AERA). Investors are sometimes nervous about substantial discretionary power granted to independent regulators and have advocated regulatory contracts with greater predictability in tariff regimes and, therefore, revenue streams. In this way, independent regulators combined with regulatory contracts may inspire greater confidence. It is sometimes said that regulatory contracts may be stronger when supported by independent regulators because the contracts are necessarily incomplete and when unaddressed situations arise, an independent regulator may take the necessary call. In addition, because concession contracts are frequently renegotiated, there is a need for independent regulatory institutions who can do this.

Let us discuss the important regulatory systems in some more detail.

2.1 *Regulation by Contract*

We have seen that given the huge investment requirements, asset specificity, and lack of an independent regulator in many sectors, regulation by contract may be necessary. The essence of a concession contract is that it embodies the rules of determining tariff as an agreement between the private investor and the government. Because of them being in the contract, the investor's consent is necessary to change the rules. This legal protection of tariff expectations gives the investor the confidence to invest in infrastructure.

However, even in sectors where there are independent regulatory agencies, their mere existence may not be sufficient for regulatory certainty. For example, in the case of Delhi Power Distribution PPP, the High Court of Delhi on 23 May 2011 had observed that[9]

> ...the Commission (Delhi Electricity Regulatory Commission, DERC) has to function with responsibility, intellectual integrity, consistent objectivity, and transparent functionalism appreciating the essential nature of the regulatory body. We emphasize on intellectual

[9]The context of the observation was regulatory flip flops by Delhi Electricity Regulatory Commission whereby it gave conflicting recommendations about tariffs within a period of 6 months—from decrease tariffs to increase tariffs.

integrity and transparent functionalism as we are totally dissatisfied with the way the Commission has proceeded with the manner of (tariff) determination.

As we have seen, most Concession Agreements would have provisions regarding tariff determination and performance standards—this may provide greater predictability and enforceability. In this way, Concession Agreements define the "rules of the game" so that prospective bidders for service provision can build financial models and bid. Regulation by contract is already in existence in India, e.g., in the road sector.

There are ***three variants of regulation by contract*** depending on how it is enforced. In the first variant, key contract provisions, such as tariff-setting formulae, are ***self-administered*** by the parties to the contract, which implies regulation without a regulator or the assistance of third parties. However, the most important problem of this variant is that parties to the contract are both "players and referees." For example, challenges regarding impartiality and credibility of government can arise if it is a party to the contract and is also directly administering the contract, including tracking performance provisions, particularly if it is failing to fulfill any contractual commitments such as investment obligations.[10]

To build credibility and a semblance of impartiality, in the second variant, provision could be made for ***certain aspects of the contract to be undertaken by third parties***—Independent Engineer who monitors performance. Independent Engineer is generally a qualified firm jointly selected by public and private partners to monitor construction during the "construction" period and monitor operation and maintenance during the "operation" period. The public party is concerned as it is delegating some of the public functions to the private sector. However, rather than the public party monitoring the performance, the private partner's preference would be that this function is carried out by a third-party firm or an Independent Engineer. However, effectiveness of these contracts depends on penalties for poor performance, which have rarely been imposed in India. For example, the Comptroller and Auditor General of India has ticked off the National Highway Authority of India that penalties due are not collected.

In the last variant, the detailed tariff-setting agreement, is ***administered by a regulator*** although it is embedded in a concession contract. Here the regulatory contract complements but does not replace the regulator. However, there is a problem: while tariff-setting formula may be specified in the contract, the regulator may feel obligated by its mandate to intervene in public interest. In these cases, it is essential that regulatory boundaries are clarified between the concession contract and the independent regulator.

[10]In the airport sector in India, the airport company for Delhi Airport, Delhi International Airport Limited is 26% owned by Airports Authority of India, which is a majority public sector owned company.

2.2 Independent Sectoral Regulator

In the classic Anglo-American tradition, the regulator has the legal right to set the tariff at a "reasonable" level. However, with such a legal right, it gets the power to override the tariff-setting rules in the contract, threatening the contractual certainty that the investor so desires. On the other hand, if the regulator is bound by the rules in the contract, then it becomes merely a contract management unit. This model can provide greater certainty for the future investor, but questions the independence of the regulator.

To elaborate, there is potential of conflict between Sector Regulator and Concession Agreement if both coexist. A regulatory agency can partner more successfully with a regulatory contract where the contract is incomplete and additional regulatory mechanisms are essential. Alternatively, the areas could be explicitly segregated between the two through law and/or the contract like restricting the regulator to periodic tariff setting, or performance monitoring or mediation and arbitration.

In the electricity sector in India, for instance, there are the independent regulators, Central Electricity Regulatory Commission at the federal level and the State Electricity Regulatory Commissions at the state level, as well as the Concession Agreement (Power Purchase Agreement) between the private power generator and the public distributor and there is a possibility of conflict between these two regulatory systems. In this case, without defining the regulatory domains of the two systems, the regulatory risk may be of such a level that it may preclude the private sector from bidding and investing.

In Manila, confusion resulted from the coexistence of a regulator with a concession contract. There, the water system for the east and the west sides of the city was transferred to private firms under two concession contracts. The contracts lay down the service standards and tariff-setting rules. The government has however also created a quasi-autonomous Regulatory Office, on the lines of the UK's Ofwat.[11] In the wake of the Asian currency crisis (1997), the viability of the concessionaires required changes in regulatory rules. But it was unclear whether the Regulator should be changing the rules (an independent agency using discretionary authority in public interest) or purely enforce the terms of the contract and leave any negotiation to the board of MWSS (Metropolitan Waterworks and Sewerage System, the public agency), the legal signatory to the contract. In the end, multiple regulatory players had to be involved, including the Regulator, the board of MWSS, the arbitrator under the contract, and even the president of the Philippines!

Using a contract to attract private participation and then superimposing a regulator with unilateral powers to override that contract may appear as a sure recipe for failure. This calls for the need for harmonization between these two regulatory

[11]The regulator for the water sector in the UK.

systems through a consultative process; other options are untenable: for example, exempting PPP contracts from provisions of sector regulation implies that the most important beneficiary of independent regulation is precluded from its benefits; or leaving tariff and service standards to the regulator may be equally preposterous because as we have discussed, tariffs and performance standards are the most important regulatory tasks and without them the concession contract may be pretty useless; or compensating the private partner in the event that regulatory decisions are inconsistent with the concession agreement may not be agreed by the sector regulator (though this has happened in the case of Uganda through a World Bank PRG as we have already seen).

One model of harmonious coexistence of contract and regulatory agency is that the regulatory body monitors the contract, enforces it, provides the analytic input when tariffs or other aspects of the contract are reset or renegotiated, publishes information about the private operator's compliance vis-à-vis the contract,[12] benchmarks the performance of a number of contracts to ensure performance improvement based on competitive benchmarking, ensures that regulatory decisions (for example, for tariff reviews) are taken after public participation,[13] and creates a customer complaints unit to help customers with unresolved complaints with the utility.

One question that is often asked is: How much discretion should be given to regulatory bodies? Highly specified contracts may limit regulatory discretion which gives comfort to investors, but may cause renegotiation. More discretion to regulator can facilitate adjustment to new unforeseen events and thus prevent renegotiations but may cause regulatory risk to investors. So, there is a need for balance between regulator's discretion and regulatory certainty through the concession contract. However, it is also agreed that some form of discretion may be given to the regulator.

2.3 *Outsourced Regulatory Functions*

Challenges associated with a regulator's independence, capacity, or legitimacy may suggest outsourcing as an option. Similarly, where regulatory contracts require additional support for their effective administration, the outsourcing option may be explored. Cost–benefit reasons may also favor outsourcing and contracting out work. This system entails use of external contractors to perform certain functions such as tariff reviews, monitoring of compliance with contract conditions, or dispute

[12]Giving the regulator the responsibility to publish the private party's contract compliance information as well as the performance of government agencies involved in the sector would increase transparency and accountability.

[13]This could be done in a number of ways: for example, by allowing the public to interact with the utility in public in which the utility justifies tariff changes to the regulator.

resolution among the parties. A survey of 51 infrastructure regulators by Tremolet et al. (2004) found that 75% contracted out at least some regulatory tasks and devoted 20–33% of their budgets for outsourcing. This system can provide a powerful ancillary or transitional mechanism to build confidence in the regulatory system and ensure greater consistency and credibility in regulatory decisions.

For operationalizing the outsourcing option, strategic decision will need to be made about the functions that should be outsourced and this will differ over time, e.g., as regulatory capacity and credibility gets built up, the number of outsourced regulatory functions may go down.

Even in relatively developed regulatory systems, some functions may be outsourced. In this arrangement, government or independent regulators use the services of experts to help them arrive at reasoned regulatory decisions. When contracting out work, a standing panel is preferable. The appointment process of experts needs to be transparent and credible. Besides panelists should have the necessary qualifications, skills, experience, and no conflict of interest. If the appointed experts have conflict of interest, their advice could likely be biased impacting their credibility and the credibility of the derived regulatory decisions.

There are two variants of this regulatory system

- *Weak advisory regulator model*: In this model, advice is generally confidential, which the authority in question may accept or ignore. Public consultation is absent or scarce and credibility of the advice therefore is low.
- *Strong advisory regulator model*: This model is strong in terms of transparency and accountability (public participation in regulatory decisions is extensively used) and could help build a political constituency for independent regulation at a later stage.

2.4 Hybrids

Regulatory models often coexist depending on country and sector contexts and challenges. Regulatory models need to be more nuanced, and customized to individual country contexts keeping in mind regulatory commitment and capacity. Hybrid models fit for individual country settings can be selected from the menu of options. Also the nature of these hybrid models should be dynamic and in consonance with changes in regulatory independence and capacity.[14]

In India, we have regulation by contract in the road sector, which does not have an independent regulator. In the power and the aviation sectors, there are independent regulators as well as concession contracts. It is also true that in many instances, some outsourced expert advice is used while making regulatory decisions. In the water sector, there are concession contracts in cities like Nagpur and

[14]Eberhard (2007b).

government also regulates the sector. This last feature (regulation by government) subjects the sector to considerable regulatory risks impeding the flow of private investment in the sector despite immense unmet need for efficient water services. Thus, India could be considered an example of a country where hybrid regulatory system is prevalent.

3 Infrastructure Regulatory Institutions in India

Regulatory framework in Indian infrastructure sectors has developed autonomously rather than by design. Political constraints, ministerial preferences, and suggestions from multilateral agencies have played a major role in the emergence of infrastructure regulatory system in India. Because of these factors, there is no common philosophy or uniformity in regulation across infrastructure sectors in the country.

The main infrastructure regulatory agencies are: Central Electricity Regulatory Commission/State Electricity Regulatory Commissions (CERC/SERCs) in the Power sector; Telecom Regulatory Authority of India (TRAI) in the Telecom sector; Tariff Authority for Major Ports (TAMP) in the Port sector; and Airports Economic Regulatory Authority (AERA) in the Airport sector. In addition, the Rail Tariff Authority has been approved by the Government and is likely to be set up soon.

- ***Power sector—CERC/SERC***

In the power sector, we have independent regulatory institutions in the form of Central Electricity Regulatory Commission (CERC) at the federal level and State Electricity Regulatory Commissions (SERC) at the provincial level. This is because Electricity is a Concurrent subject with both the federal government and the state governments empowered to legislate on the subject.

CERC was constituted in 1998. The mission of CERC includes promoting competition, making bulk power markets more efficient, improving the supply quality, promoting investments in power and advising government to eliminate institutional barriers to better match demand and supply and protect consumer interest.

In pursuance of the mission, the main mandatory functions of the Electricity Regulatory Commissions (ERC) are: to regulate the tariff of generation and transmission companies; to issue licenses to function as transmission licensee and electricity trader; to adjudicate upon disputes involving generating companies or transmission licensee; and to specify and enforce the standards with respect to quality, continuity and reliability of service by licensees.

The main advisory functions of ERCs are: promoting competition, making power markets more efficient, and promoting investments in the sector.

As would be apparent from the functions stated above, the CERC and SERCs have extensive functions and regulatory powers with regard to tariff setting, enforcing performance standards, and dispute resolution.

- ***Telecom—TRAI***

As private service providers entered the telecom markets, there arose, inevitably, the need for independent regulation. The government established the Telecom Regulatory Authority of India (TRAI) in February 1997 through an Act of Parliament. Its mandate is to regulate telecom services, including fixation/revision of tariffs for telecom services, a function earlier performed by the Central Government.

The other functions of TRAI are to recommend the terms and conditions of license to a service provider; ensure compliance to terms and conditions of license; settle disputes between service providers; protect the interest of the consumers of telecom service; and facilitate competition and promote operational efficiency of telecom services so as to facilitate growth in such services.

In 2000, the TRAI Act was amended through an ordinance, that established a Telecommunications Dispute Settlement and Appellate Tribunal (TDSAT) to take over some functions from TRAI. TDSAT now adjudicates any licensor-licensee dispute, those between two or more service providers, as well as between a service provider and consumer group. It also hears appeals against any action of TRAI.

- ***Ports—TAMP***

The Tariff Authority for Major Ports (TAMP) was created in 1997 with tariff setting as its sole function. Its jurisdiction covers only the 12 major ports and not the 200+ non-major ports that have emerged in India. TAMP sets tariff ceilings for Major Ports. Non-major ports are largely autonomous and enjoy market driven pricing. Tariffs at major ports are rarely below ceiling as they run at full capacity. There is no recourse to TAMP on other matters such as dispute resolution, performance standards, consumer protection, and competition. The orders notified by the Authority are final with no appellate authority except, of course, the state High Court.

However, given the competition, it has been suggested that tariff setting should be deregulated and it should be left to market forces. Only when competition among terminals in a port or among ports is seen insufficient, or when some serious market imperfections arise, there would be need for pricing control. Therefore, the operating principle should be tariff regulation as exception rather than by rule. In this set up, TAMP could also act as the Appellate Tribunal where tariff is determined by service providers.

- ***Airports—AERA***

Airports Economic Regulatory Authority (AERA) was created in 2008. Its main functions are: determine the tariff for aeronautical services; determine the amount of the Development Fee, and Passenger Service Fee in respect of major airports; and monitor the set performance standards relating to quality, continuity and reliability of service. However, AERA only regulates PPP airports (Delhi, Mumbai, Hyderabad and Bengaluru). Other over one hundred airports are regulated by the public sector incumbent, Airports Authority of India (AAI). This seems like a major flaw because AAI is the operator as well as the regulator for these airports.

As the name suggests, AERA does only economic regulation while technical regulation is the domain of the Director General of Civil Aviation (DGCA). However, Government is mulling the creation of a unified regulatory agency, the Civil Aviation Authority replacing DGCA and AERA.

- ***Rail Tariff Authority in the works***

The Rail Tariff Authority (RTA) was approved by the highest decision-making authority of the Government of India, the Union Cabinet, in January 2014. Its sole function would be to advise the Ministry of Railways on passenger and freight rates. This will reduce persistent cross-subsidization[15] between freight and passenger services and restore freight traffic to railways. The current share of railways and roads in freight traffic is 30:70 and should change towards optimality if freight and passenger tariffs are rationalized. The recommendations of the RTA would be non-binding on the Ministry of Railways. They could be binding only after amending the Railways Act, 1989.

4 Regulatory Reforms

The Electricity Regulatory Commissions and TRAI enjoy extensive regulatory powers compared to TAMP and AERA. The ERCs and TRAI also satisfy many of the fundamental tenets like separation of powers (among legislative, executive and judicial powers), democratic accountability, and the federal principle that we discuss below.

Separation of Powers: The institutional framework that has emerged in electricity and telecom sectors in India broadly conforms to the doctrine of separation of power (legislative, executive, and judicial). The regulators themselves (ERCs and TRAI) function as quasi-judicial bodies. Appeals against their orders are heard by separate quasi-judicial Appellate Tribunals (Appellate Tribunal for Electricity, APTEL and Telecom Dispute Settlement and Appellate Tribunal, TDSAT).

Democratic accountability: Direct accountability of the regulator to a Ministry (executive) may undermine its independence. The regulatory agency is therefore given functional autonomy in its day-to-day functioning. But the Ministry is granted powers to issue broad guidelines and directives. Regulators may be made

[15]Freight rates are kept well above economic levels so that passenger fares may be kept low. The extent of cross-subsidization of passenger fares by freight rates has been estimated at Rs. 320 billion annually (which is a third of the budget of the Indian Railways) and needs to be rationalized.

accountable to the legislature through the requirement of submitting an annual report; to the people through the requirement for public hearings before arriving at decisions, and appointment of competent regulators.

Federal principle: Subjects are divided into center (i.e., federal Government), state and concurrent competence. This has been followed in the electricity and telecom sectors. In the electricity sector, which is a concurrent subject, there are multilevel regulatory institutions as per the federal principle. However, there is a need for developing a uniform philosophy through creation of institutions like the Forum of Regulators, which has membership of both CERC and SERCs. As telecom is in the central list, there is the TRAI at the national level and no separate agencies dealing with telecom regulation at the state level.

However, there is a need for a uniform regulatory framework across regulatory agencies. This uniformity is desired in terms, for example, of the relationship of the regulator with the Ministry. While the Ministry may give general policy guidelines to the regulator like in the case of Delhi power distribution privatization, it should never interfere with regulatory decisions, which implies that regulatory agencies should otherwise be autonomous and accountable to Parliament in terms of both reporting requirements and removal of members of the regulatory body.

There is also a need for uniformity in composition and service conditions in terms of selection process, qualifications, and experience, which varies across infrastructure regulatory agencies; e.g., appointment tenure varies from 3 to 5 years, and the regulators may be reappointed in electricity appellate tribunals, not in others.

In terms of functions, CERC enjoys extensive powers, including licensing, enforcement, and penalties, while the role of TAMP is restricted to only tariff setting and that too only for major ports. One guiding principle for functions of regulatory agencies is to appreciate the difference between *carriage* and *content*. *Carriage* (like power transmission lines or water pipelines) has natural monopoly non-competitive elements, so players should have non-discriminatory open access to these facilities. *Content* like electricity (power generation) or voice telephony can be provided competitively. Regulatory system should ensure this.

There is no specialized forum of appeal (appellate tribunals) except for electricity and telecom. There are issues also with accountability of regulators.

There are no regulators in the road and coal sectors where ministries are playing this role. However, it is an international best practice to separate the roles of policy making, operation, and regulation where the policy-making function should be with the government, while operation is with service providers who can be from the public or private sectors, while regulation should be with independent and autonomous regulatory agencies to promote competition and fair play. If ministries double up as umpires (regulators), the regulatory risk may become too high, leading to the private sector shying away from service provision or demanding a hefty risk premium, or even project cancelation as we have seen in the Dar-es-Salaam Water and Sewerage case.

But, care should be taken against proliferation of regulatory agencies. India probably already has the unique distinction of having the maximum number of independent regulatory agencies. This has complicated and delayed decision-making and has increased uncertainty regarding the business environment. These issues are further compounded by regulatory "surprises." So, there is a strong case for reducing the number of independent regulators rather than increasing them. In this context, there may be no advantage in having separate regulators for coal and roads. For the coal sector, the charter of the CERC may be expanded. For issues that arise in PPP projects, government already has an institutional mechanism in the road sector (Inter-Ministerial Group) to suggest appropriate contractual adjustments rather than require regulators to do this.

4.1 What Can India Learn from Other Countries?[16]

While reforming the Indian infrastructure regulatory system, what can we learn from other countries? The idea is to learn from the experience of countries with robust regulatory systems.

United States: The creation of independent regulatory agencies pretty much started in the USA. Independent regulation had emerged in the US in the early part of the twentieth century in response to public resentment at the abuse of monopoly powers by private firms in the provision of essential services. However, no new regulators have been created in the US in recent decades.

These regulatory agencies are not uniform in scope and design and we have sector-specific (Federal Aviation Authority) and multi-sectoral regulators (Federal Communications Commission). However, the US infrastructure regulatory agencies are relatively autonomous and are not subject to everyday political interference. There is also democratic accountability in that these agencies are closely supervised by the US Congress in terms of appointments and reports. Another facet of democratic accountability is that rule making by these agencies is subject to public hearing. Also, the Administrative Procedure Act requires agencies to publish all proposed regulations in the Federal Register at least 30 days in advance for public comments.

United Kingdom: The UK infrastructure regulatory agencies are also characterized by a lack of common approach and consistency. However, conventions ensure that selection is credible and there is autonomy in functioning. The UK has undertaken regulatory reforms since the mid-1990s and the thrust of these reforms is on creation of multi-sectoral regulators to streamline regulatory framework and eliminate overlapping regulations, and reduction of regulatory burden.[17]

In some ways, the present Indian situation resembles the legal framework for utilities regulation in the UK at the turn of the century. There sector-specific statutes

---

[16]Secretariat of Infrastructure (2008).

[17]Reduction in regulatory burden is designed to bring about a balance between public interest and interests of persons. Burden is defined to include a financial cost, an administrative inconvenience, or obstacle to efficiency.

governed existing regulators with diverse regulatory objectives as well as different regulatory structures and processes. India may require a period of consolidation and cross-sector standardization of regulation through a consolidating regulation applicable to all existing regulators.

Australia: Just like India, there is separation of powers between the Commonwealth and States in Australia. Similarly, in that country, there is no uniformity in regulatory institutional formats, objectives, or regulatory processes across regulators in consonance with India. Most states in Australia have multi-sectoral regulators. The trend is towards development of a common regulatory approach through federal-state coordination. National markets in electricity and gas have developed through extensive consultations among federal and state governments, utilities and consumers.

Sri Lanka: In Sri Lanka also, the trend is towards multi-sectoral regulator in electricity and water services. The reasons are: objectives of regulation are similar, e.g., tariff regulation and universalization of service, which calls for deployment of common skills avoiding unnecessary duplication of personnel and costs. In an environment where regulatory capacity is in short supply, this would be a very important consideration. Multi-sectoral regulator also facilitates cross-learning across sectors and may be less amenable to capture by the government or the private sector. This (regulatory capture) is a very frequent occurrence in developing countries and may be a very important consideration in favor of multi-sectoral regulators.

The above survey makes it apparent that the regulatory challenges faced by India are not unique, but are being faced by many other countries, both developing and developed. It is in this context that the government has mulled regulatory reforms, a topic that we turn to next.

4.2 Regulatory Reforms in India

The Indian Prime Minister's 2011 Independence Day Speech included the following paragraph:

> In recent years, we have established independent regulatory authorities in many areas. These authorities discharge many responsibilities which were earlier in the domain of the government itself. We have no legislation which would enable monitoring of the work of these regulatory authorities and make them more accountable, without, however, compromising their independence. We are also considering enactment of such a law.

As we have seen, regulatory reforms may be needed in a number of areas and in fact a Regulatory Reforms Bill was prepared in 2013, but could not receive parliamentary approval for conversion into law. The areas of regulatory reforms could include the following:

Clarity of roles: There should be a separation among functions related to policy making, operations, and regulation. Policy making is the domain of the government; operators can be from both public and private sectors; and regulator should regulate with clearly defined objectives and tasks. Grantor of the contract and the Regulatory Agency must be two separate entities—Regulatory Agency should be the "judge" between the grantor and the grantee (operator). These functions should not be combined either in the government or the regulator.

Objectives: Enabling competition and protecting consumer interest resulting in accessible, affordable and quality infrastructure ought to be the objectives of regulation. As we have seen, the two most important regulatory tasks are setting tariffs and enforcing performance standards. In this context, it is well known that competition is the best safeguard of consumer interests. This is apparent, for example, from the experience of the telecom sector where the telecom tariffs have gone down from being among the world's highest about two decades ago to being among the world's lowest now. Performance standards should be enforced for ensuring quality of service.

In competitive market segments, regulation should preferably be light with tariff-setting left to markets (e.g., voice telecom services, which is the *content* segment). In segments with elements of natural monopoly, on the other hand, (e.g., airports, transmission lines, which is the *carriage* segment) regulation ought to be strict. In order to promote competition in *content*, *carriage* should be strictly regulated to ensure non-discriminatory open access for service providers including reasonable tariffs.

Independence and Autonomy: Regulatory institutions ought to be independent and autonomous—both in administration as well as financially—to achieve the desired objectives. In terms of administrative autonomy, regulator should have fair degree of autonomy in selecting its staff and the remuneration payable to its staff—expert staff may be hired on market-determined compensation. In terms of financial autonomy, budget of the regulator should be presented by the Ministry concerned for parliamentary approval as a grant or from levy of such fees that may be authorized. Once approved, the entire budget should be put at the disposal of the regulatory commission.

The Ministry should be entitled to give only general policy guidelines to the regulator. To re-emphasize, policy guidelines should be "general" and not specific to any case under consideration of the regulator. There should be no perceived interference from the executive in the selection and removal of members constituting the regulatory body. The members of the regulatory body should be selected by the President on recommendation of the Prime Minister. The members should have a fixed tenure of 4 years. The qualifications and experience of members may be specified by law to ensure a multidisciplinary composition of the regulatory body. Composition at present is generally retired and serving bureaucrats. It is no coincidence that all the four major infrastructure regulatory bodies in India currently are headed by ex-bureaucrats. This should change and people with other than public sector background (academics, lawyers, Chartered Accountants, managers, etc.) should also be selected for these institutions to have sufficient credibility. Removal of members of the regulatory body should be sufficiently difficult so that an inconvenient ruling may not be a ground for removal. Terms of service of the regulator should be remunerative enough to attract suitably qualified and experienced persons. Members should be ineligible for reappointment and should also be debarred from employment with any entity dealing in matters under the jurisdiction of the regulator at least for some "cooling off" period.

Functions: As seen above, there are two essential regulatory tasks: tariff setting and enforcing performance standards. The functions of the regulatory body relate to these tasks. So, tariff determination in sectors subject to limited competition is the most important function. Here, the guideline is that tariffs should be affordable while at the same time viable for the private sector. One indication of viable tariffs for the private sector is that the project should be able to attract financing on commercial terms. The second major function relates to protecting consumer interest by ensuring quality of service and lowering costs. The quality of infrastructure services should be benchmarked to international standards. Very often the quality standards are a part of license conditions and so a related function of any regulatory body would be enforcing the license conditions.

Transparency: Transparency requires that regulators take decisions under clearly defined, published procedures. Stakeholders' inputs and comments should be taken into account through public hearings, for example, and rationale for decisions should be explained.

Predictability: Following published regulatory procedures and methods consistently and in a timely fashion is key to a regulator's predictability. Predictability and consistency of decisions and decision-making, in turn, make for credibility of the regulatory process. One mechanism for ensuring predictability is setting multi-year tariffs during which tariffs would be relatively fixed and any variation in the tariffs during the multi-year period would be as per a predetermined formula.

Accountability: Though independent and autonomous, regulators should have democratic accountability. It is an accepted practice that regulators should not be accountable to the concerned ministry (like TRAI being accountable to the telecom ministry and ERCs being accountable to the Ministry of Power), lest there be inappropriate interference in the functioning of the regulatory agencies. However, regulators should be accountable to the people and the legislature. This could be ensured through transparency in regulatory rule-making with compulsory requirement of prior publication, public hearings, and time for comment. Once a regulation is made, it should be communicated through an Annual Report to Parliament outlining the regulatory approach and decisions. Regulation/report should be tabled in Parliament and scrutinized by the appropriate legislative committee and the regulator should be available to answer questions. The annual accounts of the regulatory agency should be subject to audit by the Comptroller and Auditor General (CAG), which should however be restricted to expenditure control and not policy review of regulatory decisions.

Legal accountability should be ensured through making it possible for any person aggrieved by a regulatory decision to be able to file an appeal with the Appellate Tribunal. In addition, there should be provision for Judicial Review of regulatory and appellate decisions, which should however only be restricted to questions of law and procedures and not policy choices.

Capacity-building: Competence of regulatory staff determines, in a large measure, the quality and credibility of regulatory decisions. In the regulatory field, it has been stated that quality human resources are harder to find than money. Capacity-building should be a vital element for improving regulatory performance. Some strategies to alleviate capacity constraints are: some key rules (such as tariff setting) may be specified in the contract, rather than being left to the regulators discretion; build up core of qualified and skilled staff and rely on external advice for specialized tasks; make employment terms at the regulatory agency attractive so that it can attract qualified personnel; and establish multi-sectoral agencies to conserve staff resources.

Multi-sectoral regulators: It has been suggested that there should be multi-sectoral regulators for communications, energy, and transport at federal level in India. At the state level, there should be a single infrastructure regulatory commission spanning all infrastructure sectors. This would reduce the number of regulatory agencies, help develop capacity, enhance consistency, and reduce costs. While there is a clamor of new regulators in the coal and road sectors in India, regulatory goals in these sectors may as well be served by enlarging the scope of the existing regulators in related sectors, e.g., the scope of the existing ERCs may be extended to the coal sector.

4.3 Present State and Desired Status of Infrastructure Regulation in Developing Countries

The figure below summarizes the present state and desired status of infrastructure regulation in developing countries. The current state in most developing countries is characterized by weak commitment—both regulatory and political—to independent regulation and significant institutional and human capacity constraints, placing them in the lower left quadrant of the figure. The desired state is characterized by strong regulatory commitment and competent institutions, which is the upper right quadrant. While an independent regulator might be effective with a strong regulatory commitment and institutional competence, it is likely to be less successful in settings with weak government commitment and limited institutional capacity. This movement from lower left to the upper right quadrant will take considerable time (Fig. 4).

It took decades for the US to reach an equilibrium in which the independence of regulatory agencies was recognized and supported by administrative procedures, rules, and judicial review. In developing countries, regulatory structures have been

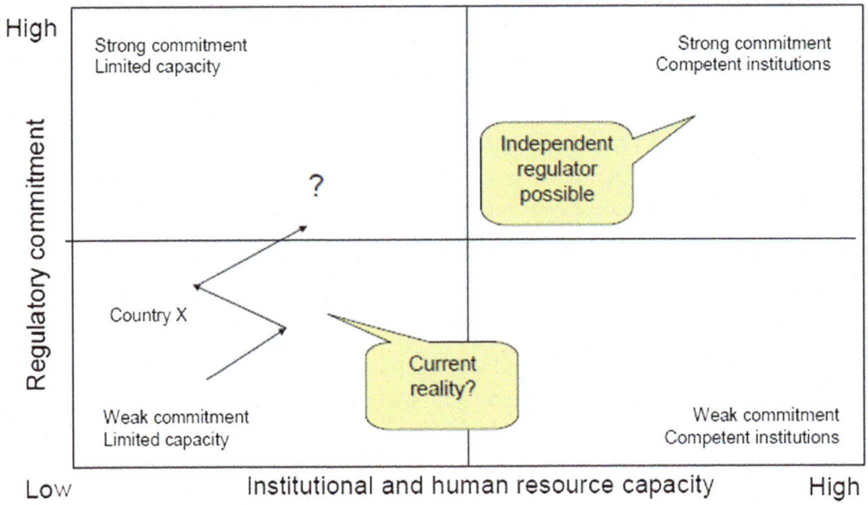

Fig. 4 Regulatory commitment and institutional capacity. *Source* Eberhard (2007b)

created from scratch and are still in early stages of development. Although progress towards regulatory effectiveness has been slow, at least the trend is in the right direction—greater independence, accountability, and transparency. The effort towards regulatory reforms in India is also in the same positive direction.

Part II
Infrastructure PPPs in India: Managing the Challenges

Chapter 9
PPPs in India

1 Current Status of PPPs in India

Public–Private Partnerships (PPPs) are the default option for implementing infrastructure projects in India. As a result, India stands second in the developing world both by number of projects and investment as per the Private Participation in Infrastructure database of the World Bank. In terms of number of projects, India stands second to China while in terms of investment, it stands second to Brazil.

The condition of PPPs in India is, however, not sanguine. There are several cases of distressed and failed PPPs. For example, Delhi Airport Metro Express line was shut down due to financial woes and is now being run by the public sector. Tata's Mundra Ultra Mega Power Project of 4,000 MW capacity was shut down due to high coal prices, but is now producing power as the coal prices have moderated. The marquee Delhi International Airport Limited (DIAL) has also had issues.

These three flagship projects were implemented on PPP basis by the best of the Indian private sector infrastructure companies, namely Reliance Infrastructure, Tata Power, and GMR Infrastructure, respectively, but fell on bad times for a variety of reasons. Some of the generic reasons for the woes of several trophy PPPs[1] were badly designed contracts (only 40% of the Indian PPPs are based on Model Concession Agreements, MCAs); high leverage that had made things inflexible and increased risks; and inadequate land acquisition and long-drawn environmental clearance process that delayed projects with severe adverse implications on their financial viability. The issues differed across sectors. In the road sector, the poor state of PPPs was attributed to firms bidding aggressively for Build-Operate-Transfer projects using the "Jugaad" principle of first bagging the project and renegotiating later. The DIAL project may also be facing problems because of aggressive bidding. In the power generation sector, coal prices had shot through the

[1]The Economist (2012).

K.V. Pratap and R. Chakrabarti, *Public-Private Partnerships in Infrastructure*,
India Studies in Business and Economics, DOI 10.1007/978-981-10-3355-1_9

roof while its availability was constrained. For all these reasons, fresh PPP activity had stalled but things have started looking up lately.

Another piece of evidence about the country's rickety infrastructure is India's ranking on global competitiveness. As per the World Economic Forum's (WEF) Global Competitiveness Report (GCR) 2015–16, India ranks 55th out of 140 countries,[2] which is a massive improvement over 2014–15 rankings when it was ranked 71. Despite the improvement in India's ranking in the current year, India is still ranked lower than its 48th rank in the GCR 2007–08, which implies that India is steadily losing its competitiveness. India's rank differential with China is 27, up from 14 in 2007. Infrastructure is one of the 12 parameters that is considered by the WEF in preparing the global competitiveness ranking. For India, WEF has found that one of the most problematic factors for doing business is the inadequate supply of infrastructure—quality of overall infrastructure is ranked at 81 out of 140, which implies that the quality of infrastructure is pulling down the overall Indian competitiveness. Quality of electricity supply is ranked at a lowly 98 out of 140 countries.

India's Infrastructure deficit: India's significant infrastructure deficit spans multiple sectors. Though the power supply situation in India has improved lately (peaking deficit of 3.2% and energy shortage of 2.3% in 2015[3]), the quantum of Aggregate Technical & Commercial (AT&C) losses is very high at an estimated at 25.4%.[4] In the road sector, there are about 100,000 km of National Highways, which constitute 2% of the network but carry 40% of the traffic.[5] These are the best roads in India but only 24% are 4-lane or more, 52% are 2-lane, 24% are single lane, the single lane implying that if two vehicles have to cross each other, one has to get down to the shoulder to allow the other to pass. This suggests severe road congestion and wastage of time and fuel in ubiquitous traffic jams in the country.

In the Airport sector, the traffic has just exploded in recent years. Delhi Airport's three runways have 75 aircraft movements per hour during peak hour and over 950 movements a day. As a result, there is inadequate capacity in terms of runways, aircraft handling capacity, and terminal buildings. Before the third runway became

[2]The ranking uses evaluation on 12 parameters for 140 countries. The parameters include macroeconomic environment, infrastructure, institutions, and health and education. In the Global Competitiveness Report 2015–16, India is ranked lowest among the BRICS countries except for Brazil—China is ranked 28, Russia 45, South Africa 49, and Brazil 75. After 5 years of decline, India jumped 16 ranks to 55th place in 2015–16. While the impression of India's institutions has improved (60th rank, up 10), business leaders still consider corruption to be a major hindrance to doing business in the country. Infrastructure has also improved (81st, up 6) but continues to be a major growth bottleneck with electricity particularly being a problem.

[3]Government of India (Ministry of Power) (2016).

[4]The figure is for 2012–13 (Source: Government of India (Central Electricity Authority) 2016).

[5]India has world's second largest road network at 4.8 million km. The road network transports more than 60% of all goods and 85% of total passenger traffic in the country.

operational at Delhi Airport, it was not unusual to have aircrafts circling in the holding area of the Airport for half-an-hour or more wasting precious fuel and time. In the port sector, there are inadequate berths, rail-road connectivity, and shallow draft. The average turnaround time of vessels[6] at Indian ports was 2.13 days in 2014–15[7] compared to a few hours in Singapore. In the railway sector, there are saturated routes and slow average speeds of both passenger and, particularly, the freight trains.

Besides the large infrastructure deficit in India, there are other issues with publicly provided infrastructure: poor quality of infrastructure, e.g., Delhi airport was worse than a bus terminal at the turn of the millennium and was rated among the worst in the world; persistent losses, e.g., the subsidy to the integrated power utility of Delhi, Delhi Vidyut Board, on the eve of the privatization of its distribution function in 2001–02 was Rs. 11.96 billion and this number was increasing by about 0.5 billion every year; and time and cost overruns—as per the status report of major central-sector projects in India costing Rs. 1.50 billion or more for the month of September 2012, out of the 566 such projects, 46% had been delayed vis-a-vis their latest scheduled date of completion. Delays in land acquisition, municipal permissions, material supply, work awards, as well as operational issues continued to drag down implementation of these projects. The overall cost overrun amounted to 16.8% of the original cost. All these issues imply that there is overall low efficiency in most publicly provided infrastructure.

This huge infrastructure deficit and other issues with publicly provided infrastructure beg for a remedy. The government cannot fund infrastructure to the extent of the shortfall as it is bound by the annual fiscal deficit target emanating from the Fiscal Responsibility and Budget Management Act (2003). As we have seen, there are other issues with publicly provided infrastructure, partly because of the poor incentive mechanisms in the public sector. Therefore, the Government has invited the private sector for taking on select infrastructure provisioning responsibilities to address the issues including improvement of on-time and within cost delivery of projects. PPPs also shift the focus from asset creation to service delivery. In addition, private sector operations in the same industry provide a benchmark to the public–sector for improving efficiency (as apparent from the telecom, airlines, port, road, and power industries, which have both public and private sector operators).

Because of the emphasis placed on PPPs, there is increasing importance of private participation in infrastructure. In the Tenth Plan (2002–07) period, 25% of Rs. 9 trillion (or ~\$225 billion) came from the private sector. In the Eleventh Plan (2007–12) period, this percentage went to over a third (38%) of Rs. 20 trillion (~ \$500 billion) that came from the private sector. In the Twelfth Plan (2012–17)

---

[6]The total time spent by a vessel at the port from its arrival at to its departure from the reporting station.

[7]Source: Government of India (Ministry of Shipping) (2016).

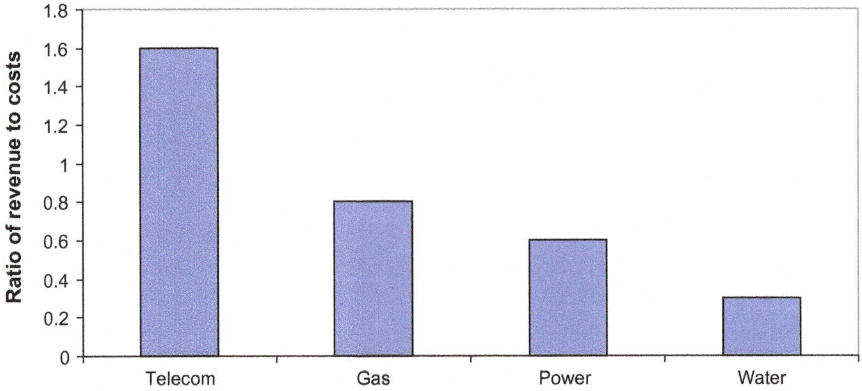

Fig. 1 Costs are fully recovered only in few infrastructure sectors. *Source* World Bank (1994)

period, about half (47%) of the total projected infrastructure investment of Rs. 40 trillion (~ $1 trillion) was expected to come from the private sector.[8] So, we find that not only is the proportional contribution of the private sector rising (from a quarter to a third to about half over the Tenth, Eleventh, and Twelfth Plan periods, respectively), but it is also increasing on an increasing base, thus demonstrating the salience of private participation in infrastructure in India.

Not all Infrastructure Sectors are equally amenable to PPPs: The private sector would want sustainable revenue streams to be interested in investing in any project. One of the crucial determinants of private participation in infrastructure (PPI) is the ratio of revenue to costs (see Fig. 1). This ratio is the highest in the telecom sector, and not surprisingly the sector accounts for the highest PPP investment among all infrastructure sectors. Similarly, the water sector has the least cost recovery and could be the most important reason for the least PPI in the sector. In between there is the power sector, where private investment has flown in, but mainly in the generation sub-sector, where the political economy issues are the least, compared to power distribution.

Share of private investment in different sectors in the 11th Plan period in India: In line with the above argument, we find that private investment constitutes the preponderant share of investment in the port, telecom, and the airport sector (see Fig. 2). Other areas of private interest are electricity (mainly generation) and road sectors, while the water sector did not attract any interest mainly because of low cost recovery and the associated political sensitivity of any effort to improve cost recovery in the sector.

Given the experience, government policy has been to increase reliance on PPPs for additional investment and for improved efficiency in sectors that can be

[8]All numbers in this paragraph are at constant 2011–12 price level and exchange rate (Rs. 40 = $1).

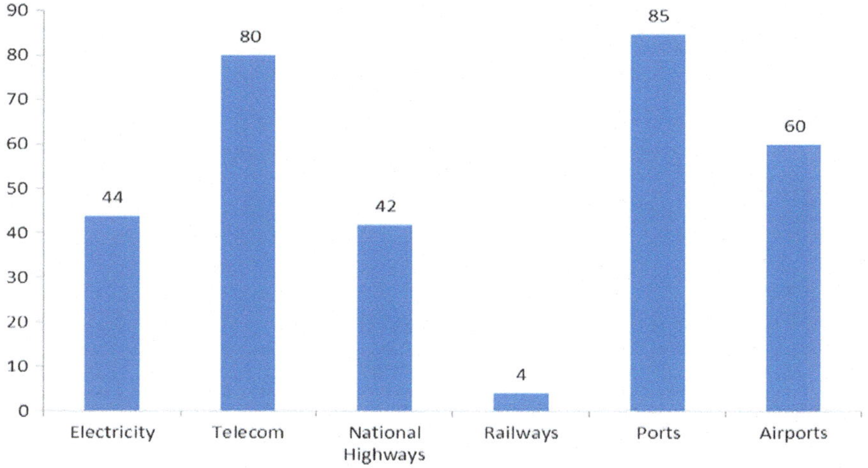

Fig. 2 Share of private investment in different sectors in India in 11th Plan (2007–12) period

commercialized, e.g., highways, ports, airports, and rail concessions. Another strand of public policy is that public sector has to continue and even expand especially in sectors that cannot be commercialized, such as rural roads. The increased private investment in the commercialized sectors makes this move (public investment to concentrate more on non-commercialized sectors) possible.

Overall Status of PPI in India: As we have seen, India is ranked second among developing countries both by number of PPP projects and investments. Figure 3 shows the sector-wise distribution of number of projects and investment for private participation in infrastructure in India.

Figure 3 shows that most PPP projects are in the transport sector (in terms of numbers), constituted mainly by 386 road projects. However, most investment has come in the energy sector, where this investment has come mainly in the electricity generation sector ($132 billion of the $143 billion investment in the energy sector). On the other hand, the least number of projects and the least investment has come in the water and sewerage sector because of low cost recovery and the associated political sensitivity of any effort to raise water tariffs to cost recovery levels.

Most private investment has flown into electricity generation and not in distribution as political economy issues are fewer in generation (Fig. 4). There are a small number of projects and correspondingly low investment in water and sewerage sector in India. This is because, though there is immense need for PPI, political economy issues emanating from low cost recovery in the sector are the maximum. A large chunk of investment has flown into telecom because of adequate cost recovery. Road sector accounts for the maximum number of projects, but these projects are comparatively smaller as compared, for example, to telecom projects.

The top 10 PPP infrastructure sponsors in India account for more than half of the total PPP projects (52%) and investments (56%) (see Fig. 5). Of them, 9 are indigenous, implying that the PPI program in India is mainly homegrown. One of

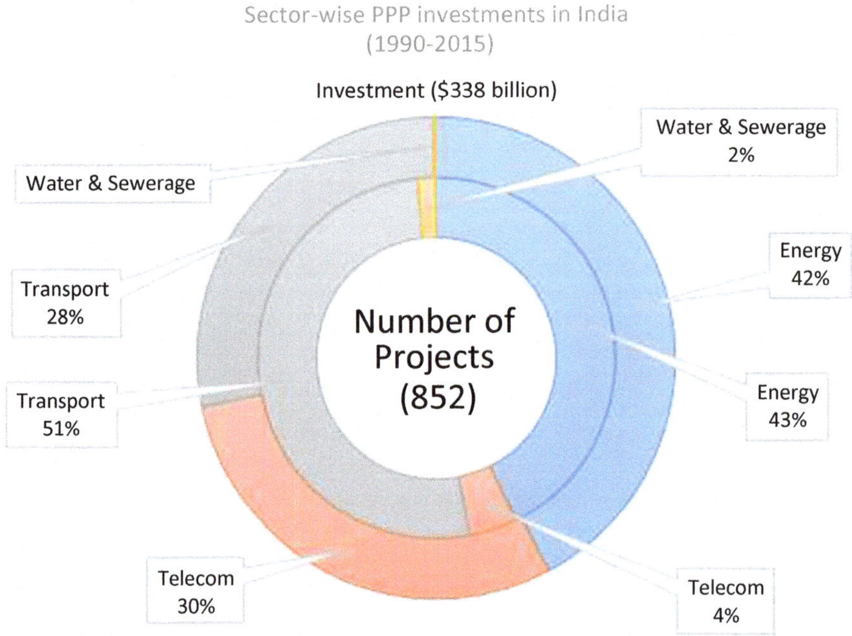

Fig. 3 Private Participation in Infrastructure in India (1990–15). *Source* Private Participation in Infrastructure database of the World Bank (http://ppi.worldbank.org) (viewed on 28 January 2016)

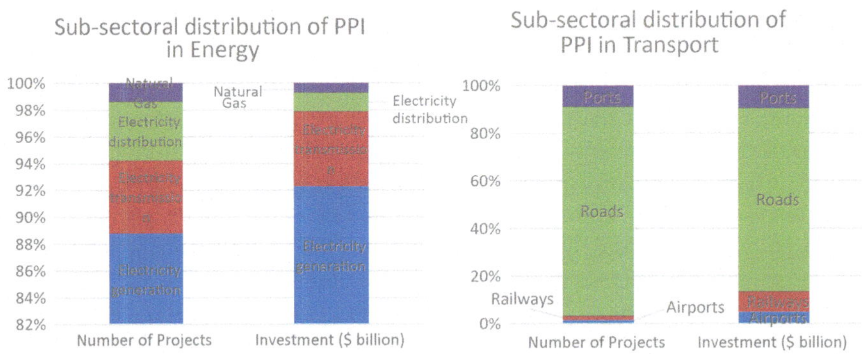

Fig. 4 PPI flows in India, by sub-sectors. *Source* Private Participation in Infrastructure database of the World Bank (http://ppi.worldbank.org) (viewed on 28 January 2016)

the reasons for this could be the high foreign exchange risk in infrastructure sectors (other than port and airport sectors where a reasonable proportion of revenues is in foreign currency). In infrastructure sectors, the revenues generally are in local currency while foreign investment would generally mean the use of foreign currency financing, thus giving rise to currency mismatch and foreign exchange risk. Domestic investment, on the other hand, is subject to lower political sensitivity and

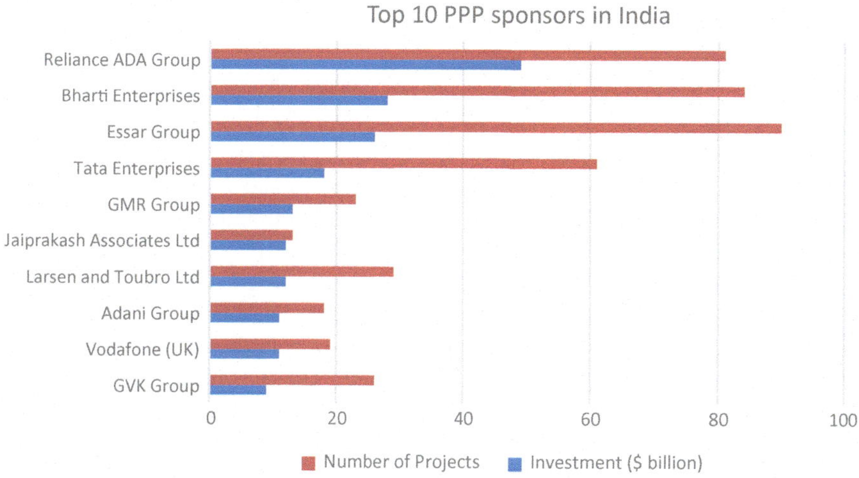

Fig. 5 Top Project Sponsors in India. *Source* Private Participation in Infrastructure database of the World Bank (http://ppi.worldbank.org) (viewed on 28 January 2016)

foreign exchange risk. Another characteristic of sponsor information is the heavy presence of telecom firms in consonance with the rest of the world.

PPP Trends: PPP trends in India, both by number of projects and investments, are shown in Fig. 6. While the overall trend is positive, PPPs experienced an upsurge only in the 11th Plan period (2007–12), when they contributed to more than a third of the total infrastructure investment of about $500 billion. This was also commensurately reflected in the number of PPP projects. There was little impact of the Global Financial Crisis of 2008 on the pace of PPP investments, both because of limited role of foreign investment in Indian infrastructure and because of the proactive measures taken by the government and the Reserve Bank of India to contain its impact. Another trend that is discernible is that since 2012, there has been a sharp deceleration in both the number and investment in PPPs. In the last 2 years (2014–16), the deceleration may have been reversed, because of proactive policy measures evidenced by new models in the road sector (hybrid annuity

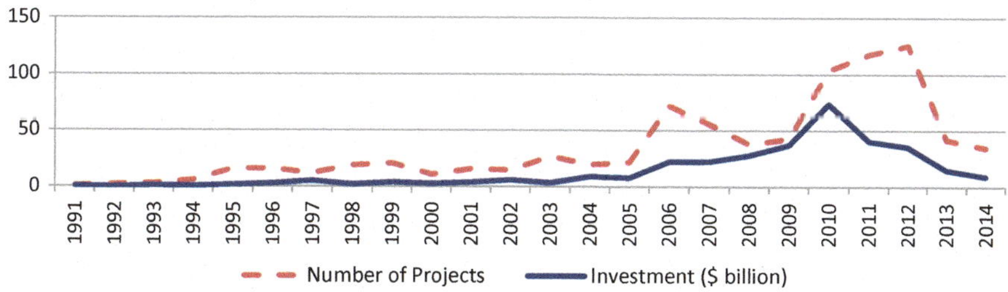

Fig. 6 PPP trends in India. *Source* Private Participation in Infrastructure database of the World Bank (http://ppi.worldbank.org) (viewed on 30 January 2016)

model) and addressing some of the constraints in the other sectors like availability of coal in the power generation sector.

Given that there is a gestation period of a few years between financial closure of a project and its commercial operations, the figure also implies increase in the number of projects under operation.

PPP in States: India is a federal country with 29 states and 7 union territories. The top five states account for 58% of total PPP investments in India. Undivided Andhra Pradesh is the leading state both by number of PPP projects and investments (17.5%). Some of the PPP projects undertaken in undivided AP are: Rajiv Gandhi International Airport, Gangavaram Port, and Krishnapatnam Port. AP Infrastructure Development Enabling Act, 2001 was the first such act in the country. It applies to all infrastructure projects implemented by the state. The Act specifies guidelines for developer selection, gives options in terms of PPP types, and sets limits on state support to infrastructure projects. The Government of Andhra Pradesh uses the following forms of support: Direct financial support in the form of state's share of viability gap funding (VGF) to promote economically viable but financially unviable projects; exemptions in terms of sales tax and stamp duty; asset-based support in the form of Government-owned land at concessional lease charges; administrative support to get clearances, undertake rehabilitation and resettlement, power and water supply at project site, etc. (Fig. 7).

Maharashtra, Karnataka, and Gujarat average around 11% each of the total PPP investments in the country. The most popular sector for PPP in leading states are roads. The bottom 10 states represent only 3.5% of total PPP investments indicating differences in investment environment.

2 PPP Framework in India

As we have seen, India is second in the developing world both by number of and investment in PPP projects. The measures for attracting private infrastructure investment include: policy, institutional, and regulatory framework for PPPs that has been put in place; financial support to bridge viability gap of PPP projects; creation of India Infrastructure Finance Company Limited (IIFCL) for long-term debt; and simplification and standardization of documents and processes.

Policy, institutional and regulatory framework: The policy is to encourage private participation in economic and social infrastructure for: on-time and within cost delivery of infrastructure; higher efficiency in operations; and diverting scarce fiscal resources to non-commercial sectors like rural roads.[9] The institutional structure is

[9]The idea is that PPPs should be encouraged in sectors that can attract private investment (commercial sectors) so that scarce fiscal space can be released for non-commercial sectors like rural roads where private sector would not be interested.

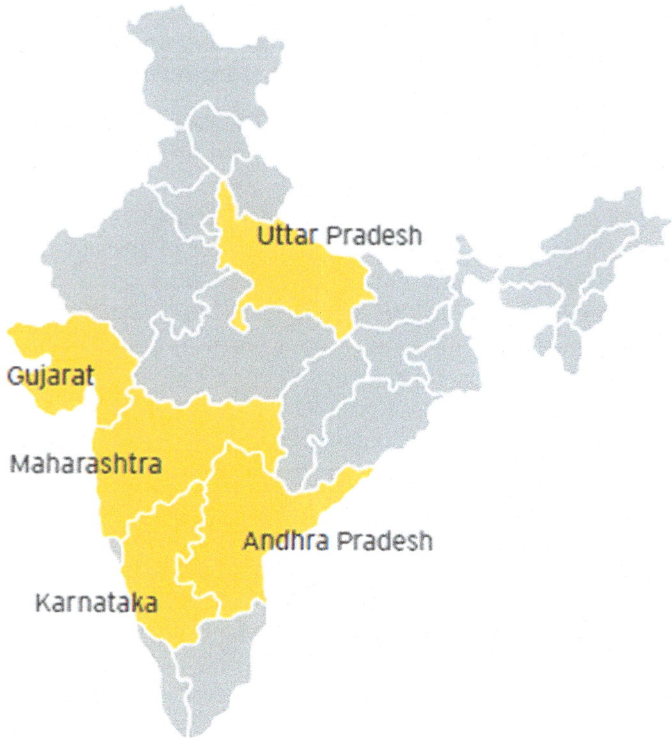

Fig. 7 Most popular states for PPPs in India. *Source* Ernst & Young. *Accelerating Public–Private Partnerships in India*

in the form of Public–Private Partnership Appraisal Committee (PPPAC), Empowered Institution (EI), and Empowered Committee (EC). PPPAC has been constituted to streamline appraisal and approval of PPP projects. The Committee is chaired by Secretary, Department of Economic Affairs (DEA) with Secretaries of the Niti Aayog, Department of Expenditure, Department of Legal Affairs and the Administrative ministry as its members. Since its constitution in January 2006, the PPPAC has approved 307 central project proposals with total project cost of over $50 billion. For focused and top level attention to infrastructure, a Cabinet Committee on Infrastructure (CCI) was constituted in 2009 under the chairmanship of the Prime Minister. It reviewed and approved initiatives for augmenting private investment in infrastructure projects. However, CCI has recently been discontinued. EI and EC are for appraising and approving state level projects.

As we have seen, independent regulatory agencies have been created in many infrastructure sectors like telecom (Telecom Regulatory Authority of India, TRAI), electricity (Central Electricity Regulatory Commission, CERC at the federal level and State Electricity Regulatory Commissions, SERCs, at the state level), ports (Tariff Authority of Major Ports, TAMP), and airports (Airport Economic

Regulatory Authority, AERA). The Rail Tariff Authority has also been announced in the railway sector. The existence of these regulatory bodies is instrumental in reducing regulatory risk for private investors, thus incentivizing such investment.

Financial Support to PPPs: Since the externalities created by infrastructure projects cannot always be internalized by project sponsors, the government has notified the Viability Gap Funding (VGF) Scheme in 2006 to enhance the commercial attractiveness of competitively bid infrastructure projects which are justified on the grounds of economic returns, but fall short on the score of financial returns. Under the scheme, the Central Government can grant assistance up to 20% of project capital costs to PPP projects, thus leveraging budgetary resources by accessing a larger private capital pool. The sponsoring ministry or authority or State Government can provide an additional grant of up to 20% of project costs. VGF is the bidding parameter in many road projects and thus the amount of VGF that a project gets is based on competitive bidding. 324 central and state projects with an investment of about Rs. 2.5 trillion have been cleared with a VGF commitment of Rs. 0.5 trillion.

A new financial institution has been created for providing long-term funding to infrastructure projects. This is a necessity because usual commercial bank funding suffers from asset-liability mismatch as the liabilities of banks are short-term (time deposits of banks are usually for a maximum period of 5 years) and infrastructure assets are long term. The Ministry of Finance and the Planning Commission incorporated the India Infrastructure Finance Company Limited (IIFCL) to provide long-term loans to infrastructure projects with long gestation periods. IIFCL provides direct lending support to project companies as well as refinancing of banks and financial institutions up to 20% of the project cost. It leverages government guarantees to raise funds from domestic and overseas markets. By late 2016, IIFCL has sanctioned Rs. 404 billion for 229 projects.

Simplification and Standardization of documents for PPP projects: The terms of the project agreements as well as the tendering arrangements are usually complex, mostly because of the nature of the risks and the involvement of multiple participants in PPPs including project sponsors, Engineering, Procurement, and Construction (EPC) contractors, operators, fuel suppliers, lenders, off-takers, government agencies, and regulatory authorities. Given the complexity of PPP contracts and the risk exposure of government in such contracts, it is extremely useful to have standardized documents and arrangements that provide predictability of obligations to main parties to the contract and mitigate risk for private capital and government sponsoring authorities. Standardized documents are regarded as the best practice for implementing a PPP program of the magnitude that India is implementing. The use of standard documents also simplifies and expedites decision-making by the public sector authority.

The standardized framework should address the issues that are typically important for non- or limited-recourse project financing, like unbundling and mitigation of risks; matching of risks and rewards; ensuring symmetry of obligations between the principal parties; accuracy and predictability of costs and obligations;

reduction of transaction costs; force majeure; and termination. It should also address other key concerns like user protection, independent monitoring, dispute resolution, and Government financial support. The objective is to secure value for public money while providing efficient and cost-effective user services.

Substantive standardized documents have been created and are exemplified by Model Concession Agreements (MCAs), Manual of Specifications and Standards, and Rules governing user charges. The erstwhile Planning Commission has published MCAs for PPP in National Highways, State Highways, Port Terminals, Operation & Maintenance of Highways, Urban Rail Systems (Metro rail), Operation of Container Trains, Redevelopment of Railway Stations, Development of Non-metro Airports, Greenfield Airports, Procurement-cum-Maintenance of Locomotives, and Transmission of Electricity. The MCA for PPP in Urban Water Supply is under preparation at the Ministry of Urban Development.

The standardized Process Documents that have been created for PPP projects are exemplified by Request for Qualification (RfQ) for prequalification of bidders and Request for Proposal (RfP) for financial bidding across infrastructure sectors. India's model documents are acceptable to domestic and foreign investors as evidenced by the large number of such projects that have been awarded.

Going forward, the objective is to create world-class infrastructure at affordable prices in India comparable in quality to that existing in the developed world. This would involve opening up the power sector to more competition especially through more PPPs in transmission and distribution sub-sectors (as we know, most PPPs in electricity sector of India has come in power generation as compared to transmission and distribution), accelerating the roll out of PPP projects in highways, ports, and airports, and enhancing the flow of long-term debt to infrastructure sectors which is a major bottleneck.

3 Evolving PPP Policy: The Kelkar Committee Report

Given the problems faced by PPPs in the country, the Government of India constituted a Committee in 2015 on revisiting and revitalising the PPP model chaired by Dr. Vijay Kelkar. The Terms of Reference of the Committee included a review of the PPP policy experience, including the variations in contract content; analysis of risks involved in PPP projects in different sectors and existing framework of sharing of such risks between the project developer and the Government; propose design modifications to the PPP contractual arrangements based on the Indian experience, and international best practices; and suggest measures to improve capacity building in Government for effective implementation of PPP projects. The Committee has since submitted its Report (see Appendix).

A critique of the Kelkar Committee report on PPPs: Many of the recommendations of the Kelkar Committee report are unexceptionable, like divesting equity and monetization of public sector assets after construction is complete.[10] The project risks come down considerably after project completion and when the project is in operation phase. It is also well known that, in general, returns of infrastructure projects have low volatility and these returns are not correlated with business cycles. Therefore, such projects that are in operation phase may be ideal for investment by pension, insurance and sovereign wealth funds whose investment horizon is long-term and look for returns with these characteristics. In fact, the National Investment and Infrastructure Fund (NIIF), the sovereign wealth fund of India, is creating a sub-fund for the road sector with a corpus of Rs. 5,000 crore[11] to exploit this opportunity. The road sector has many projects where construction is complete and could provide good investment avenues for financial investors, both domestic and foreign.

Another valid recommendation is that "RFPs (Request for Proposals) may not be issued until at least 80% of land required is available." Inadequate land acquisition has been a major cause of project delays and therefore cost escalation as National Highways Authority of India has realized to its peril. Therefore, financial bidding should only be done after most of the required land has been acquired.

However, the authors have four issues with the Kelkar Committee recommendations. One, the report has issues with standardized Model Concession Agreements[12] (MCAs), which is an international best practice. Negotiating a concession agreement with all stakeholders will increase transaction costs, open up contracts to litigation (on account, for example, of providing different risk sharing clauses to one investor compared to others in the same sector), cause delays, and would make public sector officials liable for mistakes and answering for them, thus adding to the delays and adversely impacting the credibility of the PPP contracting system. Negotiating individual contracts with preferred bidders would also lower transparency and the value for money that is expected from private participation in infrastructure to public authorities. While some clauses in the existing MCAs may be tweaked to make them more adapted to current realities, sector-wise MCAs with project-specific flexibility built-in should be the way forward for India to maintain its lead in the PPP firmament.

---

[10]Monetization of viable projects that have stable revenue flows after EPC delivery maybe considered. This should be seen as a monetization opportunity that can attract risk averse long-term funding like pension and institutional investors. By providing O&M PPP opportunities, the authority will be able to free up budgetary funds for fresh EPC and start a virtuous cycle of fresh investment fed by additional revenues. (Report of the Committee on Revisiting and Revitalising Public Private Partnership model, page xiii.)

[11]Times of India. 14 September 2016. *Infra pool to have separate funds for roads, clean energy.*

[12]For example, the "Committee notes that the adoption of the Model Concession Agreement (MCA) has meant that project-specific risks are rarely addressed by project implementation authorities in this "One-size-fits-all" approach. A rational allocation of risks can only be undertaken in sector and project-specific contexts." (Report of the Committee on Revisiting and Revitalising Public Private Partnership model, page x.)

India prides itself for being among the top two countries for private participation in infrastructure both by number of projects and quantum of investments.[13] The road sector accounts for a major proportion of these projects (45% in terms of number of projects and 22% in terms of investment, see Figs. 3 and 4). The road sector PPP laurels are primarily attributable to the adoption of MCAs in the sector.

Two, the Report pitches for independent sectoral regulators for all those sectors that are going in for private investment.[14] As it is, India has among the highest number of infrastructure sectoral regulators. While we agree that there should be separation of policy formulation, operation, and regulatory functions, we do not agree that independent sectoral regulators are the only answer for ensuring independent regulation. The same objective of independent regulation can be achieved by well-written contracts and we can have "regulation by contract" as in the road sector. The initial tariff and the trajectory of its increase may be stated in the contract as has been done in the Model Concession Agreement for roads. This would provide more certainty, reduce risk premium demanded by bidders and therefore result in lower user charges for the consumers. It may not be a coincidence that India has contracted the highest number of PPP road projects (among all infrastructure sectors) without having a road regulator and practicing "regulation by contract."

Independent sectoral regulators are neither necessary nor sufficient for regulatory credibility. We must not forget what the Delhi High Court said about Delhi Electricity Regulatory Commission (DERC) in 2011, when, within a space of six months, DERC sent contradictory statutory advice to the Delhi Government with respect to the financial position of the Delhi power distribution companies and the need for tariff increase.[15] In this context, the Delhi High Court, the appeal forum for DERC tariff orders, had observed that:

> …the Commission (DERC) has to function with responsibility, intellectual integrity, consistent objectivity, and transparent functionalism appreciating the essential nature of the regulatory body. We emphasize on intellectual integrity and transparent functionalism as we are totally dissatisfied with the way the Commission has proceeded with the manner of (tariff) determination.[16]

---

[13]Private Participation in Infrastructure database of the World Bank (http://ppi.worldbank.org) (viewed on 31 January 2016).

[14]Recommendation that it is "Essential to set up independent Regulators in sectors going in for PPP". (Report of the Committee on Revisiting and Revitalising Public Private Partnership model, page xvii.)

[15]On 30 June 2010, Chairman, DERC conveyed to the Delhi Government that the three private distribution companies have a surplus of Rs. 3,577 crore that needs to be adjusted through a tariff reduction in FY 2010–11. On 15 December 2010, DERC sent 'Statutory Advice' to Delhi Government acknowledging the resource crunch being faced by Delhi discoms and calling for a tariff increase.

[16]High Court of Delhi, Judgment pronounced on 23 May 2011 on WP (C) No. 4821/2010 (2011) (p. 31) [http://delhicourts.nic.in/MAY11/NAND%20KISHORE%20GARG%20VS%20GOVT%20OF%20NCT%20OF%20DELHI.pdf, accessed 30 December 2012].

Another option for ensuring independent regulation could be to expand the mandate of the existing independent regulators. Thus, while there is some talk of independent regulators in the railways and road sectors, it is for consideration whether the same objective cannot be achieved by expanding the mandate of the Airport Economic Regulatory Authority, for example. This would promote cross-sectoral learning, prevent regulatory capture by both the private and public sectors, and be economical in terms of human resources and costs. After all, it has been said that quality human resources are scarcer than money in regulation.

Three, the recommendation about renegotiations is problematic and risks bringing the gains from Indian PPP experience to a standstill. For example, the report states that the final decision on a renegotiated concession agreement must be based *inter-alia* on (1) comparison with the financial position for government at the time of signing the concession agreement and (2) comparison with the existing financial position for government just prior to renegotiation. This will permit the Authority regulating the concession to take a decision based on a full comparison of the likely outcomes over the future of the concession.[17]

In this regard, let us take the case of the Tata Mundra Project (a 4,000 MW Ultra Mega Power Project, UMPP, based on imported coal in coastal Gujarat, formally called Coastal Gujarat Power Limited), in which efforts were made to renegotiate the contract. Even before the commercial operation date of the entire project, the project company petitioned the Central Electricity Regulatory Commission (CERC) that as Indonesia had changed its law whereby all coal sourced from that country needed to be benchmarked to prevailing coal prices, it would not be able to meet its obligations under the Power Purchase Agreements entered into with public sector distribution companies in 5 states (Gujarat, Maharashtra, Rajasthan, Punjab and Haryana). The CERC gave it relief to the extent of 55 paise per kWh and in the process the bidders who were rejected (L2–L4) all became competitive and have a genuine grievance that why was this relief not on the table when the project was bid out.

In terms of the criteria suggested by the report, since all the discoms with which Tata Mundra had signed PPAs are in the public sector, the relief amounts to over Rs. 25,000 crore over the contract period in the form of transfer from the public to the private sector. However, if the project was rebid now, the asking price of replacement power would be higher at Rs. 4.10 per kWh as determined by Appellate Tribunal of Electricity (APTEL) [even after accounting for the relief, Rs. 2.26 per kWh (the levelized tariff) + 0.55 per kWh (relief given by CERC) would be less than the cost of replacement power] and therefore, the relief would be allowed in terms of the criteria set out in the report. We believe that this is a wrong prescription as there should be sanctity of contracts.

The change of law event in Indonesia was also not "unprecedented" and "unforeseen," the grounds on which relief was given to Tata Mundra by CERC, as that country is known to abrogate contracts unilaterally. To take an example in the

[17]Report of the Committee on Revisiting and Revitalising Public Private Partnership model, page 33.

powers sector itself, Indonesia entered into negotiated contracts for the Dieng, Patuha, and Karaha Bodas geothermal projects around the turn of the century, only to find the tariffs unaffordable, and brought about new regulations reducing the contracted price of power. The government had to ultimately take over these projects at great cost imposed by international arbitrators (Wells and Ahmed 2007). Thus, the breach of contract by Indonesia is not "unprecedented" and therefore should not have been "unforeseen."[18]

For all these reasons (violating the sanctity of contracts, revenue outcomes mostly in favor of the private sector and against public sector, etc.) renegotiations should not come easy and may be done only in exceptional circumstances, a stance that is not supported by the report.

Finally, the recommendation about excluding public sector companies from bidding for PPP projects[19] also seems illogical. There is a separation of ownership and management in the company form of organization. In theory, as long as the management is professional, it does not matter whether the ownership is private or public. We have several well-run public sector companies like NTPC in the power sector. NTPC bids for PPP projects in power generation sector and increases competition. For example, NTPC bid for the Sasan UMPP and though it did not win the bid, it nevertheless increased competitive pressure for the benefit of the users. Therefore, ex-ante debarring of the biggest power sector generating company in India that is also run professionally to bid for PPP projects does not stand to reason.

One of the authors is reminded of the infamous part-allocation of the Talabira Coal Block to Hindalco in 2005, which was the subject of considerable controversy and a CBI case. This author was Deputy Secretary at the Prime Minister's Office at the time and was handling, among others, the proposals of the Ministry of Coal. One of the proposals in this infamous allocation was that Mahanadi Coalfields Limited, a public sector undertaking, should not be allowed to bid for mining coal subsequent to the part-allocation of Talabira Coal Block to Hindalco. This sub-proposal was rejected by the Prime Minister mainly because this author opposed the sub-proposal of the Ministry of Coal that public sector companies should be excluded from competitive bidding for mining of the Talabira Coal Block.

In conclusion, it can be said that the Kelkar Committee, in its effort to make the PPP regime extremely friendly to the private sector, may have erred at what in some aspects, that we have highlighted above.

---

[18]Pratap (2013).

[19]The Committee is of the view that since state owned entities SoEs/ PSUs are essentially government entities and work within the government framework, they should not be allowed to bid for PPP projects. (Report of the Committee on Revisiting and Revitalising Public Private Partnership model, page xii.)

4 Broad Current Critical Debates Around Infrastructure Projects

4.1 Growth Versus Environment

India is abundant in coal and so it is natural that the energy needs of the country would be met by the resource endowments in which the country is rich and so coal would increasingly be used for electricity generation. However, much of the present coal is located in forested regions thus bringing to prominence the tussle between growth and environment. It has been estimated that since 2007, more than 26,000 hectares (ha) of forest land in India has been used for coal mining. Then there is the question of inter-generational inequity in that environmental degradation now would compromise the environment of the future generations.

Related to this is a question that is often asked: Should growth have a higher priority than the environment? The primacy of growth is justified on the grounds of over a quarter of the Indian population living below the poverty line and the need to provide electricity to about 40% of the Indian population that does not have access to grid-based power. It is expected that provision of electricity to this section of the Indian population would remove an important constraint to its economic status.

One of the issues that has gained central stage recently is that of stalled projects. It has been estimated that there are stalled projects to the tune of Rs. 18 trillion (about 13% of GDP) of which an estimated 60% are in infrastructure. The necessary acceleration in clearing the backlog of stalled projects has already begun. The coal and gas supply bottlenecks are likely to be alleviated through the planned reforms of the coal sector and the auctioning of coal blocks de-allocated by the Supreme Court. The rise in the price of gas is expected to increase gas supply. Faster environmental clearances, as well as reforms in land and labor laws are also crucial. This thinking is apparent from the frenetic pace at which the Government has cleared projects recently while glossing over (or so it seems) the environmental sensitivities.

One of the important legislations in environmental conservation in India is the Forest Rights Act (FRA). FRA seeks to recognize the rights of forest dwelling communities (not just tribals) to land, water, forests, and forest resources. The law has a consent clause that is seen to be problematic by industry: no project can come up on forest land without the consent of affected Gram Sabha (Village Council), and completion of the process of recording locals' rights. Dongria Kondhs—a tribe in Niyamgiri, Orissa—used this clause to reject Vedanta's plan to mine on their sacred mountain in the Indian state of Orissa.

One of the important examples of the conflict between environment and growth is the case of approval given for mining of Mahan and Chattrasal coal blocks for power generation projects (see Box 1).

Box 1: Case of Approval of Mahan and Chattrasal Coal Blocks[20]

Forest areas were earlier declared "go" (blocks that could be allowed to be mined) or "no-go" (blocks that would remain untouched) for coal mining. In March 2010, Mahan and Chhatrasal were in "no-go" zone because of rich forest cover and impact on forest dwelling and tribal communities. In October–November 2012, Mahan was approved for thermal power plants of Essar and Hindalco and Chhatrasal for Reliance's Sasan UMPP plant as these power plants were already up and running—so it was a sort of *fait accompli* for these coal blocks.

The Mahan coal block, located in one of the densest sal forests in India, was allocated in 2006 to a joint venture between Essar Power and Hindalco Industries. It was earmarked to supply 5 million tons of coal per year for 14 years to two power projects—a 1,000 MW power plant of Essar and a 650 MW project of Hindalco.

But this would require felling at least 500,000 trees over an area of close to 1,000 ha requiring a central government clearance. The allottees applied for one in 2008. The Forest Advisory Committee, the Union environment ministry's statutory appraiser of such projects, hesitated to issue one. It could neither refuse nor was it willing to consent. By 2010, the then environment minister, Jairam Ramesh, promulgated the no-go policy for coal mining to provide some predictability to the forest clearance process by listing beforehand forests that were too good to be destroyed. Mahan fell in that category. The Forest Advisory Committee ultimately rejected the forest clearance pointing out that the state government had understated the quality of forests and the rights of the tribals on the land had not been settled under the Forest Rights Act.

The allottees, however, did not give up, reaching out to the then Prime Minister Manmohan Singh, Finance Minister Pranab Mukherjee, who was also heading the Group of Ministers on coal and environment issues, and Environment Minister Jairam Ramesh. Essar pointed out that its plant was over 60% complete irrespective of the coal block clearance.

After initially protesting, pointing out that "Clearance of the Mahan coal block will open up a Pandora's Box which we should avoid at all costs," Ramesh eventually relented and left the matter to the Group of Ministers to take a final call.

Greenpeace India, an aggressive international environment non-governmental organization (NGO) known for its attention-grabbing techniques, has campaigned against many new coal projects in India for a while. The Mahan coal block provided it with its most visible campaign issue. A group of citizens from 11 affected villages had come together under the banner of Mahan Sangharsh Samiti (MSS), and begun protesting at the

[20]Draws on Kohli (2013).

site against handing over their forests. Greenpeace supported MSS at the local level and soon took it to national and global visibility.

Ramesh's successor Jayanthi Natarajan took the same stance as Ramesh, but was overruled by the Group of Ministers (GoM) headed by Mukherjee. She reluctantly cleared the project, noting, "Despite reservations against the diversion of the dense forest land expressed strongly by the environment ministry at the GoM, and the fact that the entire civil work and construction of the plant is already complete after procurement of environmental clearance—and resulting inter-alia in huge exposure to nationalised banks—Forest Clearance (first stage) may be granted to the Mahan coal block."[21]

What this case shows is that "higher" approval bodies like Empowered Group of Ministers (EGoM) and the Cabinet Committee on Infrastructure (CCI) can simply over-rule positions taken by the Ministry of Environment and Forests (MoEF) (the classification of "go" and "no-go" areas was done by MoEF).

The rights of the tribals over the forests under the Forest Rights Act (FRA) was another issue. Under the law, the forest clearance required the settlement of the tribal's rights and their consent was obtained. However, there were charges of fraudulently obtained consent.

The protests turned dramatic with Greenpeace activists, unfurling a banner on the glass facade of the Essar Group headquarters in Mumbai saying "We kill forests: Essar." The company sued them for criminal defamation.

Environment ministry, now led by Veerappa Moily, issued the final clearance in February 2014 overriding concerns about tribal rights. MSS challenged it before the National Green Tribunal.

While the hearings were on, the National Democratic Alliance (NDA) government took over at the Center. Soon an Intelligence Bureau report was leaked naming, among others, Greenpeace India for being anti-development and anti-national. Using the report, the government blocked funding support to the organization from its mother organization abroad.

In September 2014, Supreme Court canceled allocation of Mahan coal block to Essar and Hindalco and in May 2015, Government canceled allocation of Chhatrasal coal block to Reliance putting an end to the matter.

The tussle between Growth and Environment is not unique to India. One recent example of this playing out is the Adani coal mining project in Australia (Carmichael Coal and Rail Project, Total Project Cost: $16 billion), its largest coal project. The project involves mining coal in the hinterland, transporting it to the coast, and shipping it to consumers in Asia through the Great Barrier Reef, the largest collection of corals on earth.

[21]http://www.business-standard.com/article/economy-policy/nda-govt-s-grouse-with-greenpeace-mahan-coal-block-protests-115022000023_1.html.

Australian government gave environmental clearance to the project. However, the Australian federal court rejected the clearance for not taking into consideration two endangered species—yakka skink (Australian native lizard) and ornamental snake. In addition, it is felt that dredging will destroy the Great Barrier Reef, a world heritage site. International banks like Standard Chartered, Commonwealth Bank of Australia, and National Australia Bank have withdrawn support for the project.

However, despite the contest between environment and growth in India as elsewhere, there is hope. Typically, countries start in forested *poverty*. As they get richer they also get barer—until alarm bells ring and they attempt to recover their losses. The trigger points and period differ, but the trajectory is similar in most: a reverse J, steeply down, then bottoming out, then back up again, but only partially —the "forest transition curve." According to research done by the Economist magazine, India is already in the rising part of the reverse J, while countries like Brazil seems to be nearing the bottom. The world may be, as well. India is replanting forests it once cut down. In 1980, India had about 640,000 km^2 of forest left. Now, it has 680,000 km^2, and is replanting about 1,450 km^2 a year.

It should also be realized that some damage to the environment is inevitable. The answer, therefore, should be sustainable development including rules that provide that if you cut trees, you should do compensatory afforestation.

Environmental concerns in Project Finance: Non-governmental organizations (NGOs) and civil society organizations (CSOs) focused on environmental sustainability and the rights of indigenous peoples have shifted their tactics away from project sponsors and development institutions like the World Bank, and have begun targeting private financial institutions involved with project lending. As the confrontations have become more frequent and more strident in recent years, bankers have come to recognize the reputation, deal, and credit risks associated with contested projects. In 2003, four project finance banks voluntarily created and then announced a set of guidelines known as the *Equator Principles* (EP) intended to guide project lending decisions. The principles are largely based on the environmental safeguards established by the International Finance Corporation (IFC), the private sector arm of the World Bank, in 1998. To address the evolving standards for sustainable lending and to expand the principles' scope and reporting requirements, the Equator banks issued a revised set of principles colloquially known as "EP II" in July 2006. In June 2013, they issued a third version of the Equator Principles. The main developments of the EP III are: (a) expansion of the scope to include project-related corporate loans and bridge loans; (b) alignment of compliance standards; (c) required assessment of carbon emissions and human rights issues; and (d) equirement for greater transparency and reporting. As of May 2014, 78 financial institutions in 34 countries have adopted the Equator Principles. These institutions collectively provide more than 70% of project finance debt in developing countries.[22]

[22]Esty et al. (2014).

In the past few years, awareness of carbon risk—the idea that greenhouse gas emissions, particularly carbon dioxide (CO_2), are damaging the environment—has increased. The Carbon Disclosure Project (CDP), an independent, non-profit organization that now holds the largest collection of self-reported climate change, water and forest-risk data, was launched in 2000 in the United Kingdom. Its investor initiatives, which are currently backed by more than 767 institutional investors with more than $92 trillion in assets under management, aim to help drive investment flows towards a low carbon and more sustainable economy by giving the financial community access to this information. Three banks (Citibank, JPMorgan Chase, and Morgan Stanley), in conjunction with leading power companies and environmental NGOs, joined forces to create the *Carbon Principles*, which provide a consistent methodology to evaluate and address carbon risk in power projects. As of May 2014, six banks have adopted the Carbon Principles.

The *Climate Principles* are a similar framework for climate change best practice for the financial sector launched by The Climate Group. The adopting institutions include Crédit Agricole, BNP Paribas, F&C Investments, Standard Chartered, Swiss Re and HSBC. Financial institutions and institutional investors have even denied funding for the proposed projects in an effort to self-regulate their activities.[23]

4.2 Land Acquisition

Insufficient land has emerged as the single biggest constraint to speedy implementation and consequent cost escalation of infrastructure projects in India. The problem is widespread across infrastructure sectors and includes many road PPP projects (e.g., Delhi–Jaipur Highway) and power projects (e.g., Tilaiya UMPP).

Land supply is limited by its very nature (total area of India at 329 million ha is fixed) while the population is increasing relentlessly. The increasing population pressure on land is reflected in decreasing geographical area per person (0.27 ha per person in 2011). The economy has not been able to cope with the increasing demand of land for two interrelated reasons: a large part of the landmass is held by households who earn their livelihood from land, which implies that if incremental demand is to be met, some households would have to give up land; bulk of the people dependent on land (through agriculture and related activities) do not have the skills to make a living without land, nor are there enough job opportunities in other sectors to absorb unskilled labor.[24]

What is land acquisition? Land acquisition is the forcible takeover of privately owned land by the government or private companies for developmental projects in the larger interest of society. This is different from voluntary purchase and sale of land in which land owner does not have the compulsion to part with the land.

[23]Esty et al. (2014).

[24]India Infrastructure Report (2009).

"Eminent domain"—the sovereign's right of compulsory acquisition of land (albeit with compensation) for "public purpose"—is well established in law worldwide. The term "public purpose" is rather wide in its implication and may include privately executed projects if they result in an indirect public good or some larger social good (including increased tax revenue or employment). There is strong justification in the theory of political economy for acquisition to resolve certain types of market failure like "hold up problems."[25] Second, land titles are often disputed, as in Indian conditions, and acquisition by the Government, statutorily cleans the title.

Land Acquisition—A major issue for infrastructure projects: In India, implementing agencies like the National Highway Authority of India (NHAI) have lately awarded projects with only small percentage of the land acquired,[26] sometimes as low as 30%. This is contrary to the global best practice of completing land acquisition before tendering projects. Global best practice suggests that 100% of the land should be acquired before tendering, a challenging provision in India given the high private land ownership. In cases where it is feasible, acquiring 100% of the land before tendering will increase the attractiveness of Indian projects for investors, both domestic and foreign. Delay in subsequent land acquisition is possibly the single largest factor causing project delays of about 15–20% compared to the original schedule.

A study commissioned by the erstwhile Planning Commission, as well as a McKinsey survey of construction companies, suggests that about 80% of road projects, like in many other sectors, are marked by land acquisition delays. Since continuous tracts of land are needed for optimal progress of construction, this delay also raises the project costs by under-utilizing the committed labor and equipment. With time and cost overruns, projects could stall as exemplified by the Delhi–Jaipur highway where the private partner has run out of money to be able to complete the project causing nuisance to the traveling public which is faced with poor quality unfinished road.

One of the major reasons for delay in land acquisition is under-valuation of land. While the new law on land acquisition in India takes care of this, it may have moved too far in this direction.

How is land acquired?

Land Acquisition Act, 1894: Land acquisition is a ***concurrent subject*** under the Indian Constitution, so both federal and state governments can legislate on the

[25]Many development projects require large tracts of land. Any individual can stall the process of private market purchase by refusing to sell or demanding a price disproportionate to the market value, even if the majority of owners are willing to sell.

[26]Land Acquisition is the responsibility of the public authority in Indian Model Concession Agreements across infrastructure sectors.

matter.[27] Before the enactment of the new law, land was being acquired under Land Acquisition Act (LAA), 1894. Under this Act, land was acquired for "public purpose;" companies and government had to compensate land-owners according to "market value" of property, but there was no provision for Rehabilitation & Resettlement.

It is generally held that the old land acquisition procedure suffered from serious defects: unsatisfactory consultation with affected communities, meager attention to minimizing the extent of land acquired and exploring alternatives, lack of provisions for rehabilitation and resettlement (R&R) of those dependent on the land (like tenants and share croppers), scope for misuse of "urgency" provisions in non-urgent cases, and a strong tilt toward inadequate compensation for the land acquired. A new Act, it was felt, was needed to specifically addresses all these issues.

Right to Fair Compensation and Transparency in Land Acquisition, Rehabilitation and Resettlement (RFCTLARR) Act, 2013: RFCTLARR, a federal statute, has replaced LAA, 1894 and has come into force on 1 January 2014. It applies to all infrastructure projects. As per the new Act, in case of land acquisition for private company by government, consent of 80% of Project Affected Persons (PAPs) has to be obtained; for PPP projects, consent of 70% PAPs is required; no consent is required for government projects. The Act lays down that process for land acquisition would involve a preliminary notification stating the intent for acquisition, compensation to be given by a certain time, Social Impact Assessment (SIA) survey,[28] and R&R[29] to be provided to the persons affected by the acquisition.

The most controversial aspect of the new law is that after coming into force from 1 January 2014, a private company would pay 4 times the market value of acquired land in rural areas and double the value in urban areas[30]; and there is a provision of 25 infrastructure facilities like schools, electricity and road connection, etc., for resettlement of PAPs. The houses should also reflect the needs of the PAPs like houses with cattle sheds.

Since land acquisition is a concurrent subject, States can have their own land acquisition laws. But, there have to be certain minimum acceptable standards. The 2013 Act enforces a certain minimum acceptable standard on four things—consent,

---

[27]Under Article 254(2) of the Constitution, states have the authority to frame specific laws on subjects on the concurrent list with central/presidential assent. Using the provision, eight states had their own versions of the Land Acquisition Act, 1894, before the new 2013 Act was passed.

[28]If land acquisition results in the displacement of 400 families in the plains or 200 families in the hills or tribal areas, the government must conduct a Social Impact Assessment in consultation with Gram Sabha to look at public and community properties. The report will then be evaluated by an expert group comprising two non-official social scientists, two experts on rehabilitation, and a technical expert. It will also be examined by a committee to ensure that the proposal for land acquisition meets certain specified conditions. Industry has felt that this will lead to cumbersome delays and encourage red tapism.

[29]R&R is must for projects bigger than 50 acres in urban areas and 70 acres in rural areas.

[30]Compensation will be based on circle rates as well as the average of top prices for proximate land parcels of the last 3 years, whichever is higher.

SIA, compensation and R&R. States may want to better them in their own laws but cannot fall below what is provided in the RFCTLARR Act.

The new law has been enacted because of two primary reasons: increased public concern on land acquisition issues, and absence of a national law to provide for the rehabilitation & resettlement and compensation for loss of livelihoods. In the new law, there is an attempted balance between the concerns of farmers and those whose livelihoods are dependent on the land being acquired while facilitating land acquisition for industrialization, infrastructure, and urbanization. It was also felt that LAA, 1894 was outdated—notwithstanding multiple amendments, its main structure remained the Land Acquisition Act of 1894.

The impact of enactment of RFCTLARR on land acquisition, infrastructure, and industrial projects is shown in the table below (Table 1).

What industry wants?: Given the adverse affects of the new law on industry and infrastructure, industry wants the following: Define Gram Sabha and lay down process for its consent to be conclusive because it has happened many times that the Gram Sabha has gone back on its consent; Consent of the owner should be irrevocable (no reopening of projects); For linear infrastructure projects such as railways, highways, etc., R&R process should be significantly reduced and simplified as displacement is comparatively smaller; Include manufacturing under public purpose to facilitate setting up of large projects like steel, cement, etc.

Table 1 Impact of RFCTLARR on land acquisition and infrastructure projects

Positive	Negative
Fairer to farmers—no forceful acquisition (it may curb Maoism); increased compensation; rehabilitation and resettlement	Land acquisition has become expensive, e.g., Land cost for 272 km proposed Delhi–Jaipur Expressway project has gone up 3 times to over Rs. 18,000 crore. This will affect viability of industrial projects and erode competitiveness; adversely affect investment climate Identifying PAPs would be difficult as they may not have title deeds of their land
More transparent; Reduces investor uncertainty; increases supply of land for development	Long delays[a] (could take 50 months for various processes to be completed leading to cost escalation as well), litigation, complicated and complex, especially the consent provision
	Providing R&R (alternate livelihoods)—Companies do not provide land in lieu of land, and if they provide jobs, it is generally short-term; some companies like NTPC provide annuity payments instead of jobs. Villagers facing loss of livelihood are unsure how long compensation money will last. With the law to be applied retrospectively, even projects being set up now will be revisited later, increasing project risks

Source Authors' compilation

[a]As it is, it takes about 295 days to acquire or lease public land in India, more than twice the global average (*Source* World Bank). Getting private land takes 99 days, versus a global average of 61 days.

Given the concerns raised by industry and the fact that PPP projects account for 60% of the Rs. 18 trillion worth of stalled projects, the Government wanted to balance the development needs of the country while protecting the interests of the farmers, and therefore, it had issued an Ordinance to amend the RFCTLARR Act, 2013 for the third time in 2015. The amendments related to: No social impact assessment (SIA) and mandatory *consent* for select sectors (defence, rural infrastructure, affordable housing, industrial corridors and infrastructure projects including PPPs.[31]). However, the government proposed no change in compensation for the land acquired. It was hoped that the proposed changes in the RFCTLARR would benefit specified sectors which would be able to acquire land faster while reducing legal hassles.

Opposition parties alleged that the changes were introduced to benefit corporate groups and are anti-farmer. The farmers were opposed to removal of consent clause and social impact assessment in the 5 industrial sectors. The farmers were also opposed to the proposed repeal of Section 24(2) of the 2013 Act, relating to the acquired land being returned to the original owners if it remained unused for more than 5 years.

In August 2015, a joint parliamentary panel suggested that the government withdraw six key amendments, including the plan to remove the consent clause and the social impact assessment. Both the houses of Parliament failed to pass the amendments and ultimately there was no change in the RFCTLARR law.

The box below provides examples of a successful and an unsuccessful land acquisition in India.

Box 2: Examples of a Successful and an Unsuccessful Land Acquisition in India[32]

JSW Bengal Steel Project: A successful Land Acquisition Model

In 2007, the OP Jindal Group signed a Memorandum of Agreement (MoA) with the West Bengal Government to set up a 10-million ton steel plant at Salboni with the total project cost estimated at Rs. 350 billion and a requirement of 4,860 acres of land. Of this, the government acquired about 4,300 acres of fallow land. The Group still needed to purchase about 560 acres. After negotiating directly, JSW Bengal Steel (JBS) successfully formed a partnership with 700 marginal farmers. JBS offered an attractive compensation package and one job per family, valued approximately at Rs. 0.6 million per acre. Other formalities required to start construction of the plant proceeded in parallel. The West Bengal government also granted Special Economic Zone status to the company. There have been no news reports of any role of middlemen and other rent-seeking agents. On 2 November 2008, the company laid the foundation stone of the project.

[31]In PPPs, many-a-times, ownership of the assets including land rests with the government while the private partner is only given the right to operate these assets over the concession period.

[32]Draws from India Infrastructure Report (2009).

Tata Motors Small Car Project: An unsuccessful Land Acquisition Model

Around the same time, the Tata Group expressed interest in setting up their small car project in West Bengal and after visiting several locations, signed a Memorandum of Understanding (MoU) with the West Bengal Government for setting up a plant at Singur with an estimated investment of Rs. 1,000 crore and requiring 1,000 acres of land.

Later, when the State went to acquire the land it offered just Rs. 0.1 million per acre of fertile land drawing considerable opposition from locals. The project started a controversy, as over 5,000 locals opposed the land acquisition under the local Member of Legislative Assembly (and a member of the opposition party), under the banner of Krishi Jomi Bachao (Save Farmland) Committee. It got increasing support from the media, political parties, and the intelligentsia opposing the project. Tata Motors Managing Director expressed unhappiness over the State Government's progress in land acquisition and signaled that the company may withdraw from West Bengal if the State is unable to provide land by the end of the year. As a result, farmers were forced to sell their land. With the end-of-the-year deadline in mind, the Land Revenue Minister of West Bengal announced that land acquisition at Singur was complete and distribution of the compensation checks was in the final stage. Tata Motors made a notional beginning of construction at the plant site in January 2007, under heavy police presence. A revelation of the terms of the deal between private business and the State, meanwhile indicated large freebies and subsidies by the latter. A farmer whose land was acquired committed suicide, and his family refused to collect compensation saying the acquisition was forced. Meanwhile Tata Motors announced an early 2008 launch date of the small car, Nano, with large-scale export plans.

On 18 January, 2008, the Calcutta High Court upheld the Singur land acquisition. As the project progressed, the State Opposition political party chief agreed to hold talks with the Tata officials to resolve the impasse but the situation deteriorated into a long-drawn agitation. The Tata Group CEO threatened to pull out if violence and disturbance continued. The State Chief Minister promised to meet the Tata Group Chairman to resolve the "Singur deadlock;" however, criticizing the opposition for the continued stand-off there. Tata Motors finally announced its decision to pull out from Singur in October 2008.

The Singur Land Rehabilitation & Development Bill, 2011 was passed in the Legislative Assembly on 14 June 2011. Tata Motors challenged the High Court Order upholding the Singur Act, 2011. On 22 June 2012, the Division Bench of the Calcutta High Court struck down the Bill. On 6 August 2012, the state government of West Bengal moved Supreme Court and on 31 August 2016, the Supreme Court ruled that land acquisition in Singur was illegal.

5 Urbanization and PPPs: Role of PPPs in the Indian Smart City Mission

A major new initiative of the Government for building urban infrastructure is the launch of the Smart City Mission (SCM) with increased role of PPPs in the provision of urban infrastructure. This section provides a snapshot of the Mission.

The Indian Smart City Mission was launched in June 2015. The selection of cities to be developed into smart cities is through a two-stage competitive process. Stage I of the competition that provides for intra-state competition is complete, and 98 potential Smart Cities have been announced. In Stage II of the competition, which is an inter-city competition across India, 33 Smart Cities have been announced so far.

The Smart City Mission aims at providing basic infrastructure, decent quality of life to the people, clean and sustainable environment and Information Technology (IT) driven smart solutions. The idea is to begin with a compact area in the city, develop that area as a Smart City by providing a package of core infrastructure and smart solutions. This will then have catalyzing effect, extending similar smart area development to rest of the City as well as creation of similar Smart Cities in other parts of the country (Table 2).

Architecture of the Smart City Mission (SCM): The Mission provides for flexibility. There are three models of implementation of the SCM: Retrofitting (where existing area in the cities are improved), Redevelopment (existing areas are rebuilt incorporating the essential elements of a smart city), Greenfield (new smart cities are developed) or a mix thereof. Cities would choose the model depending on their vision, local context, and resources. The SCM lays emphasis on citizen participation and the chosen model of SCM development depends on what citizens want,

Table 2 Essential features of a Smart City

Core (basic) infrastructure	**Smart solutions**: *The idea is to do more with less.*	**Livability**: *This is an area that is especially problematic in Indian cities.*
• Adequate water supply, including waste water recycling and storm water reuse • Assured electricity supply • Rain water harvesting • Proper sanitation including solid waste management	• Smart metering • Smart parking • Intelligent traffic management • Robust IT connectivity and digitalization	• Pedestrian friendly pathways • Encouragement to non-motorized transport (e.g., walking and cycling) • Non-vehicle streets/zones • Innovative use of open spaces • Energy efficient street lighting • Visible improvement in the area (e.g., replacing overhead electric wiring with underground wiring, encroachment-free public areas) • Ensuring safety of citizens especially children, women and elderly

Source Government of India, Smart Cities Mission (www.smartcities.gov.in)

including their willingness to pay for smart city development. This is critical as good infrastructure would cost money and part of this would have to come from user charges. So, those portions of existing cities would be developed into smart cities where citizens are willing to pay the higher cost of smart city development. This would be manifested in the form of higher property taxes (because the cost of their property would increase with good infrastructure and the government should get a part of this increase—through what is called “value capture financing”) as well as reasonable user charges for say water supply and electricity.

The concept of smart city development is inclusive. Since smart city development emphasizes the development of a compact area, all residents of the selected area would be benefitted from the Smart City initiative. While the major beneficiaries of the smart city development would be the citizens residing in the compact area chosen for smart city development in terms of improved infrastructure, etc., a Pan City feature has been added as an essential requirement for every smart city proposal so that there is something for all city residents in it. This would hopefully build a political constituency to support the smart city initiative.

Competitive selection of smart cities sets it apart from entitlement based schemes generally employed to roll out national programs in India. All cities to be developed into smart cities will compete for selection. This is the first time that competition has been incorporated in the design of any centrally sponsored scheme in India. As already stated, there is a two-stage competition for the selection of smart cities. In Stage I, there is intra-State competition, based on laid down criteria including city capacity for development into smart cities. Stage II of the competition is on all-India basis among shortlisted Stage I cities. 33 cities (out of 98) have been declared winners of the competition and are being developed into smart cities.

The implementation of the SCM at the city level would be done through a Special Purpose Vehicle (SPV), which would be a company registered under the Companies Act, 2013. The SPV initially will be a 50:50 Joint Venture between State Government and Urban Local Body (ULB), which will implement each approved Smart City Proposal. SPV will plan, appraise, approve, release funds, monitor and evaluate all projects in the Smart City. Initial paid-up capital of SPV would be Rs. 2 billion made up from first-year contribution of the Government of India (which could be used by the ULB for funding its own contribution) and State Governments. To reiterate, Government of India would be having no equity in the SPV, which would be having majority equity of the State Government and the ULB. However, given the financial condition of the ULBs in India, the provision of using Government of India funding for ULB equity has been made.

SPV mechanism helps in that an independent, healthy balance sheet is created to enable mobilization of resources, and gives flexibility of implementation, especially with regard to engaging professional expertise. Both these objectives are critical for implementation of the SCM and were found to be wanting in the existing institutional setup at the local level. Most of the existing urban local bodies are in the red and have to go through a long-drawn out recruitment process to hire professional expertise. Therefore, the SPV mechanism is critical for the success of the Mission.

The successful implementation of the Mission would involve substantial financial outlays. It has been estimated that total urban infrastructure investment requirement is about $1 trillion over the 20-year period (2012–31).[33] The total planned investment in 33 shortlisted Indian Smart Cities is about $13 billion. Assuming the same scale of infrastructure investment, investment in the proposed 100 smart cities would be about $40 billion till 2020. Of this, about $16 billion will come from governmental sources (Government of India, State Governments/ULBs), which would have to be leveraged from both internal and external financing sources.

Given the huge investment requirement, business-as-usual will not work. The Indian Smart City Mission aims at a paradigm shift in how urban infrastructure is financed—from grant based to more commercial sources of funding. Urban infrastructure in India till now has been financed mainly by grants from the Central and the State governments, which have been woefully short of the requirements. This type of funding is also inefficient with poor accountability. This needs to change and commercial sources of financing need to be emphasized if world-class smart cities are to be built. The alternative sources of funding that are being emphasized in the Smart City Mission are Public–Private Partnerships (PPPs), Municipal Bonds, Loans from multilateral banks including World Bank and ADB, Land monetisation through Value Capture Financing and Tax Incremental Financing, etc., and appropriate User Charges. User charges should at least cover the Operation and Maintenance expenditure of urban infrastructure.

PPPs in urban infrastructure are especially challenging because of low-cost recovery and the associated political sensitivity of any effort to increase user charges to cost recovery levels. The proposed PPPs in the Smart City Proposals of the 33 winning cities are shown in the table below. The most important reason for cities proposing PPPs is the resource crunch that they face and any unmet infrastructure need may have adverse political consequences (Table 3).

Some illustrative cases of PPPs in urban infrastructure are discussed below.

PPPs in Multilevel Parking: PPPs can play an important role in creating and maintaining better parking infrastructure, particularly in the central business districts of major metropolitan cities. The figure below compares Parking Fees in various cities in 2011. While we are not saying that the parking charges in say, Delhi be increased to that of London in one go, what the figure shows is that parking charges in India have considerable scope for providing added revenues to the Urban Local Bodies. In addition, increased parking charges would disincentivize use of private transport like cars and encourage the use of public transport like buses with attendant environmental, economic, and social benefits (Fig. 8).

The aim of PPPs in multilevel parking is to improve services without public capital outlay and provide an additional revenue stream to the SPV/ULB that can be used for other priority expenditures. New multilevel parking structures would

[33]*Source* The High Powered Expert Committee (HPEC) for Estimating the Investment Requirements for Urban Infrastructure Services in India (2011).

Table 3 PPPs in winning Smart City proposals

Sector	Number of Smart Cities
Smart/multilevel parking	30
Power/smart grid/solar panel	23
Solid waste management	18
Water supply/waste water recycling	16
Housing/slum redevelopment	15
Public bike sharing system and E-rickshaw	14
Sewerage	12

Source Smart City Proposals of the winning cities (http://smartcities.gov.in/winningCityp1.aspx) (viewed on 30 June 2016)

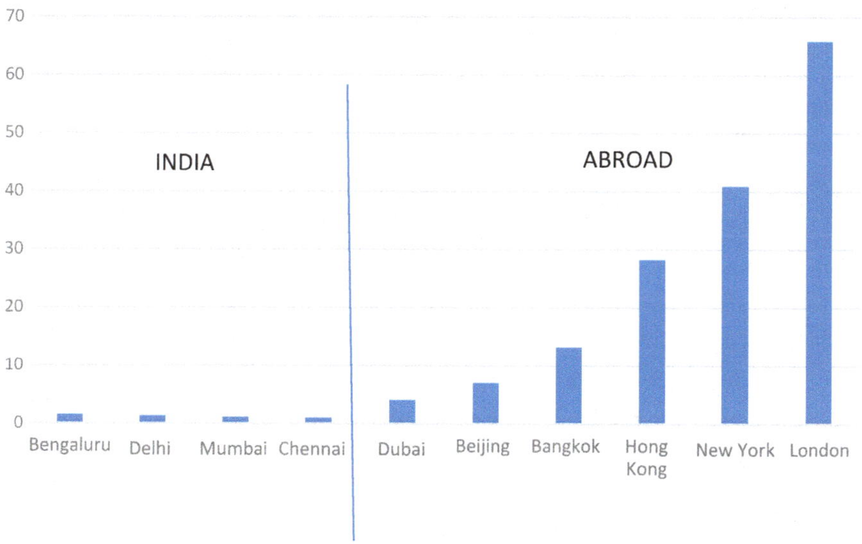

Fig. 8 Parking Fees (in US Dollars) for a 12-hour period. *Source* Ministry of Urban Development (2016)

ensure that there is no clogging of streets and therefore would improve parking experience. Regulation of parking charges would be with public agencies and the assets would be transferred to the SPV/ULB at the end of the concession period.

***PPPs in Municipal Solid Waste (MSW) Management*.** Annual Municipal Solid Waste generation is expected to grow 3 times from the current level to 377 million tons by 2030 in India (McKinsey 2010). Solid waste management accounts for 25–50% of ULB's expenditure (World Bank 2006). There is low-cost recovery in the sector estimated at less than 50% of the O&M cost (MoUD 2010). Investment requirement for solid waste management over 20-year period (2012–31) is estimated at $10 billion (HPEC 2011). Smart City Proposals of 18 (out of 33 selected) cities include PPP projects in Solid Waste Management.

Table 4 presents the salient features of an illustrative PPP project in solid waste management (SWM) in India. A few features are noteworthy. The capital cost is divided evenly between the public and the private sector. In low-cost recovery sectors like SWM, this sharing of capital costs may be necessary for a project to be financially viable with politically acceptable user fees. Construction and operating risk are transferred fully to the private sector as it has more control over these risk factors. It may also be noticed that this is an integrated project covering collection, transportation, and processing of MSW and reclamation of the landfill site, which may again be a best practice. Division of these responsibilities across operators may lead to blame game to the detriment of municipal services.

PPPs in Urban Water Supply: There is an immense need for private sector participation in urban water supply so as improve the quantity and quality of services. No Indian City has 24 * 7 piped water supply; quality of water supply is poor; there is low-cost recovery (<20% of costs); and there are large uncovered areas and population. Investment requirement in water supply sector is estimated at $80 billion for the 20-year period (2012–31) (HPEC, 2011). Reflecting the poor state of the urban water supply in India, Smart City Proposals of 16 (out of 33 winning) cities include PPP projects related to Urban Water Supply including Bhubaneswar, Ludhiana, Kochi, Indore, and Bhopal cities in India.

The profile of the water supply PPP in Nagpur is presented in Table 5. Like in the MSW case, we see that there is capital cost sharing between the public and the private sectors because of low-cost recovery in the sector and the difficulty in

Table 4 Profile of Integrated Solid Waste Management PPP in Hyderabad, India

Award date	February 2009
Bid process time frame	6 months
Bids	2
Bid parameter and winning offer	Tipping fee per ton of MSW received at disposal facility gate = Rs 1,431
Private operator	M/s Ramky Enviro Engineers Ltd. (REEL)
Cost	Rs. 4.35 billion
Investment	Private player (50%), Jawaharlal Nehru National Urban Renewal Mission (JNNURM) (35%), Government of Andhra Pradesh (15%)
Operator obligations	MSW collection, O&M, construction and reclamation of landfill sites
ULB obligations	50% of total project cost, road connectivity, transfer of existing assets to concessionaire
Risk allocation summary	
Investment risk	Private player (50%), Government (50%)
Construction and operating risk	Private player (100%)

Source Authors' compilation

Table 5 Profile of PPP in Nagpur Water Supply

Mandate	Rehabilitation + O&M
Duration (years)	25
Bid parameter	Lowest bid price (Fee/kilo liter of user charge)
Operator	Veolia & Vishwaraj[a]
Total project cost	Rs. 3.88 billion
Private investment	30%
Government grant	JNNURM (70%)
Performance targets	100% coverage; 24-hr water supply; 96% water samples meeting quality targets
Contract signed	late 2011
Contract management	City

[a]Veolia is a multinational corporation while Vishwaraj is the local partner. In low-cost recovery, politically sensitive sectors like water supply, keeping a local partner in the consortium may help manage political risks

Source Authors' compilation

raising retail tariffs. The bidding parameter (user fees) allocates a lot of risk on the private partner and could have been designed better (e.g., competitively bid annuity, which would have provided considerable risk mitigation for the private sector). The performance target (100% coverage), besides improving the revenue for the PPP by reducing non-revenue water is also expected to build political constituency of support for the PPP as the poor are generally the ones who are rationed out of piped water supply and end up paying much higher charges for water.

Appropriate PPP models for Urban Sub-Sectors: While implementing SPVs and ULBs would decide on the appropriate PPP model depending on their requirements and political will, the following table indicates the preferred PPP models across urban infrastructure sub-sectors in India (Table 6).

To make PPPs sustainable in urban infrastructure like in other infrastructure sectors, outcomes should be benign [24 * 7 water supply, improved quality of water supply, covering uncovered areas (benefitting mainly the poor), reducing wastage and leakage, i.e., reducing Non-Revenue Water]. There would also be the need to cultivate stakeholders—users and employees. "Stakeholder" strategies may not

Table 6 Appropriate PPP models for Urban Sub-sectors

Urban sub-sector	Appropriate PPP model
Multilevel parking	BOT (toll)
Integrated solid waste management	Operation and maintenance (O&M) contract; BOT annuity model
Water supply	O&M contract; BOT annuity model

Source Authors' compilation

always work out from a purely financial perspective, but may be needed to make PPPs politically feasible,[34] and, once established, sustainable. PPPs should also provide Value for Money for the public agencies. This would preclude the use of revenue and rate of return guarantees to attract the private sector to urban infrastructure. It is essential to examine whether PPP projects are beneficial to government in the net, or they merely move liabilities to the future as in revenue and rate of return guarantees. Performances can differ widely across countries. The average value for money to the government from PPP projects in UK was estimated to be 17% as compared to only 9% in Australia.

The next chapter takes a look at the issue of renegotiations and cancellation of PPP projects, that have become fairly frequent and could have significant adverse financial impact on the country.

Appendix: Summary of the Report of the Committee on Revisiting and Revitalising Public Private Partnership Model[35] (The Kelkar Committee)

A. Highlights of the Report

1. The availability of high-quality infrastructure and the overcoming of India's infrastructure deficit is crucial to attaining and sustaining rapid growth that generates the right kinds of jobs. PPPs in infrastructure represent a valuable instrument to speed-up infrastructure development in India. This speeding up is urgently required for India to grow rapidly and generate a demographic dividend for itself and also to tap into the large pool of pension and institutional funds from aging populations in the developed countries.
2. India offers today the world's largest market for PPPs. It has accumulated a wealth of experience in getting to this premier position. As the PPP market in infrastructure matures in India, new challenges and opportunities have emerged and will continue to emerge. Periodic review of PPPs, as is the present Committee's remit, are a must to help address issues before they become endemic and to mainstream innovations and foster new ones that improve the successful delivery of PPP projects. This has to be a dynamic process. Such reviews should ideally, therefore, be done frequently, perhaps once every 3 years, and more often if they

[34]Pratap (2011).

[35]Draws from Ministry of Finance (2015).

become part of the work program of the Institute of Excellence in PPPs that the Committee has recommended to be set up urgently.

3. India's success in deploying PPPs as an important instrument for creating infrastructure will depend on a change in attitude and in the mind set of all authorities dealing with PPPs, including public agencies partnering with the private sector, government departments supervising PPPs, and auditing and legislative institutions providing oversight of PPPs. This change in attitude requires (1) moving away from a narrow focus on transactions to focusing on the relationship and on service delivery for citizens (2) building-in an approach of "give and take" between private and public sector partners, and (3) developing a mechanism for dealing with uncertainties inherent in long-term contracts. It must be kept in mind that given market and technological uncertainties, both public and private managers of long-term PPPs take decisions based on incomplete information. A decision that looks problematic ex-post cannot automatically be deemed to be *malafide*. The Committee urges all parties concerned to foster trust between private and public sector partners when they implement PPPs. Implementation of projects under PPP frameworks should be based on an equitable partnership between different stakeholders in a manner that best delivers services to the citizens of India.
4. The Government may take early action to amend the Prevention of Corruption Act, 1988 which does not distinguish between genuine errors in decision-making and acts of corruption. Measures may be taken immediately to make only *malafide* action by public servants punishable, and not errors, and to guard against witch hunt against government officers and bureaucrats for decisions taken with bonafide intention. The government may speed-up amendment of the Prevention of Corruption Act, Vigilance and Conduct rules applicable to government officers.
5. The PPP eco-system in the country is well developed and has been continuously evolving to meet the many challenges encountered in the implementation of such projects. Experience has also underlined the need to further strengthen the three key pillars of PPP frameworks namely Governance, Institutions and Capacity, to build on the established foundation for the next wave of implementation.
6. In addition to changing mindsets, there is an urgent need to rebuild India's PPP capacities. Structured capacity building programs for different stakeholders including implementing agencies and customized programs for banks and financial institutions and private sector need to be evolved. The need for a national level institution to support institutional capacity building activities must be explored. Every stakeholder without exception has strongly emphasized the urgent need for a dedicated institute for PPPs as was announced in the previous Budget. The Committee strongly endorses the "3PI" which can, in addition to functioning as a centre of excellence in PPPs, enable research, review, roll out

activities to build capacity, and support more nuanced and sophisticated models of contracting and dispute redressal mechanisms. A dynamic 3PI can support a dynamic process of infrastructure design, build, and operate in India and thereby help deliver on the promise of reliable infrastructure services for all citizens.

7. The Committee cannot overstate the criticality of setting up of independent regulators in sectors that are going in for PPPs. The Committee recommends setting up these independent regulators with a unified mandate that encompasses activities in different infrastructure sub-sectors to ensure harmonized performance by the regulators.
8. The Committee welcomes the current review and amendment of the Arbitration Act and strongly endorses the need for time limits on hearings.
9. The dominant, primary concern of the Committee was the optimal allocation of risks across PPP stakeholders. Inefficient and inequitable allocation of risk in PPPs can be a major factor in PPP failures, ultimately hurting the citizens of India. The Committee notes that the adoption of the Model Concession Agreement (MCA) has meant that project-specific risks are rarely addressed by project implementation authorities in this "One-size-fits-all" approach. A rational allocation of risks can only be undertaken in sector and project-specific contexts. This arrangement has to only be developed by the project proponents concerned in collaboration with other stakeholders. While risk allocation can be specific to the sector and project, the Committee also emphasizes that a generic risk monitoring and evaluation framework should be developed encompassing all aspects across project development and implementation lifecycle. The Committee urges all stakeholders to then use this framework and allocate risk optimally in accordance with the basic principle that "the entity that is best suited to manage the risk is allotted that risk." The MCAs adopted in some sectors were extremely valuable in reducing transaction costs for the Authority. It is the Committee's view that MCAs for each sector are reviewed to capture the interests of all participating stakeholders—users, project proponents, concessionaires, lenders and markets. The Committee has suggested some changes which would require review to facilitate successful project delivery. Responding to inputs provided by stakeholders, some sector-specific recommendations have been made which are an indicative (though not an exhaustive) list of suggestions which will need detailed expert study.
10. For the next generation of PPP contracts, the Committee suggests the following broad guidelines while allocating and managing risks: (1) an entity should bear the risk that is in its normal course of business; (2) an assessment needs to be carried out regarding the relative ease and efficiency of managing the risk by the entity concerned; (3) the cost effectiveness of managing the risk needs to be evaluated; (4) any overriding

considerations/stipulations of a particular entity need to be factored in prior to implementing the risk management structure; (5) DEA, or preferably the 3PI, should deploy sophisticated modeling techniques that exist to assess risk probabilities and the need to provision for them; and (6) there should be ex-ante provisioning for a renegotiation framework in the bid document itself.

11. Typically, infrastructure PPP projects span over 20–30 years and a developer often loses bargaining power related to tariffs and other matters in case there are abrupt changes in the economic or policy environment which are beyond his control. The Committee feels strongly that the private sector must be protected against what has been called an "Obsolescing Bargain"—the loss of bargaining power over time by private player in PPPs—through the mechanisms including the setting up of Independent Sector Regulators.
12. PPP projects can become distressed when risks emerge that may not have been contemplated at the time of signing. This could give rise to a call for amending the terms of the Concession Agreement to reflect new project realities better. The Committee has suggested benchmarks to be applied to each proposed renegotiation as well as set out a set of conditions that should not be accepted as valid reasons for a request for amendment of a concession agreement.
13. The final decision on a renegotiated concession agreement must be based on (1) full disclosure of the renegotiated estimated long-term costs, risks and potential benefits; (2) comparison with the financial position of government at the time of signing the concession agreement; and (3) comparison with the existing financial position for government just prior to renegotiation. This will permit the Authority regulating the concession to take a decision based on a full comparison of the likely outcomes over the future of the concession.
14. The Committee notes that a number of stalled PPP projects need to be kick started. There is an urgent need to evolve a suitable mechanism that evaluates and addresses "actionable stress"—using stress and adversity to deal with the underlying systemic problems. Sector-specific institutional frameworks should be developed to address these stalled infrastructure projects. The Indian highways sector has proven experience in dealing with stressed PPP projects, and learnings from this sector should be utilized for other sectors and frameworks established for other sectors with the necessary customization. At the same time, umbrella guidelines should be developed for stressed projects that provide an overall framework for development and functioning of sector-specific frameworks. The proposed Tribunal and IPAT approach, in the Committee's view, are the possible solution. The Committee is of the view that only a statutorily established, credible, empowered, multidisciplinary expert

institutional mechanism may be able to deal with the complex issues involved.

15. The Committee recognizes the need for a quick, equitable, efficient, and enforceable dispute resolution mechanism for PPP projects. It is suggested that PPP contracts have clearly articulated dispute resolution structures that demonstrate commitment of all stakeholders and provide flexibility to restructure within the commercial and financial boundaries of the project.
16. In the wake of new project proposals emerging in various infrastructure sectors, the Committee recommends that appropriate legal frameworks be developed against which these can be evaluated.
17. The authorities may be advised against adopting PPP structures for very small projects, since the benefits of delivering small PPP projects may not be commensurate with the resulting costs and the complexity of managing such partnerships over a long period. The transaction costs of well-structured PPP projects are significant, including essential but expensive expert advisory services.
18. Unsolicited Proposals ("Swiss Challenge") may be actively discouraged as they bring information asymmetries into the procurement process and result in lack of transparency and fair and equal treatment of potential bidders in the procurement process.
19. Inherent in the concept of PPP is the role of a "Private Sector Partner" that will implement the project, based on the need to leverage private sector financing and also the managerial and operational efficiencies of the private sector party. It is in this context that the Committee is of the view that since state owned entities SoEs/PSUs are essentially government entities and work within the government framework, they should not be allowed to bid for PPP projects.
20. The authorities should not treat PPPs as an off-balance sheet funding method for the government's responsibility of providing reliable infrastructure services to its citizens. PPP should not be used as the first delivery mechanism without checking its suitability for a particular project. States and other agencies should also not treat Central PPP VGF as a source of additional grants that can be accessed by adopting a PPP delivery mode for projects that are not suitable for such a long-term financing structure.
21. There have been concerns raised by all stakeholders (Government and Private Sector alike) on the demand for developer books of account being subjected to government audit and for access under RTI and Article 12 of Constitution. Conventional audit by authority of private partner's books as per standard procurement process risks delivery of poor quality of service/public asset provision if there is no certainty of processes in the medium term. To address this, the Committee recommends that the government notify comprehensive guidelines on the applicability and

scope of such activities. The laid down process would enable review only of government internal systems, and not that of SPVs, but SPVs would need to follow best practices, incorporate governance systems including those related to related party transactions, financial disclosures, etc., as in the Companies Act, 2013.

22. Monetisation of viable projects that have stable revenue flows after EPC delivery maybe considered. This should be seen as a monetisation opportunity that can attract risk averse long-term funding like pension and institutional investors. By providing O&M PPP opportunities, the authority will be able to free up budgetary funds for fresh EPC and start a virtuous cycle of fresh investment fed by additional revenues.
23. Equity in completed, successful infrastructure projects may be divested by offering to long-term investors, including overseas institutional investors as domestic and foreign institutional investors with long-term liabilities are best suited for providing such long-term financing, but have a limited appetite for risk. Cash generated out of divestment of equity would be available for the creation of new infrastructure projects in the country.
24. Improving a PPP project's risk profile so that it is more suitable for overseas and domestic long-term investors can be accomplished through partial recourse to credible third-party institutions. This could be implemented through a partial credit guarantee or cash flow support mechanisms.
25. It is necessary to explore options for sourcing long-term capital at low cost. Towards this, the Committee recommends, encouraging the banks and financial institution to issue Deep Discount Bonds or Zero Coupon Bonds (ZCB). These will not only lower debt servicing costs in an initial phase of the project but also enable the authorities to charge lower user charges in initial years.
26. Some countries have a legal framework for PPPs in the form of PPP Act/Law/Policy. MoF may develop and publish a national PPP Policy document. Ideally, such a policy document should be endorsed by the Parliament as a policy resolution to impart an authoritative framework for implementing executive agencies as well as to legislative and regulatory agencies charged with oversight responsibilities. The Committee recommends an assessment of whether formulating and enacting a PPP Law will facilitate successful expansion of PPP into new sectors, including health, other social sectors, and urban transport.
27. In the final analysis, the success of deploying PPP as an additional policy instrument for creating infrastructure in India will depend on the change in attitudes and mindsets of all the authorities including public agencies partnering the private sector, government departments supervising the PPPs, and auditing and legislative institutions providing oversight of the PPPs. The PPP reflects a paradigm shift involving the private sector. It

means moving away from "transaction to relationship,"accommodating "give and take" between private and public sector partners, and finally accepting uncertainties and appropriate adjustments inherent in implementing long-term contracts. Given the market and technological uncertainties, the PPP management will take decisions based on incomplete information. Hence, a decision which looks problematic "ex-post" need not necessarily be considered as *malafide*. The Committee urges all parties concerned to foster trust between the private sector and public sector partners in implementing PPP. As mentioned earlier in the Report, PPP is an additional policy instrument to enable India to save time. Since the "demographic deadlines" are staring at us, there is need to accelerate growth. By all accounts, there are only two or three decades left for India to complete the transition from a low-income country to a high-income and developed economy by overcoming the "middle income trap."

B. Key Recommendations

28. Revisiting PPPs: Achievements and Challenges

    a. Contracts need to focus more on service delivery instead of fiscal benefits.
    b. Better identification and allocation of risks between stakeholders.
    c. Prudent utilization of viability gap funds where user charges cannot guarantee a robust revenue stream.
    d. Improved fiscal reporting practices and careful monitoring of performance.

29. Why it is Urgent for India to get Infrastructure PPPs Right

    a. Given the urgency of India's demographic transition, and the experience India has already gathered in managing PPPs, the government must move the PPP model to the next level of maturity and sophistication.
    b. The Committee feels strongly that maturing the PPP model in India is an urgent priority also to take advantage of this historical conjunction of India's infrastructure needs and the availability of long-term funding.
    c. PPPs have the potential to deliver infrastructure projects both faster and better. Building on India's 15 years of experience with PPPs, there is need to iron out the difficulties in the performance of PPPs at every stage of the contract.

30. Rebalancing of Risk Sharing

    a. An assessment needs to be carried out regarding the relative ease and efficiency of managing the risks by the entity concerned.

b. Cost effectiveness of managing the risks needs to be evaluated.
c. Sophisticated modeling techniques are prevalent to assess probabilities of risks and the need to provision for them. DEA may hone its skills in this and provide guidance to project authorities.
d. The final decision for a renegotiated Concession Agreement must be based on:

- Full disclosure of long-term costs, risks, and potential benefits;
- Comparison with the financial position of government at the time of signing the Concession Agreement;
- Comparison with the financial position of government at the time prior to renegotiation.

31. Resolving Legacy Issues

a. Only a statutorily established credible empowered multidisciplinary expert institutional mechanism can deal with the complex issues involved:

- An Infrastructure PPP Project Review Committee ("IPRC") may be constituted to evaluate and send its recommendations in a time-bound manner upon a reference being made of "Actionable Stress" in any Infrastructure Project developed in PPP mode beyond a notified threshold value.
- An Infrastructure PPP Adjudication Tribunal ("IPAT") chaired by a Judicial Member (former Judge SC/Chief Justice HC) with a Technical and/or a Financial member, where benches will be constituted by the Chairperson as per needs of the matter in question.

b. In case procurement of land or clearance is pending from government authorities for more than prescribed number of days, the outstanding work should be de-scoped (under the provisions of Change in Law of Concession Agreement), and allow rest of activities for completing work. Balance work could be completed on a cash-contract basis, provided land and required clearances are in place.
c. Cancel projects that have not achieved a prescribed percentage of progress on the ground. Rebid them once issues have been resolved or complete them through public funds and if viable, bid out for Operations and Maintenance.

32. Generic, including Legacy Projects

a. Sector-specific institutional frameworks may be developed to address issues for PPP infrastructure projects. An entity should bear the risk that is in its normal course of business (for instance, acquisition of land is a normal course of business for public entities). Overriding considerations/stipulations of each entity to be factored in prior to implementation of risk management structure.

b. Learnings from the Highways sector to be utilized for other sectors to customize and adopt such frameworks.
c. Umbrella guidelines may be developed for stressed projects that provide an overall framework for development and functioning of the sector-specific frameworks.
d. DEA to finalize a national PPP Policy document.
e. Unsolicited Proposals ("Swiss Challenge") to be discouraged to avoid information asymmetries and lack of transparency.
f. PPP structures not to be adopted for very small projects in view of the transaction costs involved. DEA to issue threshold guidance.

33. Strengthening Policy, Governance, and Institutional Capacity

a. Amend the Prevention of Corruption Act, 1988 to distinguish between genuine errors in decision-making and acts of corruption.
b. Build up capacity in all stakeholders, including regulators, authority, consultants, financing agencies, and developers.
c. Set up an institution for invigorating private investments in infrastructure, providing guidance for a national PPP policy and developments in PPP, developing a mechanism to capture and collate data for decision-making, undertaking capacity building activities. The 3PI institute for PPPs announced in 2014 may be set up without delay.
d. Prequalified PPP consultancies could be empaneled by DEA as earlier which could be tapped at short notice.
e. Revive the PPP Cells supported by the DEA over the last decade in Infrastructure Ministries and State Governments.
f. An institutionalized mechanism like the National Facilitation Committee (NFC) to ensure time-bound resolution of issues including getting timely clearances/approvals during the implementation of projects for smooth running of such projects.
g. Ministry of Finance to coordinate with other implementing ministries to develop a policy to promote secondary market for operational assets.
h. Disallow statutory audit of books of SPVs governed by the provisions of the Companies Act. Ensure adoption of principles of good governance by the SPVs.
i. Standard public authority requirements of audit till point of award (public books) and post-construction discharge by Authority of monitoring and oversight of project operations as per the concession agreement (public books) to be in the purview of statutory/government audit agencies.
j. Essential to set up independent Regulators in sectors going in for PPP.

k. Discourage government participation in SPVs that implement PPP projects unless strategically essential. DEA to issue guidance on Government participation in such JV-SPVs.

34. Scaling Up Finance

a. Restrict the number of banks in a consortium.
b. Banks to build up their own risk assessment/appraisal capabilities.
c. Check list of items listed as a guidance for lenders.
d. RBI may provide guidelines to lenders on encashment of bank guarantees in line with ICC norms.
e. Monetisation of viable projects that have stable revenue flows after EPC delivery should be considered.
f. Equity in completed, successful infrastructure projects may be divested by offering to long-term investors.
g. Ministry of Finance to allow banks and financial institutions to issue Zero Coupon Bonds which will also help to achieve a soft landing for user charges in the infrastructure sector.

35. Revitalising Contractual Processes

a. Need for review of the MCAs.
b. Sample suggestions for generic changes, including for resolution of disputes, and sector-specific changes.

36. Reinvigorating the Sectors

a. Independent sector regulators essential.
b. Build upon maturing landscape in Roads and Ports PPP and move into the next phase; Roads: avoiding delays, institutionalized dispute resolution, improved project development activity, monetization of operational assets, efficiency and transparency by electronic tolling, etc.
c. Ports: review of role and need of Tariff Authority for Major Ports (TAMP), review of MCA, quicker clearances, rationalized leases and stamp duties.
d. Airport: PPPs to be encouraged where viable in Greenfield and brownfield projects, have policy that addresses potential demand for airport services in the country, notify a unified regulatory structure, clarity in delineation of Till policy, calculation of aeronautical and other cash flows essential.
e. Encourage use of PPPs in sectors like Railways, Urban, etc. Railways to have an independent tariff regulator, tap potentially useful PPP opportunities including brownfield assets.

37. Fast Forward PPPs
    a. Set up an institute of excellence in PPP to *inter-alia* guide the sector, provide policy input, timely advice and undertake sustainable capacity building.
    b. Ensure integrated development of infrastructure with roadmaps for delivery of projects.
    c. India's demographic deadlines are staring at us. There are only two or three decades left to complete the transition from a country that has just attained middle-income status to that of a high-income and developed economy. Besides the basic problems for provision of adequate infrastructure, the middle-income trap is also to be averted. Without adequate infrastructure, this will simply not be possible. India is currently in a global win-win situation with a large young population that will need good jobs and a huge pool of global savings that can be tapped for building out our infrastructure. PPPs are an important policy instrument that will enable India to compress time in this journey toward economic growth and development. A successful and growing stream of PPPs in infrastructure will go a long way in accelerating the country's development process.

Chapter 10
When Things Go Wrong: Renegotiation and Cancelation of Infrastructure Projects

In April 2013, the Central Electricity Regulatory Commission granted relief to the Tata Mundra and Adani Mundra imported coal-based power projects by agreeing to reopen signed long-term power purchase agreements. Many road projects, including GMR's Kishangarh–Udaipur–Ahmedabad project, are also seeking relief after contract award through renegotiations. The road ministry had planned to include renegotiations explicitly in the terms of reference of the proposed road regulator.

Among the most important reasons for the country making rapid strides in private participation in infrastructure is the drawing up of Model Concession Agreements across infrastructure sectors, which define the risk-reward framework for stakeholders in precise terms. Use of standardized documents is an international best practice, which lends transparency to and expedites the project award and implementation process. Renegotiation of existing contracts appears to compromise the sanctity of agreements, but have become uncomfortably frequent in recent years. This chapter seeks to understand the background leading up to the recent cases of renegotiations, the practical implications, and the policy imperatives.

1 Renegotiations—A Brief Conceptual Background

Renegotiation involves changing the original contractual terms and conditions. This is distinct from an adjustment that occurs as a result of a mechanism already defined in the contract. Standard scheduled tariff adjustments[1] and periodic tariff reviews,

This chapter draws heavily upon Pratap, Kumar V., 2011, *Sustaining Privatization of Infrastructure,* Ph.D. dissertation, University of Maryland.

[1]In the Indian Model Concession Agreements, user tariffs are linked to inflation. Any tariff increase resulting from the mechanism provided in the Concession Agreement would not be considered Renegotiation.

K.V. Pratap and R. Chakrabarti, *Public-Private Partnerships in Infrastructure*,
India Studies in Business and Economics, DOI 10.1007/978-981-10-3355-1_10

for instance, are built into the contracts and not considered renegotiations. Renegotiation suggests a failure to comply with agreed-upon terms and departures and deviation from expected promises of sector improvements.

Renegotiations have a wide-ranging scope, e.g., change in the risk allocation matrix, change in terms of the contract (tariffs, guarantees, investment plans and levels, lump-sum payments or recurring fees, coverage objectives, service standards, concession period, etc.).

Why renegotiate? There could be many reasons for renegotiations. Chief among them are:

- **Incomplete and poorly designed contracts**—One popular line of argument is that since all contingencies cannot be foreseen in a long concession period (coal shortage, etc.), renegotiations would take place anyway. Since contracts are incomplete by their very nature, renegotiations is a way to deal with unforeseen contingencies. Writing a contract with all possible contingencies may be too expensive and may make the contract too unwieldly. In addition, people writing the contract have limited ability and bounded rationality and so aiming for a contract covering all contingencies may also not be possible.
  Poor risk allocation in a concession contract may also be a reason for renegotiations. If the public sector has given revenue or rate of return guarantees, it may be too onerous for the public sector to fulfill its obligations in the face of persistent shortfall in revenues or profits. The Delhi–Noida Toll Bridge could be an example of this as the public sector gave a rate of return guarantee of 20% annually on the total project cost with any shortfall in this to be added to the total project cost to be serviced in the following year. Since the project is making much less than this, an optimum strategy for the public sector would be to renegotiate the project. A court rating in October 2016 has achieved as much by disallowing collection of tolls on the Delhi–Noida Toll Bridge.
- **Macroeconomic shocks** can undermine the financial equilibrium of infrastructure projects as revenues are generally in local currency but investments could be in foreign currency. When the domestic currency loses value as in a macroeconomic shock, the ability of these revenues to service foreign debt and equity is severely impaired leading to renegotiation or even cancelation. Macroeconomic crises are a regular occurrence in the world as exemplified by Mexico (1994), East Asia (1997), and Argentina (2002). A highly successful water project in Argentina, Aguas Argentinas, could not survive the Argentine macroeconomic crisis of 2002 and ultimately had to be canceled. To prevent renegotiations on account of macroeconomic shocks, contracts should provide clear guidelines for adjustments in such situations to the extent possible.
- **Opportunistic behavior**: Aggressive bidding and private sector seeking more favorable terms after contract award can also engender renegotiation requests. This is akin to the "Jugaad" principle at work in India and is apparent from the experience of many projects including the Tata Mundra (or Coastal Gujarat Power Limited) and the Delhi International Airport Limited (DIAL) projects, both of which we discuss later in the book.

A simplified version of the "Jugaad" principle is illustrated in the following equation: $R = PQ - OC - T - D = rKi$, where R represents profits, P prices or tariffs, Q quantity of output, OC stands for operation and maintenance costs, T represents taxes, D is depreciation, r is the opportunity cost of capital, and Ki is invested capital. This equation shows that the excess of revenues over costs should provide an appropriate return on investment at equilibrium. If the award criterion is a transfer fee, it is covered in Ki. If it is the lowest tariff, it is captured in P. As Guasch[2] points out, any appropriate bid, whether based on K or P, has, the principle of this equation in its background.

In a strategic or opportunistic bid, profits are less than the required return on capital or $R = PQ - OC - T - D < rKi$. Strategic, opportunistic, or aggressive bidding, therefore, refers to bids that do not provide firms with desired returns—that is, the cost of capital for the submitted bids exceed cash flows from it. The demand for renegotiations in such cases aims at higher tariffs (or P) or lower transfer fee (or Ki) to balance the equation. In the case of the Tata Mundra bid, the relief sought was in terms of P. The intention here is to win the bid with the expectation of a later renegotiation, arguing that the equation does not balance, and higher tariffs or additional investment sources (through levy of Development Fee in the case of DIAL) are needed to restore financial equilibrium. Underbidding improves the chances of winning an auction, while the possibility of renegotiation lessens the likely losses arising from it.

The "Jugaad" principle can play out in a number of ways: Once a private enterprise wins a concession in an infrastructure sector, it may behave opportunistically and be able to "hold up" the government—for example, by insisting on renegotiating the contract, seeking more favorable terms. The "Jugaad" principle may have been used in earlier telecom bidding in India too, where the bids based on license fees were too high and the government had to renegotiate these projects to sweeten the deal for the private sector by making revenue share as the operational parameter as against license fees. Similarly, the bids received in the recent solar auctions (where solar tariffs reached below Rs. 4 per kwh) may be too aggressive and are likely to be renegotiated in the future.

Typology of Renegotiation

Based on the above, one can classify renegotiations among the following types.

- Initiated by Government: Governments are generally not keen to shut down infrastructure projects because of concerns about service continuity (Tata Mundra Project), possible termination payments (Delhi–Noida Toll Bridge), and negative publicity surrounding these perceived failures. Therefore, they may renegotiate contracts for the following reasons.

[2]Guasch (2004).

- Opportunistic: This could be politically motivated say, when a new government reduces contracted tariffs or increases investment obligations after the private sector has put in the investment.
- Change in priorities: A new government may have new priorities of sector development and this may lead to renegotiation of existing contracts. This is often linked to the electoral cycle as we exemplify by the Dabhol Power Project case. The opposition political alliance won elections in Maharashtra in March 1995, and in May the new government appointed a committee of state ministers to review the Dabhol Project. The Committee recommended scrapping the Dabhol project in August 1995 on the grounds that the capital costs of the project were inflated, that the foreign currency denomination of tariff payments would cause unjustly high power rates, that there were outstanding environmental issues, and that the project would harm the economic development of Maharashtra. Ultimately, the state and the Dabhol Power Company finalized the terms of the renegotiated agreement in the same year. Dissatisfaction with services and perceived non-compliance by operator with agreed-upon terms may also lead to renegotiations.

• Initiated by Operator: As compared to renegotiations initiated by the Government, an overwhelming majority of such contracts are renegotiated at the behest of the private sector operator (see Fig. 1).

  The various types of renegotiation initiated by the operator could be:

  - Opportunistic: This happens, for example, when the private sector submits a low unrealistic bid to win a contract with the hope of later renegotiations. The chance of winning the bid increases if a low bid is submitted, but the consequences of the low bid do not play out if the contract is renegotiated to the advantage of the bidder.
  - Macro-shock related: The private sector operator may want to renegotiate a contract if the economy experiences a macroeconomic shock and foreign currency funding has been extensively used. This may cause massive financial stress resulting in the demand for revision of user tariffs, for example, beyond what is provided for in the contract.

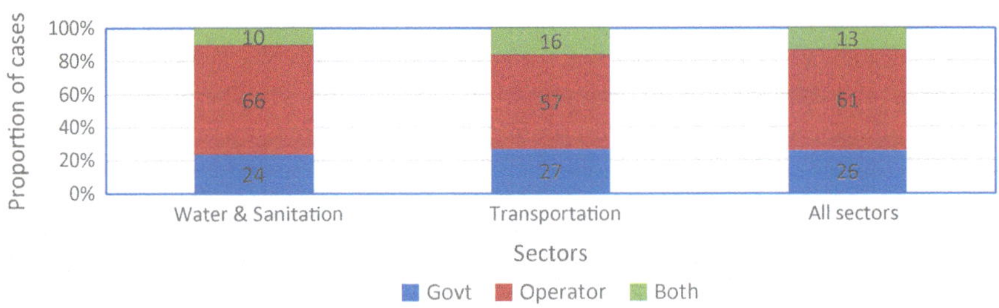

Fig. 1 Initiator of renegotiation. *Source* Guasch (2004)

- Ambiguous: It may also happen that renegotiations do not fit in any of the above types. For example, in the case of the Aguas Argentinas project, there was increase in investment obligations for the private sector, coupled with a macroeconomic shock.

When conditioned by the type of tariff regulatory regime, operators were predominantly the initiators of renegotiation (83%) in the price-cap regime, but under a rate of return regime, the government-initiated renegotiation, although with a much lower incidence (34%). This is because a price-cap regulatory regime is more demanding on the private operator, whereas the level of risk is higher for the government in the case of rate of return regulation. The low incidence of government-initiated renegotiation even in the case of rate of return regulation may be because of reluctance on the part of the government to acknowledge that mistakes may have been made in the past as in the case of Delhi–Noida Toll Bridge.

2 Renegotiations—International and Indian Experience

Guasch, in his seminal study on renegotiations,[3] analyzed over a thousand infrastructure concessions granted over the period 1985–2000 in the Latin America and Caribbean (LAC) region, and found that about 30% of the concession contracts are renegotiated and that the average time to renegotiations is 2.2 years from start of operations, despite original contract agreements being for 20–30 years. The telecommunications sector is usually far less subject to renegotiation. This is mostly because of the sector's higher viability and availability of potential new entrants. Excluding the telecommunications sector raises the incidence of renegotiation to 41.5%. Significantly, Guasch also found that concessions in the electricity sector are much less prone to renegotiations (9.7%) mainly because the sector has competing suppliers, thus reducing the bargaining power of individual providers. Projects in the transport sector (55%) and water and sewerage sector (74%) are, however, much more prone to renegotiations (see Fig. 2). Renegotiations also came fastest in water and sanitation concessions, on average within 1.6 years after concession award. In contrast, in the transportation sector, the average time to renegotiations was 3.1 years, possibly owing to the sector's longer construction period.

Updated figures for the LAC region for the 1988–2010 period indicates that the contracts are increasingly becoming more fragile as indicated by their average time to renegotiation from start of operations shown in Fig. 3.

The high incidence of renegotiations shown in the figures above makes renegotiation the norm rather than the exception. This high incidence violates the sanctity of contracts and creates a rational expectation that governments are willing to give into renegotiation demands, which might be promoting more opportunistic behavior on the part of the private sector. Thus, a vicious cycle of bidding low, with

[3]Guasch (2004).

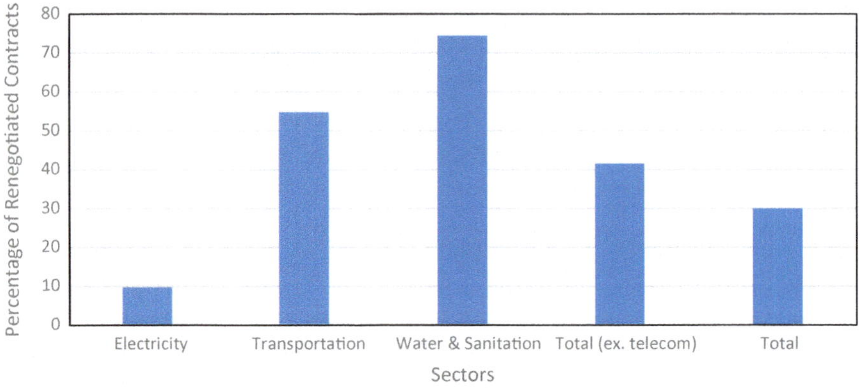

Fig. 2 Sector-wise distribution of renegotiated contracts. *Source* Guasch (2004)

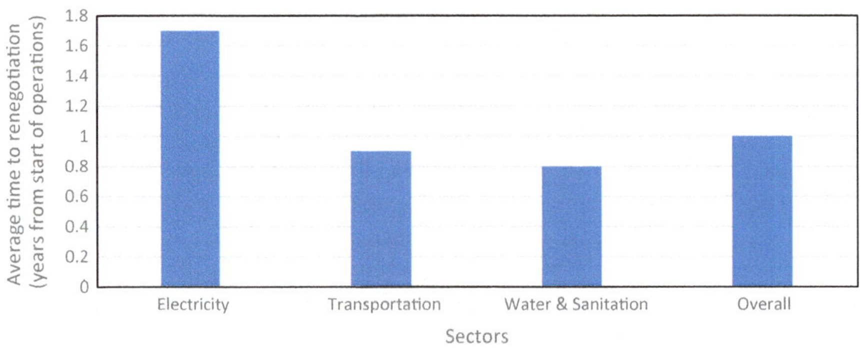

Fig. 3 Fragility of contracts. *Source* Guasch (2013)

the objective of winning the concession and then renegotiating better terms is created, making aggressive bidding the equilibrium strategy for rational bidders.

According to Guasch, while some renegotiations may be desirable when they address the essentially incomplete nature of concession contracts, the prevalent high incidence of renegotiations points toward opportunistic behavior, including efforts to mitigate cases of aggressive bidding.

Contract features have an impact on risk allocation and therefore have a bearing on the incidence of renegotiations. Thus, if the bidding parameter is the lowest tariff to be charged to consumers, there is considerable risk allocated to the private operator, and the incidence of renegotiation associated with this feature is high at 60% compared to when the award criteria is the highest transfer fee (11%). Chances of renegotiation went up significantly when concession contracts contained investment requirements (70%) (e.g., Aguas Argentinas) as compared to performance indicators (18%). Moreover, the incidence of renegotiation was much higher under price-cap regulation (42%) than rate of return regulation (13%). The presence of a regulatory agency appears to reduce it significantly from 61% (in its absence)

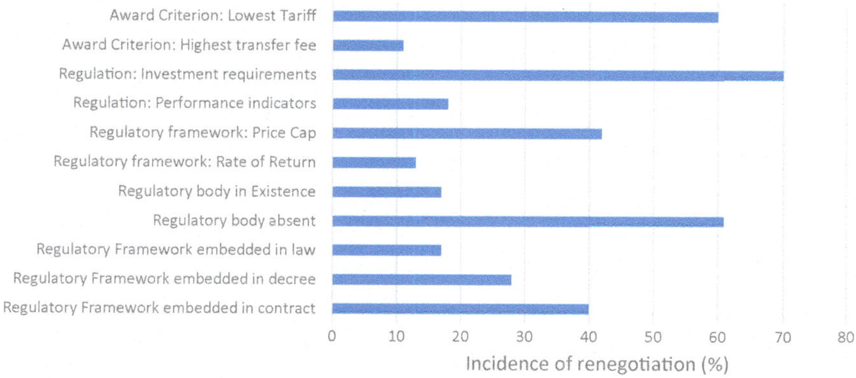

Fig. 4 Contract features and incidence of renegotiations. *Source* Guasch (2004)

to 17%. Where the regulatory framework was embedded seemed to matter as well. Renegotitaions happened most frequently when it is embedded in the contract (40%) than in a decree (28%) or a law (17%) (Fig. 4).

Outcomes of renegotiations: What is worrisome is that the outcomes of renegotiation frequently turn out to be in favor of the private sector and against the government and users. Thus, Guasch finds that renegotiations lead to increases in tariffs (62% of the cases), delays and decreases in investment obligations (69%), increases in the number of cost components with an automatic pass-through to tariffs (59%), and decreases in the annual fee paid by the operator to the government (31%). A small number of renegotiations, however, led to tariff decreases (19%), increases in the annual fee paid by the operator to the government (17%), and unfavorable changes for the operator of the asset base (22%) (see Fig. 5).

The costs of renegotiation could be classified into:

- Fiscal: Often outcome of renegotiation carry a fiscal cost to the government through reduction in the annual fee to be paid by the operator, etc.
- Political: Renegotiations tend be quite visible as there is large coverage in print and electronic media. When the results are seen to be unfair to users and government, the PPP model tends to lose credibility and public support and the PPI program comes under threat.
- Financial: Time and resources are needed to address and resolve the conflicts.
- Economic/Social: Users tend to be adversely affected by renegotiations (reduced access, higher prices or lower quality of service).

On average, these costs have been quantified to be 3–15% of the investment.

Indian experience in renegotiations: The incidence of renegotiations in India is much less than that experienced in the Latin America and Caribbean countries. This could be because of the robust institutional structure for approval of PPP projects (Public–Private Partnership Approval Committee seated in the Ministry of Finance), extensive use of Model Concession Agreements, which has in built

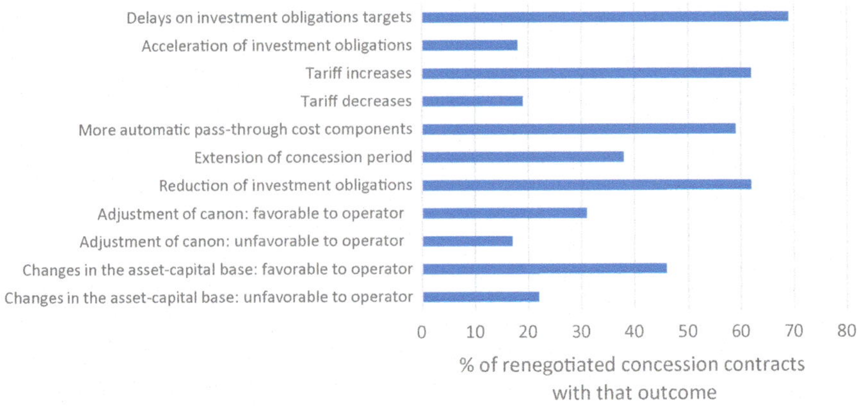

Fig. 5 Outcomes of renegotiation. *Source* Guasch (2004)

flexibility in the form of tariff indexation, etc., and independent sectoral regulators that have been established in major infrastructure sectors like telecom, power, civil aviation, and ports.

Despite all this, some Indian projects have been renegotiated and are mentioned below.

- Power: Dabhol Power Project in 1996; GVK Jegurupadu electricity generation project[4]; Tata Mundra UMPP Project (see Box 1 below about the details of this case)
- Road: Kishangarh–Udaipur–Ahmedabad Project
- Metro rail: Delhi Airport Line—now canceled
- Telecom: Change from high license fee to revenue sharing regime
- Some cases fit to be renegotiated (courts have recently disallowed levy and collection of tolls): Delhi–Noida Toll bridge

In India, renegotiations have occurred mainly at the instance of the private sector. The government does not seem to be keen to initiate renegotiations even to protect its own interest. This corresponds with the results of the Guasch study, which found that 61% of the renegotiations occurred at the instance of the concessionaires while only 26% of the renegotiations were initiated by the government (see Fig. 1). But, this is where the similarity ends. Guasch found that in the price-cap regulatory regime, operators were mostly and almost exclusively the initiators of renegotiation (83%), but under a rate of return regime, the government sought it more often, although much less frequently (34%). This gap is explained, at least in part, by the increased risk to the operator in a price-cap regulatory regime. However, many Indian regulatory regimes are hybrid with a 16% rate of return on

[4]GVK Jegurupadu electricity generation project in Andhra Pradesh was renegotiated twice prior to commercial operations.

Table 1 Ranking of bidders for Tata Mundra Project

	Bidder	Levelised tariff (Rs./kWh)	Ranking
1	Tata Power Company Limited	2.264	L1
2	Reliance Energy Generation Limited	2.661	L2
3	Adani Enterprises Limited	2.696	L3
4	Essar Power Limited	2.801	L4
5	Larsen and Toubro Power Limited	3.220	L5
6	Sterlite Industries (India) Limited	3.746	L6

equity guaranteed in many infrastructure sectors. So, it is a bit strange why the government has not been keen to protect its own interests by initiating renegotiations.

Box 1: Renegotiation of Tata Mundra Project or Coastal Gujarat Power Limited

Project Background

Tata Mundra Project is an Ultra Mega Power Project (UMPP) of 4000 MW capacity and is based on imported coal. Four UMPPs, each with an installed capacity of 4000 MW, have been bid out till date—Mundra, Sasan, Krishnapatnam, and Tilaiya. Power price is low in these projects because of economies of scale and superior, energy efficient and environment-friendly technology.

The Total Project Cost for the Tata Mundra Project is $4 billion. As is typical of a PPP project, there is limited recourse financing with a high debt-equity ratio of 3:1 in the project. The entire equity is from Tata Power. More than 50% debt is in foreign currency with foreign loans of $1.8 billion provided by Korean Exim, Korean Insurance, ADB, etc. Domestic loan is $1.2 billion through a consortium of banks led by State Bank of India. The main project equipment has been imported from Korea and Japan with excise and custom duty exemption.

The contract type is Build-Own-Operate-Maintain (BOOM). The concession period for the project is 25 years. The project has been commissioned (last unit commissioned in March 2013).

Bid description

The Bid Process Coordinator was Power Finance Corporation (PFC), which made the Detailed Project Report. The Special Purpose Vehicle for implementing the project was formed by PFC and is called Coastal Gujarat Power Limited (CGPL). Project Development Risk was mitigated through the

Table 2 Analysis of financial bids of Tata Mundra Project

	NECC	ECC	NEC	EC	NET	ET	NEIH	EIH	Total
Tata	0.83	0.05	0.37	0.5	0.14	0.22	0.055	0.098	2.26
	CC = 0.88		Coal = 0.87		Transportation = 0.36		Inland handling = 0.15		
Reliance	1.07	0.001	0	0.93	0.21	0.32	0.05	0.08	2.66
	CC = 1.07		Coal = 0.93		Transportation = 0.53		Inland handling = 0.13		
Adani	1.05	0	1.15	0	0.31	0	0.18	0	2.69
	CC = 1.05		Coal = 1.15		Transportation = 0.31		Inland handling = 0.18		

Note NECC non-escalable capacity charge; *ECC* escalable capacity charge; *NEC* non-escalable coal charge; *EC* escalable coal charge; *NET* non-escalable transportation charge; *ET* escalable transportation charge; *NEIH* non-escalable inland handling charge; *EIH* escalable inland handling charge

SPV on whose name land was acquired, environmental clearance obtained, and transmission arrangements made.

Like in any large project, there was a two-stage bidding process consisting of Request for Qualification (RfQ) and Request for Proposal (RfP) stages. The RfQ was issued in March 2006 and 13 bidders submitted bids out of which 11 qualified for the RfP stage. The RfP was issued in November 2006 and 6 bidders submitted financial bids. The RfP Bidding Parameter was lowest levelized tariff. The levelised tariff of the 6 bidders at the RfP stage may be seen in Table 1. Tata Power was declared successful based on least levelized electricity tariff of Rs 2.26 per kilowatt hour (kWh) of electricity. Tata Power acquired CGPL in April 2007 from PFC for about Rs. 280 million.

According to the RfP, the tariff to be quoted by the bidders comprised two components, Energy Charge and Capacity Charge, which were further divided into escalable and non-escalable components. The bids of the top three bidders are analyzed in Table 2.

The renegotiation process

Although at the point of bidding, none of the bidders owned any captive coal mine abroad, both Tata and Adani appear to have assumed significant risks by quoting large component of their coal charges (Tata—43%, Adani—100%) as non-escalable.[5]

This implied that their tariffs would not reflect any significant variation in international coal prices over the term of the PPA despite this being an imported coal-based project, as such variations are assumed to have been factored-in in their bids.

Tata Power, later in March 2007, acquired 30% stake in two of the largest mines (Arutmin and KPC) in Indonesia under Bumi Resources Tbk, the largest coal mining company in Indonesia. This provided them a basis for long-term coal procurement on a contractual basis for Mundra UMPP.

Although Reliance Power quoted 100% of its coal charges as escalable in Mundra, they changed strategies for the Krishnapatnam UMPP, another imported coal-based project, where they quoted 100% of their coal charges as non-escalable. This opened them to substantially higher risks, as they were completely delinked from variations in international coal prices. It is not surprising therefore that Reliance's Krishnapatnam UMPP was seriously affected by the regulatory changes in Indonesia (their source for coal). Reliance had stalled all work at Krishnapatnam stating that the feasibility of developing the project no longer existed with the regulatory changes in Indonesia.

[5]Only the escalable fuel charge component of the tariff can be escalated as per the escalation indices of Central Electricity Regulatory Commission (CERC).

The high level of risk borne by Tata Power by making a major part of its variable costs non-escalable led to unmanageable risks for CGPL. Tata Power bagged the project at a levelized tariff of Rs. 2.26 per unit of electricity, after keeping 43% of its fuel charge non-escalable. So, it willingly accepted the commercial risk of keeping a major component of its tariffs non-escalable, which was instrumental in Tata Power winning the bid. Subsequently, Tata Power petitioned Central Electricity Regulatory Commission (CERC) that because of change in Indonesian regulations, whereby all existing coal contracts have to benchmark coal prices to international market prices, its Power Purchase Agreement (PPA) with power procurers has become unviable.[6]

The estimated coal requirement for the project is approximately 12 million metric tons per annum (MMTPA). Fuel price and availability risk are largely borne by the private sector, which had sought to mitigate it through back to back Coal Supply Agreements (CSA) with IndoCoal Resources, Caymen Islands. As per the petition, the new Indonesian law[7] and higher imported coal prices have made the UMPP unviable at PPA rate—there is a loss of Rs. 18.73 billion per annum and Rs. 475 billion over PPA period of 25 years. To buttress its case, CGPL stated that its accumulated loss in 2013 was Rs. 38.10 billion and more than 80% of the net worth had already eroded. However, in the event of breach of the Coal Supply Agreement, the liability of IndoCoal on account of all losses, costs, and expenses incurred by the Petitioner as a result of the loss under the CSA and in entering into any alternative arrangement for the supply of coal, is limited to US $55 million only. The

[6]CGPL had filed the petition seeking relief under Article 12 (Force Majeure) and Article 13 (Change in Law) of the PPA and Section 79 of the Electricity Act to mitigate the impact of the unprecedented increase in the price of imported coal.

[7]Government of Indonesia promulgated the "Regulation of Minister of Energy and Mineral Resources No. 17 of 2010 regarding Procedure for Setting Mineral and Coal Benchmark Selling Price" on 23.9.2010. According to the new Indonesian Regulations, the holders of mining permits for production and operation of mineral and coal mines are required to sell mineral and coal in domestic and international markets including to their affiliates by referring to the benchmark price and the spot price of coal in the international market. All long-term coal contracts for supply of coal from Indonesia are required to be adjusted with the Indonesian Regulations within a period of 12 months, i.e., by 23.9.2011. CGPL amended the CSA in 2012 to align with the new Indonesian Regulations. Due to adoption of the Indonesian Regulations, CGPL petitioned that it is supplying power to the procurers by purchasing coal at a higher price than the price envisaged at the time of bid. The petitioner has submitted that Tata Power Company Ltd. submitted its bid for Mundra UMPP in December 2006 after considering the prevailing economic situation at the time of the bidding. The petitioner has submitted that the then price for benchmark coal of Gross Calorific Value (GCV) 6322 kcal/kg was USD 49.75 which was equal to USD 42 for GCV 5350 kcal/kg. The petitioner has submitted that due to certain subsequent unforeseen and unprecedented developments such as promulgation of Indonesian regulations and rise in international coal prices from USD 40–50/MT in 2006 to USD 110–120/MT in 2011, mainly due to increase in its spot price on account of increase in coal import by India and China, it has become commercially impracticable for the Petitioner to supply power at the bid out tariff. (Source: Central Electricity Regulatory Commission order dated 15.4.2013).

new set of Standard Bidding Documents of the Ministry of Power make fuel price pass-through to the power procurers. But, this is also problematic as the retail tariffs are politically capped and any increase in input prices would only be reflected in increased losses of public sector distribution companies.

The CERC gave relief to the company,[8] through a majority decision on 15 April 2013, after contract award by requiring a committee[9] to be formed, including power procurers and CGPL, to compensate the project for the "unprecedented" and "unforeseen" increase in coal prices. It however correctly ruled that the change in Indonesian regulations do not constitute "Force Majeure" or "Change in Law" for the project as defined in the Power Purchase Agreement (PPA)[10] between Coastal Gujarat Power Limited (CGPL, the Special Purpose Vehicle company created for implementing the project) and the state-owned distribution companies in Gujarat (for 47.5% of CGPL's generation), Maharashtra (20%), Punjab (12.5%), Haryana (10%), and Rajasthan (10%), This relief[11] was given under regulatory powers of the CERC under Section 79(1)(b) of the Electricity Act,[12] thus negating the provisions of Section 63 of the Act,[13] which provides for the CERC adopting the tariff arrived at through competitive bidding.

However, the CERC order was appealed against at the Appellate Tribunal of Electricity (APTEL), which upheld the decision of CERC on CGPL in July

---

[8]Central Electricity Regulatory Commission (2013): "Order dated 15 April 2013 on Petition No. 159/MP/2012", Viewed on 20 April 2013 (http://www.cercind.gov.in/2013/orders/159_mp_2012.pdf). CERC passed a "compensatory tariff" order to offset losses on account of costly imported coal in favor of Tata Power in April 2013. The difference between actual and quoted energy charges was to be the compensatory tariff mechanism.

[9]The Compensatory Tariff Committee was set up under Deepak Parekh. The Committee recommended 0.59/kWh as the compensatory tariff for 2013–14. It also recommended true-up/reconciliation of actual costs every year vis-à-vis normative assumptions. Thus, the Committee effectively converted the tariff arrived through competitive bidding (Section 63 of Electricity Act, 2003—tariff determination through competitive bidding) to a cost-plus regime (Section 62 of Electricity Act—tariff determination through Electricity Regulatory Commission) after contract award. This amounts to renegotiation of the contract.

[10]PPA between CGPL and distribution companies was signed in 2007.

[11]Tata sought tariff increase of 0.67/kWh; 'Compensatory Tariff' Committee recommended 0.59/kWh; CERC ordered 0.55/kWh; APTEL agreed for 0.52/kWh. The benefit to CGPL amounted to Rs. 250 billion over the PPA period. In the process, the private sector liability was transferred to the public sector. This corresponds with Guasch's view that the predominant beneficiary in most renegotiations is the private sector.

[12]Section 79(1)(b) of the Electricity Act, which has been used by CGPL to obtain relief from CERC, deals with the following function of CERC: "to regulate the tariff of generating companies other than those owned or controlled by the Central Government specified in clause (a), if such generating companies enter into or otherwise have a composite scheme for generation and sale of electricity in more than one State".

[13]Section 63 of the Electricity Act states that "the Appropriate Commission shall adopt the tariff if such tariff has been determined through transparent process of bidding in accordance with the guidelines issued by the Central Government".

2014, but reduced the relief (gross compensatory tariff) to 0.52/kWh, thus providing a benefit of Rs. 250 billion to CGPL over the life of the project. The justification given for the relief was that the resultant tariff rate of Rs. 2.78/kWh was much lower than the cost of replacement power at Rs. 4.10/kWh. However, the Supreme Court has stayed APTEL's order and subsequently annulled CERC's orders.

Is the outcome of renegotiation perverse?: The compensatory tariff order reopened a signed long-term PPA and violated the sanctity of contract. It was a closely contested bid where the levelized tariff difference between L1 (Tata Power) and L3 (Adani) was Rs. 0.43/kWh. The relief on account of increase in Indonesian coal prices given by APTEL is Rs. 0.52/kWh. Therefore, the bidders L2 and L3 have reason to feel aggrieved for this benefit given to Tata Power after contract award and have a genuine question that why was this relief not on offer at the time of bidding.

The international market price of coal would fluctuate and so the exact impact of the Indonesian regulations will vary from time to time and may get neutralized over the 25-year contract period. In addition, PPA is a legally binding document between CGPL and the power procurers and should have been honored. The CERC should also have looked at the claim that the change in Indonesian regulations was "unprecedented" and "unforeseen" as the country has been known to abrogate contracts unilaterally. To take an example in the power sector, Indonesia entered into negotiated contracts for Dieng, Patuha, and Karaha Bodas geothermal projects around the turn of the century, only to find the tariffs unaffordable, and brought about new regulations reducing the contracted price of power. The Government of Indonesia had to ultimately take over these projects at great costs imposed by international arbitrators.[14] Thus, the breach of contract by Indonesia is not "unprecedented" and therefore should not have been "unforeseen".

There are wider implications of this CERC order. The order transfers fuel price risk from the private sector, which it took on willingly by keeping 43% of the fuel charge non-escalable, to the public sector. When retail tariffs are *politically capped*, increase in fuel price for power projects would only be reflected in the increased losses of the state power distribution companies.[15] This also sets a very bad precedent for all long-term infrastructure contracts in the country[16] making them vulnerable to renegotiations after contract award –

[14]Wells and Ahmed (2007).

[15]As per the CGPL petition, the additional financial implication due to increase in Indonesian coal price works out to Rs. 1,873 crore per annum and Rs. 47,500 crore over the 25 year PPA period. This adverse financial implication was sought to be transferred to the account of the state-owned power procurers.

[16]Pratap (2013).

Reliance has already filed petition with CERC for other 3 UMPPs (1 out of which has been canceled recently).

Timeline to Renegotiation

- Apr 2007—Power Purchase Agreement signed with procurers of 5 states
- Sept 2007—CERC adopts tariff of Mundra UMPP discovered through competitive bidding
- Apr 2008—CGPL achieves Financial Closure
- Sept 2010—New Indonesian coal pricing regulation notified
- Mar 2012–Mar 2013—Commercial Operation Date (COD) of all 5 units of Mundra UMPP
- July 2012—CGPL files petition before CERC
- Apr 2013—CERC issues order directing CGPL and procurers to constitute a committee to suggest compensatory tariff
- Feb 2014—CERC orders compensatory tariff increase of Rs. 0.55/kWh of electricity; Renegotiations within a year of COD
- July 2014—Appellate Tribunal for Electricity (APTEL) upholds decision of CERC and awards Rs. 0.52/kWh to CGPL from March 2014
- April 2017—Supreme Court annuls CERC and APTEL's relief to CGPL

In terms of outcomes of renegotiations, the world-wide pattern has been repeated in India, as it appears to show greater willingness to accommodate the concerns of the private sector, than display similar urgency when it comes to protecting the public interest. The outcomes of renegotiation would also be looked at unfavorably by agencies like the Central Vigilance Commission, the Comptroller and Auditor General of India (CAG), and the Central Bureau of Investigation leading to difficulties for the private sector, regulators, and the government, and ultimately for the future of private participation in infrastructure in the country.

Let us look at a few Indian examples of renegotiations to illustrate this point. The infamous Dabhol Power Project was renegotiated in 1996 increasing the size of the project more than threefold to 2,184 MW and ultimately adding to the liabilities of the government when the project failed. Government eventually paid Rs. 8,485 crore[17] to the owners of the Dabhol Project in 2005, and a smaller project would have cost much less. The "fast track" GVK Jegurupadu electricity generation project in Andhra Pradesh was renegotiated twice prior to commercial operations.

[17]Lok Sabha Unstarred Question number 536 answered on Nov 24, 2006.

The renegotiations largely favored GVK by providing for a central government counter-guarantee and a better plant load factor incentive formula. As pointed out by the CAG in its report on the Delhi International Airport Limited (DIAL), there was no provision of the Development Fee in the Operation, Management and Development Agreement that DIAL signed with the government. But, the government agreed to levy of a Development Fee in 2009 at the cost of passengers, the financial implication being Rs. 34.15 billion according to the CAG.[18] The outcomes of all these cases turned out to be against the government and in favor of the private sector.

But, when it comes to protecting the public interest, there is no similar urgency. The Delhi–Noida Toll Bridge project needs to be renegotiated in public interest, but there is no urgency shown by either the Noida Authority or the Uttar Pradesh Government to renegotiate it, though it is widely acknowledged that the project is a case of bad contracting by the government. One of the clauses in the contract is that the Noida Authority guarantees 20% return on the total project cost annually and any shortfall is added to the project cost to be serviced in the following year. Projections show that while the project can provide a rate of return of about 10%, there would still be a significant shortfall in the guaranteed returns. So, a project costing Rs. 4.08 billion in 2001, when it was commissioned, would become a huge liability of over Rs. 800 billion at the end of the original concession period in 2031.[19] Therefore, it is in public interest to either renegotiate the project abrogating the guaranteed returns clause or cancel it after paying off the current liabilities, including guaranteed overdue returns, of over Rs. 50 billion.

Thus, on balance, after renegotiations, the terms of the contract improve for the operator/investors through changes in the risk allocation favorable to operator, efficiency gains are reduced, users are on average worse off, there is adverse fiscal impact, including increases in direct and contingent liabilities, and there is overall reduction in value for money to the Government.

Summary of Evidence on Renegotiations

- Significant number of PPP infrastructure transactions have been renegotiated after the contracts have been signed. India is also catching up;
- Renegotiations frequently occur soon after financial close;

[18]"Report of the Comptroller and Auditor General of India for the year ended March 2012 on Implementation of Public Private Partnership in Indira Gandhi International Airport, Delhi" (Report No. 5 of 2012–13, Viewed on 18 February 2013) (http://saiindia.gov.in/english/home/Our_Products/Audit_Report/Government_Wise/union_audit/recent_reports/union_performance/2012_2013/Commercial/Report_No_5/5.pdf). This view is, however, contested by the DIAL sponsor, GMR.

[19]Pratap et al. (2012).

- Problem is particularly acute in certain sectors, notably water and sanitation;
- Mostly renegotiations are started by the private sector operators, but there are also cases of government-initiated renegotiations;
- Outcomes of renegotiations are generally favorable to the private sector and against government and the users.

3 What Can Be Done to Prevent Opportunistic Renegotiations?

Renegotiations tend to undermine the sanctity of contracts. Making everything negotiable even after contract award, negates the benefits of a competitive auction. Since many infrastructure projects enjoy monopoly in the delivery of services, competitive bidding ensures competition *for* the market (as distinct from competition *in* the market) and competes away the monopoly rents available to service providers, thus keeping user charges for infrastructure services low. Once renegotiations are institutionalized and they become routine, competitive bidding would not lead to the selection of the most efficient service provider, but the one who is most adept at renegotiation, which is a perverse outcome.[20] Thus, opportunistic infrastructure players would bid low to get the projects awarded, but would not suffer the consequences of their low bids as contract terms are changed through renegotiations. And renegotiations are a bilateral process between the selected service provider and the government, untempered by the discipline of competition.[21]

However, it is also true that renegotiation can help when it addresses the fundamentally incomplete nature of concession contracts. In fact, some renegotiations should be expected, and such efforts can actually improve welfare. Renegotiations can be used to correct past mistakes and salvage bad projects. However, the high incidence of renegotiations that we have seen in Sect. 2, exceeds reasonable levels and suggests opportunistic behavior by operators and governments. This high incidence of renegotiations undermines welfare and denigrates sanctity of bid and contract by distorting the gains from competitive bidding.

---

[20]If the auction is designed well and provides adequate incentives, competitive bidding for the right to operate a concession for a given number of years should elicit the most efficient operator. If bidders believe that renegotiation is feasible and likely, however, their incentives and bidding will be affected, and the auction will likely select, not the most efficient provider, but the one most skilled at renegotiations. This result helps explain why many concessions in LAC region have been renegotiated just after concession award. (Source: Guasch 2004.)

[21]Renegotiation takes place between the government and the operator only, so it is not subject to competitive pressures and their associated discipline. Opportunistic renegotiation, can reduce or eliminate the expected benefits of competitive bidding.

Renegotiations can also undermine the integrity of a concession and compromise welfare as well as threaten the desired structural reform program in infrastructure. This is particularly true when it is used opportunistically or strategically by an operator or even the government, to secure additional benefits, rather than being driven by the inherent incompleteness of a contract. This gives us a guiding principle for renegotiations: it should occur only when justified by the initial contract's incompleteness (over and above the built-in contingencies) or by major unexpected events and not for reducing the commercial losses of the concessionaire.

As the Greek philosopher Heraclitus famously observed, there is nothing permanent, except change. So, one needs to design better contracts containing mechanisms to adjust terms when situation warrants, e.g., tariff or payment adjustment on account of inflation and exchange rate. For example, the Indian Model Concession Agreements in the road sector link toll rates to 40% of the inflation rate on the assumption that debt is generally at fixed (and not floating) rates and not all costs increase in line with inflation. Contracts should also clearly define (i) the treatment of assets, evaluation of investments, outcome indicators,[22] (ii) procedures and guidelines for adjusting and reviewing tariffs, (iii) criteria and penalties for early termination of concession, and (iv) procedures for resolution of conflict. Clear contract provisions reduce potential disputes and associated demand for renegotiations.

Concession contracts should clearly allocate risks and be based on a detailed "risk matrix," identifying all possible risks, and assigning each risk to the party best able to manage that risk. It should also incorporate mechanisms to deal with other contingencies.

Concession contracts should be awarded competitively as opposed to negotiations (directly adjudicated concessions), preferably following a two-stage bidding process, and be designed to avoid ambiguities. The two-stage bidding process would ensure that only technically and financially sound firms put in the financial bid based on a single bid parameter, which could be Lowest Present Value of Revenues for mitigating traffic risk in the road sector.

There should be a detailed analysis of seemingly aggressive bids before awarding a concession. However, there is a problem in disqualifying aggressive bids. The fear of being accused of corruption or favoritism prevents even well-meaning governments from disqualifying aggressive bids.

Once signed, there should be sound implementation of contracts. The sanctity of the bid should be upheld—operator should be held accountable to the submitted bid.[23] This could be ensured by requiring performance bonds of significant value[24]

---

[22]As far as possible, there should be outcome targets (regulation by objectives), rather than investment obligations (regulation by means).

[23]This approach forces operators to bear the costs of aggressive bids and of normal commercial risks—even if doing so results in the abandonment of concessions. It is necessary to establish a reputation of canceling concessions, when appropriate.

[24]Low value of performance bonds increases the chances of renegotiations by private operators and is associated with higher incidence of noncompliance with contractual clauses. Performance bonds in the form of bank guarantees rather than bankers' cheques would reduce blocking of financial resources of the concessionaire.

(5–10% of Total Project Cost in the form of bank guarantees). In addition, given that there is a lower incidence of renegotiations associated with the existence of regulatory agencies, appropriate regulatory framework, and agency, if necessary, should be put in place before the award of concessions. These should be armed with enough autonomy and implementation capacity to ensure high-quality enforcement as well as to deter political opportunism. However, this does not mean independent regulatory body for every sector or subsector. There is a menu of regulatory options including widening the scope of existing regulators, "regulation by contract," etc., and the appropriate option may be chosen.

Contracts should contain clauses committing governments explicitly to a policy of no renegotiation barring the activation of well-defined triggers. Public agencies should establish a reputation for not easily conceding renegotiation demands—say, maintaining a 5 years freeze period on renegotiation after contract award. The first tariff review should not be allowed for a significantly long period (at least 5 years) except if contract contingencies are activated. Concession contracts should also provide for significant compensation to operators in the event of unilateral changes made by the government to the contract, including penalties and this should be applicable symmetrically, i.e., if government induced changes bring in benefits for the private operator, compensation should be due to the government.

Summarizing the approach to renegotiations, to limit demand for renegotiations, we need to write better contracts with unambiguous delineation of risks and rewards across stakeholders and including all foreseeable eventualities in the contract document. Once written, these contracts need to be enforced strictly because the sanctity of bids needs to be upheld through, say, high performance bonds. As a further deterrent to opportunistic renegotiations, government needs to specify that it would not entertain any demand for renegotiations for the first 5 years of a contract. After this period, the private sector would need to deposit a fee, which should be related to the total project cost, for the regulators to consider any request for renegotiation. This fee would be refunded in case the renegotiation request is approved by the regulator. In evaluating these requests, regulators should be able to distinguish between renegotiation demands based on incomplete contracts and those based on opportunistic behavior and only the former kind needs to be considered. Opportunistic renegotiation demands based on aggressive bidding and conceding of these demands are bad in principle and practice, produce perverse incentives and outcomes, and therefore should not be entertained.

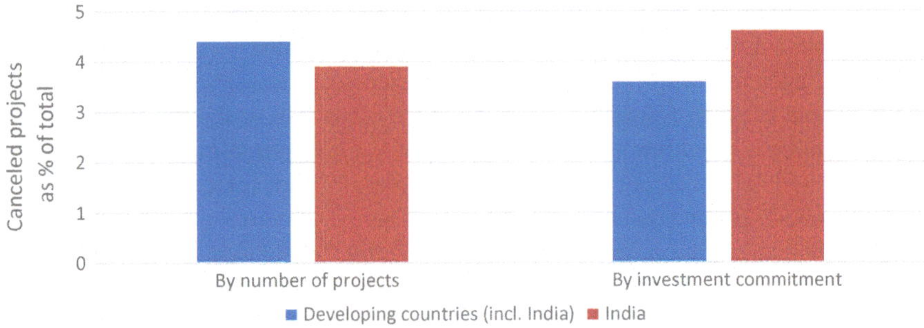

Fig. 6 Canceled infrastructure projects with private participation, (1990–2015). *Source* Private Participation in Infrastructure (PPI) database of the World Bank (ppi.worldbank.org)

4 The Record of Infrastructure Project Cancelations in India[25]

Twenty six Public–Private Partnership (PPP) road projects have been canceled in India since 2013. With this, India has caught up with the world-wide average rate of PPP project cancelations[26] (see Fig. 6). While 4.4% of the 6,547 PPP projects were canceled[27] in developing countries world-wide, India has seen 3.9% of its 852 PPP projects being canceled in the period 1990–2015. As a percentage of total investments, India has seen 4.6% of these investments canceled compared to the world-wide rate of 3.6%.

Admittedly, these percentages seem low as "freedom to fail" is part of the reason to turn to the private sector in infrastructure provisioning. Some project cancelations should be expected, since some projects or concessionaires will underperform. The low proportion of project cancelations could be because infrastructure projects acquire a resilience of their own once they are set up owing to concerns about service continuity (Tata Mundra Project), possible termination payments (Delhi–Noida toll bridge), and negative publicity surrounding these perceived failures.

But the government seems to have learned on the job. As the Report of the Committee on Revisiting and Revitalizing PPP Model of Infrastructure (Kelkar Committee Report) states "It is recommended to cancel projects that have not achieved a prescribed percentage of progress on the ground. Such projects may

[25]Based on Pratap (2016).

[26]The incidence of project cancelations in India was less than 1% till 2012.

[27]As per the Private Participation in Infrastructure database of the World Bank, a project is deemed to have been canceled if, before the end of the contract period, the private company physically abandons the project (such as withdrawing all staff); or the private company ceases operations or halts construction for 15% or more of the license or concession period, following the revocation of the license or repudiation of the contract by the relevant authority; or the private company sells or transfers its economic interest in the project to the public sector.

receive rebids, once the issues have been resolved, or constructed through public funds and if viable, bid out for Operations and Maintenance." The Report goes on to say that "For delays resulting from the concessionaire's default or financial stress not related to project delays, concessions may be terminated or bridge financing as permitted may be allowed but a penal charge or a haircut may be imposed on the concessionaire." As if following the prescription, and running out of patience for their "lack of commitment and lackadaisical approach," the government has warned non-serious developers and bankers of terminating 19 highway projects worth Rs. 200 billion—"perform or get terminated."

Reasons for PPP Project cancelation: There has been relatively little systematic analysis of the cancelation of private infrastructure projects reflecting the still low overall cancelation rate. However, some light on relevant factors is shed by case studies of individual projects or groups of projects as well as the more general literature on foreign investment and privatization.

Vernon argued[28] that foreign investment is welcomed initially for bringing in new technologies, good management and capital. Over time, as the recipient country becomes wealthier, and develops better technological and management skills, its perception of the bargain changes in nature. Outright expropriation may occur, though creeping expropriation, for example, through emphasis on local inputs, might be more likely.

Gomez-Ibanez[29] reviewed the nationalization of electric utilities in Latin America over the period 1943–1979, covering the experience of Argentina, Brazil, Colombia, Mexico and Venezuela. Foreign private investment in their power sectors was often associated with the development of complex engineering projects (hydroelectric plants) or the large scale of infrastructure finance required. As cities were initially electrified, the investment was welcomed. However, as access to electricity became more widespread, concerns about natural monopolies, and perceptions that investors, in particular foreign investors, were making excess profits grew and began to impact the regulatory framework. He notes that the few electric utilities not nationalized by the 1980s were domestically owned: all foreign-owned utilities had been nationalized. He also notes that where the sector was regulated at the national level—in Brazil, Colombia and Mexico—the regulatory frameworks were more robust but still not strong enough to provide continued incentives for investment. In Argentina, utilities were regulated by municipalities, and were the first to be nationalized. Finally, he notes the impact of macroeconomic factors on

[28]Vernon (1971).

[29]Gomez-Ibanez (1999).

Table 3 Canceled infrastructure projects with private participation in developing countries, 1990–2015

	Projects reaching financial closure		Projects canceled		Canceled projects as % of total	
Sector	Number	Investment commitment[a]	Number	Investment commitment[a]	By number	By investment commitment
Energy	3185	832	86	16	2.7**	1.9**
Telecom	847	1034	60	31	7.1**	3.0
Transport	1609	473	92	24	5.7*	4.2
Water and sewerage	906	80	51	16	5.6*	20.0**
Total	6547	2419	289	87	4.4	3.6

[a]In current US $ billion
* Indicates a significant difference at 5% level of statistical significance
** Indicates a significant difference at 1% level of statistical significance
Source World Bank, Private Participation in Infrastructure (PPI) database

the financial viability of utilities, given the reluctance of regulators to allow prices to rise to reflect inflation and currency devaluation.

In the list of canceled projects, toll road projects in Mexico, power generation projects in Indonesia, and water projects in Argentina are featured prominently. All these projects suffered from macroeconomic shocks occurring at different times in these countries—Mexico in 1994, East Asia in 1997, and Argentina in 2002. Macroeconomic shocks can dramatically increase the cost of project financing, through exchange rate depreciation when foreign currency financing is used or through increases in domestic interest rates. These shocks may also affect demand for services from the projects through lower economic growth.[30]

In the water and sewerage sector, there are many important challenges—low-cost recovery, dilapidated assets, and the need for substantial investments—and political sensitivities[31] around the very involvement of the private sector in the water supply can make for a difficult operating environment. In fact, 51 of the 906 PPP projects (5.6%) in the water and sanitation sector in developing countries world-wide have been canceled accounting for $16.1 billion of the $80 billion (20%) investments—the highest cancelation rate in terms of investments across all infrastructure sectors.

Water and sewerage projects and power distribution projects that were canceled encountered problems as a result of opposition to needed price increases, difficulties in getting consumers to pay for services (usually in a situation where they were accustomed to getting the service free) and opposition to the principle of the private

[30]Harris and Pratap (2009).

[31]Two water and sewerage contracts in the province of Maldonado (Uruguay) reverted to the public sector (to Obras Sanitarias del Estado, OSE) after 2004 when the electorate approved a constitutional amendment that made access to water a fundamental human right and transferred water and sanitation services to the public sector.

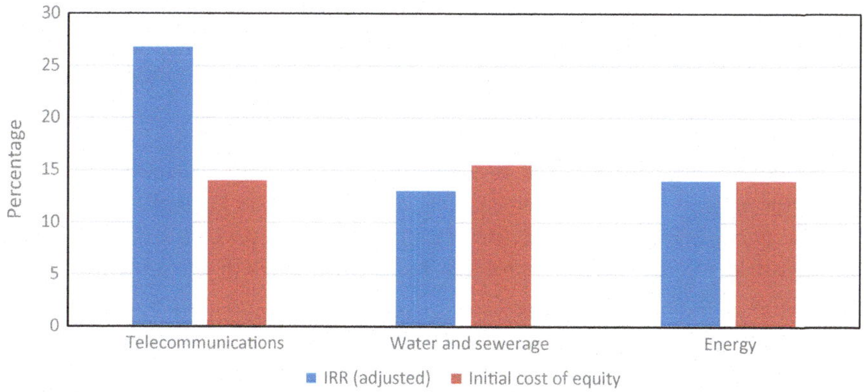

Fig. 7 Average profitability by sector of privatized and concessioned firms and the cost of equity in Latin America and Caribbean Countries, 1990–2000 (%). *Source* Guasch (2004)

sector providing these "essential" services. Most countries see power and, in particular, water being priced well below costs. Though the private sector may bring in efficiencies, in terms of reducing costs and increasing revenue collections, the initial gap between revenues and costs may be too large to bridge with politically feasible price increases, which may result in project cancelation (Table 3).

It is very difficult to get the private sector interested in provision of water because of low-cost recovery, etc. If it is a foreign company providing water, the risk of project failure increases even more. Once private companies start providing water, the risk of project failure is disproportionately high in terms of both numbers and investments, as we see in the table above.

The low level of user charges and difficulties in raising prices in the water sector explain the mismatch between internal rate of return and cost of equity in the sector. This may, in turn, explain the increased project cancelation and the flat private investment commitments in the water sector in recent years (Fig. 7).

The presence of foreign sponsors engenders greater political sensitivity than domestic sponsors, and foreign sponsors may also feel more able to abandon a project in difficulty. Some have argued that domestic firms are likely to be more accommodating in renegotiations than foreign multinational firms. As a result, projects with domestic sponsors are less likely to be canceled even after a macroeconomic crisis, as with some of the Indonesian power projects after the 1997 East Asian financial crisis (Wells and Ahmed 2007). In addition, projects with foreign sponsors may be more likely to use foreign financing, which can cause mismatches when revenues are earned in local currency[32] as in most infrastructure projects.

Interactions among these variables may increase the probability of project cancelations dramatically. Thus, the foreign-sponsored water and sewerage project

[32]Harris and Pratap (2009).

in Argentina, Aguas Argentinas failed in the aftermath of the Argentinean macroeconomic crisis of 2002.

It is apparent from the above that the three most important factors for project cancelation include macroeconomic crises, challenges associated with PPPs in the water sector, and foreign sponsorship of these projects.[33]

Project cancelations in India: Besides the 26 road projects canceled since 2013, other PPP projects that have been canceled in India include Dabhol Power Project —Phase I and II, and Central Electricity Supply Company of Orissa (CESCO). The two non-road projects recently canceled include the Delhi Airport Metro Express and Tilaiya UMPP.

Many of the above factors for project cancelation may be playing out in India too. Dabhol Power Project (now called Ratnagiri Gas and Power Private Limited, RGPPL), which is featured among the canceled projects in India in the World Bank's Private Participation in Infrastructure Project database, was canceled partly because it had foreign sponsors (project sponsors of Dabhol included Enron, Bechtel, and General Electric, all of the USA). Foreign-sponsored projects in underpriced sectors like power are highly susceptible to cancelation because such projects become extremely visible and politically contentious as in the case of Dabhol Power Project (DPP). The presence of foreign sponsors adds to the problems as increases in retail power tariffs to make projects viable are viewed as sell-out of national interests to foreigners. DPP also suffered from inappropriate risk allocation with most risks allocated to the public sector, becoming practically a no risk project for the private sector, which became too expensive for the public sector to service. After the Dabhol debacle and given the sorry financial state of the main power off-takers (the State Electricity Distribution Companies), foreign investors view the political and commercial risks of investing in India to be excessive (though the sentiment seems to have improved lately). This partly explains the growing importance of domestic firms (like NTPC, Reliance Energy, and Tata Power) in the Indian power sector. It is also no coincidence that another canceled project in India, the Central Electricity Supply Company of Orissa also had a foreign sponsor (AES Corporation of the USA). CESCO is also a power distribution project, which is vulnerable to political sensitivity.

Tilaiya UMPP or Jharkhand Integrated Power Limited was awarded to Reliance Power. But, it pulled out of the Project in April 2015 on the ground that the state had failed to make adequate land available. Out of the 1,700 acres required for the project, the state had acquired only 417 acres, as per the project sponsors. The cancelation of the Delhi Airport Metro Express has been extensively discussed earlier in the book.

The union territory of Delhi was trying to induct the private sector in both power and water distribution at the turn of the millennium. However, it failed in the water

[33]Pratap (2011).

sector partly because of the low-cost recovery and the presence of foreign consultants in the water distribution sector as compared to the power distribution sector.

The post-2013 project cancelations in the Indian road sector are mainly a result of aggressive bidding by the private sector and inadequately prepared projects by the public sector (in terms of insufficient land acquisition and delay in forest and environment clearances). Featured among these cancelations is the Shivpuri-Dewas project in Madhya Pradesh promoted by the GVK group and involving a total project cost of Rs. 30 billion. Specifically, there are no foreign sponsors in these canceled road projects.

Private companies often bid aggressively[34] to make sure that they bag the projects and the possibilities of renegotiation mean that they would not suffer the costs of aggressive bidding as in the case of Tata Mundra and Delhi and Mumbai airports. Tata Mundra (formally, Coastal Gujarat Power Limited) was able to obtain relief from the Central Electricity Regulatory Commission while Delhi and Mumbai airports were able to impose development fees on users though such fees were not envisaged in the Operation, Management and Development Agreement that the sponsors for both these projects (GMR and GVK, respectively) signed with the government.[35]

What has happened lately is that the renegotiation route to financial sustainability of PPP projects is closed. Corruption-wary decision makers are circumspect about giving relief through the renegotiation route and therefore there is no option for the project sponsors that bid aggressively but to walk out of the projects to cut losses. It is also true that the road sector has seen the maximum number of projects in the Indian PPP program [386 of the 852 Indian PPP projects (or 45%) that saw financial closure in the 1990–2015 period are in the road sector as per the World Bank's PPI Project database] and quite a few of them are stalled. Giving the renegotiation relief to many of these projects would have been problematic, and so cancelation was probably the only remedy for such projects.

The similarity between Indian and Mexican road project cancelations: India and Mexico have the overt infamy of being countries with the second (33 projects) and third highest (21 projects) number of PPP project cancelations, respectively.[36] If one sees the sectoral break-up of the canceled projects in these countries, one would realize that about three-fourths of these projects were in the road sector. India

[34]As the Report of the Committee on Revisiting and Revitalizing PPP Model of Infrastructure states "Over-aggressive bidding with inadequate due diligence by bidders has sometimes led to unviable offers. Since determining whether a bidder's capital structuring permits such optimistic bidding is difficult for the Authority, despite its own conservatism in its project report, bids were accepted and later failed." (http://finmin.nic.in/reports/ReportRevisitingRevitalisingPPPModel.pdf) (page 34, viewed on 30 December 2015).

[35]Allowing Delhi International Airport Limited to levy and use the development fees violates one of the basic provisions of Operation, Management and Development Agreement, which was part of the bid documents.

[36]China with 36 cancelled PPP projects has the highest number of such cancelations.

and Mexico also account for 60% of the road projects that have been canceled world-wide to date.

In the period 1989–94, the Government of Mexico undertook an ambitious program of constructing about 5,500 km of private greenfield toll roads to benefit from the opportunity provided by the North American Free Trade Agreement (NAFTA). By 1995, about 53 contracts had been awarded. However, construction costs were frequently underestimated while traffic was overestimated in the bids [traffic volumes averaged 25–65% of originally forecasted levels as per one estimate; Standard and Poor's (2006) has found that traffic forecasts turned out to be too optimistic in more than 75% of cases], making the bids aggressive just as in the case of India.

Additionally, just like India where the concessioning authority, National Highways Authority of India (NHAI) in its rush to show better results bid out road stretches with land acquisition much lesser than the desired 80% of the required land, concessions in Mexico were awarded before all permits, approvals, and the right-of-way were secured, introducing delays and exposing concessionaires to community pressures for route realignment—putting upward pressure on costs (Standard and Poor's 2006).

Most of these projects were canceled in the wake of the Mexican peso crisis of 1994 when highly leveraged foreign-financed firms suffered financial bankruptcy because of the macroeconomic crisis that the country experienced in that year. Toll road traffic declined by 12% in 1995, foreign currency denominated loans became huge liabilities as the domestic currency lost value, and floating rate debt also became expensive to service when short-term interest rates increased to over 71% in April 1995. As per the PPI database of the World Bank, a total of 16 private toll road projects were canceled in the wake of the Mexican macroeconomic crisis of 1994. Unlike Mexico, India did not suffer a macroeconomic crisis which resulted in a wholesale cancelation of PPP projects.

In Mexico, the concessions were taken over by the federal government because of concerns about the health of the construction and the banking industry. Some of these projects were reconcessioned later after improving the PPP policy regime, given the fiscal resource constraints and the need for increased road infrastructure. Taking a cue from the Mexican experience, India would do well to reconcession some of the projects that have been taken over for similar reasons. What will work in favor of the reconcessioning is that these highway projects have seen some progress and would have better data with more predictable cash flows and growth projections than being totally greenfield projects where it is difficult to make traffic forecasts with reasonable degree of accuracy.

What happens to canceled projects? Eighty five percent of the canceled projects revert to the government, often at substantial financial cost[37] (e.g., Delhi Airport Metro Express, Dabhol Power Project, etc.). This outcome is diametrically opposite to what was originally envisaged, as the starting point of many PPP projects is the

---

[37]Pratap (2011).

inability of governments to provide for the infrastructure needs of their citizenry because of the fiscal crunch. The Government of India has paid a high price for the canceled Dabhol Power Project. The total cost of revival of DPP is estimated at Rs. 100.38 billion, out of which the "acquisition price" was Rs. 84.85 billion at which Ratnagiri Gas and Power Private Limited (RGPPL, the new SPV) acquired the assets from the owners of DPP.

The high fiscal costs associated with canceled projects are sometimes associated with inappropriately high level of arbitration awards foisted on developing countries by the international tribunals, when the private investors are compensated not only for the costs incurred, but also the foregone profits over the expected lifetime of the project. Failure to reform the system of international arbitration to redress the imbalance between its attention to the legitimate economic and social concerns of host countries and those of investors will surely mean a retreat by those nations affected by the arbitration awards from the system.

In many cases, governments try to rebid the project, but without much success. This is because it is difficult to get the private sector interested again when experience has demonstrated that private operations are not sustainable.

Some of the same factors that explain project cancelation (like sector viability) in the first round of privatization seem to be playing a part in reprivatization as well. For example, telecom sector enjoys the highest reprivatization rate mainly because of its high sector viability compared to power and water sectors. Projects reprivatized in the energy sector were small greenfield generation projects. None of the canceled electricity distribution/integrated projects were reprivatized. Many characteristics of the water sector, like severe underpricing of services, dilapidated assets and the need for substantial investments, and high levels of leakage, illegal connections, low billing and collection efficiency, and the associated political sensitivity, make it unattractive for private participation. Once a water project gets canceled, these same factors make its reprivatization difficult as is apparent from the case of Dar-es-Salaam Water (Tanzania), the lease contract for which was signed in 2003, which was canceled in 2005, and was taken over by a government entity, Dar-es-Salaam Water and Sewerage Corporation (DAWASCO). The private company suffered operating losses of Tanzanian shillings 15.6 billion in its less than 2 years of operations, which was an important reason for project cancelation. Since the time DAWASCO has taken over operations, revenue collection is up, costs have been cut, and a new billing system has been put in place. However, problems of mismatch between collections and costs remain: DAWASCO collects only about Tanzanian shillings 1.6 billion a month, while its operational costs are 2.2 billion, forcing the government to pick up the tab more than once.

In Summary

As we have seen, the private sector exits only a small fraction of private infrastructure projects before the contract ends (<5%).[38] Yet such cancelations can have a sustained impact on a country's PPP program, reducing the private sector's confidence in the government's commitment as well as the government's confidence in the robustness and "value for money" of these arrangements.[39] This seems to be playing out in India with limited private interest in infrastructure projects (World Bank 2014)[40] and government emphasizing the public sector route to infrastructure financing. As the Economic Survey 2014–15 says: "India needs to tread the path of investment-driven growth. Can the private sector be expected to rise to the occasion? Highly leveraged corporate balance sheets, and a banking system under severe stress suggest that this will prove challenging. Against this backdrop, public investment may need to be augmented to recreate an environment to crowd-in private investment" (2015:74–75).

Although trends in cancelation may not be an issue for private infrastructure projects as a whole, it is a concern in the water and sewerage sector. The high probability of cancelation and relatively low level of fresh investment in the sector suggests a declining role for the private sector in making available this essential service. With cash-strapped governments not in a position to satisfy the need, the net result is deteriorating quantity and quality of water and sewerage services across much of the developing world.

However, it also needs to be borne in mind that the recent bout of PPP project cancelations in India is not necessarily bad. Rather than go in for repeated renegotiations to try and sweeten the deal for the private sector, cancelations are probably the way to go to elicit more realistic bidding from the private sector. The pain that the stakeholders (including private sponsors) are suffering now because of increasing cancelations is probably the necessary price that needs to be paid for a better tomorrow entailing more realistic bidding.

[38]Increased role of domestic investors—seen in countries such as India, Mexico and Brazil—and development of local capital markets will likely make projects even more robust to cancelation.

[39]Harris and Pratap (2009).

[40]In 2014, India recorded $6.2 billion investment in private infrastructure projects—a 9 year low.

Chapter 11
Analysis and Case Studies of a Few Infrastructure PPPs in India

In this final chapter of the volume, we look at a few selected issues and experiences of Infrastructure PPPs in India. We begin with a brief analysis of Value for Money (VfM) in the road sector of India. We then look at three extensive case studies: the Dabhol Power Project; the Delhi Power Distribution experience; and the Delhi International Airport Project to provide an in-depth view of the real-life issues involved with infrastructure PPPs in India.

1 Analysis of Value for Money (VfM) from PPPs in the Indian Road Sector[1]

In attempting to calculate VfM in India, as explained in the Appendix to Chap. 4, we expect to lessen some of the uncertainty about PPPs by adding to the PPP evaluation literature in developing countries.

It should also be noted that the UK Private Finance Initiative (PFI), which has driven much of the world's thinking about public–private partnerships, and Japan[2] require that before the PPP mode is adopted, a careful evaluation is undertaken to establish that the government is likely to get value for its money. However, "no such analysis is presently being done in India."[3] This makes this a pioneering study for India.

---

[1]Based on Pratap (2011, 2015).
[2]In Japan, government guidelines require that the public sector must construct a Public Sector Comparator (PSC) and demonstrate that the PPP option provides better value for money (VfM) before adopting a PPP project. (Source: Grimsey and Lewis 2005).
[3]Government of India, Planning Commission (Secretariat for Infrastructure) (2010).

K.V. Pratap and R. Chakrabarti, *Public-Private Partnerships in Infrastructure*,
India Studies in Business and Economics, DOI 10.1007/978-981-10-3355-1_11

Data description

Some India-related data on PPP projects is publicly available over the internet (http://www.pppindiadatabase.com). While the India PPP database has provision for wide-ranging information on individual PPP projects, most of the data fields are empty, which made it imperative to supplement data from various other sources—ministry websites and annual reports, answers to parliament questions, presentations of government officials, audit reports of the Comptroller and Auditor General of India, websites of project companies, newspapers, and a Price Waterhouse Coopers report entitled "*Public–private partnership financing in India*" (2007).

Data collection posed many challenges, as some of the data used in the analysis is not public, while part of the data is real time. Some of the data is from newspapers and had to be validated from multiple sources. Data availability has limited our ability to draw sharper conclusions.

Estimation of Value for Money in Indian road sector PPPs[4]

PPP projects would seem to provide immense value for money to the Indian government as the average drawdown on fiscal resources through government grants in Indian PPPs is only 4% of project costs[5] (as against the maximum permissible grant of 40%), and a functional asset is created. However, some anecdotal evidence is out of sync with this—like the case of the Delhi–Noida Toll Bridge project, which does not seem to provide any VfM to the government. In fact, this project shows that PPPs can impose a substantial financial burden on the public sector and result in commensurate negative VfM for the government because of sub-optimal risk sharing between the public and private sectors. Given the anecdotal evidence, the chapter attempts a more structured analysis for calculating value for money in the road sector of the Indian economy.

Since the beginning of the millennium, there was a major move away from "item-rate" contracts to public–private partnerships in build–operate–transfer (BOT) mode for implementing road projects so that scarce budgetary resources could be leveraged to access a larger pool of private capital. In addition, it was also expected that PPP projects would be delivered on time and without cost overruns, and the quality of service would improve.

Two major methods for implementing BOT road projects in India are BOT (Annuity) and BOT (Toll).[6] The major difference between the two relates to allocation of traffic risk, which is assumed by the government in the former to make the

[4]This section draws heavily upon Pratap (2011).

[5]Price Waterhouse Coopers (2007).

[6]In BOT projects, the private sector builds the road, operates it for the contracted period, and then transfers it to the public sector. In return, the private sector receives a fixed amount of money from the government every 6 months, which we call annuity. BOT (toll) projects are similar except that the government allows the private sector to toll the road for the contract period instead of providing annuity.

Table 1 India: Distribution of road projects between BOT (annuity) and BOT (toll) (status as on March 31, 2013)

	Awarded		Total project cost (Rs. crore)	Annuity/Viability gap funding (Rs. crore)	Completed	
	Number of contracts	Length (km)			Number of contracts	Length (km)
BOT (annuity)	51	3,547	30,287	3,097 (10%)	20	1,104
BOT (toll)	188	18,200	159,954	21,020 (13%)	55	3,337

Source National Highways Authority of India (2013)

project attractive to the private sector,[7] while it remains with the concessionaire in the latter case. The distribution of BOT contracts in India between BOT (Annuity) and BOT (Toll) is given in Table 1. As would be apparent, BOT (Toll) roads constitute a majority of PPP road projects in India.

In this chapter, we calculate VfM for all BOT road projects in NHDP Phase I.[8] The BOT (Annuity) and BOT (Toll) projects considered in this study constitute the entire universe of such projects implemented under such contracts, under the National Highways Development Program (Phase I) of the Government of India. Since we are analyzing the entire universe of such projects, this ensures against selection bias to some extent. But, only the more viable projects may have been considered for bidding out to the private sector, so some selection bias remains.

BOT (Annuity) projects: In such projects, the responsibility for construction, operation, and maintenance rests with the concessionaire who gets availability-based annuity payments from the government-contracting agency to service his investment. Annuity payments, determined by competitive bidding, are borne by the public sector in the form of deferred budgetary payments and the concessionaire receives a fixed sum directly from the contracting agency, the National Highways Authority of India (NHAI), biannually for the services provided by the road over the life of the contract.

We have analyzed all eight BOT (Annuity) projects under NHDP Phase I that are under operation.[9] The following assumptions have been made in the VfM analysis for BOT (Annuity) road projects using the simplified Public Sector Comparator (PSC) method:

[7]In many low-demand road projects, tolls may not be sufficient to enable financial closure of the project even after availing the maximum possible Viability Gap Funding (40% of the Total Project Cost). Therefore, availability based annuity payments from the government may be an important means to generate private interest for such projects.

[8]National Highways Development Program (NHDP) is the flagship program of the Government of India for road development. The main component of NHDP Phase I is the Golden Quadrilateral Project which connects the four megacities of Mumbai, Chennai, Kolkata, and Delhi.

[9]It is important to choose operational projects as promised benefits may not always materialize. To the extent that there are slippages in implementation, the value for money to the government from PPPs would come down.

- The estimated project cost by NHAI is increased by 25% to allow for optimism bias.[10]
- Project construction is spread over 3 years ending in the planned year of completion in the ratio 1:2:2.[11]
- Operation and maintenance (O&M) costs are Rs. 1 million per kilometer per year[12] at constant prices from the year in which operation commences.
- The project revenues for the concessionaire consist of annuity only.[13] The annuity payments are made for 15 years after the construction period of 3 years unless stated otherwise.
- The discount rate is 11% (6% on account of the time value of money,[14] corresponding to the yield on treasury bonds of comparable maturity at the time the projects were awarded, plus 5% on account of inflation, which corresponds to the actual historical rate of inflation in the country).
- Toll collection after concession period of the BOT (annuity) projects is not accounted for, as the tolling option would be available to government even with conventional procurement.
- Asset residual value of PPP project is not taken into account because it is assumed to be the same as under the PSC option to keep the VfM estimate conservative.
- No adjustment has been made for differential taxation and transaction costs of the PPP projects for simplification.

The methodology used to calculate value for money to the government in BOT (Annuity) projects is shown in Eq. (1) below (reproduced here from Chap. 4):

$$\sum VfM_i = \sum [PVPC_i + PVOM_i - PVA_i)] \quad (1)$$

[10]Column 4 of Tables 2 and 4 shows the project cost estimated by the contracting agency, NHAI. Optimism bias in project estimates arises, *inter alia*, from underestimating project costs. We assume (conservatively) an optimism bias of 25% in the NHAI estimates on the basis of data on 4 projects [2 BOT (Annuity) projects and 2 BOT (Toll) projects] where the average difference between the project cost estimated by NHAI and the cost at financial closure was 39.5%. These projects are: Nellore Bypass (optimism bias 19%), Maharashtra Border–Belgaum (78%), Nellore–Tada (15%) and Tumkur–Neelmangala (46%).

[11]See the Report of the Core Group on Financing of the National Highway Development Program (http://www.pppinindia.com/pdf/NHDP.pdf) for phasing of the construction cost.

[12]Report of the Core Group on Financing of the National Highway Development Program (http://www.pppinindia.com/pdf/NHDP.pdf) page 23.

[13]Government of India (Department of Road Transport and Highways). *Model concession agreement for annuity-based projects* (http://www.nhai.org/annuity.pdf).

[14]The UK public sector authorities also assessed projects with a 6% real discount rate until recently.

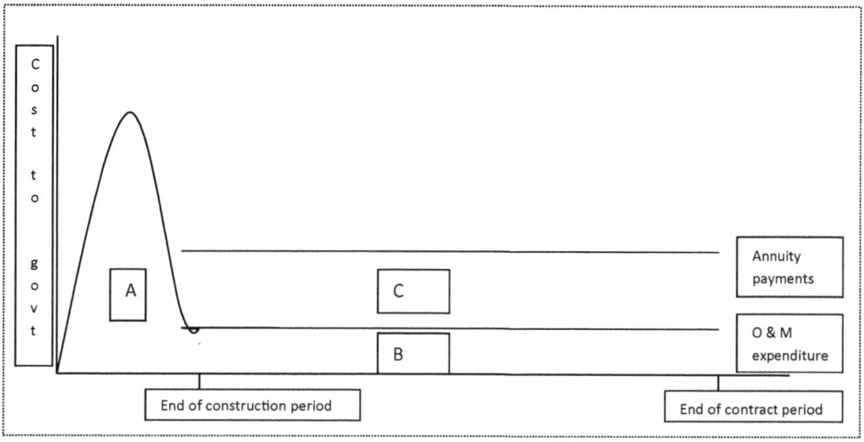

Fig. 1 Value for money in BOT (annuity) road projects. *Source* Author's conceptualization

where

VfM_i	is the Value for Money to the government from *i*th project,
$PVPC_i$	is the present value of the estimated Project Cost of the *i*th project,
$PVOM_i$	is the present value of the estimated Operation and Maintenance (O&M) expenditure over the life of the contract for the *i*th project, and
PVA_i	is the present value of the annuity payments over the life of the contract for the *i*th project.

More simply, the above equation can be written as:

Value for Money to the government = Present Value of (estimated Project Cost + estimated O&M expenditure over the life of the contract − annuity payments).

The methodology is illustrated in the Fig. 1. The government, instead of making lumpy investments at the start of the project for constructing it (area A in Fig. 1) and subsequently making small Operation and Maintenance expenditures (area B), is making annuity payments for the duration of the contract (area C). Value for money to the government is given by the area (A + B − C).

The results of the analysis are presented in Table 2.

Overall, there is a positive value for money to the government from these eight operational projects of Rs. 2.624 billion (8% of the present value of estimated project and O&M costs) under NHDP Phase I. It is also significant to note that not all BOT (annuity) projects provide a positive VfM.

The estimate of the value for money to the government is conservative for a number of reasons. Though we have assumed an optimism bias of 25% in the cost estimates of NHAI, the actual optimism bias could be higher. In addition, conventionally procured road projects are routinely delayed (59% of projects are

Table 2 Value for money in NHDP Phase I for BOT (annuity) projects

Road stretch	State	Road length (km)	Project cost (Rs. million)	Semiannual annuity payments (Rs. million)	Value for money (Rs. million)	Value for money (as % of PV of project and O&M costs) (%)	Date of commencement of construction	Due for completion	Date of completion
Ankapalli–Tuni	Andhra Pradesh	59	2,832	294.8	911	23	May 2002	Nov 2004	Jan 2005
Tuni–Dharmavaram	Andhra Pradesh	47	2,319	279.1	329	10	May 2002	Aug 2005	Aug 2005
Dharmavaram–Rajahmundry	Andhra Pradesh	53	2,060	296.2	−48	−2	May 2002	Mar 2005	Mar 2005
Nellore Bypass[a]	Andhra Pradesh	17	1,432	129.6	421	22	Oct 2002	Oct 2004	Sep 2004
Maharastra Border–Belgaum[b]	Karnataka	77	3,320	505.1	−482	−10	June 2002	Dec 2004	Oct 2004
Tambaram–Tindivanam[c]	Tamil Nadu	93	3,750	418.6	964	17	May 2002	Nov 2004	Oct 2004
Panagarh–Palsit	West Bengal	64	3,500	555	−1,011	−21	June 2002	Dec 2004	June 2005
Palsit–Dankuni	West Bengal	65	4,324	400	1542	27	Oct 2002	Feb 2005	July 2005
Total for 8 projects		476	23,537	2,878	2,624	8			

[a]Contract period of 17 years with construction over 2 years and O&M over the next 15 years
[b]Contract period of 15 years with construction over 2.5 years and O&M over the next 12.5 years
[c]Contract period of 17.5 years with construction over 2.5 years and O&M over the next 15 years
Source India PPP Database (http://www.pppindiadatabase.com); Comptroller and Auditor General of India (2008). Union Audit Reports: *Public–private partnership in implementation of road projects of National Highways Authority of India* (Performance Audit—Report 16 of 2008). (http://www.cag.gov.in/html/reports/commercial/2008_PA16com/contents.htm); NHAI website—NHAI Contracts with BOT-Annuity Funding (http://203.200.117.60/CPISWeb/Reports/ViewReport.aspx). Value for money calculations are those of the authors

delayed, with delays of between 1 month and 92 months),[15] while the timeliness of delivery of the BOT (Annuity) projects seems to be better[16]: three projects were delivered ahead of schedule, three suffered slippages, and the balance two were delivered on time (see Table 2). In addition, not all slippages may be treated as cases of concessionaire default: in the case of the Panagarh-Palsit project, it has been observed that there was a delay of 5 months in making the required land available and finalizing the change of scope orders.[17] There is also the limited risk of cost overrun for the government[18] under PPP procurement[19] as construction cost risk is transferred to the private sector through fixed price construction contracts with liquidated damages.

All these factors (higher than assumed optimism bias in cost estimates, timeliness of delivery, and limited risk of cost overrun) would improve the overall VfM. Finally, given the fiscal crunch, it may not even have been possible for the government to undertake all these projects through conventional procurement. So, the overall economic benefits should be much higher.

Sensitivity analysis of value for money to changes in the discount rate and optimism bias was also carried out. It was found that the VfM in BOT (Annuity) projects is very sensitive to change in discount rate (see Table 3). With an assumed optimism bias of 25%, the VfM increases to 20% from 8% if we increase the discount rate from 11 to 13%, while it decreases to −7% if we decrease the discount rate to 9%. This is because of the impact of the discount rate on large future annuity liabilities in such PPPs. This disproportionate impact of the discount rate on VfM is in line with that found in the Australian evaluation[20] of PPPs, where opposite conclusions were reached when using a 8.65% discount rate (leading to the conclusion that the PPP mechanism was 9% cheaper than traditional delivery) compared to an evaluation adopting a 5.7% discount rate (when the PPP mechanism was apparently 6% more expensive).

---

[15]Government of India (Ministry of Statistics and Program Implementation) (2008).

[16]PPPs offer strong incentives to finish the project early, since profits rise with increased annuity payments. Such incentives are usually absent (or weaker) under traditional procurement.

[17]Comptroller and Auditor General of India (2008).

[18]According to a World Bank study, the average cost overrun in 28 completed national and state highway projects was 24%. (Source: World Bank 2008).

[19]Consolidating over 14 studies for UK, Australia, France, and Norway, Bain finds that the average construction cost overrun in PPPs (at 13%) is around half that observed in conventionally procured projects, and the range of outturn costs is significantly narrower. Even the lower construction cost overrun may not represent a risk to the public sector as Bain finds that experienced PPP contractors with strong balance sheets and reputations will complete their obligations as intended and at their own risk. To illustrate the point, Bain says that in the case of the Spencer Street Station PPP in Melbourne, the contractor (Leighton) admitted it had suffered significant losses yet completed the works with no additional payments from the public sector. (Source: Bain 2010).

[20]Fitzgerald (2004). In the Fitzgerald study, when the discount rate was reduced from 8.65 to 5.7%, the value for money went down from 9 to −6%.

Table 3 Sensitivity analysis of VfM in BOT (annuity) projects

		Optimism bias		
		15%	25%	35%
Discount rate	9%	−14%	−7%	−1%
	11%	2%	8%	13%
	13%	15%	20%	25%

Source Author's calculations

BOT (Toll) Projects: BOT (Toll) projects are the preferred mode of implementing PPP road projects in India apparently because there is no direct burden on the fisc (such as annuity payments impose) and the traffic risk is borne by the concessionaire[21] in such projects. In these projects, the concession includes construction, operation, and maintenance by the concessionaire and the investment is serviced through toll revenues. Budgetary support to the concessionaire is restricted to an upfront grant determined through competitive bidding which is limited to a maximum of 40%[22] of the project cost. This upfront grant (called Viability Gap Funding) is expected to compensate the concessionaire for undertaking projects that are economically viable but fall below the threshold of financial viability because of externalities that the market is not able to capture.

We have analyzed all nine BOT (Toll) projects under NHDP Phase I that are in operation. Thus, the BOT (Annuity) and BOT (Toll) road projects analyzed in this chapter constitute the entire universe of such projects implemented under NHDP Phase I, which addresses the issue of selection bias to some extent. However, as we have discussed earlier, there could be qualitative differences in PPP and Government-implemented projects, and therefore, selection bias may still exist.

The assumptions used in the analysis are the same as for BOT (Annuity) projects presented above, except for the following additional assumptions:

- Tolls are foregone by the government in favor of the concessionaire in such projects. Actual annual toll collection has been taken for the period 2010–13 (three financial years), and based on these, projections have been made for the entire concession period. 93% of the potential toll receipts have been considered.[23]

---

[21]Projects are first bid out on BOT (Toll) basis; if they are unviable on BOT (Toll) basis, they could be implemented on BOT (Annuity) basis. Projects that are not viable on either BOT (Toll) or BOT (Annuity) could be implemented through Engineering, Procurement and Construction (EPC) contracts. (See, for example, Lok Sabha unstarred question number 2437 answered on 27 August 2012).

[22]Maximum 20% of the Total Project Cost from the Government of India and another 20% from the project sponsoring authority like a state government.

[23]According to the Committee on Infrastructure (Government of India), NHAI could put up toll facilities only on 58.7% of 11,037 km of completed highways across the country (as quoted in The Economic Times. May 1, 2009). This percentage has gone up lately with NHAI being able to put up toll facilities on 93% of the 13,911 km of completed highways in the country (Source: National Highways Authority of India 2013). In our sample of 17 BOT projects, while the private sector

- Equity brought in by the concessionaire is spread over 3 years in proportion to progress in construction of the project and is assumed to be in the ratio 1:2:2. Since any upfront grant (Viability Gap Funding) is released in proportion to the equity brought in by the concessionaire, we assume the same spread for it in first 3 years of the concession period.
- Budgetary support is restricted to an upfront grant (VGF) to the concessionaire, determined through competitive bidding and is up to a maximum of 40% of the project cost. This upfront grant is expected to compensate the concessionaire for undertaking projects that are economically viable but fall below financial viability threshold because of externalities that the market is not able to capture.

The methodology for calculating VfM stands slightly modified given the nature of BOT (Toll) projects and is calculated as a two-step process, shown in Eqs. 2 and 3.

$$\sum CS_i = \sum [PVPC_i + PVOM_i - VGF_i] \tag{2}$$

where

CS_i is the Cost Savings to the government from the ith project,
$PVPC_i$ is the present value of the estimated Project Cost of the ith project,
$PVOM_i$ is the present value of the estimated Operation and Maintenance expenditure over the life of the contract for the ith project, and
VGF_i is the present value of the Viability Gap Funding over the first 3 years of the contract period for the ith project.

$$\sum VfM_i = \sum [CS_i - PVTR_i] \tag{3}$$

where

VfM_i is the Value for Money to the government from the ith project,
CS_i is the Cost Savings to the government from the ith project, and
$PVTR_i$ is the Present Value of potential Toll Receipts from the ith project.

The methodology, in words, for calculating VfM for BOT (Toll) projects is presented below:

- Cost savings to government = Present Value (PV) of (estimated Project Cost + estimated O&M expenditure over the life of the project − VGF)

(Footnote 23 continued)

could put up toll facilities in all 9 BOT (toll) projects, the public sector was able to put up toll facilities on only 4 of the 8 BOT (annuity) projects, with no toll facilities on the following projects: Tuni-Dharmavaram, Dharmavaram-Rajahmundry, Nellore Bypass, and Panagarh-Palsit projects. [Reply to Lok Sabha (Lower House of Indian Parliament) Question No. 1869; replied on December 1, 2009].

- VfM to government = Cost savings to government − PV of potential toll receipts.

The results of the analysis are presented in Table 4. Overall, there is a negative value for money to the government from these nine projects of Rs. 19.809 billion (−39% of the present value of estimated project and O&M costs). Another striking feature is that all but two BOT (Toll) projects are producing negative value to the government.

However, this estimate of VfM in BOT (Toll) road projects is conservative for the same reasons as for BOT (Annuity) projects: higher than assumed optimism bias in cost estimates; timeliness of delivery of PPP projects[24]; limited risk of cost overrun in PPPs[25]; and given the fiscal crunch, it may not have been possible for the government to undertake all these projects. The first three factors would improve the overall VfM, while the last one, economic returns.

We also carried out a sensitivity analysis of value for money over potential toll receipts and optimism bias. The results are presented in Table 5. The striking feature of the table is the generally negative VfM from BOT (Toll) projects. Given that the collection ratio of potential tolls is ascending to the theoretically maximum level of 100%, the likely VfM to the government from the 9 BOT (Toll) projects would be negative irrespective of the level of assumed optimism bias.

To reemphasize this point, if we assume 100% potential toll receipts, *ceteris paribus*, the VfM from BOT (toll) projects is negative irrespective of the level of optimism bias. This stands to reason as the differential advantage of the private sector goes down (this is captured as VfM) with increasing efficiency of the public sector as reflected in the collection ratio of potential tolls. The 100% toll collection ratio could be a more realistic toll collection ratio, as in 2013, this ratio had already jumped to 93%.

The weighted average VfM from eight BOT (Annuity) projects and nine BOT (Toll) projects that constitute the entire universe of such projects in NHDP Phase I is (–) 20.5%. However, if we incorporate the transfer of cost-overrun risk to the

[24]Out of the 9 BOT (toll) projects considered, one was delivered before time, three were delivered on time, while five suffered a time overrun of an average of 12.2 months. However, in the case of the Satara—Kagal road, out of the overall delay of 21 months, there was delay of nine months in the implementation of additional items of work. If allowance is made for such delays, that are not due to deficient performance of the concessionaire, the time overrun in the case of the entire sample of BOT (toll) projects decreases to just over 2 months. (Source: Comptroller and Auditor General of India 2008).

[25]Cost overrun is only applicable to item-rate contracts and not to PPP contracts, whether given on BOT (Toll) or BOT (Annuity) basis. In item-rate contracts, there is a provision of payment of escalation due to delays. In case the PPP project is delayed due to reasons attributable to the contractor, liquidated damages are to be imposed and no escalation is paid. For example, the Total Project Cost (TPC) of Delhi–Gurgaon Highway is Rs. 7.10 billion (Rs. 5.55 billion as per concession agreement and Rs. 1.55 billion as per change of scope of the project) whereas the completion cost to the concessionaire (up to 31 March 2011) is Rs. 14.06 billion as per their balance sheet. But, the concessionaire is liable for all this cost overrun. Escalation is paid only in case where the delay is beyond the control of the concessionaire.

Table 4 Value for money in NHDP Phase I BOT (Toll) projects

Road Stretch	State	Road length (km)	Project cost (Rs. million)	Viability gap funding (Rs. million)	Value for money (Rs. million)	Value for money (as % of PV of project and O&M costs) (%)	Date of commencement	Due for completion	Date of completion
Nandigama–Vijayawada	Andhra Pradesh	35	1386.50	402	−2295.2	−92.6	Aug 2001	Dec 2003	June 2004
Nellore–Tada (AP-7)	Andhra Pradesh	110.5	6213.50	1273	−2284.2	−23.2	Aug 2001	Dec 2003	Feb 2004
Tumkur–Neelmangala	Karnataka	32.5	1550	248.3	−1171.6	−51.7	June 2002	Dec 2003	Dec 2003
Satara–Kagal	Maharashtra	133	6000	2400	2847.5	27.8	Feb 2002	Aug 2004	May 2006
Mahapura (near Jaipur)–Kishangarh	Rajasthan	90.38	6440	2110	−8367.3	−96.6	April 2003	Sep 2005	March 2005
Rail overbridge at Kishangarh	Rajasthan	1	180	166.60	32	15	March 1998	Feb 2000	Feb 2000
Vivekananda bridge and approach	West Bengal	6	6410	1200	−2655.3	−36.6	Sept 2002	Apr 2007	June 2007
Durg bypass	Chhattisgarh	18	700	0	−3362.9	−266.8	March 1999	Jan 2001	Jan 2001
Delhi–Gurgaon highway	Delhi	28	7100	(–) 610	−2552.5	−30.6	Apr 2002	July 2005	Jan 2008
Total for 9 projects		454	35,980	7189.30	−19,809	−39.2			

Source India PPP Database (http://www.pppindiadatabase.com); Comptroller and Auditor General of India (2008). Union Audit Reports: *Public–Private Partnership in implementation of road projects of National Highways Authority of India* (Performance Audit—Report 16 of 2008). (http://www.cag.gov.in/html/reports/commercial/2008_PA16com/contents.htm); NHAI for revenue data in the period 2010–13; NHAI website—NHAI Contracts with BOT Funding (http://203.200.117.60/CPISWeb/Reports/ViewReport.aspx). Value for money calculations are those of the authors

Table 5 Sensitivity analysis of value for money in BOT (Toll) projects

		Collection ratio of potential tolls		
		60%	80%	100%
Optimism bias	15%	−20.5%	−56.5%	−92.4%
	25%	5.7%	−21.5%	−48.7%
	35%	24.3%	3.2%	−17.9%

Source Author's calculations

private sector (24%) (see footnote 18) in the analysis, we find that the value for money to the government from all NHDP Phase I projects implemented in the PPP mode is mildly positive at 3.5% (24–20.5%).

The VfM will increase with increasing optimism bias and discount rate. However, it will decrease, ironically, with an increase in the collection ratio of potential tolls. But, this stands to reason, as the increased government efficiency (reflected in an increased collection ratio of potential tolls) would reduce the differential advantage of the private sector in performing the same tasks, which is captured by VfM.

As we have seen, the Government of India assigns priority to the BOT (Toll) mode of procurement of road projects over BOT (Annuity). Our results, which could be explained in terms of risk–return framework,[26] question this priority on the basis of value for money to the government. We find that while the returns to the government from BOT (Annuity) projects are mildly positive, they are drastically negative in the case of BOT (Toll) projects. This may be because of the high rate of growth of toll revenues seen in India in the period 2010–13, which represents the opportunity costs of BOT (Toll) projects. On the other hand, in BOT (Annuity) projects, since the traffic (and commercial) risk is allocated to the government, the government has been gaining from the high traffic growth on Indian roads.

Inferences

Overall, the following conclusions flow from our analysis of NHDP Phase I PPP projects:

- There is a negative value for money to the government from road PPP projects (−20.5% on average). And a minority (7 out of 17) of PPP projects provide positive value for money to the government. The government should, therefore, be mindful of the drivers of value for money in PPP projects[27] (especially competition and transfer of construction risk), which should be harnessed to improve VfM from PPP projects.

[26]Since Government assumes higher risk in BOT (Annuity) projects compared to BOT (Toll) projects, its returns are higher in the case of BOT (Annuity) projects.

[27]As we have seen in Chap. 4, the key drivers of VfM have been identified as risk transfer, long-term nature of contracts (including whole life costing), use of an output-based specification, competition, performance measurement and incentives, and private sector management skills. (Source: Arthur Andersen and Enterprise LSE 2000).

- BOT (Annuity) projects produce better value to the government compared to BOT (Toll) projects (8% compared to −39.2%). The government may, therefore, have to reconsider its explicit preference for BOT (Toll) projects.
- PPP projects perform significantly better in terms of timeliness of delivery. PPPs offer strong incentives to complete the project early since profits increase when users can be charged or annuities claimed from an earlier date. Such incentives are usually absent under traditional public procurement. Other important points to note are: a quarter of the PPP projects in our sample were delivered before their due date; for many of those which were delayed, the delay was not due to any concessionaire default; and BOT (Annuity) projects perform significantly better than BOT (Toll) projects in terms of timeliness of delivery.
- There are fewer problems of cost overrun in PPPs as construction cost risk is passed on to the private sector. If we account for this, then the overall VfM to the government from BOT projects becomes mildly positive.[28]
- Sensitivity analyses of our results show that value for money to the government from PPPs increases with any increase in the discount rate and optimism bias, and, ironically, any increase in the assumed inefficiency of toll collection by the government.

However, the value for money calculations in the road sector is subject to an important caveat. As already discussed, the selection of projects to be implemented by the public sector and the private sector is not a random process. If there are qualitative differences between the projects that are implemented by the public sector and by the private sector, we cannot be sure that the positive value for money from PPP projects are for real or merely reflecting qualitative differences between projects. This endogeneity issue has not been adequately dealt with in this chapter and is a subject for future research.

2 Case Study: Dabhol Power Project

2.1 The Dabhol Saga

Dabhol Power Project, in the Indian state of Maharashtra, was the largest private sector power project taken up in the country till 2007 and was its biggest single foreign investment. It was initiated in 1992 as a greenfield build-own-operate (BOO) project and reached financial closure in 1996. It was one of the eight "fast-track" power projects that did not require competitive bidding. The contract period was 20 years. The installed capacity of the project was 2,184 MW to be built

[28]As we have seen, there is a negative value for money to the government from NHDP Phase 1 projects. However, when cost overrun in conventional procurement is accounted for (24%, see footnote 18), the overall VfM becomes (+) 3.5%.

in two phases (after the renegotiation of the project in 1995–96) at a total cost of $2.9 billion. Phase I was of 740 MW comprising a 695 MW plant fueled by Naptha with an additional peaking capacity of 45 MW, and Phase II was of 1,444 MW fueled by liquefied natural gas (LNG). The project partners were Enron Corporation, Bechtel Enterprises Inc. (primary contractor for the engineering, procurement, and construction of the project), General Electric Corporation (supplier of the project's turbines), and the Maharashtra State Electricity Board (principal power offtaker). There were two payment guarantees for the project—one from the State Government of Maharashtra and a counter guarantee (for Phase I) from the federal (Central) Government. It was among the largest gas-fired power plants in the world, and Enron's most significant overseas endeavor in terms of size, cost, and political visibility.

In 1991, India began its power privatization program as part of the overall liberalization of the economy. It amended the Electricity (Supply) Act (1948), allowing private participation and foreign direct investment in generation, and stimulating a wave of experimentation by state governments, who share authority over electricity with the central government in India's federal system. Enron Corporation and General Electric signed a memorandum of understanding with the Maharashtra State Electricity Board (MSEB) in 1992 to build the project.[29] The operating entity was called the Dabhol Power Company (DPC), a joint venture with Enron as the majority owner. During most of the project development period, Enron owned 80% of the project, while General Electric and Bechtel Enterprises owned 10% each.[30] The parties negotiated the project terms over an 18-month period, which culminated in the Dabhol Power Company and MSEB signing a 20-year power purchase agreement in December 1993. Over the next year, Enron organized project finance, obtaining $635 million in financing, insurance, and loan guarantees from Bank of America, ABN AMRO, IDBI, the US Export-Import Bank, and the Overseas Private Investment Corporation (OPIC).

The opposition political alliance won elections in Maharashtra in March 1995, and in May the new government appointed a committee of state ministers (the Munde Committee) to review the Dabhol project. The Munde Committee recommended scrapping the Dabhol project in August 1995 on the grounds that the capital costs of the project were inflated, that the foreign currency denomination of tariff payments would lead to power rates being much higher than justified (MSEB was bearing the currency risk), that there were outstanding environmental questions, and that the project would adversely affect the economic development of Maharashtra. The state government canceled the project in August 1995 on the recommendation of the Munde Committee. As a result, Enron threatened arbitration and sought $300 million in compensation. The state government also filed a suit in

[29]US House of Representatives (Minority Staff, Committee on Government Reform) (2002).

[30]In late 1998, MSEB purchased part of Enron's equity stake, which dropped Enron's share to 65%. In 2004, GE and Bechtel acquired the bankrupt Enron's stake in the project for a paltry sum of $23 million to raise their own share to 85%. Since 2005, the entire equity of the project is held by Indian public sector companies and financial institutions.

September 1995 to void the agreement, alleging fraud and misrepresentation. Trying to resolve the problems, the company entered into renegotiations with the state government, which announced, in early 1996, that it will accept a revised agreement. The state and the Dabhol Power Company finalized the terms of the revised agreement in the same year. The revised agreement (1996) exacerbated the risks (commercial and foreign exchange) borne by the state government as it was committed to take-or-pay power at 90% plant load factor (PLF), and the capacity of the project was effectively expanded to about three times its original size (from 740 to 2184 MW), by removing the optional nature of Phase II of the project. Under the revised agreement, which included some other capacity and cost changes, DPC's post-tax internal rate of return was expected to be around 20%, down from the earlier expected 26–32%.

After a series of legal challenges to the project, which were eventually dismissed, Dabhol Phase I (740 MW) began generating power in May 1999. While MSEB had contracted to buy a minimum amount of power at 90% PLF under a take-or-pay commitment, it was purchasing only 33–60% of the plant's output from Phase I under its merit order dispatch rules. The high DPC power rates were due to rising crude oil prices in 2000 and a falling rupee, given that MSEB was bound to a US dollar-denominated tariff. The state was obligated nonetheless to pay the plant's full fixed charges, which further increased the rates. The total tariff payments by MSEB from May 1999 to December 2000 were Rs. 2,931 crore, at an average of Rs. 4.69 per kWh,[31] compared to the projected tariff of Rs. 2.40 per kWh and Rs. 1.89 per kWh at the time of signing the PPA and the amended PPA in 1993 and 1996, respectively, claimed by the proponents of DPC[32] as also Rs. 2.20 per kWh that MSEB was paying[33] for power sourced from other sources. This was imposing a heavy financial burden on the MSEB. These financial problems were expected to dramatically worsen after Phase II became operational towards the end of 2001, as it would add an additional 1,444 MW of power capacity and the entire project would be converted to run on imported LNG, which is a relatively cheaper fuel, but the cost of the entire LNG facility (with high spare capacity) was added to that of the project and thus would feed into the fixed charges. MSEB also undertook take-or-pay obligations for the LNG under a 20-year contract.

By early 2001, MSEB stopped paying DPC for its power saying that the "power from the plant is unneeded and too expensive" and imposed a major penalty (about $86 million) on the company for "technical underperformance." In May 2001, after DPC was served a 6-month pre-termination notice, MSEB rescinded the PPA claiming that DPC had misrepresented the project's ramp up capability, and stopped drawing power from the project. The Dabhol Power Company ceased operation of Phase I of the plant and halted construction of the 90% complete Phase II portion (1,444 MW) in mid-2001. The state urged Enron to renegotiate the contracts at

[31]Rao (2001).

[32]Prayas Energy Group (2001)

[33]Lamb (2006).

lower prices, but Enron refused. Enron instead sought to sell its 65% stake in the project for $2.3 billion to the government. A few months after these developments, the majority sponsor of DPC (Enron Corporation) filed for bankruptcy (December 2001) causing further problems to the project. The Enron saga in India can be summed up in the following sentence: "Since its conception … the Dabhol power project in the Indian state of Maharashtra has generated more problems than power."[34]

The Maharashtra Government appointed Energy Review Committee (Godbole Committee, 2001) had the following to say about the project: "The committee is concerned with numerous infirmities in the process of approvals granted in the project, which bring into question the propriety of the decisions…The committee is troubled by the failure of governance that seems to have characterized almost every step of the decision-making process on matters relating to DPC. The failure of governance has been broad, across different governments at different points of time, at both the state and the central level, and across different agencies associated with examining the project, and at both the administrative and political levels. It strains belief to accept that such widespread and consistent failure to execute assigned responsibilities is purely coincidental."

The Dabhol Project was a negotiated project (as opposed to being competitively bid). It came under intense criticism from the media on grounds of lack of transparency, corruption, and human rights violations. According to court testimony, Enron had spent $20 million on training Indians in the working of the capitalist business.[35] Because of its alleged non-transparency, it had become especially politically contentious and controversial. The World Bank had also not supported the project: "As far back as April 1993, the World Bank evaluated the Dabhol project and concluded that it was "not economically viable, and thus could not be financed by the Bank." Specifically, the World Bank found that "the project was too large for base load operation in Maharashtra"[36] and the project's power was very expensive. The high cost of power was corroborated by Central Electricity Authority, the Indian federal statutory agency responsible for evaluating and approving power projects when it stated that "Dabhol CCGT (Combined Cycle Gas Turbine) plant was not the least cost option."

After the shutdown of the project in May 2001, the foreign shareholders and lenders of DPC filed a string of lawsuits and arbitration proceedings against the MSEB, the government of Maharashtra and the federal government, in India and abroad, claiming expropriation of assets by the government. The disputes centered around the jurisdiction of Maharashtra Electricity Regulatory Commission (MERC) in relation to the PPA of DPC; the validity of the various guarantees and counter guarantees that Maharashtra government, the federal government, and domestic

[34]The Economist (2001).

[35]Financial Times. January 12, 2002. *The Enron Affair—Shadowy Path to State Approval.*

[36]As reported in 'US House of Representatives (Minority Staff, Committee on Government Reform) (2002).'

lenders had issued to foreign lenders of the project, in the event of payment default; and the order in which to deal with the claims of a now bankrupt company.[37] US Courts and International Court of Arbitration (Paris) decided in favor of the foreign shareholders of DPC and pronounced awards.[38] One of the awards directed OPIC to pay $28.57 million each to Bechtel and GE as their interests in Dabhol Power Company were improperly expropriated. Negotiations, claims, and counterclaims among stakeholders continued till 2005 when the ownership of the project changed hands to Indian public sector companies.

The foreign investors in DPC put up their stake for sale (85% including Enron, GE, and Bechtel) in 2001 itself, and there was a lot of interest in the market, including the private sector, for acquiring it. The Dabhol assets comprised of the semi-finished 2,184 power complex and an LNG terminal with related facilities. Some of the interested parties were Tata Power, BSES, GAIL (public sector), Reliance Industries, Shell, British Gas and Gaz de France. However, the deal did not come through partly because some of the bidders found the asking price too high. In 2002, the Bombay High Court appointed a court receiver for the assets of DPC and barred it from participating in any bankruptcy, winding-up, liquidation or restructuring proceedings abroad or from selling its assets. This was important for protecting the interests of the DPC creditors after Enron went bankrupt in 2001.

As there was excess demand for electricity in the state of Maharashtra (18% overall shortage and 23% peaking shortage in 2005–06[39]), the Government of India and Government of Maharashtra have revived the project through public sector enterprises in 2005. Ratnagiri Gas & Power Private Limited (RGPPL), the project special purpose vehicle, has taken over the DPC assets in order to operate the power project and the associated LNG terminal. The shareholders of RGPPL are the biggest power generating company of India, NTPC (28.33%), the gas marketer and distributor, GAIL (28.33%), Indian Financial Institutions (28.33%), and the MSEB Holding Co. Ltd (15.01%).[40] The total subscribed capital in the project is Rs. 1,765 crore out of an authorized capital of Rs. 4,000 crore.[41]

The total cost of revival of DPC is estimated at Rs. 10,038 crores ($2.4 billion at the then exchange rate), out of which the "acquisition price" was Rs. 8,485 crore ($2 billion) at which RGPPL acquired the assets[42] from the erstwhile owners of Dabhol Power Company. The cost of power was sought to be reduced through reduction in the claims of various stakeholders, to a commercially—and politically—acceptable level: Bechtel settled its claims for $160 million while GE recovered

[37]Economic and Political Weekly. 2004. *Power: Costly Mess.*

[38]Business Wire (2005).

[39]Ministry of Power (2007).

[40]As per an answer given by the Indian Minister of Power in the Indian Parliament (Lok Sabha Unstarred Question number 1509 answered on August 4, 2006).

[41]Project Finance International (2008).

[42]As per an answer given by the Indian Minister of Power in the Indian Parliament (Lok Sabha Unstarred Question number 536 answered on Nov 24, 2006).

about $145 million, OPIC received $220 million and the other offshore lenders received 77 US cents to the dollar[43] for a total of $230 million. As part of the settlement, the foreign stakeholders agreed to withdraw all lawsuits filed against the Indian government, including an arbitration claim for as much as $6 billion, and help restart the plant.

The present capacity of RGPPL is 2150 MW out of which 1480 MW (two of the three power blocks) has already been commissioned in 2006–07. As per a one-time arrangement between RGPPL and Maharashtra State Electricity Distribution Company Limited (MSEDCL), 349 million units of power was supplied @ Rs. 4.25 per kWh during the period May–June 2006 for about 55 days to meet the peak summer requirements of MSEDCL.[44] Thereafter, RGPPL supplied power using Naphtha as fuel to the MSEDCL, as per their demand, till June 28, 2007. After that, the unit was kept in reserve shutdown on account of low demand in monsoons by MSEDCL.

Meanwhile, in April 2007, RGPPL and MSEDCL entered into a long term 25-year PPA for the supply of power from the project using gas as fuel. The PPA is based on a capacity charge of Rs. 1.01 per kWh and fuel charge of Rs. 1.99 per kWh and thereby the cost of power was expected to be a little over Rs. 3 per kWh.[45]

Since commercial viability of the project is based on LNG as fuel and the operation of the plant to its full rated capacity, RGPPL has tried to source gas from various sources. On the basis of supplies from GAIL, the project switched from Naphtha to Regassified Liquefied Natural Gas (R-LNG) as its primary fuel on July 31, 2007. RGPPL has entered into a gas sale agreement with GAIL, Indian Oil Corporation Limited (IOCL) and Bharat Petroleum Corporation Limited (BPCL) for the supply of 1.5 million metric tons per annum (MMTPA) R-LNG up to September 2009. This quantity is sufficient to operate two out of the three Power Blocks of the RGPPL plant. GAIL and Petronet LNG Ltd. (PLL) have yet to tie-up balance 0.7 MMTPA gas for the third unit and also the gas supplies for the entire project for the period beyond September 2009.[46] The beleaguered power plant required about 5.6 Million Metric Standard Cubic Meter Per Day (MMSCMD) by October 2009 to double its generation capacity to 1,200 MW. Running it at its full capacity of 2,150 MW would need 8.4 MMSCMD of gas.

RGPPL is using domestic gas from KG D-6 basin for power generation since September 30, 2009. Prior to that, RGPPL was using imported R-LNG supplied by GAIL (India) Limited, IOCL and BPCL from Dahej Terminal of Petronet LNG Limited. After switching over to domestic gas, the fuel cost has reduced by 65 paise/kWh with respect to September 2009 R-LNG price (considering 1 USD = Rs.

[43]Project Finance International (2005).

[44]As per an answer given by the Indian Minister of Power in the Indian Parliament (Lok Sabha Unstarred Question number 3588 answered on August 25, 2006).

[45]As per an answer given by the Indian Minister of Power in the Indian Parliament (Rajya Sabha Unstarred Question number 243 answered on August 13, 2007).

[46]As per an answer given by the Indian Minister of Power in the Indian Parliament (Rajya Sabha Unstarred Question number 2871 answered on September 10, 2007).

Table 6 Average sale price of electricity from RGPPL

Financial year	Fuel type	Annual average rate (Rs./kWh)
2006–07	Naphtha	5.25
2007–08	Naphtha & R-LNG	3.58
2008–09 (Provisional)	R-LNG	3.25

46.50). The average sale price of electricity from RGPPL for financial years (FY) 2006–07, 2007–08 and 2008–09 is shown in Table 6.

In November 2015, the Indian Railways started buying 300 MW power at a rate of Rs. 4.70 per unit from RGGPL. While the Indian Railways would buy power from RGPPL at Rs. 4.70 per unit, the Central Government would add an additional Rs. 1.45 per unit as a subsidy, allowing RGPPL to get a net Rs. 6.15 per unit from the sale of power. The amount will be collected directly in an IDBI Bank account, which will then be used to pay for fuel, O&M expenses, and the balance will be retained by lenders for servicing the company's loans.

Box 1: Major Milestones of the Dabhol Power Company Project

1991: India amends Electricity (Supply) Act (1948), allowing private participation and foreign direct investment in power generation.

1992: Enron and General Electric sign a memorandum of understanding with the Maharashtra State Electricity Board (MSEB) to build the project.

1993: Dabhol Power Company and MSEB sign a 20-year power purchase agreement (PPA).

1995: A government committee (Munde Committee) recommends scrapping the Dabhol project.

1996: Dabhol Power Company and the state of Maharashtra finalize the revised PPA, which increases the effective size of the project about three-fold (from 740 to 2184 MW).

1998: MSEB purchases 15% of DPC's equity, which drops Enron's share to 65%, while Bechtel Enterprises and GE have 10% each.

1999: Dabhol Phase I (740 MW) begins generating power.

2000: Revenue shortfall of MSEB grows to over $275 million owing partly to the high price of power sourced from DPC.

2001: MSEB rescinds the PPA and stops drawing power from the project. DPC ceases operation of Phase I of the project and halts construction of the 90% complete Phase II of the project (1,444 MW).

2004: GE and Bechtel buy off the bankrupt Enron's stake in the project to raise their own share to 85%.

2005: Ratnagiri Gas & Power Private Limited (RGPPL), a special purpose vehicle with public sector sponsors (power generator NTPC, gas major GAIL, MSEB, and Indian financial institutions) takes over the project. The total acquisition price is Rs. 8,485 crore (about $2 billion).

2006: First phase (740 MW) of the project is recommissioned.
2007: Second phase (740 MW) of the project is recommissioned bringing the total recommissioned capacity to 1480 MW. RGPPL and Maharashtra State Electricity Distribution Company Limited (MSEDCL) enter into a 25-year PPA for the supply of power from the project using gas as fuel.
2015: Indian Railways starts buying 300 MW from the project.

2.2 *How Unique Was Dabhol? Other Power Sector PPP Projects in India*

Though hundreds of contracts were signed, by end-2007 only about 10,502 MW of greenfield PPP generation capacity was operational in India[47] (of which Dabhol led in terms of size). Table 7 shows a partial list of the operational greenfield PPP power generation projects in India.

Many of the projects that are operational have characteristics similar to Dabhol. For example, the GVK Jegurupadu electricity generation project in Andhra Pradesh has been modestly successful. The 216-MW Jegurupadu project, sponsored by GVK Industries (40%) and CMS Energy (24%), was a "fast-track" project developed under the 1991 amendments to India's electricity law (like Dabhol). The project was awarded via negotiation and was renegotiated twice prior to commercial operations. The renegotiations largely favored GVK by providing for a federal government counter guarantee and a better plant load factor (PLF) incentive formula, which remained at a low 68.5% PLF. It was the first fast-track power project to start operations in 1997.

As a fast-track power project, the tariffs were cost-plus. Though the capital cost of Rs. 3.8 crore per MW for the project is considered high (though lower than Dabhol), it was a much smaller project compared to Dabhol and therefore the much needed, though expensive, power could be absorbed by the state offtaker, AP Transco. Another mitigating factor that makes the tariffs affordable is that the project has been running on natural gas recently, which is a cheaper fuel compared to Naptha.

Another positive factor in the case of GVK Jegurupadu project is the condition of the state power sector. The Andhra Pradesh power sector has been rated the best in the country[48] on account of its relative financial viability (cash expenses in excess of 96% were covered by revenue from sale of power net of state subsidies in 2004–05), strong regulatory processes (Andhra Pradesh Electricity Regulatory Commission has been operational since 1999), strong and improving operational

[47]Ministry of Power (2008).
[48]CRISIL and ICRA (2006).

Table 7 India: Operational greenfield PPP power generation projects in India (status as of April 2008)

Project/Company name	State	Fuel choice	Installed capacity (MW)	Estimated cost including IDC (Rs. crore)	Fast track	Commissioned in
Paguthan CCGT (Gujarat Torrent Energy Corp Ltd)	Gujarat	Natural Gas/Naptha	655	2,298	No	Oct 1998
Hazira CCGT (Essar Power Ltd)	Gujarat	Natural Gas/Naptha	515	1,667	No	May 1997
Baroda CCGT (GIPCL)	Gujarat	Natural Gas/Naptha	167	368	No	Nov 1997
Surat Lignite TPP (GIPCL)	Gujarat	Lignite Coal	250	1,167	No	Jan 2000
Dabhol CCGT (Dabhol Power Co.)	Maharashtra	Phase I: Naptha Phase II: Natural Gas	740 1,444	9,051	Yes	Project canceled; 1480 MW temporarily recommissioned in 2006-07
Jegurupadu CCGT (GVK Industries)	Andhra Pradesh	Natural Gas/Naptha	216	827	Yes	June 1997
Godavari CCGT (SPGL)	Andhra Pradesh	Natural Gas/Naptha	208	748	Yes	March 1998
Kondapalli CCPP (Kondapalli Power Corpn. Ltd.)	Andhra Pradesh	Natural Gas/Naptha	350	1,035	No	Oct 2000
Torangallu TPS (Jindal Tractebel Power Co. Ltd.)	Karnataka	Blast Furnace Gas/ Coal	260	1,094	No	May 1999
Tanir Bavi Power	Karnataka	Naptha	220	NA	No	2001
Belgaum Power	Karnataka	Heavy Distillate Fuel Oil	81	NA	No	NA
Neyveli TPS (ST-CMS Electric Company)	Tamil Nadu	Lignite	250	1,325	Yes	Oct 2002
Pillaiperumalnallur CCGT (PPN Power Co.)	Tamil Nadu	Natural Gas/Naptha	331	1,122	No	April 2001

(continued)

Table 7 (continued)

Project/Company name	State	Fuel choice	Installed capacity (MW)	Estimated cost including IDC (Rs. crore)	Fast track	Commissioned in
Basin Bridge DGPP (GMR Vasavi Power Corpn. Ltd.)	Tamil Nadu	Heavy Distillate Fuel Oil	200	757	No	Dec 1998
Samayanallur DGPP (Balaji Power Corp.)	Tamil Nadu	Heavy Distillate Fuel Oil	106	384	No	Sept 2001
Samalpatti DGPP (Samalpatti Power Co.)	Tamil Nadu	Heavy Distillate Fuel Oil	106	392	No	March 2001
Karuppur CCPP	Tamil Nadu	NA	120	NA	No	July 2005
Jojobera	Jharkhand	NA	360	NA	No	
Baspa HEP (Jaiprakash Hydro Power Ltd.)	Himachal Pradesh	Hydro	300	949	No	May 2003
Malana HEP (Malana Power Co. Ltd.)	Himachal Pradesh	Hydro	86	342	No	July 2001
Vishnu Prayag HEP	Uttarakhand	Hydro	400	NA	No	Oct 2006
Total			7,365	23,526		

IDC Interest during Construction; *NA* Not Available

Source Central Electricity Authority website (http://www.cea.nic.in); Jaypee Group website (http://www.jilindia.com/privatehydropower.htm); Lamb (2006); Project Finance International (www.pfie.com)

performance of generating plants (PLF above 88%), improvement in consumer metering, reduction in subsidy levels in gross terms and as a percentage of revenue of the utilities' and the state budget, and unbundling of the sector on functional lines with separation of trading function from the transmission company.

On the other hand, the ranking of Maharashtra power sector (where DPC is located), though improved to the eighth position in the current rankings for all states of India, still lags behind Andhra Pradesh on account of a host of factors. One major result of the unfavorable fundamentals of the power sector is that the state has lagged in capacity additions. During the period 2000–05, there has been no addition to generating capacity, which has led to huge demand–supply gap of 4,500 MW during peak hours in the state leading to blackouts across the state. To fill the demand gap, MSEB and the successor entities have to make power purchases at significantly higher rates as compared to the state's own cost of generation causing further financial stress.

State Electricity Boards (SEBs) are otherwise considered the weakest link in the Indian power sector but are nevertheless indispensable with a near monopoly over distribution and accounting for a major portion of the generation and transmission capacity. The total commercial losses (excluding subsidy from the government) of the State power sector had been estimated at Rs. 28,825 crores (about $7 billion or over 1% of GDP) in 2006–07. This was mostly because of technical line loss, commercial line loss (electricity theft) and the cross-subsidy tariff structure. The last subsidized agriculture steeply at the expense of commercial and industrial consumers. Consequently, the average price of electricity sold (estimated at 4.62 cents in 2005) was below the average cost of supply (estimated at 5.6 cents), resulting in large losses incurred by the SEBs and leaving no surplus for capital investment.[49] However, the rate of return of the State power sector which was (−) 24% in 2006–07 was estimated to have improved to (−) 18% in 2007–08.[50]

Notwithstanding the financial state of the SEBs in general, GVK Jegurupadu has been paid under the terms of the PPA by AP Transco, the entity handling the transmission function in the state. Payment security is being provided through escrow facilities through which all AP Transco revenues pass, and promoted in part by significant discounts from both the fixed and variable tariff components for prompt payment. The tariff formula is calculated to provide a 16% rate of return at 68.5% PLF. However, the plant has often run at or above 90% PLF and should be performing well financially. Although the foreign investor, CMS Energy, has exited the project in 2002 to concentrate on the US market, the local partner, GVK, is continuing with plans for expansion and additional power sector investment.

Similarly, the Lanco Kondapalli Power Project in Andhra Pradesh is doing well. It is a small project (350 MW) compared to Dabhol, competitively bid on the basis

---

[49]Annual Report of the Central Electricity Authority of India for FY 2005–2006 (www.cea.nic.in).
[50]Government of India (Ministry of Finance) (2008).

of a single tariff, has foreign partners but with limited foreign exchange risk. It had rights to natural gas allocation as it was competitively bid and has run on natural gas since 2001 making the power affordable. The project has payment security mechanism in place in the form of an escrow account, like many other private power producers, for payment from its state offtaker (AP Transco).

Another Indian state with significant private power activity is Gujarat. None of the Gujarat private power projects is a "fast-track" project like Dabhol or GVK Jegurupadu. Looking at Paguthan (655 MW) and Essar Power (515 MW) projects as examples of the power privatization program in Gujarat, we find that there are two major factors in the success of these projects vis-à-vis others like Dabhol. One was the relatively low capital costs per MW (at Rs. 3.2 crore and Rs. 3.5 crore per MW for Essar Power and Paguthan, respectively). This caused the tariffs to be lower for these projects, which was partly responsible for them being less politically contentious. The second factor was that the projects had two-way firm private gas contracts owing to the development of LNG terminals and gas fields in the state. Such contracts ensured that the projects would either receive the committed gas supply or the price differential if the contracts were not honored. Both these projects are expanding their capacity, which is remarkable especially in the case of the Paguthan project as it is currently 100% foreign-owned by the Hong Kong-based China Light and Power.

The Gujarat private sector projects are also helped by the second position (after Andhra Pradesh) that the Gujarat power sector holds among all states of India.[51] The main reasons for the positive rating of the state power sector are a significant reduction in losses in recent years, on the basis of improved operational efficiency and optimization of power purchase costs, and continued support from the Government of Gujarat in terms of reforming and restructuring the sector.

2.3 In Conclusion

What the Dabhol experience, as well as the reality of many other power sector projects in India, points out is the criticality of sanctity of contracts to infrastructure projects, and the role of support from the political dispensation and climate that can make or mar massive projects and can lead to very different outcomes from comparable circumstances. This arbitrariness of outcomes is, in no small measure, an outcome of insufficient regulatory structure and lack of institutions with the stature to reduce political risk. The next case study deals with this critical aspect of the infrastructure sector—regulations and regulatory risk.

[51]CRISIL and ICRA (2006).

3 Case Study: Delhi Power Distribution PPP

3.1 Introduction

In consonance with the rest of the developing world, in recent years, India has attracted substantial private investment in power generation segment compared to power distribution segment. The principal cause of this dichotomy is the low-cost recovery in distribution and the associated political sensitivity of any proposed retail tariff hike. There is a loss of more than Rs. 1.07[52] per unit of electricity sold in the country adding up to Rs. 600 billion loss per annum for the power distribution segment in the country as a whole. Power generation, by contrast, is a typical business-to-business transaction with public and private power generators selling power to and receiving payment from mostly public distribution companies. However, recognizing that this is an unsustainable situation and the poor financial condition of the distribution segment has cast a shadow on generation investments, the Indian government has been making efforts to harness private sector efficiencies to improve the finances of the power distribution segment. This has taken the form of statewide privatizations of power distribution in Orissa and Delhi and use of distribution franchisee models in five towns and cities (namely Bhiwandi, Agra, Nagpur, Aurangabad, and Jalgaon).

Out of the many efforts to introduce private participation in power distribution, and one with a substantial tenure post-privatization is the case of Delhi. Delhi being the country's capital, Delhi power distribution privatization has great political sensitivity in that anything that happens in Delhi is keenly watched across the nation. Despite this, the government could gather the political courage to push through power distribution reforms and with relative success because of a number of innovative measures.

The Delhi power distribution segment was privatized in July 2002 by carving the city into three zones and privatizing them by giving majority shareholding (51%) to the two largest private power sector players in India, Tata Power (North and North-West Delhi) and BSES [BSES Rajdhani Power Limited, BRPL (South and West Delhi) and BSES Yamuna Power Limited, BYPL (Central and East Delhi)].[53] The balance 49% equity is held by the state-owned holding company, Delhi Power Company Limited.

[52]Local currency is Rupees (Rs.). The exchange rate as on 26 August 2016 is US$1 = Rs. 67.03.

[53]Reliance Infrastructure subsequently acquired 51% stake in BRPL and BYPL. Besides the three zones that were privatized, Delhi coverage area includes the areas under the New Delhi Municipal Council (NDMC) and those in the Cantonment served by the Military Engineering Services (MES). NDMC is a Municipal Council entrusted with the responsibility of distribution of electricity to some consumers in the New Delhi area under Sections 195–201 of the New Delhi Municipal Council Act (1994). It has obligations of a Licensee under the Electricity Act (2003) in respect of these portions of the New Delhi area. MES is also a deemed Licensee. NDMC and MES provide electricity in these areas as public sector distribution organizations.

Because of the political sensitivity of this segment and the relatively low ratio of revenues to costs, power distribution privatization is inherently difficult and there are many examples of failed initiatives across the world. Initially, what helped privatization was the inefficiency of the erstwhile Delhi Vidyut Board (DVB), the predecessor government utility that carried out the power distribution function, and the associated public discontent, which made the DVB employees mute their opposition to privatization and the Delhi citizens yearn for a change. The Delhi Government showed strong political will,[54] was willing to provide subsidies during the transition period,[55] and transferred only a sustainable level of liabilities to the distribution companies,[56] because of which the Delhi privatization effort has been relatively successful.

A map of Delhi showing the geographical spread of the power companies and their profile is given below. It would be apparent that, besides the private distribution companies (discoms), Delhi has two other state-owned organizations serving smaller areas as has been alluded to earlier: NDMC area and the cantonment served by the MES (Fig. 2).

The basic data about the Delhi Power Distribution companies is presented in Table 8.

In the above context, this case study seeks to assess the results of privatization after more than a decade of Delhi power distribution privatization so as to evaluate whether ownership change may provide an answer to the large losses and inefficiency of the power distribution segment in India and other developing countries.

3.2 *Returns to Privatization of Delhi Power Distribution Segment*

Privatization has produced healthy returns for Delhi. This assessment is based on the following facts: low level of subsidy from the government to the private discoms since privatization (except for the initial transitional subsidy); substantial progress in Aggregate Technical and Commercial (AT&C) loss reduction, which is a much better performance than that seen internationally and in Orissa, the only

[54]This political commitment was reflected in, for example, making government entities pay their electricity bills and providing security personnel in law enforcement drives against power theft.

[55]A transitional subsidy of Rs. 34.50 billion was provided to the three private distribution companies in the first 5 years of privatization (2002–07). It is likely that the privatization initiative would have failed without this subsidy, unless the government was willing to raise retail power tariffs substantially above politically feasible levels.

[56]By 2001, Delhi Vidyut Board's (the predecessor government-owned utility) total liabilities were more than 6 times its asset base [Source: Kennedy School of Government (2007)]. Over 85% of the existing liabilities were left with the government-owned holding company and only the balance was transferred to the three newly formed distribution companies (Source: Agarwal et al. 2003, p. 2).

Fig. 2 Geographical spread of the power companies in Delhi

Table 8 Delhi private distribution company profile

	Particulars	Unit	BRPL	BYPL	NDPL	Total
1	Area	Sq km	750	200	510	1460
2	Total registered customers	Million	1.73	1.23	1.20	4.16
3	Peak demand	Mega Watt (MW)	2,045	1,210	1,350	5,028[a]
4	Consumption per year (2010–11)	Million Units (MU)	8,576	4,707	6,400	19,683
5	Customer density	Consumers per sq km	2,192	6,139	1,961	2,486

[a]Peak demand in Financial Year (The Indian Financial Year is from April 1 to March 31) (FY) 2012 including NDMC and MES.

Source BSES website (http://www.bsesdelhi.com/Aboutus/bsesataglance.asp, accessed September 26, 2012); NDPL website (http://www.ndpl.com/Display-Content.aspx?RefTypes=3&RefIds=142&page=Profile, accessed September 26, 2012); Saxena (2010)

other instance of state-wide power distribution privatization in the country; limited increase in retail electricity tariffs since privatization compared to the pre-privatization period; and improvement in the quality and access to power in terms of lower load shedding, reduced distribution transformer failure rate, and increased pace of electrification of unelectrified colonies.

Subsidies: There is clear financial value for money for the Delhi government from power distribution privatization. From providing an annual subsidy for

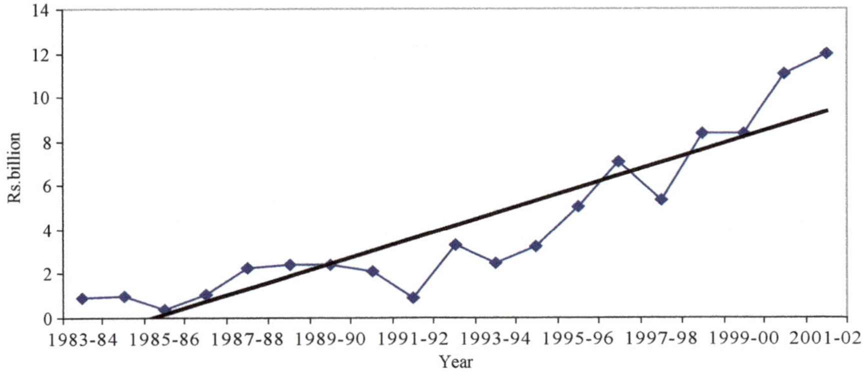

Fig. 3 Net commercial loss of DESU/DVB, by year (Rs. billion). *Note* Delhi Electricity Supply Undertaking (DESU) and DVB were predecessor government utilities, which carried out power distribution in Delhi. *Source* Sagar (2003)

bridging the revenue gap of nearly Rs. 12 billion before privatization,[57] and the positive trajectory adding over Rs. 0.50 billion every year to the subsidy (see Fig. 3), there is little outgo from the budget on account of power distribution subsidy now.[58] Though there was a transitional subsidy of Rs. 34.50 billion in the first 5 years of privatization (2002–07), this subsidy was about half of the amount that the government would have to otherwise provide in the business-as-usual scenario.

Aggregate Technical and Commercial (AT&C) loss reduction: Two main priorities of the Delhi government on the eve of privatization were to provide reliable and uninterrupted electricity supply to Delhi consumers at reasonable costs and to reduce the subsidies on account of power distribution. The principal cause for both these issues was the high level of AT&C losses (AT&C loss is the difference between the units input into the distribution system and the units for which payment is realized from the consumers by the distribution company), which was over 50% at the time of privatization. Therefore, the Delhi Government was probably right in making AT&C loss reduction as the bidding parameter as, ideally, the bidding parameter should be related to the problem that needs to be addressed through privatization.

Figure 4 shows the targeted and actual AT&C loss reduction by year for the Delhi discoms. The efficiency gains reflected in reduced AT&C levels are substantial. As against an opening AT&C loss level of 48.1% for BRPL at the time of privatization, the loss level in 2010–11 was 18.8%. Similar efficiency gains were

---

[57]Net commercial loss of Delhi Vidyut Board in 2001–02 was Rs. 11.96 billion.

[58]The only customer segment that is subsidized is the segment that consumes 0–200 units of electricity per month. This is akin to 'lifeline tariffs' for this segment. The amount of subsidy is estimated at Rs. 2.50 billion per annum.

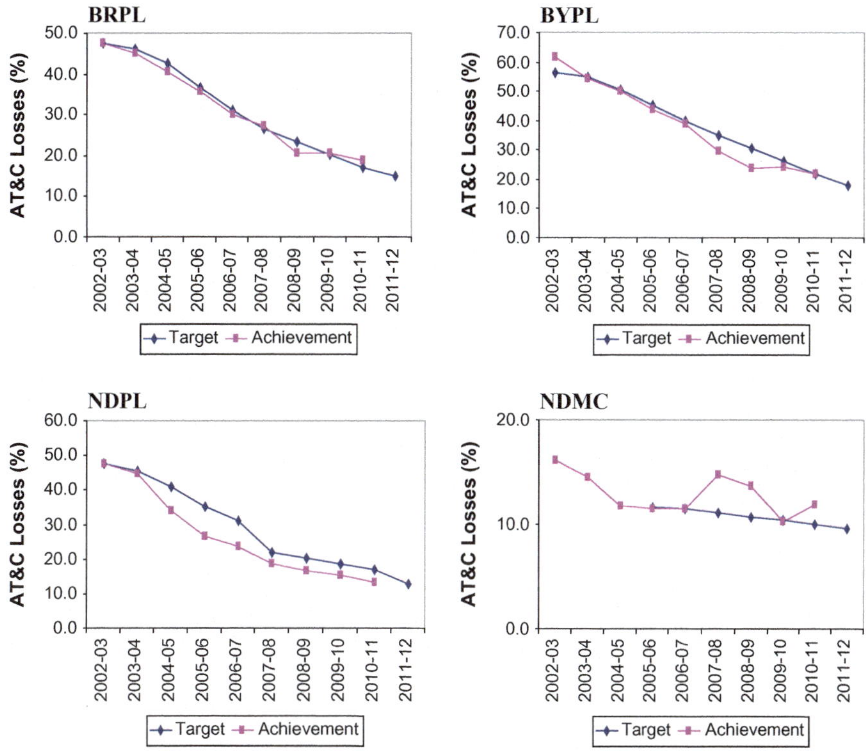

Fig. 4 AT&C losses—targets and achievement, by year and discom (percent). *Note* For some years, achievement is as claimed by the discom, but not approved by Delhi Electricity Regulatory Commission (DERC). *Source* Delhi Electricity Regulatory Commission, "Annual Report 2008–09," 2009; Delhi Electricity Regulatory Commission, "Staff Paper based on true up petition for FY 2009–10 and ARR petition for FY 2011–12 of BRPL, BYPL, and NDPL," 2011; Delhi Electricity Regulatory Commission, "Staff Paper based on petition for true up of FY 2010–11 and ARR for FY 2012–13 to FY 2014–15 of TPDDL," 2012; Delhi Electricity Regulatory Commission, "Order on True up for FY 2010–11, Aggregate Revenue Requirement for FY 2012–13 to FY 2014–15 and Distribution Tariff (Wheeling & Retail Supply) for FY 2012–13 for TATA Power Delhi Distribution Limited, BRPL, BYPL, and NDMC, 2012; Delhi Electricity Regulatory Commission, "Tariff orders for NDMC" (various years)

seen in the case of BYPL (57.2–22%) and NDPL[59] (48.1–13.1%). The average AT&C losses for all private Delhi discoms taken together came down from 51.1% in 2001–02 to 18% in 2010–11. The substantial efficiency gains are also reflected in the ability of the private discoms to beat the AT&C loss reduction targets in most years.

Comparing the performance improvements brought about by private discoms and the public sector outfit (NDMC) is akin to a natural experiment where there is an ownership change in the case of areas served by BRPL, BYPL, and NDPL,

[59]Now known as Tata Power Delhi Distribution Limited (TPDDL).

Table 9 Compound annual growth rate (CAGR) of AT&C losses in Delhi discoms, 2002–11

Discom	CAGR of AT&C Loss	
	Target (%)	Achievement (%)
BRPL	−12.1	−10.9
BYPL	−11.1	−12.2
NDPL	−12.1	−14.9
NDMC[a]	−2.9	0.8

[a]Data for NDMC is from 2005–06 to 2010–11 as its targets for AT&C losses began to be set from 2005–06

Source Delhi Electricity Regulatory Commission, 'Annual Report 2008–09', 2009; Delhi Electricity Regulatory Commission, 'Staff Paper based on true up petition for FY 2009–10 and ARR petition for FY 2011–12 of BRPL, BYPL, and NDPL', 2011; Delhi Electricity Regulatory Commission, 'Order on True up for FY 2010–11, Aggregate Revenue Requirement for FY 2012–13 to FY 2014–15 and Distribution Tariff (Wheeling & Retail Supply) for FY 2012–13 for TATA Power Delhi Distribution Limited, BRPL, BYPL, and NDMC, 2012; Delhi Electricity Regulatory Commission, "Tariff orders for NDMC" (various years)

while NDMC area continues to be catered to by the public sector. We find that NDMC has not been able to beat the AT&C loss reduction targets in most years, unlike the private discoms. The magnitude of loss reduction for NDMC, both in absolute and percentage terms, is also much lower than the private discoms[60] (see Table 9) even after taking into account the increasing difficulty of reducing AT&C losses as they come down (this aspect is reflected in the relatively flat trajectory of the targeted AT&C losses in the NDMC chart in Fig. 4). While the achievement of NDMC for AT&C losses in 2010–11 at 11.9% may be near the best possible level technically, there is a need to reduce these losses further as all distribution licensees still have areas where losses are significantly higher than the average AT&C losses achieved by them (above 40% in many areas).

The above efficiency improvements in terms of over-achievement of AT&C loss reduction targets in most years by the private discoms have become possible as a result of the substantial capital investments that have been made by them for improving the distribution network,[61] which has been incentivized through the regulatory system,[62] government support in the form of special courts for power theft related cases, police support during theft control drives, which reflects strong political support for the

[60]AT&C loss in NDMC area was 11.9% in 2010–11 up from 11.5% in 2005–06.

[61]For example, NDPL has invested Rs. 3.50 billion in the first 5 years (2002–07) to upgrade the distribution system in its area.

[62]Capital expenditure is being incentivized through the regulatory system as the Delhi Electricity Regulatory Commission (DERC) approved capital expenditure earns a return and the over-achievement of AT&C loss reduction targets resulting from such capital expenditure earns extra returns for the discoms. For example, NDPL has claimed that it has achieved the AT&C loss level of 13.1% in FY 2010–11 as against the targeted 17%. NDPL has claimed a total benefit of Rs. 1.32 billion on account of this over-achievement.

initiative, and the use of technology like advanced metering infrastructure (AMI) for metering, reading, and monitoring consumption of large consumers.[63]

Transfer from consumers: It can be argued that the low level of subsidy support from the Delhi Government to power discoms now may just be reflecting a transfer from the consumers in the form of higher retail tariffs. However, it has been observed that the overall tariff hike over the pre-privatization period (FY 1991–FY 2002) was at an average rate of 15% per annum while post-privatization (FY 2003–FY 2012), this hike has been only 6.3% per annum.[64] Though there has been a resultant build-up of regulatory assets[65] in recent times, these numbers show that the current low level of subsidy support from the Delhi Government to power distribution sector is not a result of increased current transfers from the consumers. Projections also show that if the same trajectory of retail tariff hike would have been maintained post-privatization as prevalent pre-privatization, this unfunded liability of Rs. 83.21 billion (regulatory assets) till March-2012 would not have arisen.

Other performance parameters: On the quality of power, we find that the *load shedding* in Delhi has come down to 128 million units (MUs) in FY 2008–09 against 558 MUs during 2001–02. As a percentage of the energy supplied, the load shedding has come down to 0.6% in 2008–09 from 3% in 2001–02. Similarly, the discom-wise. *Distribution Transformer Failure Rate* (leading to unscheduled load shedding) during 2008–09 and the previous year shown in Table 10, is also showing improving performance.

Other performance indicators are also showing significant improvements. As against poor *metering practices*/manual reading/and electromechanical meters in FY 2002–03, there is direct downloading of meter reading[66] from electronic meters in FY 2009–10. As compared to the preponderance of inaccurate/provisional *billing* in FY 2002–03, there is actual billing (more than 99.5%) in FY 2009–10. The *collection efficiency* has gone up to nearly 100% in 2009–10. As compared to

---

[63]In the case of NDPL, advanced metering infrastructure (AMI) has been implemented for all consumers with demand of 15 kilo Watt (kW) and above, who represent 30,000 users, or about 3% of its total consumer base, but contribute to almost 60% of the revenue. As per an estimate, implementation of AMI for large consumers is the reason for more than 90% of the quantitative achievements of NDPL.

[64]In the pre-privatization period (FY 1991–FY2002), there were 6 Tariff Orders and the overall tariff hike was about 15% per annum with the range across consumer categories being 13–18%. In the post-privatization period (FY 2003–FY 2012), there have been 7 Tariff Orders and the tariff hike has been at an average rate of 6.3% per annum.

[65]Regulatory assets reflect the unfunded difference between the actual DERC approved costs of discoms and what has been accounted for by DERC in the form of tariff hike. The estimated revenue deficit for FY 2012–13 of the three discoms at the 2011–12 tariff levels is Rs. 14.02 billion, while the accumulated revenue deficit till FY 2010–11 (along with carrying cost) is Rs. 69.19 billion (corresponding numbers for NDPL are Rs. 2.96 billion and Rs. 20.65 billion). Regulatory assets would have to be liquidated through future tariff hikes. Keeping the tariffs low with provision for future hikes would burden the consumers by interest cost which, in any case, has to be recovered from the consumers. Longer the delay, the higher the interest cost.

[66]As per the company, BRPL is the only company in India and one of the few companies in the world that uses Optical Download System for downloading meter data.

Table 10 Distribution transformer failure rate

Discom	2007–08 (%)	2008–09 (%)
BRPL	0.45	0.2
BYPL	1.38	1.13
NDPL	1.65	1.29

Source Delhi Electricity Regulatory Commission, *Annual Report 2008–09*, 2009

rampant theft of electricity in FY 2002–03, theft has been effectively controlled in FY 2009–10 and this is reflected in lower AT&C losses. All 207 *unelectrified colonies* have been electrified in BYPL area and 808 unelectrified colonies have been electrified in BRPL area showing improvement in electricity access.[67] The working of *customer care centers* and timely reading of meters and billing have also been showing progress.

3.3 Benchmarking the Delhi Privatization Experience

The achievements of Delhi discom privatization are much superior to that of Orissa, the only other case of state-wide distribution privatization in India. In contrast to the compound annual growth rate of (–) 12.5% of AT&C losses in private Delhi discoms, the achievement in Orissa has been a meager (–) 3.6%.[68]

The achievements of Delhi discom privatization also seem to be superior to that found internationally. Using a large database (160 electricity utilities that experienced private participation between the beginning of the 1990s and 2002 and 90 state-owned electricity enterprises across the developing world), Gassner et al. (2007)[69] find that private sector participation (PSP) is associated with 11% reduction in distribution losses (by contrast, Delhi privatization experience is associated with over 34% point reduction in AT&C losses) and a 45% increase in bill collection rates (by contrast, collection efficiency has already reached the theoretical maximum of 100% in the case of private Delhi discoms).

Delhi privatization experience is all the more creditable as distribution privatization is inherently difficult because of low-cost recovery and the political sensitivity of inducting the private sector for the provision of a "basic need." The table below shows that though energy projects as a whole are least likely to be canceled[70]

[67]Saxena (2010).

[68]The period considered for Delhi is 2001–02 to 2010–11 while for Orissa, the period is 1999–00 to 2009–10.

[69]Gassner et al. (2007, p. 3).

[70]As per the World Bank-PPIAF Private Participation in Infrastructure Database (ppi.worldbank.org), a project is deemed to have been canceled if one or more of the following events occur before the end of the contract period: the private company physically abandons the project (such as withdrawing all staff); the private company ceases operation or halts construction for 15% or more

Table 11 Canceled infrastructure projects with private participation in developing countries, by sector, 1990–2011

	Projects reaching financial closure		Projects canceled		Canceled projects as percent of total	
Sector	Number	Investment commitment[a]	Number	Investment commitment[b]	By number	By investment commitment
Energy	2259	625.0	79	13.7	3.5[b]	2.2[b]
Electricity generation and transmission	1658	461.1	37	10.9	2.2[b]	2.4[b]
Electricity distribution or integrated utilities	259	95.8	27	1.6	10.4[b]	1.7[b]
Natural gas	342	68.1	15	1.2	4.4	1.8[b]
Telecommunications	848	826.9	49	23.9	5.8[b]	2.9[b]
Transport	1373	310.7	67	17.7	4.9	5.7[b]
Water and sewerage	762	65.2	51	16.1	6.7[b]	24.7[b]
Total	5242	1828.0	246	71.4	4.7	3.9

Note Numbers may not add up due to rounding off
[a]In current US $ billion
[b]Indicates a significant difference at the 1% level of statistical significance
Source World Bank, PPI Project database (ppi.worldbank.org, accessed September 16, 2012)

(both in terms of number of projects and investment commitments) among all infrastructure sectors, we find that distribution or integrated utility power projects have the highest incidence of cancelation among all infrastructure sectors. This proportion at over 10% is more than double the average for all infrastructure projects by numbers (see Table 11).

3.4 *Regulatory Risk for Private Discoms*

Private infrastructure players are generally subject to considerable regulatory risk. *Tariff risk* is the most common type of regulatory risk and refers to the risk that the regulator will not enforce cost-recovering level of tariffs. The Delhi discoms are subject to significant tariff risk as apparent from the insufficient tariff increases, large delays in the issue of tariff orders by the Delhi Electricity Regulatory Commission (DERC) creating a cash crunch for the discoms, and consequent build-up of regulatory assets. Such is the cash crunch in the discoms that in April

(Footnote 70 continued)

of the contract's expected life following the revocation of the license or repudiation of the contract by the relevant authority; the private company sells or transfers its economic interest in the project to the public sector.

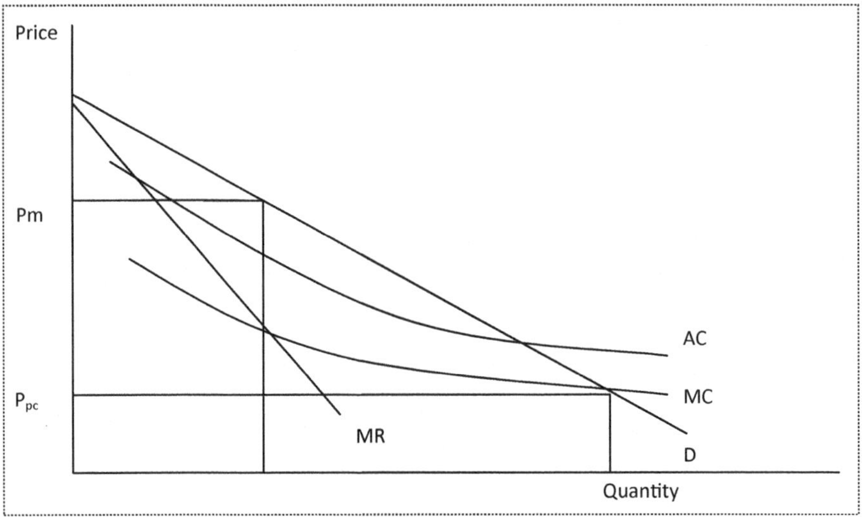

Fig. 5 Conflict between economic efficiency and financial viability in a natural monopoly

2012, the Delhi Government had to infuse Rs. 5 billion each in the equity of Delhi's private discoms, BRPL and BYPL as the financial institutions had agreed to loan them Rs. 40 billion on the condition that the promoters bring in 20% of the proposed additional capital as equity. If this had not been done, the Delhi Government would have had to allow its equity holding in the discoms to slip,[71] leverage in the discoms to remain at unsustainable levels,[72] and these discoms would have defaulted on their overdues to power generators like NTPC, which would have brought darkness to many parts of Delhi.

The genesis of regulatory risk in natural monopolies: Power distribution has natural monopoly elements. In such projects, economic efficiency is achieved, in some cases, at the output level (the socially desirable level of output) which is not financially viable. As the mandate of regulatory agencies[73] generally includes promotion of economic efficiency, besides ensuring financial viability, they have an

[71]Delhi Government owns 49% of these companies through the holding company, Delhi Power Company Limited.

[72]The debt–equity ratio (a measure of leverage) of the three private Delhi discoms in 2009–10 was BRPL (18), BYPL (13), and NDPL (1.40). The leverage was very high in the case of BRPL and BYPL.

[73]Delhi Electricity Regulatory Commission (DERC) was constituted by the Delhi Government on March 3, 1999 and became operational from December 10, 1999. DERC's approach to regulation is driven by the Delhi Electricity Reform Act (2000), the Electricity Act (2003), the National Electricity Policy (2005), and the Tariff Policy (2006). These Acts mandate the Commission to take measures conducive to the development and management of the electricity industry in an efficient, economic and competitive manner which, inter alia, includes tariff determination.

Table 12 Ratio of power purchase cost to revenues (%)

Discom	2008–09	2009–10	2010–11 (Apr–Sept)
BRPL	83	94	119
BYPL	73	77	135
NDPL	76	98	113

Source Delhi Electricity Regulatory Commission, 'Statutory Advice from DERC to Delhi Government', 2010 (http://www.derc.gov.in/Mainpercent20Pagepercent20Matter/Advicepercent20Ubderpercent20sectionpercent2086(2)/Advice.pdf, accessed May 5, 2011)

economic rationale for setting tariffs below cost-recovery levels. This issue is illustrated in Fig. 5.

Natural monopolies are characterized by downward sloping marginal cost (MC) curves. The socially optimal price is at Ppc, where Price = MC. While the monopolist would want to set the price at the level of Pm, where MC = MR (Marginal Revenue), the regulator would want to set the price at Ppc, where price does not cover average costs. Therefore, a sustainable regulatory approach that allows investors satisfactory returns whilst being perceived to charge fair prices to consumers is challenging. This exposes power distribution projects to considerable regulatory risk. In addition, political sensitivity of any decision to raise power tariffs renders distribution reforms especially difficult, which adds to the tariff risk.

High ratio of power purchase costs to revenues: This regulatory risk (tariff risk) is manifested in the high proportion of power purchase costs to revenues of Delhi discoms, and ultimately in the form of "regulatory assets" that would need to be paid for by hiking consumer tariffs in the future. Power purchase costs should normally not exceed 80% of revenues for financial viability,[74] but in 2010–11, this proportion was over 100% for all three private discoms of Delhi. The high proportion of such costs to revenues indicates the inability of the companies to pass on the increase in power purchase costs to their consumers, a finding that replicates the international experience[75] (Table 12).

Regulatory Capacity: In addition, there are capacity constraints in the case of DERC, which need to be addressed. Issues with regulatory capacity were most evident in 2010 when DERC sent contradictory statutory advice to the Delhi Government over a space of 6 months about the financial position of the discoms and the need for a tariff increase.[76] In this context, the High Court of Delhi, the appeal forum for DERC tariff orders, had observed that:

---

[74]Other norms are: Operation & Maintenance expenses like employee expenses (9%), depreciation (3–4%), Return on Capital Employed (6–7%), and income tax (0.5–1%).

[75]Gassner et al. (2007). This study found that, except for electricity concessions, there is no evidence of a systematic change in residential prices as a result of PSP, pointing to the economic and political difficulties in aligning tariffs with the cost of service across the developing world.

[76]On 30 June 2010, Chairman, DERC conveyed to Delhi Government that the three private discoms have a surplus of Rs. 35.77 billion that needs to be adjusted through a downward tariff revision in FY 2010–11. On 15 December 2010, DERC sent 'Statutory Advice' to Delhi

> ...the Commission (DERC) has to function with responsibility, intellectual integrity, consistent objectivity, and transparent functionalism appreciating the essential nature of the regulatory body. We emphasize on intellectual integrity and transparent functionalism as we are totally dissatisfied with the way the Commission has proceeded with the manner of (tariff) determination.[77]

Multi-Year Tariff Orders: As has been stated earlier, the Delhi discoms are subject to considerable tariff risk. One way in which regulatory uncertainty is sought to be reduced is through the issue of multi-year tariff (MYT) orders. The MYT framework sets long-term performance targets for entities engaged in the distribution of power and aims at rewarding performance, promoting efficiency, and providing regulatory certainty to the investors by encouraging transparency, consistency, and predictability.

DERC segregates costs into two categories: those which are expected to be controlled by the distribution licensee, and those over which the licensee does not have significant control. The Commission sets targets for each year of the "Control Period" for parameters considered controllable. Any financial losses arising out of underperformance vis-a-vis these targets are to be borne by the licensee. *Controllable parameters* include: AT&C losses, Distribution losses, Collection Efficiency, Operation and Maintenance (O&M) expenditure, etc. On the other hand, *uncontrollable parameters* are not within the licensee's control and any variations in these parameters from the levels laid down in the MYT Order can be factored into the revised "Aggregate Revenue Requirement" (ARR) computations for the following year through the "truing-up[78] process." These include: Cost of power purchase from various sources, as well as Revenue from sale of power to consumers.

The first Multi-Year Tariff Order (MYTO) for the discoms was issued on February 23, 2008. The original Control Period of the first MYTO ended in end-March 2011, which was later extended to end-March 2012. The second MYTO was notified in January 2012 and is valid for the financial years 2012–13 to 2014–15. MYTOs are issued after going through the public hearing process, designed to incorporate views of the stakeholders in the tariff determination process.

Retail tariffs: It should be realized that infrastructure services have to be paid for, either from the budget or user fees. As one of the important objectives of inducting the private sector in the Delhi distribution segment was to control the subsidy outgo, retail tariffs have to be cost reflective. While the tariff risk for Delhi discoms has kept retail tariffs down, on a more general plane, *India currently has*

(Footnote 76 continued)

Government acknowledging the resource crunch being faced by Delhi discoms and calling for a tariff increase.

[77]High Court of Delhi, Judgment pronounced on 23 May 2011 on WP (C) No. 4821/ 2010 (p 31) [http://delhicourts.nic.in/MAY11/NAND%20KISHORE%20GARG%20VS%20GOVT%20OF%20NCT%20OF%20DELHI.pdf, accessed 30 Dec. 2012].

[78]Truing-up exercise is designed to fill the gap between the actual expenses at the end of the year and anticipated expenses estimated at the beginning of the year. Truing-up exercise is necessary as there would always be variation between projections and actuals.

some of the lowest and most uneconomic average electricity tariffs in the world—Rs. 4 per unit (kilo watt hour, kWh) at the retail level, compared to about Rs. 6–Rs. 7.50 per kWh in countries much better-endowed with coal or gas (Canada, South Africa, the USA), and Rs. 9.50–Rs.10 per kWh elsewhere (much of Europe, developing countries).[79] On an aggregate basis, the gap between the average cost of supply and tariff is Rs. 1.07 per kWh which results in financial loss for every unit of power sold[80] in the country. This makes the current tariff levels unsustainable that cannot elicit needed investments, drain resources, and are not targeted at the poor.

To address these concerns partly, the Appellate Tribunal for Electricity (APTEL) in a recent far-reaching judgment has ordered State Electricity Regulatory Commissions to make a periodic review of tariff mandatory, even if the distribution companies (discoms) do not submit their tariff petitions on time.[81] In addition, since fuel and power purchase cost is a major expense of the distribution company which is uncontrollable, the APTEL has ordered that the fuel and power purchase cost adjustment should preferably be done on a monthly basis. This would make the tariffs more cost reflective.[82]

There is support for the above judgment of the APTEL from the Tariff Policy (2006), which provides that:

> Uncontrollable costs should be recovered speedily to ensure that future consumers are not burdened with past costs. Uncontrollable costs would include (but not limited to) fuel costs, costs on account of inflation, taxes and cess, variations in power purchase unit costs including on account of hydro-thermal mix in case of adverse natural events.[83]

Accordingly, DERC has taken some decisions lately that may make the tariffs more cost reflective. In July 2012, DERC has decided to implement a Power Purchase Cost Adjustment on a quarterly basis, which would benefit the discoms. Further, to even out the load curve, the DERC has approved a system of Time of Day (ToD) tariff for large industrial and commercial consumers (300 kW and above) on a pilot basis. Here peak hour consumption is charged at higher rates with a rebate on off-peak hour consumption. This is aimed at reducing load during peak hours and thus control the rise in power purchase costs. This is critical for Delhi as the daily load can vary from 3000 to 5000 MW in summer causing surplus during off-peak hours, usually sold cheaper than the power purchase cost primarily because it is available during off-peak hours. DERC had revised the tariff for all consumer categories (by an average of over 20%) to enable the discoms to recover the

[79]Government of India, Ministry of Finance (2011).

[80]Letter dated 21 January 2011 from Secretary, Ministry of Power to Chairman, Appellate Tribunal for Electricity.

[81]Six states have not revised tariffs for more than 5 years.

[82]Appellate Tribunal for Electricity, 'Judgment dated 11 November 2011 in OP No. 1 of 2011' pp. 85–88 (http://aptel.gov.in/judgements/OP%20NO.1%20OF%202011.pdf, accessed 30 Dec. 2011).

[83]Ministry of Power, 'Tariff Policy' (6 Jan. 2006), clause 5.3(h)(1) p 7 [http://powermin.nic.in/whats_new/pdf/Tariff_Policy.pdf, accessed 20 April 2013].

approved revenue requirement for FY 2012–13. It also introduced a surcharge of 8% over the revised tariff to meet the carrying cost of the revenue gap till FY 2010–11 and for the liquidation of revenue gap.[84]

Conclusion

It is true that everything is not perfect after Delhi power distribution privatization. There is no open access for large consumers, which would have attracted investments, and delivered price and efficiency gains to consumers.[85] Related to this is the lack of development of a competitive power market wherein a public monopoly has been replaced with a private monopoly and a "single buyer" model persists at the distribution level. Outages are also common and there are complaints about over-billing.[86] Some of these problems can be addressed through enforcing performance standards by the regulator, which has not been done and thus again reflects on regulatory capacity.

However, given our imperfect world, any improvements would have to be incremental and a judgment as to the direction of change would depend on the counterfactual: what would have happened had the public sector Delhi Vidyut Board still continued to be responsible for Delhi power distribution operations? And the answer is unambiguous: after privatization, the state government subsidy is much lower, and qualitative and quantitative indices of power supply to consumers are better. So, privatization of Delhi power distribution is better than what it would have been, had the status quo been maintained.

4 Case Study: Delhi International Airport Ltd (DIAL)

4.1 Introduction

On January 31, 2006, a consortium led by GMR Infrastructure Limited, and including Fraport of Frankfurt, Germany, and others won the contract to modernize the international airport at India's capital, New Delhi. This came about slightly over two and a half years from the approval of the proposal for modernization (via privatization) of the Delhi airport by the Airport Authority of India (AAI).

GMR Infrastructure Limited is part of the GMR Group, one of India's fastest growing infrastructure companies with interests in airports, energy, highways and urban infrastructure and with a presence in several countries beyond India,

---

[84]No surcharge is necessary in case of NDMC where a surplus of about Rs. 4 billion exists as on 31 March 2011.

[85]Haldea (2011, pp 159–90).

[86]However, as per TPDDL, during 2010–11, as against the standards of performance with regard to percent billing mistakes (0.2%) and percent faulty meters (3%), actual achievement has been 0.03% and 0.34%, which implies that the company has over-achieved even these targets.

including Turkey, South Africa, Indonesia, and Singapore. It had been partnering with the government in the increasingly popular Public–Private Partnership (PPP) model that the Indian government had adopted since the late 90s. GMR has also built the iconic Rajiv Gandhi International Airport at Shamshabad near Hyderabad.

The modernized international airport in Delhi was opened for traffic in 2010 just in time for the 2010 Commonwealth Games. It became South Asia's largest hub, which in 2011–12 handled about 36 million passengers. Its Terminal 3 is the eighth busiest international hub in the world and was completed within the time for the Commonwealth Games. In the years 2012 and 2013, the IGIA was consistently ranked the second-best airport in the world in the 25–40 million passengers category by the Airports Council International.[87]

But this journey of privatization and modernization of the Delhi airport was neither smooth nor free from controversy. The projected costs ballooned nearly four times from Rs. 3,297 crore at the time of bidding to an eventual Rs. 12,857 crore as per DIAL (see Appendix 1). This increase in cost, in turn, was initially thought to be funded through a rights issue which ran into difficulty owing to AAI's inability to subscribe to it. The final recourse, therefore, was to the markedly unpopular levy of Development Fees. While all these steps were obviously taken with the knowledge and approval of Airport Economic Regulatory Authority (AERA) and relevant government agencies, that was not enough to avoid subsequent controversies and acrimonies.

Of the controversies surrounding the project, two main sets of issues were the most important and visible—one surrounding the process of awarding of the contract, highlighted most by a court case alleging unfairness on the part of the government in awarding the contract to the GMR-led group by a competing group led by Reliance Infra. The second controversy was one that stemmed from the Indian Comptroller and Auditor General's (CAG) audit report in 2012 for the period 2006–11 of Delhi International Airport Limited (DIAL) pointing out several ways in which the government appeared to have undersold the airport operation to DIAL at significant opportunity loss to the exchequer.

The court case got dismissed and the debate around the CAG allegations ultimately subsided. DIAL saw significant losses in 2010–11 and 2011–12 before turning into profits in 2012–13 (see Financials in Appendix 2). Of course in this entire period, AAI was getting its share of about 46% of a rising revenue stream. However, the issues raised by the much publicized CAG report indicated the nature of conflict and misunderstanding that large and iconic PPPs can generate in emerging market environments. Hence, it is perhaps instructive to go through these two controversies in-depth to understand some of the contracting challenges highlighted in the previous chapters of the book.

---

[87]Airports Council International website (http://www.aci.aero/Airport Service Quality/) viewed on 13 July 2014.

The rest of the case study is structured in the following manner. The next section talks about the background and nature of the contracting process and the challenges and allegations that were made about its fairness while the one following it deals with the set of controversies raised by the CAG.

4.2 Issues in and Controversies Around the Bidding Process

4.2.1 Economic Scenario and Policy Developments

The Indian civil aviation industry has shown robust growth in both passenger and cargo traffic during the Eleventh Plan period (2007–12) when India became the ninth largest civil aviation market in the world. In 2013–14, total passenger traffic at Indian airports reached 169.05 million comprising domestic passenger traffic of 122.43 million and international passenger traffic of 46.62 million. The corresponding numbers for cargo were 2.28 MMT, 1.44 MMT, and 0.84 MMT, respectively.[88] It has been observed that air transport generally grows at twice the GDP growth rate. During the 3 year period (2009–10 to 2011–12), the total passengers handled at the Indian airports grew at a compound annual growth rate (CAGR) of 14.2%, comprising a growth rate of 8.9% in international traffic and 16.3% in domestic traffic.[89] The statistics about the Indian civil aviation sector are at Appendix 3.

This rise in air traffic growth needs to be supported with infrastructure development at airports, which requires large investments. In an attempt to reform the regulation of airports, the Government of India passed the Airports Authority of India (AAI) Act, 1994 in April 1995. Through this Act, the erstwhile National Airports Authority and the International Airports Authority of India were merged into a single entity, which would manage domestic and international airports, custom/freight airports and civil enclaves at defence airfields. AAI would also offer Air Traffic Management Services (ATMS) over entire Indian airspace with ground installations at all airports to ensure the safety of aircraft operations. Apart from these regular operations, AAI was also entrusted to move ahead with the modernization of Indian airports and ensure that India had world-class civil aviation infrastructure.

Discussions on the best way to carry out the modernization of airports were started in earnest by setting up a Task Force in 1999 which suggested that a long-term lease for outsourced management ought to be considered. In January 2000, the Cabinet approved the restructuring of airports through the long-term leasing route. In June 2003, AAI approved the modernization proposal for Delhi and Mumbai airports, each at an approximate cost of Rs. 30 billion. In September

---

[88]Government of India, Ministry of Finance (2014).

[89]Government of India, Planning Commission (2012).

2003, the Cabinet approved the restructuring of Delhi and Mumbai airports through the Joint Venture (JV) mode where AAI would retain 26% equity and the private partners would own the rest (74%). As a result, once the JV partner is selected, AAI incorporated a subsidiary company, i.e., Delhi International Airport Pvt. Ltd (DIAL), and sold 74% of the shares of DIAL to the winning JV Consortium.

At the time, the Airports Authority of India managed and operated 123 out of a total of 134 airports in India. This included 12 international airports, 99 domestic airports, and 12 customs airports. The remaining 11 airports (five international airports and six domestic airports) were managed by PPP concessionaires, State Governments, and the private sector. Of the AAI—managed airports, 32 were non-operational and only seven made a profit. Before the privatization of the Delhi airport in 2006, it was one of the most profitable airports for AAI. The revenues and net income of Delhi Airport are in Appendix 4.

4.2.2 The Bidding Process

In November 2003, a committee headed by Naresh Chandra supported AAI's plan for the modernization of India's airports. The committee noted that in the year 2003–04, the two largest airports in the country—Delhi and Mumbai—accounted for more than 49% of the passenger movements and 59% of the cargo movements for the entire country. Both the airports were handling more than twice their originally designed capacity and were suffering from overcrowding and congestion. Given the rapidly deteriorating scenario, the Committee suggested that the modernization ought to happen through privatization or joint ventures between the government and private players. The committee looked at three possible options (Table 13).

Table 13 Options for modernizing the Delhi Airport

Allocation of responsibilities	Option 1	Option 2	Option 3
Ownership	State	State	Private/Mixed
Investment	State	Private/mixed	Private
Operations management	Private	Private	Private
Strategies for private participation	Management contracts, Multiple concessions	BOT (Build–Operate–Transfer) schemes, Long term lease	Trade sales, Strategic buyouts
Examples	Hong Kong, Santiago (Chile)	Athens, Greece Bogota, Colombia	British Airports Authority, Australia, Scotland

Source World Bank (1996). Adapted from the Naresh Chandra Committee Report, 2003

The Committee, however, highlighted the following six factors which could impact the privatization program and asked AAI and other regulatory bodies to address them.

1. Airport charges in India were much higher than the charges in similar South Asian countries. The committee suggested conducting a benchmarking exercise prior to the start of any privatization process.
2. One of the features of the privatization model was the transfer of existing AAI staff to the newly privatized joint venture for a period of 3 years. The committee suggested that the government reconsider this decision by offering the AAI staff a voluntary retirement scheme.
3. Airport security ought to be taken out of the purview of AAI and transferred to the Ministry of Home Affairs.
4. Coordination between security, immigration, and passenger management services (e.g., check-in and boarding) ought to be streamlined prior to privatization.
5. Existing tenants need to be relocated or compensated.
6. The qualification criteria set by the government for privatization not be so onerous and stringent as to limit competition during the bidding process. As long as one of the members of the bidding consortium had prior experience in managing an airport, the consortium ought to be allowed to bid.

The committee warned that if these issues were not dealt with, there was a danger that highly qualified international bidders might choose not to participate in the bidding process. Furthermore, there was also the possibility that bidders who do qualify may be unable to improve the efficiency of airport operations.

The Pre-Bidding Process

Keeping the Naresh Chandra Committee Report's recommendations and needs of the aviation industry in mind, the then National Democratic Alliance (NDA) government set up an Empowered Group of Ministers (EGoM) on September 11, 2003 to decide on the key issues regarding the privatization of Mumbai and Delhi airports and build consensus among various allies of the ruling coalition government. The Ministry of Civil Aviation (MoCA) set up the Inter-Ministerial Group (IMG) in the meantime to assist the EGoM in its working. In December 2003, the IMG decided to appoint the ABN AMRO Bank as the financial consultants (FC) for the privatization process. AAI and EGoM aimed to complete the privatization process of the airports by September 2004. However, the work of these committees was interrupted by the May 2004 general elections which saw the incumbent ruling coalition—NDA—being ousted and replaced by the Congress-led United Progressive Alliance (UPA) coalition.

After coming to power, the UPA Government decided to press ahead with the privatization of the airports. The key committees, EGoM and IMG, were reconstituted in June and October 2004, respectively. In June 2004, the EGoM announced Air Plan, Australia as the global technical advisor (GTA) and Amarchand & Mangaldas & Suresh Shroff & Co (AMSS) as the legal consultants (LC). Thakur, Vaidyanath Aiyar & Co. (TVA) was appointed as the accounting and tax advisor for the bidding process. The three teams, FC, GTA, and LC under the

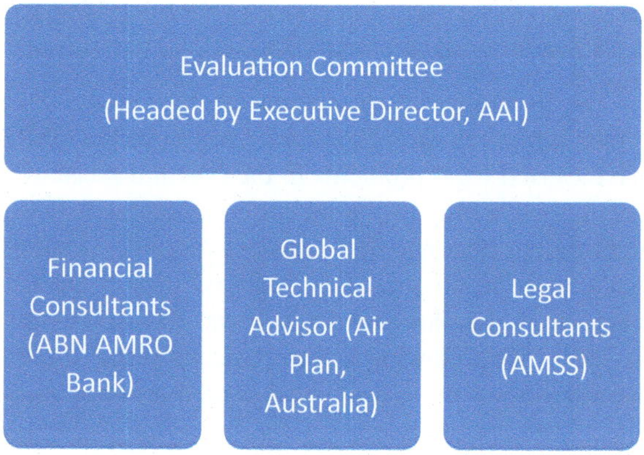

Fig. 6 Structure of the Evaluation Committee

chairmanship of the Executive Director of AAI were grouped into a single entity called the Evaluation Committee (EC) (Fig. 6).

The key responsibilities of the EC were to structure the privatization process, negotiate with bidders and move the final documents for appropriate government approvals. This required the EC to create transaction documents which made the terms and conditions of the privatization clear to the bidders. The transaction documents along with the request for proposal (RFP) were provided to the potential bidders. The transaction documents consisted of multiple documents, namely:

1. Operation, Management, and Development Agreement (OMDA): The OMDA was the most important of all transaction documents and laid out the contractual terms and conditions and granted the Joint Venture Company (JVC) the right to undertake the following functions with respect to the airport: operating, maintaining, developing, designing, constructing, upgrading, modernizing, financing, and managing. The OMDA also contained a list of mandatory capital projects that the winning JVC would have to undertake by 31 March 2010 and a list of permitted and non-permitted aeronautical and non-aeronautical activities. In short, OMDA dictated all the development work and service standards that the JVC would be asked to deliver at the privatized airports.
2. Lease Deed (LD): As per the LD, the airport and the land would be leased out to the JVC for a duration of 30 years from the effective date and, in the event of a renewal of the JVC, the property would be leased out for another 30 years. The lease is coterminus with the OMDA.
3. Shareholders Agreement (SHA): According to the SHA, AAI, Government of India, and other PSUs would hold 26% of the total shares and private participants would hold the remaining 74% of the JV's stock. Foreign shareholding of the airport was restricted to 49% while airline equity was capped at 10% of the aggregate shareholding. The authorized share capital of the JVC would be of Rs. 2.5 billion and an initial subscription of Rs. 2 billion.
4. State Support Agreement (SSA): The SSA specified conditions and nature of Government of India support, along with the mutual responsibilities and obligations of the two partners.

5. State Government Support Agreement (SGSA)
6. Substitution Agreement (SA).

The framing of these documents, especially OMDA was not a straightforward affair. While reviewing the draft version of the OMDA, several issues which could have caused legal problems in the post-bid phase were discussed in the IMG. As a result, the drafting of the transaction documents took longer than estimated. While the original plan entailed releasing the final versions of all transaction documents along with the Request for Proposal, actually the transaction documents were still being drafted at the time the RFP was released to the pre-qualified bidders on April 1, 2005. The following write-up details some of the major issues which influenced the revision of the OMDA and related transaction documents.

Issues in the Drafting of the Transaction Documents

- **Land**

The privatization of the Delhi and Mumbai airports was the first significant attempt in India to provide modern amenities to air passengers. Since both the airports were situated in an urban area and within city limits, the land value for commercial uses was significant. The consultants to AAI had recommended that the surplus land surrounding the airport be utilized for pure commercial activities independent of aeronautical activities. Classification of the land in the OMDA was as follows:

1. Aeronautical Assets
2. Non-aeronautical Assets

    a. Passenger/Cargo related commercial activities
    b. Non-associated facilities (e.g., hotels, malls, business parks, etc.)

The OMDA also classified the non-aeronautical assets as transfer and non-transfer assets. The treatment for these assets would depend upon their classification. While AAI was mandated to take over the control of the transfer assets (usually containing the land used for aeronautical services), the option of the takeover of the non-transfer assets would remain with AAI. This classification raised several issues, both legal and policy in nature. For instance:

1. At what price would AAI buy the non-transfer assets from the Joint Venture Company (JVC)? Considering the price appreciation of the land in 30/60 years' time, would AAI have enough resources to purchase that land?
2. How would the land classified as non-aeronautical be valued?
3. Could the non-transfer assets be mortgaged by the JVC to other companies?
4. Was the AAI, a statutory body, acting within its legal domain by subletting the land for commercial purposes?

These issues caused disagreement between the Ministry of Civil Aviation (MoCA) and the Planning Commission (PC). Eventually, it was decided that the non-transfer assets would be transferred back to the AAI at the fair market value of the assets less the market value of the land. The fair market value would be determined by two independent valuation companies—one chosen by AAI and the other by the JV. It was also decided that development of land for outright commercial use was not permitted. Furthermore, the OMDA restricted the land use for non-transfer assets to 5% in Delhi.[90]

- **Tariff Issues**

As per the RFP, the bidding parameter was the percentage of airport revenue shared by the JV Company with AAI, provided the JV Company scored more than 80 percentage points in the technical evaluation. The Planning Commission pointed out that if the revenue share was restricted to the aeronautical tariffs only, it would imply that JV would make losses on the aeronautical side of the business and try to cover it by promoting the non-aeronautical businesses of the airport. There was also a danger that due to these losses, the JV would not invest adequately on the aeronautical side which could have an adverse impact on performance.

It was also felt that since the JV would have a monopoly on aircraft movements at the airport, the JV could set high landing fees and other aeronautical charges on the aircrafts for profit maximization. The airlines would pass these high costs on to the passengers which would reduce the overall ridership. It was, therefore, felt that charges ought to be regulated and in the OMDA, the JV was to charge rates specified by the Government of India (GoI). Subsequently, the aeronautical rates were to be decided by the proposed Airport Economic Regulatory Authority (AERA). Principles governing tariff fixation were also incorporated in the SSA.

- **Airport Operator**

It was a mandatory requirement for bidders to have an airport operator in the consortium in order to qualify for bidding. While evaluation points would be awarded to the consortium based on the airport operator's capability, there was little clarity on whether the airport operator could hold any equity in the JV. Furthermore, since there were no guidelines regarding the agreement between the airport operator and the JV, there was a danger that the bidder could involve the airport operator simply to get past the pre-qualification stage and get some technical points. The PC was of the view that the airport operator ought to have some equity and greater direct responsibility in the operation and management of the airport. In the final OMDA, the airport operator was required to hold at least 10% equity in the JVC and was expected to enter into an agreement with the bidder for a minimum period of 7 years.

- **Bid Bond, Performance Bond, and Termination Payment**

The initial requirement in the OMDA was to have a bid bond of Rs. 50 billion and a performance bond of Rs. 50 billion. The tenure of both the bonds was 50 years. The PC objected to both the amount and tenure of the bonds and suggested a performance bond of Rs. 5 billion for a period of 5 years. The logic in

[90]Pandey et al. (2010).

support of this was that once the JV had made large capital investments and opened an escrow account, they were essentially locked in until they recoup their investments. Thus, a separate performance bond would simply add to the cost and provide no additional security. In the final OMDA agreement, the tenure of the performance bond was kept at 5 years but the amount was fixed at Rs. 15 billion for Delhi airport.

As per the initial version of the OMDA, in the case of termination due to default by the JV, the entire debt would have to be repaid by the AAI. The PC felt that placing no risk of default on the JV would create moral hazard problems and suggested that the JV should at least bear the risk of 10% of the debt. It was also noted that the SSA was explicit on the government obligations but did not clarify the consequences of default by the JV. Eventually, it was decided that the Legal Consultant (AMSS) would have to prepare a fresh document which would balance the obligations between the AAI and JV.

There were other issues in the transaction documents such as the scope of the mandatory capital projects, cost and revenue sharing. The resolution of all these issues caused the final transaction documents to be delayed.

The process of privatization of the airports had begun in 2003 but the pace only picked up from the second half of 2004. After several meetings among the FC, LC, GTA, IMG, and others, the RFP and transaction documents (which were still at the draft stage) were released to the bidders in April 2005. The bidders were also asked for inputs on the transaction documents through a pre-bid conference. However, due to various issues brought up by the Planning Commission, members of the IMG felt that the process was being rushed and not enough time was allocated for the members to go thoroughly through the transaction documents. By August 2005, the member of the IMG representing the Planning Commission felt that more work was needed to be done on the transaction documents. However, the MoCA felt that too much time had been lost since 2003 and that the privatization process ought not to be jeopardized for the sake of perfection. As a result, the OMDA along with the other transaction documents were finalized and released to pre-qualified bidders on August 30, 2005. The last date of receipt of technical and financial bids was kept as September 14, 2005.

The "Request for Proposal" Document

This part details the structure of the RFP and the evaluation procedure used by the AAI and its advisors (i.e., the Evaluation Committee) to evaluate the winning bid for the airport JV. The process was divided into four phases and only those bidders who passed through the initial phase would proceed to the next phase.

The technical evaluation approach was focused on the Government's two strategic objectives that included world-class airport development and world-class airport management. Accordingly, two global evaluation criteria ("Development Capability, Commitment, and Value Add" and "Management Capability, Commitment, and Value Add") were formulated to assess the technical bids. Detailed evaluation factors were devised to assess each of these evaluation criteria and the details of these and the weights used were provided to Bidders in the RFP document.

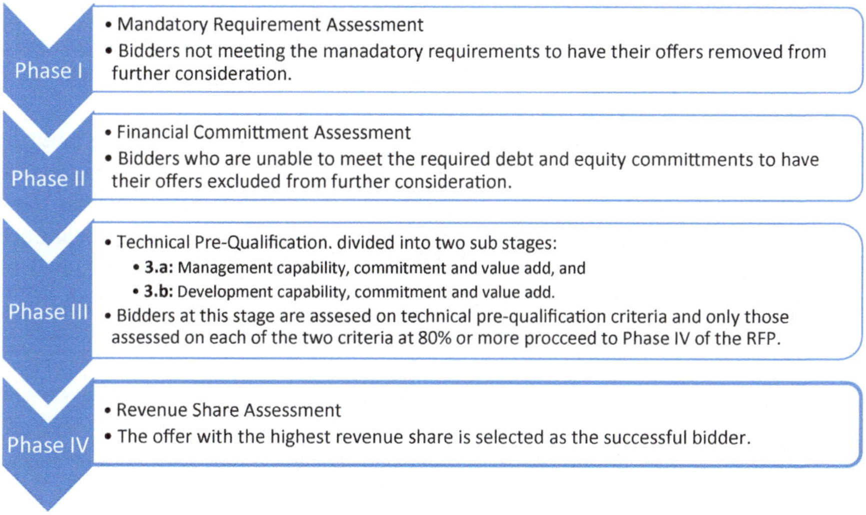

Fig. 7 Overview of the RFP process

In addition to these key transaction objectives, other objectives included timely completion, smooth transition to new ownership structure, and fair and equitable treatment of employees (Fig. 7).

Phase I involved relatively simple "checks" on the mandatory requirements such as net worth, whether FDI constraint at 49% is being met, submission of a bid bond, the participation of an Airport Operator in the consortium, etc. Phase II involved the assessment of financial parameters such as commitment for debt and equity funding, issuance of bank guarantee, etc. The assessment under the first two phases was on a pass/fail basis, with no scoring of marks.

The most crucial stage of the RFP was Phase III where bidders were to be judged and ranked on their technical merits and management ability. The requirement was that only bidders that achieved a score of 80% or higher on each of the two criteria would be technically pre-qualified. The consultants designed the Phase III evaluations such that the bidder with the best technical and management expertise, who thereby showed the most promise to implement the Government of India's master plan successfully for the Delhi airport, was awarded the project.

As stated in the RFP, the key principles underlying the evaluation approach were as follows:

- Objectivity: well defined evaluation factors, evidence-based assessment, and a multi-stage review;
- Transparency: full disclosure of approach, subject to review by Government Review Committee;
- Alignment with the Government's strategic objectives;
- Consistency of assessment.

The sub-criteria of 3.a (Management capability, commitment, and value add) were as follows:

1. **Management Capability**—Total Points Allocated: 37.5
    a. Experience of the airport operator: Points would be awarded for the number, scale, and geographic diversity of the airports operated and managed by the airport operator. Additional points would be awarded based on the track record in route and traffic development and in managing relations with airlines and other key stakeholders. Other parameters included the level of service quality performance, performance in turning around and improving aeronautical and non-aeronautical operations in airports, experience in operating and developing airports in non-OECD nations, etc.
    b. Experience of other JV members: Points were awarded to the members based on the commercial/retail experience, property, and infrastructure development experience, and experience in handling HR issues in situations where management changed hands.
2. **Management Commitment**—Total Points Allocated: 25
    a. Commitment of Airport Operator: The main criterion to award points was based on the level of equity commitment of the operator. The EC would also award points on the basis of experience and level of management resources committed to airport management in the areas of aeronautical operations, cargo handling, slot management, terminal operations, retail operations, traffic and route development, environmental management, etc.
    b. Commitment of other Prime Members: Points to be awarded based on the experience and level of management resources committed by other prime members in non-aeronautical operations and development.
3. **Management Value Add**—Total Points Allocated: 37.5
    a. HR approach and transition plan: The two main criteria for the allocation of points in this category were the proportion of AAI employees in the JVC by the end of the third year of privatization and the transition plan which would facilitate the takeover of the operation and management of the airport by the JV.
    b. Stakeholder Management: The EC would award points in this category on the basis of the identification and management of key stakeholders such as ground-staff unions, aviation companies, local municipal corporations, etc.
    c. Environment Management.

The sub-criteria of 3.b (Development capability, commitment, and value add) were as follows:

1. **Development Capability**—Total Points Allocated: 22.4

   a. Master Planning Experience: The EC would award points on the basis of the number of major international airports developed by the airport operator in the past 10 years. Additional points were awarded based on the geographical spread of the airports developed by the operator and if the airports were developed in economic situations similar to those faced in India.
   b. Development Experience: Points would be awarded based on the implementation of the following airport areas:

      i. Terminal Development
      ii. Aeronautical Development
      iii. Cargo Development
      iv. Road and Car Park Development
      v. Property Development, Indian Development Experience

The operators were asked to furnish details of their experience in infrastructure implementation of wide-ranging developments such as the scale of the airport terminals, experience in transitioning airport from single to multiple runway configurations, airport access road development, etc. Points were also awarded to operators based on the past performance of the airport developed—e.g., if commercial operations of airport terminal were successful, then more points were awarded. If the airport operator or the infrastructure company had executed airport developments in the past 10 years, then additional points were awarded.

2. **Development Commitment**—Total Points Allocated: 22.2

   a. Master planning
   b. Major airport development
   c. Indian infrastructure development

Criteria to award points in this category were the number of senior staff experienced in the design and execution of master airport plans, development of airport with multiple runway configurations, and major greenfield airport development. Additional points were awarded for the experience of proposed staff in airport planning of similarly sized airports with similar traffic mix and if the staff had previous experience of airport development in India.

3. **Development Value Add**—Total Points Allocated: 44.4

   a. Long-Term Vision
   b. Development Path
   c. Flexibility
   d. Aeronautical Operations
   e. Development Initiatives

Points in this category were awarded by the EC on the basis of the long-term plan presented by the bidder which would maximize the aeronautical capacity and capability of the airport in the most cost effective manner. Points would also be awarded on the basis of the development path of the airport (e.g., whether Phase II of the infrastructure upgrade would be synchronous with the projected growth in traffic or passengers, cargo, etc.) Points were also allocated on the flexibility plan presented by the bidders which would accommodate changes in the traffic mix and levels. Finally, points were also allocated on the service level goals set by the bidders to increase the efficiency and throughput of airport terminals and runways.

4. **Business Plan**—Total Points Allocated: 11

As stated earlier, it was decided to set the benchmark for the technical pre-qualification at 80%—only those bidders who would meet or exceed the benchmark would qualify for the final phase of the evaluation.

Phase IV was the final round of the RFP where the bidders who successfully cleared the technical evaluation would be selected on the basis of highest share offered to the AAI as a proportion of the gross revenue from the airport.

Bidder Details and Evaluation of Technical Bids

At the start of the bidding process, 10 consortia submitted ITREOIs (Invitation to Register "Expression of Interest") but only nine bidders qualified as one of the consortia had partnered with an airport consultant rather than an airport operator. By the time of the final bid submission date of September 14, 2005, four other consortia also dropped out of the process. Two of these bidders (DLF and Hiranandani) opted out citing that the OMDA document severely restricted the commercial activities which made financing the operation unviable. The other two bidders (Bharti and L&T) dropped out citing stiff conditions and development timelines. The final five bidders for Delhi Airport were as in Table 14.

On September 22, 2005 the technical bids were opened and the EC started the evaluation of the bid documents submitted by the five bidders. On November 21, 2005, the EC submitted their evaluation report and reported that the bids submitted by GMR-Fraport and Reliance-ASA were the only two consortia which passed the qualification threshold of 80%. The actual scores are given in Table 15.

A summary of the EC's evaluation of each of the offers is presented below.

Reliance-ASA: A high-level offer with a strong Indian partner and an experienced airport operator. It is noted that the airport operator has only limited experience outside Mexico, but until recently was responsible for all airports in Mexico (approximately 60 airports). Further, the group has strengthened its capability by taking an approach drawing on a range of highly experienced organizations in the

Table 14 Airport consortia who bid for the Delhi Airport at the RFP stage

	Private entity	Airport operator
1	Reliance Infrastructure	ASA (Mexico)
2	GMR Infrastructure	Fraport (Frankfurt, Germany)
3	DS Construction	Munich (Germany)
4	Sterlite Group	Macquarie-ADP (France)
5	Essel Group	TAV (Turkey)

Table 15 Airport consortia—original evaluation scores (%)

Bidder	Delhi Airport	
	Management capability, commitment and value add	Development capability, commitment and value add
Reliance-ASA	80.2	81.0
GMR-Fraport	84.9	80.1
DS Construction—Munich	72.7	69.9
Sterlite–Macquarie-ADP	57.0	61.9
Essel-TAV	39.2	40.3

areas of airport development, master planning, retail, and freight. The Initial Development Plan (IDP) is of a high standard with no significant areas of weakness.

GMR-Fraport: An excellent overall offer which got an overall high rating across most areas, management, and development, with the major exception of the Initial Development Plan. Highly experienced airport operator and Indian partner and high-quality Business Plan, Transition Plan, and Environmental Management Plan. The international experience of the airport operator in a wide range of environments was a particularly strong factor. The areas of weakness in the whole offer were in respect of Indian retail experience, handling in India of human relations issues in ownership change situations, multiple nominations for management and support positions and the IDP, which is considered unsuitable for implementation in its current form. The multiple management nominations did not reflect a lack of commitment but uncertainty about the timing of the transactions and hence which staff would be committed.

With respect to the IDP, it proposes a totally different development path to that recommended in the Airplan Development Report and to all of the plans submitted by the other bidders. The major concern is in relation to the concept of developing the whole of the midfield area as restricted airside area with no landside access. The scheme relies on high-cost automated systems for passenger and baggage movement.

DS Construction—Munich: A medium level offer with an experienced airport operator and Indian development partner. A significant weakness, which was reflected in relatively low marks in a number of management and development areas, was the lack of experience of airport operator beyond Munich and the lack of major aeronautical development experience. There were also some specific weaknesses in the offer, namely a weak Transition Plan and Environmental Management Plan. The IDP was assessed as medium earning a discount for its high cost and the large impact of developments in Stage 1, heightening risks.

Sterlite–Macquarie-ADP: The offer gives the impression of being put together in haste and has substantial gaps which have reduced the score significantly. Throughout the assessment, the score has been marked down owing to the failure to provide the required information. In addition, the Indian partner has limited relevant experience for an airport project. Further, the Indian partner utilized an SPV for its participation in the offer, meaning the Sterlite group's experience could not be considered in the evaluation. Compounding these problems is the limited information on the persons committed to management and support roles in the JVC. The IDP is feasible but is relatively aggressive in deferring developments into the future, resulting in low levels of service in the initial development stages and creates a risk that there could be capacity problems.

Essel-TAV: Overall the offer was of poor quality suffering from the combination of an airport operator with limited experience focused on operating terminals rather than airports and an Indian party with no direct relevant commercial experience and expertise. This lack of experience was reflected in low marks for operating an airport, aeronautical operations, airport development experience other than terminal development, and master planning. These problems were compounded by a failure to provide quality documents in such areas as the transition plan, stakeholder management strategy and the Business Plan. In terms of management commitment, the group relied on consultants, which is quite unsatisfactory. Both the development capability and commitment were assessed as low. The IDP was assessed as medium.

On September 19, 2005, the IMG formally set up the Government Review Committee (GRC). The GRC would conduct an independent review of evaluation undertaken by the EC. EC's evaluation report was sent to the GRC for review on November 24, 2005. The GRC made the following observations:

1. The overall approach applied is transparent and equitable across all offers that were evaluated. No bias or prejudice was observed for or against any bidder.
2. Majority of the evaluation criteria in Phase III required subjective marking and the basis on which points were awarded in this section of the RFP was not completely clear.
3. Scoring was done based on the basis of consensus rather than average of individual scores given by each member of the EC.
4. At some places, the EC had gone beyond the scope of the RFP and had not allotted points in accordance with the RFP guidelines.

The representative of the Planning Commission raised further issues with the evaluation process. A possibility of bias was raised since the financial consultant (ABN AMRO) had GMR and Reliance as major clients. Furthermore, the legal consultant (AMSS) had Reliance as a major client. Both the Financial and Legal Consultants clarified that no conflict of interest existed in terms of their assignment and as organizations they have different divisions and each division has independent business dealings with their clients. The consultants also clarified that conflict of interest has to be considered on a transaction basis and with reference to the persons on the specific project. It was mentioned that adequate internal controls/checks were in place to ensure that no conflict of interest exists.

PC also pointed out inconsistencies in the allocation of points for the airport operator. PC noted that Reliance's partner—ASA (chief operator of Mexico City Airport) was allocated three points more than DS Construction's partner—Munich

Airport (chief operator of Munich Airport). This was despite the fact that the Mexico airport ranked 119 while Munich Airport ranked 4 in international rankings.

Further issues were raised on other evaluation parameters. For instance, Reliance-ASA was awarded 2.19 points for absorbing 40% of AAI employees by the end of the third year while DS Construction—Munich was awarded 2.97 points for absorbing 95.4% of AAI employees. It was felt that DS Construction should have been awarded more than just 0.78 points extra for the absorption of more than 5,000 AAI employees. Some other parameters such as "Experience with major property development" and "Experience with major infrastructure development" were clubbed into a single parameter without assigning any weights to them. When the EC was asked to split them, the weight assignment was 0.25 and 0.75, respectively. If these weights were changed to 0.5 each, then Reliance-ASA would have scored less than 80 points and be disqualified for the next round of evaluation.

The IMG met on December 2, 2005 to discuss the issues raised on the EC's evaluation and the GRC report but was unable to reach consensus on all the issues. On December 5, MoCA decided to have all the technical bids reevaluated based on the comments in the GRC and IMG review and found the evaluation approach taken by Airplan to be "biased." IMG was instructed to finalize their recommendations in two weeks time and the EC was told to adhere strictly to the RFP document during the reevaluation exercise. The EC revised their evaluation and submitted them to the IMG and EGoM on December 14, 2005. Their revised evaluations are given below (Table 16).

The IMG met on December 14 and 16 to consider the revised evaluation. Both the Chairman and Finance Head of AAI felt that marks awarded to Reliance-ASA were high and were not comfortable with the level of subjectivity in the evaluation. At the end of the meeting, the following suggestions came forth from the participants:

Table 16 Airport consortia—revised evaluation scores

Bidder	Delhi Airport	
	Management capability, commitment and value add	Development capability, commitment and value add
Reliance-ASA	80.9 (0.7↑)	81.0 (NC)
GMR-Fraport	84.7 (0.2↓)	80.1 (NC)
DS Construction —Munich	73.1 (0.4↑)	70.5 (0.6↑)
Sterlite–Macquarie-ADP	57.0 (NC)	61.9 (NC)
Essel-TAV	37.6 (1.6↓)	41.4 (1.1↑)

NC No change; Figure in brackets is the change from the original evaluation

1. The AAI representatives suggested that fresh bids be called from all the pre-qualified bidders to affirm transparency and competitiveness in the entire bidding process.
2. The financial advisor of MoCA was of the opinion that the evaluation points awarded by the EC ought to be rejected and called for a fresh evaluation to be conducted by an independent technical committee. The representative of the Planning Commission also called for a fresh evaluation of the bids to be undertaken by AAI.
3. The representatives from Ministry of Law and Justice and Department of Economic Affairs (Ministry of Finance) endorsed the revised evaluation.

On December 21, the EGoM reviewed the results of the IMG meeting and decided to set up a Committee of Secretaries (CoS) to help prepare the final recommendations on the bidding process. The CoS, in turn, constituted the Group of Eminent Technical Experts (GETE) which would examine the evaluation process. The GETE was headed by Mr. E. Sreedharan (MD of Delhi Metro), and a respected technocrat with high credibility. The GETE was tasked with the following:

1. Validation of the evaluation exercise, including calibration of the qualifying cutoff, and carry out a sensitivity analysis to analyze the impact of interlinked sub-criteria on scoring.
2. Assess the transparency and fairness of the overall evaluation process and suggest steps (if required) to achieve a transparent and fair outcome.
3. Address issues raised by the IMG and MoCA about the evaluation process.
4. Provide suggestions for improving the selection procedure for JV partners in future.

Over the course of the first week of January 2006, GETE met many times where several issues were discussed. The members of the GETE did not request for the technical bid papers or attempt to perform a fresh evaluation of the documents but instead focused on the weights and marks allocated by the EC during the evaluation process. During their meetings, the following points emerged:

1. The evaluation process was found to have technical flaws. For instance, the EC had not based the evaluation just on the bid documents submitted by the consortia. They had used externally published material and statistics to facilitate the evaluation process. This was in violation of the RFP process.
2. Certain sub-factors within the RFP did not have explicit weights attached to them and it was unclear how the EC had allocated points across the sub-factors. The GETE corrected this by allocating equal weights to each of these criteria which subsequently reduced the scores of some of the bidders.
3. The following discrepancies were found in the case of Reliance-ASA with regard to the allocation of points:

    a. ASA (operator of the Mexico City airport) had 37% of its revenues originating from non-aeronautical services. As per the RFP, the assessment of the commercial operations of the airport operator was to be done on the airports

Table 17 Airport consortia—GETE scores

Bidder	Delhi Airport	
	Mgmt. capability (Pre-GETE)	Mgmt. capability (Post-GETE)
Reliance-ASA	80.9	74.8
GMR-Fraport	84.7	81.7
DS Constr.—Munich	73.1	73.3
Sterlite–Macquarie-ADP	57.0	53.5
Essel-TAV	37.6	40.4

having non-aeronautical revenue of more than 40%. Since ASA did not satisfy this criterion, it was unclear why the EC had awarded ASA a score of 75%. GETE reduced this score to 50%.

b. The RFP stated that additional points would be awarded to airport operators who operated airports in non-OECD countries and had increased the efficiency of those airports. ASA was based out of Mexico which is an OECD country and thus should not have received points in this subcategory. Yet, the EC had awarded ASA a score of 75%. GETE nullified this score.
c. The RFP had a sub-factor pertaining to the absorption of AAI staff into the JV. As per the requirements, at least 40% of the AAI staff must be absorbed by the end of Year 3. Additional points would be allocated for higher absorption. The EC had awarded a 50% score to all bidders who met the 40% absorption criterion and the remaining 50% on a pro-rata basis. The GETE felt that since 40% was the minimum absorption, zero points ought to be allocated for meeting the bare minimum requirement and the 100% should be pro-rated. This resulted in a reduction of 1.9 points for the Reliance-ASA consortium.
d. In the criteria "Development Capability and Value Add," GETE felt that very liberal point allocation was done for Reliance-ASA. At the same time, GMR-Fraport scored much lower despite Frankfurt airport being a major cargo hub in Europe and Fraport as the airport operator clearly having better credentials and superior experience in airport development.
e. In its final analysis, GETE was of the opinion that the Reliance-ASA bid failed to qualify for Delhi airport. While it had previously crossed the 80% threshold, it now fell short by more than five points.

The final scores submitted by the GETE to the CoS are given in Table 17.
The final recommendations by GETE were as follows:

1. There was no need to scrap the current process or invite fresh bids.
2. The GMR financial bid for Delhi airport ought to be opened and GMR-Fraport should be invited to set up the JV.
3. The second airport could be modernized in the next round of privatizations.

Final Decision by EGoM

On January 24, 2006, the EGoM met to review the report submitted by the GETE and finalized its decision. The final decisions by the EGoM were as follows:

1. The financial bids for the top four technical bidders would be opened on January 31.
2. Since GMR-Fraport was the only technically qualified bidder for both Delhi and Mumbai airports, it would be free to select the airport provided it could match the highest financial bid.
3. The EGoM changed the rules for privatizing the second airport. The remaining airport (not chosen by the GMR-Fraport consortium) would be awarded to the highest financial bidder amongst the remaining bidders. Since the Government cannot afford to spend further time in a fresh bidding process, the Government decided to decrease the technical cutoff marks to 50% for this airport.

The financial bids for the bidders are given below (Table 18).

These decisions were announced by AAI and MoCA on January 31 and the final result was as follows: GMR-Fraport matched the highest revenue-share offered by Reliance-ASA for Delhi Airport and chose to form the JV for the Delhi Airport. The members of the GMR-Fraport consortium were: (i) GMR Infrastructure Ltd; (ii) GMR Energy Ltd; (iii) Fraport AG Frankfurt Airport Services Worldwide; (iv) Malaysia Airports (Mauritius) Private Limited; (v) GVL Investments Pvt Ltd; and (vi) India Development Fund.

AAI signed an Operation, Management and Development Agreement (OMDA) with DIAL on April 4, 2006, as a state promoter. On May 3, 2006, it handed over IGI Airport, Delhi to DIAL on "as is where is" basis and granted DIAL the exclusive right to undertake the functions of its operations, maintenance, development, design, construction, modernization, finance and management.

Reliance-ASA was not satisfied with the decision taken by the EGoM and AAI and decided to challenge it in the Delhi High Court. When the petition was dismissed by the High Court, an appeal was filed at the Supreme Court but that petition was also dismissed on November 7, 2006.

Summary and Conclusions

It is evident that while the entire PPP process was reasonably detailed with a lot of thought put into the creation of the transaction documents and RFP, it became clear during the evaluation process that the process could have been designed better to ensure that it remained transparent and objective to all stakeholders. However, it should be kept in mind that privatization of this nature and on this scale had never

Table 18 Airport consortia—Financial Bids (revenue share that the bidder is willing to offer to AAI in percentage terms)

Bidder	Delhi Airport
Reliance-ASA	45.99
GMR-Fraport	43.64
DS Construction—Munich	40.15
Sterlite–Macquarie-ADP	Bid not opened
Essel-TAV	Bid not opened

been done by the Government of India earlier and some of these issues arose because of relative inexperience.

Some of the shortcomings evident in the process are detailed below:

1. The RFP and its sub-criteria were not designed keeping the goal of objectivity in mind. Since several of the criteria could not be quantified, subjectivity in the assignment of scores eventually crept into the process creating uncertainty for both evaluators and the bidders.
2. Weights for sub-factors were not made explicit at the outset of the RFP. This further increased the subjectivity in the process which eventually led to some committees being labeled as "biased."
3. The creation of additional committees (CoS and GETE) at the end of the bidding process was also reflective of the shortcomings of the process since in the ideal scenario, they should not have been required.
4. While the RFP had set the criteria for qualification and prescribed minimum scores, it had not envisaged a situation in which just one (or none) qualified. Since, by the end of the process only GMR-Fraport qualified, EGoM had to step in and use its discretionary power to change the rules (which was later criticized by one of the bidders).

However, at the end, thanks to this PPP process, India achieved one of the most significant infrastructure milestones in its history. While the process was criticized by several parties, the experience was invaluable for the government in learning how to structure a huge PPP contract in a fair and equitable manner. The timeline of the PPP process is at Appendix 5.

4.3 Issues Raised by the Comptroller and Auditor General (CAG) Report

Introduction

In 2012, the CAG of India conducted a performance audit of the company and released the findings in a report, "*Report of the Comptroller and Auditor General of India for the year ended March* 2012 *on Implementation of Public Private Partnership–Indira Gandhi International Airport, Delhi*" (Report). The main objectives of the performance audit were to assess whether:

- Important decisions like deciding on the concession period, granting right of first refusal, setting upfront fee, and the leasing of land for commercial purposes, reflected public interest and equity;
- Development of the airport complied with the Master Plan including the debt funding of the project and whether the levy of development fee was in line with the agreement;

- Whether the transaction documents like the Operation, Management and Development Agreement (OMDA), and the State Support Agreement (SSA) were properly structured to support the PPP project and adequate due diligence was carried out to safeguard the public interest;
- Receipt of the revenue share of 45.99% to Airport Authority of India was as per OMDA including share of gross revenues from the outsourced services.

The Report pointed out certain, what it perceived as, irregularities that unduly favored the concessionaire, the Delhi International Airport Limited, in the process that was followed by the Ministry of Civil Aviation. The Report, however, goes on to add “The decision to enter into a joint venture to develop and manage Indira Gandhi International Airport is a first of its kind. The present audit report thus should be viewed in terms of lessons learnt for future guidance.” The MoCA and the winning bidder, the GMR Group (GMR) rebutted the findings of the Report by submitting detailed comments on the findings of the Report (Comments).

Before we go through the main findings of the Report, and the Comments made by the winning bidder, GMR (including the response to the Public Accounts Committee of the Parliament), the 17 sets of issues covered in the Report are stated in Table 19 with the first 10 of them (the more substantial ones) detailed in this case study.

4.3.1 Conflicts Between OMDA and the Airports Economic Regulatory Authority Act, 2008 (AERA Act) in Defining Aeronautical and Non-aeronautical Services

The Report points out that certain services (like cargo handling, ground handling, parking, etc.) that are defined as “Non-aeronautical” in the OMDA are defined as “Aeronautical” in the AERA Act. This, the Report argues, excludes revenues generated from profitable services like cargo handling and ground handling from being fully accounted for, for the purposes of tariff fixation for aeronautical services at the airport (as per the SSA, the Targeted Revenue for tariff fixation considered only 30% of the non-aeronautical revenue) and therefore gives an undue advantage to DIAL.

The Comments rebutted the argument advanced in the Report by pointing out that the OMDA was executed in 2006 and the AERA Act came into force in 2009. The draft of the OMDA was part of the bidding process (and as such, all the bidders had the opportunity to bid based on the classification of aeronautical and non-aeronautical services and any winning bidder would get the benefit of the same classification). Accordingly, the MoCA said it was “absurd” to suggest that the provision was made to give undue benefit to DIAL. Regarding the issue as to Hybrid Till method of tariff fixation adopted at the IGIA, the Comments point out that this method permits moderate cross subsidy for aeronautical tariffs and also incentivizes development of non-aeronautical activities and the consequent availability of funds with DIAL for further development of the airport.

Table 19 Issues highlighted in the CAG Report

Sr. no.	Issues highlighted in the CAG report	
1	Conflict between the OMDA and the AERA Act, 2008 in defining aeronautical and non-aeronautical services	Discussed in this case study
2	The length of the Concession Period	
3	Right of First Refusal to DIAL for any proposed airport within 150 km of the IGIA	
4	(Alleged) Misuse of the Concept of the Upfront Fee	
5	Issues in connection with commercial exploitation of the land	
6	Issues in connection with Airport Development Fee charged by DIAL to the embarking passengers	
7	Issues in connection with DIAL's financing of the Project	
8	Issues concerning incentives conferred upon DIAL despite delay in execution of Mandatory Capital Projects	
9	Issues concerning outsourcing of Non-Aero Services through Joint Ventures	
10	Funds Diverted from the Passenger Service Fee account	
11	The Divergence between Original Project Cost and Actual Project Cost	Not discussed in this case study
12	Deficient Land Records at the IGIA	
13	Change in the Major Development Plan and increase in Ground Floor Area	
14	Highly Concessional Lease Rent	
15	Sharing of Revenues from Existing Leases with DIAL	
16	Delayed Payment of Retirement Compensation by DIAL	
17	Irregular Withdrawal from the Escrow Account	

GMR further added that the AERA Act recognizes the Concession Agreement executed before its formation and that the Act provides that the Concession Agreement in connection with IGIA would be taken into consideration by the AERA for the purpose of economic regulation.

4.3.2 Concession Period

The Report pointed out that DIAL enjoys the unilateral right to extend the concession period for another 30 years "on identical terms and conditions," provided no Joint Venture Company (JVC) event of default had taken place during the 20th and 25th year of the first concession period.[91] The Report argues that this provision entitles DIAL to extend "unilaterally" the period of Concession for another 30 years and that this is in "violation" of the Cabinet Note that specified that the

[91]Clause 18.1 (b) of OMDA.

Concession period could be extended "subject to mutual agreement and negotiation of terms." The Report infers that this "call option is an unfair advantage given to DIAL which is detrimental to government interest as it does not provide the government any scope for review of any of the conditions in OMDA and the SSA."

The Comments responded to this charge of the Report by stating that the EGoM was empowered to determine the terms and conditions of the Concession and the transaction structure. It enumerated examples in international context, where the Concession extended to more than 30 years and up to 60 years. GMR further added that the long concession period was provided in the OMDA to, *inter alia*, attract investments in a capital intensive sector and enhance government revenue over a longer period. Since the right to extend was part of the OMDA, it was a right available to any bidder that was selected, and therefore cannot be said to confer any undue advantage on DIAL. GMR also gave examples of other airport concessions in Hyderabad and Bangalore that followed the 30 + 30 model implemented at IGIA.

4.3.3 Right of First Refusal in Case of Second Airport

The Report found that the SSA accords a Right of First Refusal (RoFR) to DIAL for a period of 30 years in the event any other airport is planned within 150 km radius of the IGIA, provided its bid is within 10% of the winning bidder for the other airport. The Report opined that the RoFR should have relied on certain triggers like saturation point of existing airport, traffic census, rate of return on capital and expected breakeven period to arrive at a time period for which the RoFR would operate and not doing so, amounted to an unfair advantage for DIAL. Furthermore, a RoFR would inhibit the bidders for the other airport and provides DIAL an advantage over the other airport as well.

The Comments rebut the findings of the Report by pointing out that the RoFR was in line with global best practices and that it was by no means unfettered in that it would only be available to DIAL in the event its bid is within 10% of the winning bid for the other airport. In other words, in the event DIAL was also inclined to be the contractor for the other airport, it would be constrained to bid competitively and in line with other bidders at least to stand a chance of securing the same. Thus, in fact, the RoFR would promote aggressive bidding (and therefore promote competition) for the other airport. GMR pointed out that pursuant to the Policy on Airport Infrastructure (1997), "a new Greenfield airport could only be allowed within an aerial distance of 150 km of an existing civilian airport where an existing airport was unable to meet the projected requirements of traffic."

4.3.4 Upfront Fee Issue

The Report found that a one-time upfront fee of Rs. 150 crore was fixed for the Delhi Airport by MoCA. Upon an enquiry from the CAG, the MoCA explained that the amount of the upfront fee has no relation to either the extent of land or the assets of the airport. However, the CAG found that when DIAL sought the lease of an additional 190.19 acres of land, to fix a lease rent for this land, AAI used the amount of upfront fee to arrive at a rate per acre and applied it to the additional land thereby fixing a one-time fee of Rs 6.19 crore [(Rs. 150 crore/4608.9 acres) * 190.19 acres]. On the other hand, AAI leased out 7.60 acres of land to Director General of Civil Aviation and Bureau of Civil Aviation Security at a license fee of Rs. 2.41 crore per annum. Application of this license fee with the same escalation clause for 190.19 acres of land would amount to Rs. 4,534 crore for a period of 27 years. The Report claimed that AAI Board decided to lease out the required land for Rs. 6.19 crore (arrived at on the basis of upfront fee), without entering into good faith negotiations with DIAL, which the Report claimed could have fetched higher rentals for the additional leased out land.

The Comments pointed out that the use of upfront fee as a benchmark for this additional lease in fact fetched far more than would be received if the AAI and the MoCA were to rely on pro-rata calculation based on the original lease as benchmark.

GMR's response to the MoCA, rebutting the Report was that the CAG is mistaken in its view about the parcel of land that was leased out in this case. It pointed out that the land parcel leased was part of the Excluded Premises as defined in OMDA and relied on Clause 2.6.1 of the OMDA to point out that it was clearly provided that should the DIAL require the land within the definition of Excluded Premises for providing aeronautical services during the term, the parties shall enter into a lease respecting the said land; thus, there was no obligation to negotiate the lease terms unless the land parcel was included in "Carved out Assets," as defined in the OMDA. It further pointed out that the need to lease out additional land arose because the AAI wanted to retain its operational office that was located on the "Demised Premises" adjoining NH8 whereas the land around the office was earmarked for a runway as per the Initial Development Plan. Hence, as per the decision taken in the meeting held at MoCA on April 28, 2008, AAI leased 77 hectares of land from Excluded Premises, to DIAL as Additional Demised Premises, only for Aeronautical purposes. A fair way to finalize this supplementary lease deed was to lean back on to the existing terms of OMDA and Concession Agreement. Therefore, a pro-rata computation was used to arrive at the calculation of Rs. 6.19 crore.

4.3.5 Commercial Exploitation of Land

The Report pointed out that under the terms of OMDA, DIAL was allowed to utilize 5% of the total demised premises for commercial purposes, i.e., 239.95 acres. The Report alleged that the potential earning capacity of the land is Rs. 681.63 crore per acre and the current value of the land is Rs. 100 crore per acre. Thus for the total area of 239.95 acres, the possible earning from the land, according to DIAL's calculations, amounts to Rs. 163,557 crore while DIAL is permitted to use the land for commercial purposes only for Rs. 100 per year.

The Comments pointed out that a fraction of the leased land was made available for commercial exploitation in accordance with the Policy on Airport Infrastructure (1997) that identifies increasing revenues from the non-aeronautical assets as one of the major thrust areas. The Comments rebutted the figure of Rs. 681.63 crore per acre arrived at by the CAG by pointing out that the CAG has added the receivables from lease rentals to DIAL for the next 60 years without accounting for the time value of these cash flows. Accounted appropriately, DIAL would receive Rs. 27.22 crore per acre in present value terms (discounting the cash flows at 12% per annum) and adding the Rs. 32.64 crore security deposit to the same, the earning value of the commercially exploitable land would be Rs. 59.86 crore per acre. Finally, the MoCA pointed out that since the AAI held equity in DIAL and also had a revenue-share arrangement with DIAL, about 46% of the revenues of DIAL would be earned by AAI. GMR further added that the land leased out to DIAL was leased on a token rent of Rs. 100 per year because the concession pertained to the operation, development and modernization of airport assets and the lease of the land was merely incidental. The commercial value of the land was sought to be captured not through rent but the gross revenue share that the bidders were willing to provide the public partner. And thus, no undue benefit was extended to DIAL on account of commercial exploitation of land.

4.3.6 Development Fees

The OMDA specifically provided that DIAL shall arrange for financing through suitable debt and equity contributions for its obligations including the development phase of the airport. The CAG, however, found that DIAL had in fact financed approximately 27% of the development through Development Fees (DF), levied on passengers since 2009 when the MoCA approved the levy by DIAL. The Report inferred that since the levy of DF as a source of funds was only made available to DIAL, post the award of the contract (and it was not known to other bidders), the same was extension of undue benefit to DIAL in violation of the OMDA. DF enriched DIAL by Rs. 34.15 billion at the expense of the passengers.

GMR responded by pointing out that the levy of DF became necessary because AAI was unable to infuse further equity. On the other hand, provisions mandating shareholding thresholds in the OMDA prevented the private shareholders from infusing capital, since AAI would be diluted beyond its prescribed limits if the private shareholders of DIAL brought in equity capital in lieu of AAI. It further contended that since the DF is a statutory levy pursuant to Section 22 A of the Airports Authority of India Act, the contention that all the bidders were not given the opportunity to price in DF in their bids does not hold, since all the bidders should be deemed to know the law. In sum, therefore, the levy of DF cannot be said to be an extension of undue benefit to DIAL.

4.3.7 DIAL's Financing of the Project

The Report observed that out of the total capital expenditure of Rs. 12,502 crore as accepted by AERA (see Table 20), only 19% has been promoters' contribution whereas the Development Fee levied by DIAL underwrote 27% of the cost of development. Thus, the Report inferred that with an equity contribution of Rs. 24.50 billion out of which the private consortium's share was Rs. 18.13 billion, DIAL obtained a brownfield airport for 60 years in addition to commercial rights on land valued at Rs. 240 billion with an earning potential, estimated by DIAL, at Rs. 1,635.57 billion.

The Comments pointed out that contrary to the "sensationalist" allegation made in the Report (that DIAL secured the airport for 30 + 30 years in addition to the commercial rights to the land valued at Rs. 240 billion), the project has led to a creation of an asset that will yield Rs. 3–4 trillion to AAI over the balance 30 + 30 years, in addition to the receipt of all the transferable assets at the end of the concession period. Moreover, AAI controlled DIAL through its 26% equity participation in DIAL. The Comments concluded that the Report seems to have been written without any understanding of the PPP model.

GMR responded by pointing out that other than the contribution by promoters by means of equity, a part of the debt of DIAL has been backed by GMR Group through various instruments. All private promoters of DIAL have pledged 51% of their shares in DIAL as security for senior debt, while AAI has not pledged any of its shares and GMR Group has covered for AAI by pledging additional portion of its shareholding in this regard. In addition, the DF was levied in lieu of the equity contribution of AAI that AAI could not infuse and which the restrictions on shareholding in the OMDA made it impossible for the other promoters to bring in.

Table 20 Total project cost for Delhi Airport as allowed by AERA

Particulars	Rs. in crores	
Final project costs as submitted in DIAL application (Appendix 1)		12857.00
Items proposed to be excluded		
Apron	23.82	
R/W 10–28	37.50	
Escalation for reinforcement	35.67	
Upfront fee	150.00	
Gross floor area 8652 m^2 (proposed to be excluded by EIL)	107.15	
Total exclusions (B)		354.14
Total allowable project cost (A–B)		12502.86

Source AERA Order No. 30/2012–13 in the matter of Review of levy of Development Fee at Indira Gandhi International Airport, New Delhi passed on December 28, 2012, viewed on May 14, 2013 (http://aera.gov.in/writereaddata/order/281.pdf)

4.3.8 Mandatory Capital Projects

The Report stated that out of 15 Mandatory Capital Projects (MCPs) to be completed by 3 April 2008, 11 MCPs were delayed by anywhere between 87–236 days. As per the SSA, this delay should have prevented any incentives for DIAL. But instead, MoCA approved 10% increase in the aeronautical charges like landing, parking, passenger service fee, X-ray baggage and housing charges to incentivize DIAL. This was judged to be in contravention of the SSA and was an undue favor to DIAL.

The Comments respond to the allegations that MoCA increased the aeronautical charges by 10% despite the delay in completion of MCPs, by pointing out that the AAI had examined the matter in detail and that the MCPs were delayed since the works required coordination with several external agencies such as airlines, security, immigration, customs, etc. In other words, the delay in the completion of the MCPs was on account of circumstances beyond the control of DIAL. The Comments also point out that the AAI also took into consideration, comments made by the Independent Engineer in this regard and gave a one-time waiver without penalty to DIAL acting under Clause 20.3.1 of the OMDA.

GMR pointed out that the specific reasons for the delay in completing the MCPs were, *inter alia*, (i) 4 month delay in getting approvals from security agencies like Research and Analysis Wing (RAW), Intelligence Bureau (IB) and the Special Protection Group (SPG) for the relocation of VVIP areas, (ii) the "as built drawings" for underground utilities were not available with the AAI which resulted in considerable delays in their relocation and, finally, (iii) the vacation of the areas under use by the (erstwhile) Indian Airlines was significantly delayed despite the numerous verbal and written follow-up with their officers. As per SSA, DIAL would receive an incentive in the form of 10% increase in Base Airport Charges from 3 May 2008 in the event DIAL completed the MCPs required to be completed within 2 years from the Effective Date (as defined in the OMDA, i.e., 3 May 2006). However, due to the delay for the above reasons which were beyond the control of DIAL, and only on completion of all these 11 MCPs did the MoCA allow the increase of aeronautical charges with effect from February 16, 2009.

4.3.9 Joint Ventures in Non-aeronautical Services

The Report observed that DIAL has "outsourced" most of the non-aeronautical services through the joint venture (JV) route to other service providers. The revenue share of DIAL in these JVs ranged from 10 through 61% and the equity participation ranged from 26 to 50%. The Report alleged that the independent auditor appointed by DIAL pursuant to OMDA had no access to the books of accounts of the JVs with the result that the revenue-share payable to DIAL could not be independently ascertained by the CAG. Finally, the Report alleged that the three JVs dealing with car parking and cargo operationalized during the period 2009–2010 had led to reduction of revenues payable to AAI during that period because the business was transferred to the JVs. Thus, it alleged that the formation of JVs contributed to the dilution of revenues payable to the AAI.

GMR responded by pointing out that the outsourcing of non-aeronautical services is an international best practice as these are specialized functions. GMR further points out that the query about the treatment of revenue from the outsourced services came up at the pre-bid stage and it was clarified that the revenue shared in the 'regulated till' from the Revenue Share Assets will be 30% of the revenue accruing to the JVC from such assets. Thus, in case of a contract given to a third party for a duty free shop, 30% of the revenue accruing to the JVC (now, DIAL) shall be shared in the 'regulated till' and not the 30% of the revenue from the duty free shop.

Based on the above response, GMR claimed that the revenues from the outsourced services will mean the revenues that DIAL receives from the Concessionaires (and not the revenues of the Concessionaire) and as agreed, 45.99% of these revenues of DIAL were transferred to AAI. GMR pointed out that the CAGR of the revenue share of AAI is 25% since FY 2007 through FY 2012 and the CAGR of non-aeronautical revenues of DIAL is 21% due to adoption of the JV strategy.

The MoCA in its response relied on the opinion it sought from the Ministry of Law and Justice (Law Ministry). Law Ministry had opined that Article 11.1.2 of the OMDA imposes an obligation to pay 45.99% of the projected overall revenue generated by DIAL to AAI for the said year. It does not say anything about the share in the revenue created by the sub-contractors. Regarding the query about the JV model, the Law Ministry opined that formation of a JV and assigning it responsibilities is permissible so long as DIAL remains principally responsible to AAI and undertakes to indemnify AAI pursuant to Clause 8.5.7 of the OMDA. It pointed out that even before the privatization, the AAI relied on outsourcing the non-aeronautical services and the OMDA merely continues that trend by enabling DIAL to sub-contract to third parties certain airport services pursuant to Clause 2.1.2 (iv) and Clause 8.5.7 (i) (a) of the OMDA. The MoCA pointed out that the decision to adopt the JV model was a deliberate act relying on inputs from a sub-committee of the board of DIAL (that had representatives of AAI) and opinion of an ex-Supreme Court judge. The MoCA also pointed out that the independent auditors appointed by the AAI to audit DIAL also verify the revenues accruing to DIAL from the JVs. Finally, it pointed out that, the aggregate revenues to DIAL from the outsourced activities have increased from Rs. 0.46 billion in 2009–2010 to Rs. 4.04 billion in 2011–2012, thus benefitting AAI as well in the process.

4.3.10 Funds Diverted from the PSF (Security Component) Escrow Account for Purchase of Security Equipment by DIAL

Under the terms of the SSA, all the security systems were to be procured by DIAL at its own cost. The Report alleged that the MoCA permitted DIAL to utilize the security component of the passenger service fee to purchase all the security equipment since 2010. According to the Report, this led to a loss of Rs. 2.40 billion to the government and extension of undue favor to DIAL.

The Comments rebutted the allegation in the Report by pointing out that the MoCA determined that a change in the security scenario had occurred and the same necessitated upgradation of the existing security apparatus at the airports including installing highly capital intensive new security equipment (such as the Perimeter Intrusion Detection System). The permission to avail the security component of the passenger service fee was therefore given for all the airports. GMR pointed out that the MoCA notified an Order on April 16, 2010 pursuant to which it directed that expenditure related to security could be met out of PSF (SC); so, the concession was by no means only for DIAL, rather it was extended to all the airport operators. It further pointed out that since the expenses for upgrading the security were charged to the passenger security fee, the capital expenditure towards upgrading the security was not factored in at the time of calculating the tariff increase. Thus, there is no undue benefit to DIAL pursuant to the change in policy of the MoCA.

5 In Conclusion

The VfM analysis and the three detailed case studies cutting across infrastructure sectors in India provide a glimpse of the set of complex issues that can arise in real-life implementation of infrastructure PPP projects in a country with political system and maturity as that of India. They illustrate several concepts discussed in the first part of this volume but also point out that the complexity of large PPP projects can extend well beyond the topics discussed in this volume. In that sense they extend rather than simply support the discussion and analysis in the rest of the volume.

The experience with infrastructure PPPs around the world and particularly in an emerging market environment like India's has significantly enhanced our understanding of project management, risk management, politics and economics and how all these concepts and many more interact and integrate with one another. The projects remain complex, risky and often contentious but not without merit. A cautious and scientific approach to infrastructure PPPs armed with the theoretical and empirical understanding can significantly apprehend and mitigate risks and costs and save on precious public resources as well as provide a smoother experience for the private party.

Appendix 1: Total Project Cost of DIAL (Rs. crore)

Project cost (T1, T2, and T3)	Project cost as per approved master development plan	Project cost at the time of financial closure	Final project cost as per DIAL
Airfield (Runway, Taxiways, etc.)	368.80	1,765	2,634
Apron	252.50		
Passenger Terminals (including City side access roads, bridges, etc.)	4,098.40	4,669	6,836
Cargo Terminals	22	Nil	Nil
Airport Service Building and Airport Connection Building	Nil	Nil	160
General Aviation Terminal	130	762	754
Rebuilding of Terminal 1B and Revamping Arrival Terminal	340		
Revamping of Terminal 2	105		
Total Hard Costs	**5,316.70**	**7,196**	**10,384**
Preliminaries and Other Overheads	244	1,279	1,320
Funding Costs (IDC and Lenders Fee)	534		
Contingency	512		
Upfront Fee paid to AAI	150	150	150
Metro	Nil	350	350
Rehabilitation of Runway 10–28	Nil	Nil	110
Delhi Jal Board Infrastructure Funding	Nil	Nil	54
New ATC Tower with Equipment	Nil	Nil	350
Security Capex	Nil	Nil	139
Total Project Cost	**6,756.70**	**8,975**	**12,857**

Note The Total Project Cost (TPC) estimated at the time of bid was Rs. 3,297 crore for Delhi Airport

Source Engineers India Limited. *Final Report for Technical Audit of DIAL's Final Project Cost Estimates*

Appendix 2: Consolidated Financials for DIAL from FY2011 to 2013

Unless otherwise specified, all monetary values are in Rs. crore

	31/03/2013	31/03/2012	31/03/2011
Balance sheet [Abstract]			
Equity and liabilities [Abstract]			
Shareholders' funds [Abstract]			
Share capital	2,450.00	2,450.00	2,450.00
Reserves and surplus	−1,380.69	−1,453.21	−367.81
Total shareholders' funds	1,069.31	996.79	2,082.19
Share application money pending allotment	0.00	0.00	0.00
Non-current liabilities [Abstract]			
Long-term borrowings	6,047.92	5,740.94	5,229.90
Other long-term liabilities	2,149.30	2,183.21	2,409.43
Long-term provisions	89.55	108.57	118.48
Total non-current liabilities	**8,286.77**	**8,032.72**	**7,757.81**
Current liabilities [Abstract]			
Short-term borrowings	0.00	856.50	600.00
Trade payables	472.33	233.35	182.53
Other current liabilities	2,087.75	2,134.43	1,896.95
Short-term provisions	39.22	35.79	23.29
Total current liabilities	**2,599.30**	**3,260.07**	**2,702.77**
Total equity and liabilities	**11,955.38**	**12,289.58**	**12,542.77**
Assets [Abstract]			
Non-current assets [Abstract]			
Fixed assets [Abstract]			
Tangible assets	8,913.60	9,078.93	9,836.80
Intangible assets	461.90	473.07	448.48
Tangible assets capital work-in-progress	47.74	124.33	86.79
Total fixed assets	9,423.24	9,676.33	10,372.07
Non-current investments	182.59	177.86	155.45
Long-term loans and advances	97.59	128.99	197.62
Other non-current assets	892.20	717.67	16.83
Total non-current assets	**10,595.71**	**10,700.85**	**10,741.97**
Current assets [Abstract]			
Current investments	109.00	52.61	145.65
Inventories	9.59	9.47	2.72
Trade receivables	524.80	245.43	125.21
Cash and bank balances	241.28	309.44	290.10
Short-term loans and advances	71.88	89.62	316.37

(continued)

(continued)

	31/03/2013	31/03/2012	31/03/2011
Balance sheet [Abstract]			
Other current assets	403.12	882.16	920.75
Total current assets	**1,359.67**	**1,588.73**	**1,800.80**
Total assets	**11,955.38**	**12,289.58**	**12,542.77**

Unless otherwise specified, all monetary values are in Rs. crore

	01/04/2012 to 31/03/2013	01/04/2011 to 31/03/2012	01/04/2010 to 31/03/2011
Statement of Profit and Loss [Abstract]			
Disclosure of revenue from operations [Abstract]			
Disclosure of revenue from operations for other than finance company [Abstract]			
Revenue from sale of products	0.00	0.00	0.00
Revenue from sale of services	3155.91	1409.17	1164.10
Other operating revenues	88.12	83.46	79.05
Total revenue from operations other than finance company	3244.03	1492.63	1243.15
Total revenue from operations	3244.03	1492.63	1243.15
Other income	80.85	38.32	18.52
Total revenue	**3324.88**	**1530.95**	**1261.67**
Expenses [Abstract]			
Cost of materials consumed	0.00	0.00	0.00
Changes in inventories of finished goods, work-in-progress and stock-in-trade	0.00	0.00	0.00
Employee benefit expense	119.56	142.61	139.34
Finance costs	657.46	681.02	331.73
Depreciation, depletion and amortization expense [Abstract]			
Depreciation expense	399.87	412.07	254.47
Amortization expense	14.32	14.38	13.89
Total depreciation, depletion and amortization expense	414.19	426.45	268.36
Other expenses	2074.15	1190.30	1000.00
Total expenses	**3265.36**	**2440.38**	**1739.43**
Total profit before prior period items, exceptional items, extraordinary items and tax	**59.52**	**−909.43**	**−477.76**
Prior period items before tax	13.00	0.00	0.00
Exceptional items before tax	0.00	−162.12	0.00

(continued)

(continued)

	01/04/2012 to 31/03/2013	01/04/2011 to 31/03/2012	01/04/2010 to 31/03/2011
Total profit before extraordinary items and tax	72.52	−1071.55	−477.76
Total profit before tax	72.52	−1071.55	−477.76
Tax expense [Abstract]			
Current tax	–	13.85	0.00
Deferred tax	0.00	0.00	−27.56
Total tax expense	**0.00**	**13.85**	**−27.56**
Total profit (loss) for period from continuing operations	72.52	−1085.40	−450.20
Total profit (loss) for period before minority interest	72.52	−1085.40	−450.20
Total profit (loss) for period	**72.52**	**−1085.40**	**−450.20**
Earnings per equity share [Abstract]			
Basic earnings per equity share [INR/shares]	0.30	−4.43	−3.57
Diluted earnings per equity share [INR/shares]	0.30	−4.43	−3.57
Nominal value of per equity share [INR/shares]	10.00	10.00	10.00

Appendix 3: Growth of Indian Civil Aviation Sector

	1960–61	1970–71	1980–81	1990–91	1999–00	2004–05	2008–09	2009–10	2010–11	2011–12	2012–2013	2013–14
1. Total fleet strength												
(i) Air India	13	10	17	24	26	36						
(ii) Indian Airlines	88	73	49	56	53	60						
(iii) Air India Ltd. (Erstwhile National Aviation Company of India Limited)							108	113	98	9t	95	99f
2. Revenue ton-Kilometers ₹ (crore) (i) Air India	7.56	27.52	98.01	138.10	145.65	221.80						
(ii) Indian Airlines	10.0	20.00	40.03	69.92	74.03	101.73						
(iii) Air India Ltd. (Erstwhile National Aviation Company of India Limited)							328.40	353.30	367.70	360.30	3346	3910.00
3. Number of passengers carried (Lakh) (i) Air India	1.25	4.87	14.18	21.61	33.50	44.40						
(ii) Indian Airlines	7.90	21.30	54.29	78.66	59.30	71.32						
(iii) Air India Ltd. (Erstwhile National Aviation Comapany of India Limited)							117.80	117.50	127.80	134.30	141.83	154.06
4. Passengers handled at (Lakh)												
AAI Airports	N.A.	N.A.	107.38	177.23	390.35	592.84	442.54	508.71	596.43	684.00	683.87	717.8
Joint Venture Int'I Airports							646.16	72884	837.87	939.00	910.14	972.68
Total at Indian Airports							1088.70	1237.6	1434.3	1623.10	1594	1690.48
5. Cargo handled at AAI Airports (Thousand tons)												
AAI Airports Joint Venture	N.A.	N.A.	178.70	377.3	797.41	1278.47	561.42	592.95	726.52	703.43	650.41	636.48
Int'I Airports							1140.57	1366.76	1621.92	1576.56	1540.14	1641.13
Total at Indian Airports							1701.99	1959.71	2348.44	2279.99	2190.55	2277.91

Source Government of India (Ministry of Finance) (2014)

Appendix 4: Revenues and Net Income of Delhi Airport

Table 1 Total revenues of Delhi Airport (Rs. crore)

Year	Delhi
2002–03	369
2003–04	408
2004–05	489
2005–06	670
2006–07	720
2007–08	876
2008–09	958
2009–10	1,172
2010–11	1,255
2011–12	1,531

Table 2 Non-aeronautical Revenue of Delhi Airport (Rs. crore)

Year	Delhi Airport	
	Non-aero. revenue	Percentage of total revenue
2002–03	113	30
2003–04	130	31
2004–05	159	32
2005–06	183	27
2006–07	240	33
2007–08	350	39
2008–09	404	42
2009–10	574	48
2010–11	652	51
2011–12	920	60

Table 3 Net Income of AAI from Delhi Airport (Rs. crore)

Year	Delhi Airport		
	Total income	Expenditure	Net income
2001–02	347	219	128
2002–03	369	180	189
2003–04	408	180	228
2004–05	489	178	311
2005–06	670	244	426
2006–07	401	61	340
2007–08	403		403
2008–09	441		441
2009–10	539		539
2010–11	577		577
2011–12	704		704

Note 1 Revenue-share received @45.99% from DIAL from 2007 onwards. No expenditure by AAI thereafter

Source Government of India, Planning Commission (2012)

Appendix 5: Timeline of the Delhi Airport PPP

11 September 2003	Empowered Group of Ministers (EGoM) set up to decide on key issues regarding privatization of Mumbai and Delhi airports
October 2003	Ministry of Civil Aviation (MoCA) sets up the Inter-Ministerial Group (IMG) to assist the EGoM
December 2003	IMG appoints ABN AMRO Bank as the Financial Consultant
February 2004	Issue of invitation to register Expression of Interest
May 2004	General Elections in India. Incumbent NDA defeated and UPA comes to power
June 2004	EGoM reconstituted
June 2004	Air Plan, Australia appointed as the Global Technical Advisor, AMSS as Legal Consultants and TVA as accounting and tax advisor. FC, GTA and LC grouped as Evaluation Committee (EC) under the chairmanship of Executive Director, Airports Authority of India (AAI)
October 2004	IMG reconstituted
April 2005	Commencement of RFP stage with the release of RFP documents and draft transaction documents
August 2005	Issue of final transaction documents
September 2005	Submission of bids by parties; commencement of evaluation by EC
November 2005	EC submits evaluation report; only two consortia pass qualification threshold of 80%—GMR-Fraport and Reliance-ASA
November 24, 2005	Evaluation Report of EC sent to GRC for independent review of evaluation undertaken by EC
December 2, 2005	IMG meeting to discuss issues raised in the EC's evaluation but no consensus achieved
December 5, 2005	MoCA informs all bidders that no one had been disqualified on technical grounds and that all technical bids will be reevaluated based on comments by the IMG and GRC
December 14, 2005	EC submits revised evaluations to the IMG and the EGoM
December 21, 2005	EGoM reviews results of the IMG Meeting and decides to set up CoS to help prepare final recommendations. CoS in turn sets up GETE headed by E Sreedharan
January 2006	GETE submits final score with GMR-Fraport as the only qualifying consortium; recommends no further bids
January 24, 2006	EGoM reviews GETE report, decides to award Delhi airport to GMR-Fraport, but at highest bid price
January 31, 2006	Financial bids opened; Delhi awarded to GMR-Fraport
April 4, 2006	AAI signs OMDA with DIAL
May 3, 2006	AAI hands over IGI Airport to DIAL on "as is where is" basis
2008	AERA established to regulate the economic aspects of airports
2010	Modernized IGI Airport opened to traffic
2012	CAG comes out with its audit report on IGI Airport

References

Agarwal, Manish, Ian Alexander, and Bernard Tenenbaum. 2003. The Delhi electricity Discom privatizations: Some observations and recommendations for future privatizations in India and elsewhere. *Energy and Mining Sector Board Discussion Paper Series Paper No. 8*, Washington, DC: The World Bank.

Airports Authority of India. 2004. *Restructuring and modernization of Delhi and Mumbai Airports —Invitation to register an expression of interest (ITREOI)*. Airports Authority of India, February 17, 2004.

Airports Council International. http://www.aci.aero/Airport-Service-Quality/. Accessed 13 July 2014.

Andres, Luis, Vivien Foster, and José Luis Guasch. 2006. The impact of privatization on the performance of the infrastructure sector: The case of electricity distribution in Latin American Countries. *World Bank Policy Research Working Paper 3936*. Washington, DC: The World Bank.

Andersen, Arthur, and Enterprise LSE. 2000. *Value for Money Drivers in the Private Finance Initiative*, a report commissioned by the UK Treasury Taskforce.

Bain, Robert. 2010. *Construction Risk—What risk?* Project Finance International. http://www.pfie.com.

Boardman, Anthony E., Finn Poschmann, and Aidan R. Vining. 2005. "North American infrastructure P3s: Examples and lessons learned", in *The challenge of public-private partnerships: Learning from international experience*, Graeme Hodge, and Carsten Greve (eds.). UK: Edward Elgar Publishing Limited.

Business Standard. 2014. *Foreign pension plans get aggressive on India.* (http://www.business-standard.com/article/companies/foreign-pension-plans-get-aggressive-on-india-114042400012_1.html).

Business Standard. 2016. *Cheaper transport: It's time to take to water.*

Business Wire. 2005. Arbitration Tribunal Rules for Bechtel in India's Dabhol Power Project; 2nd Ruling that Indian Government Entities Have Expropriated a Private Asset Owned by US Investor.

CAG. 2013. Report on Implementation of Airport Metro Express Line Project through PPP. (http://saiindia.gov.in/english/home/Our_Products/Audit_Report/Government_Wise/union_audit/recent_reports/union_compliance/2013/Commercial/Report_13/chap_15.pdf).

Castalia Strategic Advisors. 2007. *Advice on fiscal management of infrastructure PPPs in Pakistan*.

Central Electricity Regulatory Commission. 2007. Order dated 19 September 2007 on Petition No. 18/2007. http://cercind.gov.in/03022007/No_18-2007.pdf. Accessed 5 July 2013.

Central Electricity Regulatory Commission. 2013. Order dated 15 April 2013 on Petition No. 159/MP/2012. http://www.cercind.gov.in/2013/orders/159_mp_2012.pdf. Accessed 20 Apr 2013.

K.V. Pratap and R. Chakrabarti, *Public-Private Partnerships in Infrastructure*,
India Studies in Business and Economics, DOI 10.1007/978-981-10-3355-1

Chakrabarty, K.C. 2010. *Infrastructure finance: experiences and the road ahead.* Mumbai: Reserve Bank of India. (https://www.rbi.org.in/scripts/BS_ViewBulletin.aspx?Id=11025).

Chawla, Divya. 2010. *Commercial use of land at Delhi and Mumbai Airports—An analysis of the questions of law and public policy.* Secretariat for Infrastructure, Planning Commission.

Chong, Alberto, and Cesar Calderon. 2001. *Volume and Quality of Infrastructure and the Distribution of Income: An Empirical Investigation.*

Comptroller and Auditor General, UK. 2003. *PFI: Construction Performance.*

Comptroller and Auditor General, India. 2008. Union audit reports: *Public-Private Partnership in implementation of road projects of National Highways Authority of India* (Performance Audit —Report 16 of 2008). (http://www.cag.gov.in/html/reports/commercial/2008_PA16com/contents.htm).

Comptroller and Auditor General, India. 2012. *Report of the CAG of India for the year ended March 2012 on Implementation of Public-Private Partnership–Indira Gandhi International Airport, Delhi.* http://www.saiindia.gov.in/english/home/Our_Products/Audit_Report/Government_Wise/union_audit/recent_reports/union_performance/2012_2013/Commercial/Report_No_5/5.swf.

CRISIL and ICRA. 2006. *State power sector: Performance ratings.*

DeJongh, Taylor. 2009. *Assessing the Impact of Recent Credit Constraints on Energy Sector Investment Requirements in Bangladesh*, a study commissioned by the World Bank.

Delmon, Jeffrey. 2010. *Understanding options for public-private partnerships in infrastructure.* Washington DC: The World Bank. (http://documents.worldbank.org/curated/en/999661468323693635/pdf/WPS5173.pdf).

Department of Public Enterprises, Government of India. 2016. *Public Enterprises Survey 2014–15*, vol. 1, p. 2. (http://dpe.nic.in/sites/upload_files/dpe/files/pesurvey_14_15/vol1/PES_English_Vol_1_2014_15.pdf).

DMRC. 2012. Annual Report 2011–12. (http://www.delhimetrorail.com/annual_report.aspx).

Duffield, Colin. 2008. *Report on the performance of PPP projects in Australia when compared with a representative sample of traditionally procured infrastructure projects.* Melbourne: The University of Melbourne.

Eberhard, Anton. 2007a. *Matching regulatory design to country circumstances—The potential of hybrid and transitional models.* Washington DC: The World Bank. http://documents.worldbank.org/curated/en/788491468138570182/pdf/409150Gridline1ory0designs01PUBLIC1.pdf.

Eberhard, Anton. 2007b. *Infrastructure regulation in developing countries—An exploration of hybrid and transitional models.* Washington DC: The World Bank.

Economic Times (various dates).

Ehrhardt, David, and Timothy Irwin. 2004. Avoiding customer and taxpayer bailouts in private infrastructure projects: Policy toward leverage, risk allocation, and bankruptcy. In *World Bank policy research working paper no. 3274.* Washington DC: The World Bank.

Engel, Eduardo, Ronald Fischer, and Alexander Galetovic. 2008. *Public-private partnerships: When and how?.*

Engel, Eduardo, Ronald Fischer, and Alexander Galetovic. 2011. *Public-Private Partnerships to Revamp US Infrastructure.* The Hamilton Project Discussion Paper 2011–12. http://www.brookings.edu/~/media/Files/rc/papers/2011/02_partnerships_engel_fischer_galetovic/02_partnerships_engel_fischer_galetovic_paper.pdf.

Engel, Eduardo, Ronald D. Fischer, and Alexander Galetovic. 2014. *The Economics of public-private partnerships: A basic guide.* Cambridge University Press.

Esty, Benjamin C. 2011. *An overview of project finance and infrastructure finance—2009 update.*

Esty, Benjamin C., Carla Chavich, and Aldo Sesia. 2014. *An overview of project finance and infrastructure finance—2014 update.* Boson, MA: Harvard Business School.

European Investment Bank. 2015. *Project Finance.* (http://www.eib.org/epec/g2g/annex/1-project-finance/).

Farquharson, Edward, Clemencia Torres de Mastle, and E. R. Yescombe with Javier Encinas. 2011. *How to engage with the private sector in public-private partnerships in emerging markets*. Washington DC: The World Bank.

FICCI and Ernst & Young. 2012. *Accelerating Public Private Partnerships in India.*

Fitzgerald, Peter. 2004. *Review of partnerships Victoria provided infrastructure*. Melbourne, Australia: Growth Solutions Group.

Foster, Vivien, and Cecilia Briceño-Garmendia (eds.). 2010. *Africa's infrastructure—a time for transformation*. Washington DC: The World Bank.

FRBM Act. 2003. FRBM Act aims at ensuring inter-generational equity in fiscal management and long-term macro-economic stability by achieving sufficient revenue surplus and removing fiscal impediments in the effective conduct of monetary policy and prudential debt management consistent with fiscal sustainability through limits on the Central Government borrowings, debt and deficits, greater transparency in fiscal operations of the Central Government and conducting fiscal policy in a medium-term framework. (Source: http://finmin.nic.in/law/frbmact2003.pdf).

Gassner, Katharina, Alexander Popov, and Nataliya Pushak. 2007. *An empirical assessment of private sector participation in electricity and water distribution in developing and transition countries*. Washington, DC: The World Bank.

Gassner, K., A. Popov, and N. Pushak. 2009. *Does private sector participation improve performance in electricity and water distribution?, trends and policy options*. Washington DC: The World Bank.

Gomez-Ibanez, Jose A. 1999. *The future of private infrastructure: Lessons from the nationalization of electric utilities in Latin America, 1943–1979.* Discussion Paper, Taubman Center for State and Local Government, Kennedy School of Government, Harvard University, Cambridge, MA.

Government of India. 2009. *Model request for qualification for PPP projects.*

Government of India (Central Electricity Authority). 2016. *Power sector executive summary.* http://www.cea.nic.in/reports/monthly/executivesummary/2016/exe_summary-01.pdf.

Government of India (Department of Road Transport and Highways). *Model concession agreement for annuity-based projects.* (http://www.nhai.org/annuity.pdf).

Government of India (Department of Road Transport and Highways). 2007. Presentation on PPPs in national highways in the conference of chief secretaries on PPP in infrastructure on July 21, 2007, New Delhi.

Government of India (Ministry of Finance). *Economic survey 2009–10.*

Government of India (Ministry of Finance). 2008. *Economic survey 2007–08.*

Government of India (Ministry of Finance). 2011. *Economic survey 2010–11*. New Delhi: Government of India Press.

Government of India (Ministry of Finance). 2013. *Economic survey 2012–13*. New Delhi: Government of India Press.

Government of India (Ministry of Finance). 2014. *Economic survey 2013–14*. New Delhi: Government of India Press.

Government of India, Ministry of Finance. 2014. *Mid-Year Economic Analysis.*

Government of India, Ministry of Finance. 2014. *Budget speech of the finance minister (10 July, 2014).*

Government of India (Ministry of Finance). 2015. *Economic Survey 2014–15.*

Government of India, Ministry of Finance. 2016. *Economic survey 2015–16.*

Government of India, Ministry of Finance (Department of Economic Affairs). *Scheme and guidelines for India infrastructure project development fund.*

Government of India, Ministry of Finance (Department of Economic Affairs). 2008. *Scheme and guidelines for financial support to public private partnerships in infrastructure.*

Government of India (Ministry of Power). 2016. *Annual report 2015–16.*

Government of India (Ministry of Road Transport and Highways). 2009. *Annual report 2008–09.*

Government of India (Ministry of Road Transport and Highways). 2013. *Revenue data for NHDP Phase I BOT (Toll) Projects* (unpublished).

Government of India (Ministry of Shipping). 2016. *Annual report 2015–16.* http://shipping.nic.in/showfile.php?lid=2266.

Government of India (Ministry of Statistics and Programme Implementation). 2008. *Project implementation status report of central sector projects costing Rs. 20 crore and above (July–September 2008).* (http://mospi.nic.in/mospi_pi_status_report.htm).

Government of India, Planning Commission. 2006. *Report of the core group on financing of the National highway development programme.* (http://www.pppinindia.com/pdf/NHDP.pdf).

Government of India, Planning Commission. 2007. *Concession for the Delhi Noida bridge case study.*

Government of India, Planning Commission. 2007. *Case study on concession for Nhava Sheva international container terminal.*

Government of India, Planning Commission. 2011. *Investment in infrastructure during the eleventh five year plan.*

Government of India, Planning Commission. 2012. *Interim report of the high level committee on financing infrastructure.*

Government of India, Planning Commission. 2012. *Report of the task force on financing plan for airports.*

Government of India, Planning Commission. 2014. *Second Report of the High Level Committee on Financing Infrastructure.*

Government of India, Planning Commission (Secretariat for Infrastructure). 2010. *Report of the task force on ceiling for annuity commitments.*

Government of India. *Report of the core group on financing of the national highway development programme.* (http://www.pppinindia.com/pdf/NHDP.pdf).

Government of India. Replies to various Parliament Questions [reply to Rajya Sabha (Upper House of Indian Parliament) Question number 536 answered on Nov 24, 2006; Question No. 539 answered on July 08, 2009; reply to Rajya Sabha Question No. 542 answered on July 08, 2009; reply to Rajya Sabha Question No. 1624 answered on August 27, 2007; reply to Lok Sabha Unstarred Question number 536 answered on Nov 24, 2006;reply to Lok Sabha (Lower House of Indian Parliament) Question No. 1371 answered on July 14, 2009; reply to Lok Sabha Question No. 2802 answered on December 7, 2009; reply to Lok Sabha Question No. 126 answered on November 19, 2009; reply to Lok Sabha Question No. 1279 answered on November 26, 2009; reply to Lok Sabha Question No. 1869 answered on December 1, 2009].

Government of South Africa (Department of Correctional Services, National Treasury, Department of Public Works). 2002.

Government of Victoria. 2006. Public accounts and estimates committee seventy first report to the parliament. Report on private investment in public infrastructure.

Greve, Carsten, and Graeme Hodge. 2005. *The challenge of public-private partnerships: Learning from international experience*, Graeme Hodge, and Carsten Greve (eds.). UK: Edward Elgar Publishing Limited.

Grimsey, Darrin, and Mervyn K. Lewis. 2005. Are public-private partnerships value for money? Evaluating alternative approaches and comparing academic and practitioner views. *Accounting Forum* 29 (2005): 345–378.

Grindle, Merilee S., and Thomas John W. 1991. *Public choices and policy change—the political economy of reform in developing countries.* Maryland: The Johns Hopkins University Press.

Guasch, J. Luis. 2004. *Granting and renegotiating infrastructure concessions—doing it right.* Washington, DC: The World Bank.

Guasch, J. Luis. 2013. *Presentation at the workshop on PPP contract management organized by Ministry of Finance, Government of India, New Delhi.*

Guasch, J. Luis, and Joseph Kogan. 2001. *Inventories in developing countries: Levels and determinants—a red flag for competitiveness and growth.* Washington DC: The World Bank.

GVK Power and Infrastructure Limited (Annual Report 2008–09). (http://www.gvk.com/i/GVKPIL-15th%20AR%202008-09.pdf).

Haldea, Gajendra. 2010a. *India Infrastructure Debt Fund—A Concept Paper.* (http://planningcommission.gov.in/sectors/ppp_report/4.Case%20Studies/2.IDF-A%20Concept-paper190410.pdf).

Haldea, Gajendra. 2010b. Presentation on building transmission systems: Challenges and opportunities. In *Conference on PPP in transmission of electricity*, India, New Delhi.

Haldea, Gajendra. 2011. *Infrastructure at crossroads*, 159–190. New Delhi: Oxford University Press.

Harris, Clive, and Kumar V. Pratap. 2009. *What drives private sector exit from infrastructure? Economic crises and other factors in the cancellation of private infrastructure projects in developing countries, Gridlines No. 46*. Washington DC: World Bank. http://www.ppiaf.org/ppiaf/sites/ppiaf.org/files/publication/Gridlines-46-Private%20Sector%20Exit%20-%20CHarris%20KPratap.pdf.

Heshmati, Almas, Alan Dilani, Serwan M.J. Baban (eds.). 2013. *Perspectives on Kurdistan's economy and society in transition, vol. 2*. UK: Cambridge Scholars Publishing.

High Powered Expert Committee for Estimating the Investment Requirements for Urban Infrastructure Services. 2011.

Hodge, Graeme A., and Carsten Greve. 2007. Public-private partnerships: An international performance review. *Public Administration Review, 67*, no. 3. (http://www.partnerships.vic.gov.au/CA25708500035EB6/WebObj/PAECReport/$File/PAEC%20Report.pdf).

India PPP Database. (http://www.pppindiadatabase.com).

Infrastructure Development Finance Company. 2008. *India infrastructure report*. New Delhi: Oxford University Press.

Infrastructure Development Finance Company. 2009. *India infrastructure report*. New Delhi: Oxford University Press.

International Centre for Settlement of Investment Disputes. 2008. Award of ICSID Case No. ARB/05/22: Biwater Gauff (Tanzania) Ltd. (Claimant) vs. United Republic of Tanzania (Respondent).

Irwin, Tim, and Clive Harris. 2008. *Managing the fiscal implication of PPPs*. Washington DC: The World Bank. (unpublished).

Jacobson, Charles D., and Joel A. Tarr. 1995. *Ownership and financing of infrastructure: Historical perspectives*. Washington DC: The World Bank.

Jain, Rekha, G. Raghuram, and Rachna Gangwar. 2007. *Airport privatization in India: Lessons from the bidding process in Delhi and Mumbai*.

Kennedy School of Government. 2007. *New Delhi water and power case study*. Boston: Harvard University.

Kessides, Ioannis N. 2004. *Reforming infrastructure: Privatization, regulation and competition*. Washington DC: The World Bank.

Kessides, Ioannis N. 2005. *Infrastructure Privatization and Regulation: Promises and Perils*.

Kingdom, Bill, Roland Liemberger, and Philippe Marin. 2006. *The challenge of reducing non-revenue water (NRW) in developing countries how the private sector can help: A look at performance-based service contracting*. Washington DC: The World Bank.

Kohli, Kanchi. 2013. Two coal blocks and a political story. *Economic and Political Weekly xiviii* (41) (October 12, 2013).

Kuhad, Prateek. 2010. *Bidding process for the Delhi and Mumbai Airports*. Secretariat for Infrastructure, Planning Commission.

Lamb, Peter M. 2006. *The Indian electricity market: Country study and investment context* (Working Paper # 48). Center for Environmental Science and Policy, Stanford Institute for International Studies, Stanford University, Stanford, CA.

Leigland, James, and Chris Shugart. 2006. *Is the public sector comparator right for developing countries?*. The World Bank: PPIAF Gridlines.

Llanto, G. 2008. Build-operate-transfer for infrastructure development: lessons from the Philippine experience. In *International Infrastructure Development in East Asia—towards balanced regional development and integration, ERIA research project report 2007–2*, ed. Kumar, N., 319–359. Chiba: IDE-JETRO.

Macdonald, Mott. 2002. *Review of large public procurement in the UK*. London: Mott-Macdonald.

McKinsey Global Institute. 2010. *India's urban awakening: Building inclusive cities, sustaining economic growth.*

McKinsey Global Institute. 2013. *Infrastructure productivity: How to save $1 trillion a year.*

Ministry of Civil Aviation. 2003. *Report of the Committee on a Road Map for the Civil Aviation Sector (Naresh Chandra Committee Report).* Government of India: Ministry of Civil Aviation.

Ministry of Civil Aviation. 2007. *Policy on airport infrastructure*. Government of India, Ministry of Civil Aviation.

Ministry of Civil Aviation Annual Report. (various years). Government of India, Ministry of Civil Aviation.

Ministry of Finance. 2015. *Report of the Committee on Revisiting and Revitalising Public Private Partnership model of infrastructure* (Dr. Vijay Kelkar Committee Report). http://dea.gov.in/sites/default/files/ReportRevisitingRevitalisingPPPModel.pdf.

Ministry of Power. 2007. *Power sector profile: Western region*. http://powermin.nic.in/indian_electricity_scenario/pdf/WR1007.pdf.

Ministry of Power. 2008. *Annual report 2007–08*. http://powermin.nic.in/indian_electricity_scenario/pdf/Annual_Report_2007-08_English.pdf.

Ministry of Urban Development. 2010. *Improving Service Outcomes 2008–09.*

Ministry of Urban Development. 2016. *Handbook of urban statistics.*

Mullins, Daniel, and Marvin Ward Jr. 2009. *Violating the golden rule: Fleecing the next generation from the backs of the past.* School of Public Affairs of American University: Center of Public Finance Research.

Munnell, Alicia H. 1992. Infrastructure investment and economic growth. *Journal of Economic Perspectives* 6 (4-Fall 1992): 189–198.

National Audit Office. 2007. *Benchmarking and market testing the ongoing services component of PFI projects*. (http://www.nao.org.uk/publications/nao_reports/06-07/0607453.pdf).

National Highways Authority of India. 2013. *159th monthly report on NHAI projects.*

Neufville, Richard de, and Amedeo Odini. 2013. *Airport systems: Planning, design and management.* USA: McGraw Hill Education.

New York Times. 1993. *Mexico's toll roads not taken.*

Pandey, Ajay, Sebastian Morris, and G. Raghuram. 2010. *Structuring PPPs in aviation sector: Case of Delhi and Mumbai Airport privatization.* Indian Institute of Management, Ahmadabad, India.

Planning Commission. 2009. *Model concession agreement for urban rail transit systems.*

Planning Commission, Government of India. 2009. *Frequently asked questions on model RFQ document.*

Pollitt, Michael. 2005. Learning from UK private finance initiative experience. In *The challenge of public-private partnerships: Learning from international experience*, Graeme Hodge, and Carsten Greve (eds.). UK: Edward Elgar Publishing Limited.

Pratap, Kumar V. 2011. Sustaining privatization. PhD Dissertation, University of Maryland, College Park, USA. (http://drum.lib.umd.edu/bitstream/1903/11549/1/Pratap_umd_0117E_12145.pdf).

Pratap, Kumar V. 2013a. Delhi airport metro fiasco—what can be done to redeem the project?. *Economic and political weekly, XLVIII*, no. 49 (7 Dec 2013). (http://www.epw.in/commentary/delhi-airport-metro-fiasco.html).

Pratap, Kumar V. 2013b. Renegotiations in Long-Term Infrastructure Contracts, Economic and Political Weekly, Volume XLVIII No 37. http://www.epw.in/commentary/renegotiations-long-term-infrastructure-contracts.html. Accessed 14 Sept 2013.

Pratap, Kumar V. 2015a. User fees and political and regulatory risks in Indian public-private partnerships. *Economic and Political Weekly.* (http://www.epw.in/node/146684/pdf).

Pratap, Kumar V. 2015b. *Value for money in public-private partnerships in Indian infrastructure*, University of Melbourne, Australia. http://www.aii.unimelb.edu.au/publications/emerging-leaders-reportvolume-four.

Pratap, Kumar V, Pramod Agrawal, and Syedain Abbasi. 2012. Flawed Delhi-Noida toll bridge project should be renegotiated to end contractor's undue gain. *Economic Times*, Sep 27. (http://articles.economictimes.indiatimes.com/2012-09-27/news/34127573_1_).

Pratap, Kumar V. 2016. The increasing incidence of PPP project cancellations in India. *Economic and Political Weekly L1* (39) (September 24, 2016) (http://www.epw.in/system/files/pdf/2016_51/39/The_Increasing_Incidence_of_PPP_Project_Cancellations_in_India_0.pdf).

Prayas Energy Group. 2001. Godbole Committee on Enron Project: Expose and way out. *Economic and Political Weekly.*

Price Waterhouse Coopers. 2007. *Public-private-partnership financing in India* (report prepared for the World Bank).

Project Finance International. (http://www.pfie.com) website.

Project Finance International. 1992. *More work needed on tollroads.* (http://www.pfie.com/story.asp?sectioncode=&storycode=162923).

Project Finance International. 1997. *Mexican toll roads.* (http://www.pfie.com/story.asp?sectioncode=&storycode=148797).

Project Finance International. 2005. *Dabhol resuscitation begins.* www.pfie.com.

Project Finance International. 2008. *Dabhol plant plans IPO.* www.pfie.com.

Project Finance International. 2008. *Mexican sale of toll roads set.* (http://www.pfie.com/story.asp?sectioncode=&storycode=258656).

Prud'homme, Rémy. 2004. *Infrastructure and Development*, World Bank, Washington DC. http://siteresources.worldbank.org/DEC/Resources/84797-1251813753820/6415739-1251814066992/remy1-12.pdf.

Raghuram, G., and Prashanth D. Udayakumar. 2016. *Dedicated high speed rail network in India: issues in development.* W.P. No. 2016-03-58, Ahmedabad: Indian Institute of Management.

Rao, S.L. 2001. Dabhol, Godbole report and the future. In *Economic and political weekly.*

Reuters. 2008. *How to water a parched city: a Tanzanian tale.*

Report on Indian Urban Infrastructure and Services. 2011. http://icrier.org/pdf/FinalReport-hpec.pdf.

Ruster, Jeff. 1997. *A retrospective on the Mexican toll road program (1989–94).* World Bank Viewpoint Note No. 125. Washington, DC: The World Bank.

Sagar, Jagdish. 2003. *Power sector reforms in Delhi—The experience so far.*

Saxena, Gopal K. 2010. *Presentation on Delhi privatization model.*

Secretariat of Infrastructure. 2008. *Approach to regulation of infrastructure.* New Delhi: Planning Commission. http://planningcommission.nic.in/reports/genrep/infra_reglawl.pdf.

Standard & Poor's. 2006. *A credit review of Mexico's Toll Road Sector: Stable and strong,* p. 12. http://ibtta.org/sites/default/files/Standard%20Poors%20Mexican%20Toll%20Road%20Sector.pdf.

Thakurta, and Majumdar. 2005. *How the airport bids were evaluated.* http://inhome.rediff.com/money/2005/dec/30paran.htm. Accessed 30 Dec 2005.

The Economist. 2001. *Enron in India: Generation gaps.*

The Economist. December 2012. *Infrastructure in India—RIPPP.*

The Economist. 2014. *Government outsourcing—Nobody said it was easy.* (http://www.economist.com).

The Economist. 2015. *Building Works—Infrastructure in the Rich World*, 27 Aug 2015.

The Guardian. 2007. *The water margin.* http://www.guardian.co.uk/business/2007/aug/16/imf.internationalaidanddevelopment. Accessed 16 Aug 2007.

The Guardian. July 29, 2008. *Water: Campaigners cheer defeat of Biwater's £10 m Tanzanian claim.* http://www.guardian.co.uk/environment/2008/jul/29/water.tanzania. Accessed 29 July 2008.

U.S. House of Representatives (Minority Staff, Committee on Government Reform). 2002. *Fact sheet: Background on Enron's Dabhol power project.*

Vernon, Raymond. 1971. *Sovereignty at bay: The spread of U.S. enterprises.* New York: Basic Books.

Wells, Louis T., and Rafiq Ahmed. 2007. *Making foreign investment safe: Property rights and national sovereignty.* New York: Oxford University Press.

World Bank. 1994. *World development report 1994: Infrastructure for development.* Washington, DC: The World Bank. http://documents.worldbank.org/curated/en/1994/06/734205/world-development-report-1994-infrastructure-development.

World Bank. 1996. *Privatizing airports—Options and case studies, public policy for the private sector.*

World Bank. 2004. *Global development finance—harnessing cyclical gains for development.*

World Bank. 2005. *World development report 2005: A better investment climate for everyone.* Washington, DC: The World Bank http://siteresources.worldbank.org/INTWDR2005/Resources/complete_report.pdf.

World Bank. 2006. *Improving Management of Municipal Solid Waste in India: Overview and Challenges.*

World Bank. 2008. *Emerging market investors and operators—a new breed of infrastructure investors.* (http://documents.worldbank.org/curated/en/708751468156263363/pdf/462650NWP0Box311emerging1investors7.pdf).

World Bank. 2008. *Indian road construction industry: Capacity issues, constraints, and recommendations.* Washington DC: The World Bank.

World Bank. 2008. *The Growth Report: Strategies for Sustained Growth and Inclusive Development*, 35.

World Bank. 2009. *INFRA Partners Forum—Summary Report.*

World Bank. 2012. *Public private partnerships reference guide 1.0.*

World Bank. 2013. *Doing business 2013: Smarter regulations for small and medium-size enterprises.* Washington, DC: World Bank Group.

World Bank. 2015. *World bank group support to public private partnerships—lessons from experience in client countries, FY 02-12.* Washington DC: The World Bank.

World Bank. 2015. *2014 Global PPI Update.* http://ppi.worldbank.org/features/June2015/PPI-Global-Update.pdf?v=3. Accessed 12 June 2015.

World Bank. http://data.worldbank.org/country/india. Accessed 8 June 2013.

World Bank. *Private Participation in Infrastructure (PPI) Project database.* www.ppi.worldbank.org.

World Bank, Asian Development Bank, and Inter-American Development Bank. 2014. *Public-Private Partnerships Reference Guide Version 2.0.*

World Economic Forum. 2012. *Global competitiveness report.* Geneva: World Economic Forum.

World Economic Forum. 2016. *The global competitiveness report 2015–16.*

Yescombe, E.R. 2002. *Principles of project finance.* London: Academic Press.

Index

K.V. Pratap and R. Chakrabarti, *Public-Private Partnerships in Infrastructure*, India Studies in Business and Economics, DOI 10.1007/978-981-10-3355-1

B

C

Printed by Printforce, the Netherlands